Literature
and Technology

Research in Technology Studies

Literature and Technology

Research in Technology Studies
Volume 5

EDITED BY
Mark L. Greenberg
AND
Lance Schachterle

Bethlehem: Lehigh University Press
London and Toronto: Associated University Presses

Associated University Presses
440 Forsgate Drive
Cranbury, NJ 08512

Associated University Presses
25 Sicilian Avenue
London WC1A 2QH, England

Associated University Presses
P.O. Box 39, Clarkson Pstl. Stn.
Mississauga, Ontario,
L5J 3X9 Canada

The paper used in this publication meets the requirements
of the American National Standard for Permanence of Paper
for Printed Library Materials Z39.48-1984.

Library of Congress Cataloging-in-Publication Data

Literature and technology / edited by Mark L. Greenberg and Lance
Schachterle.
    p. cm. — (Research in technology studies ; v. 5)
  Includes bibliographical references.
  ISBN 0-934223-20-3 (alk. paper)
  1. Technology in literature. 2. Literature and technology.
I. Greenberg, Mark L., 1948– . II. Schachterle, Lance.
III. Series.
PN56.T37L58   1992
809′.93356—dc20   91-60584
                                                              CIP

PRINTED IN THE UNITED STATES OF AMERICA

To the memory of Arnold Greenberg,
whose love of gadgets proved infectious

Contents

Contents

Foreword

STEPHEN H. CUTCLIFFE
STEVEN L. GOLDMAN

This volume is the fifth in the *Research in Technology Studies* series published by Lehigh University Press. As with the previous volumes in the series, the intent of this volume is to present a representative range of original essays on a single theme set by the guest editors. Mark Greenberg and Lance Schachterle have invited a group of authors to write on the theme of literature and technology. Their topics range from Medieval literature to postmodern, from high culture classics to children's books, from philosophy to feminist literary criticism. Taken together, these essays reflect the diversity and the vitality of an emerging focal area within technology studies.

Preface

Collections of essays are fundamentally collaborations. Even the need for the present jointly edited book arose from discussions among a number of scholars during a particular gathering. The idea for this collection originated in a symposium on "Literature and Technology" given at Lehigh University in March 1986 under the sponsorship of the Lehigh University Technology Studies Research Center. Greenberg and Schachterle presented earlier versions of the essays included here on that occasion; their remarks were published in *The Lehigh University Technology Studies Working Papers* series. Both editors thank Steven Goldman and Stephen Cutcliffe of the Science, Technology and Society Program at Lehigh for their invitation to pursue the conference initiative to the publication of this collection, and for their expert guidance and generous encouragement throughout its preparation.

We also thank Stephen Weininger of the Department of Chemistry at Worcester Polytechnic Institute and Carl Mitcham for helpfully commenting on drafts of our Introduction. Drexel University and Worcester Polytechnic Institute provided clerical assistance and other support for the research and preparation of this book. We are grateful for the help that permitted us to realize our thinking electromechanically and, through the agency of printing technology, to submit it to interested readers.

MARK L. GREENBERG
LANCE SCHACHTERLE

Introduction: Literature and Technology

MARK L. GREENBERG
LANCE SCHACHTERLE

Why Literature and *Technology?* When Matthew Arnold in 1882 counterpoised the study of humane letters and of the natural world, he titled the resulting essay "Literature and Science." His pairing of substantives reflected his belief that "literature" and "science" name the principal sources of knowledge about all the various parts of our experience. As a critic concerned to assess the value of these several kinds of knowing, Arnold argued that "literature" represented what could be learned about human nature, while "science" designated the systematic investigation of the physical environment.[1]

"Technology" did not enter the debate, because to Arnold's classically trained mind, *"techne"* or "craft, know-how" occupied a level of understanding considerably lower than *"episteme"* or "science, knowledge." Like Plato and Aristotle, Arnold viewed the pursuit of knowledge as a free play of intellect far removed from the manual labor of craftsmanship. Science was true peer and worthy opponent of literature precisely because it demanded learning and reason. In contrast, as Arnold makes clear in the first paragraph of the essay, technology conjured up allusions from Plato of "a bald little tinker, who has scraped together money, and has got his release from service . . . and is rigged out like a bridegroom about to marry the daughter of his master who has fallen into poor and helpless estate."[2]

In the more than one hundred years since Arnold's essay, the phrase "Literature and Science" has come to designate the poles of a continuing debate about the claims to knowledge that issue from the humanities and the natural sciences.[3] Though the accuracy of C. P. Snow's couching the debate in terms of "Two Cultures" has been much debated, his 1959 essay and the subsequent rejoinders

13

and reflections helped to fix the parameters of discussion about literature and science.[4] Since Snow's lecture, as Schatzberg's bibliography indicates, writers have continued to show a robust interest in topics loosely gathered as literature and science. The Modern Language Association compendium on the *Interrelations of Literature* devoted a chapter to Literature and Science; individual monographs and at least one series of studies on the topic have appeared.[5] Finally, in 1985 scholars from a variety of disciplines formed the "Society for Literature and Science" to promote an interdisciplinary examination of the emerging field.[6]

The interrelations of literature with technology have not enjoyed the same attention that literature and science has aroused. The tendency, especially among humanists, casually to lump together science, technology, and engineering as if they were all one undifferentiated enterprise is probably one source of this lack of interest in technology. Even when technology has been the concern of social critics from the romantics on, or has provided the "know-how" enabling authors to project a new utopia or dystopia, the blame often is placed on science. Consider the systematic confusion over "Frankenstein"—does that mythic figuration of technology name the creature or the creator? And is the creator a philosopher, scientist, engineer, or physician? (None of the above, as he is an undergraduate, brilliant but vulnerable, not the authority figure usually dignified as "Dr. Frankenstein.")

This deep-seated and permeating confusion about science and technology is curious. For all our popular concern about science and science education, what makes our daily lives different from what they would have been even a generation ago is technology (*techne,* craft)—not science (*episteme* or pure knowledge). Technology supplies most of the artifacts with which we interact every day and the structures we inhabit, and it has given rise to the modes of thought that help shape contemporary life. Technology—not quantum theory or relativity—provides the transportation and information flow crucial to scholarly conferences and publications. Technology can also eventuate in hazards and accidents, like the "airborne toxic event" in Don Delillo's *White Noise* or the mechanical-ventilation-driven plague of David Lodge's *Small World,* that interrupt those scholarly rounds. These fictive representations serve as reminders of the kinds of risks to which our technology exposes us.

Despite the pervasive presence of technology in our culture, few studies specifically treating literary relations with technology have been undertaken. The reason for this lack of attention to technology, we think, lies in the Arnoldian identification of technology with craft or skill—learned practices with measured objectives, rather than with the open-ended pursuit of pure knowledge for its own sake, as in science. To our ears, "science" like "art" conveys a sense of extraordinary demands needed to satisfy unsated curiosity. Science and art are not usually "every day," while technology is. The scientist or artist, to be successful, must accept unusual burdens and display unusual talents—or at least such is the common postromantic view. Technology and its practitioners, on the other hand, apparently operate at levels of approachable craft rather than distanced art. This technology seems closer to quotidian realities, but ironically further from intellectual scrutiny.

The word "technology," its roots and its current designations, help explain this irony. The word first appears in English in 1615, according to the *OED,* and during the Renaissance was refined to a "discourse or treatise on an art or arts," to the systematic study of the practical arts, and to technical nomenclature. By 1829, however, authors—at least in America—were making claims for the importance of technology as "the basis and distinction of modern civilization" according to John F. Kasson, who cites *Elements of Technology* by Harvard professor Jacob Bigelow as initiating the distinctive American faith in technology as source of progress.[7]

Eric Partridge in *Origins* points to a skein of English cognates of the Greek *"techne,"* which further enforce this stress on *techne* as learned craft, not a source of knowledge. Originating from the Indo-European *"tekth-,"* "to put in hand, work on, build," "technology" relates to such other craftly words as "architecture," "text," "textile," "technique," "tegument," and even "thatch."[8] *"Techne"* and "technology" are thus firmly rooted (quite literally) in the crafts of making, of applying tools skillfully, and of achieving preconceived ends. This rootedness in hand-craft should not, however, obscure an irony for our concerns: "techn*ology*" is an "ology," an intellectual discourse, a system—and even, for Heidegger and Ellul, who are examined by several authors in the essays that follow, a form of consciousness.

To Arnold, such knowing as technology designates is at best "instrument-knowledge," bound up in the specializations of such arcana as Greek accents or transcendental mathematics. (To his credit, Arnold recognized crafts in both cultures.) These forms of technological knowing are "invaluable as instruments to something beyond, for those who have the gift thus to employ them."[9] "Instrument-knowledge," technology, is thus not, like science, an end in itself but a means to some other end. Arnold's "instrument-knowledge" embraces a useful but narrow set of skills of uncertain value in pursuing real knowledge, whether in literature or in science.

Despite the high tone of Arnold and others who might consciously or unconsciously agree with his devaluation of technology, considering literature in apposition with technology rather than with science reveals certain essential qualities about both literature and technology. First and perhaps most obviously, technology is subject in literature as much as is science. The formal study of literature and science originated with literary historians such as Marjorie Hope Nicolson whose studies centered on the literary appropriation of scientific ideas.[10] But as the essays on Chaucer, Blake, Romains, and Pynchon overtly show, authors also respond to both the actual technologies and ideas about that technology in the world around them. Technology, like science, inescapably impinges on our lives, indeed often more palpably than the abstract sciences do; thus it becomes part of the environment within which literature works. Indeed, as several essays in this collection argue, technology becomes both structuring principle and theme in works whose authors are also conscious of the physical and technological dimensions of any art work, including printed text.

Second, the Indo-European root, *"tekth-"*, "to put in hand," brings the literature and science duality from the Arnoldian heights of abstractions about "the best which has been thought and said in the world" to a more immediate reality of making and doing. Reading and writing does involve craft and practice as much as knowledge and genius. Literature conveys not concepts existing in a void, but concepts worked over to present a richness of felt experience. As Partridge's *Origins* suggests, "texts" in literature "put" ideas "in hand," as it were, to frame knowledge within the dramatic fabric of experience, even as the technology of books and book production literally brings ideas "to hand." Bald little tinkers (like Socrates) make as many contributions to knowledge as do abstract philosophers.

Third, technology serves not our curiosity to learn about our environment (as science does), but instead our will to alter it. As the essays that constitute this volume acknowledge, literature not only registers our concern for science as a source of knowledge (sometimes specifically in competition with parallel epistemological claims from literature), it also records our response to how our will "works on" (*"tekth-"*) our environment, molding and displacing it to suit our needs. Such willful interventions can, of course, be joyful exertions of handicraft or threatening wastes of spirit. In either case, such interventions always express ideas or ideology. Many of the essays that follow document how authors from Chaucer to the postmodernists show forms of technology in the service of the human transformation of a given reality. Reciprocally, several of the authors concentrate on the ideologies, economics, and politics energizing such transformations.

Fourth, considering not science but technology as counterpart to literature offers at least one resolution to the dichotomy between literature and science in Arnold's essay, which, rigidified in Snow's, often characterizes (and, we believe, reduces) current interdisciplinary approaches to literary study. As Arnold and other good classicists know, *"techne"* to the Greeks did not distinguish between art and science. The present configuration of the arts began to coalesce during the eighteenth century; "science," in its current designation as a related group of professions studying phenomena systematically, emerged only during the second half of the nineteenth century.[11] According to R. G. Collingwood:

> In order to clear up the ambiguities attaching to the word "art," we must look into its history. The aesthetic sense of the word . . . is very recent in origin. *Ars* in ancient Latin, like τέχνη in Greek, means something quite different. It means a craft or specialized form of skill, like carpentry or smithying or surgery. The Greeks and Romans had no conception of what we call arts as something different from craft; what we call art they regarded merely as a group of crafts, such as the craft of poetry (ποιητικὴ τέχνη, *ars poetica*), which they conceived, sometimes no doubt with misgivings, as in principle just like carpentry and the rest, and differing from any of these only in the sort of way in which any one of them differs from any other.[12]

Collingwood's reminder that *"techne"* signified both art (literature) and craft (technology) can help us reject the too common view, voiced by Arnold but also held by many students of literature, that technology and its practitioners are narrow, blinkered, and unimaginative. As several essays show (on Blake, Romains, children's literature, and the postmodernists especially), forms of technology offer a sense of liberating spiritual engagement with the products of the material world. In the creation, manipulation, and reception of technologies, human energy need not always result in physical destruction or intellectual reduction, a truth well understood by the writers treated below and by the authors of the essays that follow. Technology is not always a demonic antagonist to art or to its sponsoring cultures.

* * *

The present collection of interdisciplinary essays on literature and technology thus attempts to remedy what the editors and contributors regard as a failure to distinguish between the operation of science versus that of technology on the one hand, and to assess various relations of literature to technology (as opposed to science) on the other. Its authors treat a wide range of subjects, and texts emerging from a range of historical periods, classical to postmodern.

Carl Mitcham and Timothy Casey's "Toward an Archeology of the Philosophy of Technology and Its Relations with Imaginative Literature" triangulates philosophy with literature and technology in order to establish "certain problematic tensions" to which such study gives rise. Their analyses anticipate issues, raised in subsequent studies in this volume, especially by Tomasch, Knoespel, and Markley, of the inevitable straining between authorized, often univocal versions of "reality" and polysemous representations of it. The "ancient quarrel" between philosophy and technology, sketched next in this essay, also offers pertinent background for enriching the work of contemporary authors like Pynchon and the writers of spy novels. Readers of this volume who are not particularly familiar with developments leading to a discrete discipline called philosophy of technology will also appreciate the lucid, brief critical chronology offered by Mitcham and Casey.

Drawing primarily upon philosophical works, the central portion of this essay elaborates four distinct approaches to philosophy of technology, one ancient and three modern, with suggestions about how each opens to a particular consideration of various "texts," including (though not limited to) imaginative literature. The authors' discussion of ancient and quite complex attitudes toward technology provides a useful background for the three essays that follow immediately in this collection. This discussion also helps illuminate attitudes toward technology expressed by such apparently dissimilar figures as Romaines and Blake, particular artists whose ideas resonate with the treatment of engineering-philosophy (especially that of Kapp) offered here. Essays by Lee, Slade, Schachterle, and Porush are similarly enriched by being read in light of Mitcham and Casey's discussions of "Technology as Social Order to Be Criticized" (section 4) and "Technology as Threat to the Human" (section 5). Additionally, the treatment of "romanticism" offered here might usefully be contrasted with remarks by Greenberg; while the treatment of Heidegger anticipates and complicates conclusions reached by Schachterle. Finally, focusing their discussion upon imaginative literature specifically, Mitcham and Casey conclude their essay with brief, suggestive philosophical analyses of a wide range of compositions devoted to depicting technology. This lucid exposition of positions adopted by major figures in philosophy of technology should prove stimulating to all who think about technology and its relations with the products of human imagination. It may also suggest (without compelling) modes of receiving or questioning the essays that follow, offering theoretical frameworks in which it is possible to situate many of the other studies in this collection.

Sylvia Tomasch's "*Mappae Mundi* and 'The Knight's Tale': The Geography of Power, the Technology of Control" assesses cartography as a technological system for exerting control. At the same time, as she demonstrates, studying maps and mapmaking tells us something about how a culture valued and disposed of the physical world. Tomasch relates these broader concerns to Chaucer's world-view by considering how maps are represented in his writings. She then uses Chaucer's cartographical imagery to provide a fresh reading of "The Knight's Tale," showing Theseus's will to assert order upon a recalcitrant reality is figured in his "mapping" of his values. His attempt to regulate the wilderness by imposing his amphitheater—whose shape is taken from the traditional medieval *mappa mundi*—reveals in the end only his vanity and impotence. Read this way, "The Knight's Tale" becomes a cautionary legend on the limits of human technology to transform the world.

The next two essays treat literature of the sixteenth and seventeenth century—an age characterized as the Scientific Revolution. Reciprocities between what we see and what we create constitute the broad theme of Kenneth J. Knoespel's "Gazing on Technology: *Theatrum Mechanorum* and the Assimilation of Renaissance Machinery." Knoespel scrutinizes depictions of mechanical devices from a number of Renaissance books, finding that such representations often invoke graphic elements from the theater. Renaissance illustrators "staged" machines, he argues, as ways of showing how technology may be assimilated, as for example in the presentation of machines in garden settings that evoke larger cultural contexts. Concomitantly, Knoespel shows that poets like Spenser, in creating verbal gardens such as that depicted in the *Faerie Queen*'s "Bower of Bliss," were heavily influenced by descriptions of gardens drawn from artificial, mechanical representations. Knoespel then analyzes several visual "narrative strategies" used in graphic and verbal portrayals of Renaissance machines. Despite individual differences, he finds that such strategies urge upon viewers certain interests and values in machinery that these artfully crafted representations succeed, finally, in mythologizing.

"Robert Boyle, Peter Shaw, and the Reinscription of Technology:

Inventing and Reinventing the Air Pump" by Robert Markley considers how Boyle created a mode of discourse appropriate to writing about the invention of one of the most novel technologies developed by seventeenth-century science. Contrary to conventional expectations that descriptions of technology are transparent and neutral, Markley's analysis shows how Boyle's description is embedded in social, political, religious, and sexual contexts. His essay traces Boyle's struggles to devise a "literary technology" to promote his claims to authority for describing a radical "scientific technology" that flaunted ancient assumptions about nature abhorring vacuums. The essay further shows how Boyle's redactor, Peter Shaw, simplified Boyle's descriptions in part by excising precisely those appeals to establishing social authority that later generations, having grown accustomed to scientific claims to truth, no longer required. Markley thus contributes to the growing interdisciplinary attempt to situate technological discourse in its sociological and historical climate.

Mark Greenberg's "Romantic Technology: Books, Printing, and Blake's *Marriage of Heaven and Hell*" begins by noting—and then questioning—the well-documented hostility toward science and technology ascribed to the major English romantic poets. Of their number, only William Blake knew at first hand the very technology that liberated the romantics from eighteenth-century patronage—the technology of letterpress printing, bookmaking, and commercial publishing. A trained engraver, Blake developed strategies for visual, verbal, and verbal-as-visual artistic presentations that often satirize and undercut the new conventions of mass produced books. Simultaneously, Blake's works in composite art offer themselves materially as alternatives to commercial printing. To Blake, printing technology resulted in the codification of vision into linear typography stored in sterile libraries. Responding to that threat in *The Marriage of Heaven and Hell*, Blake explicitly crafted engraved plates mixing flowing calligraphy and colored designs into a multigesturing media that broke out of the confines of reductionist black-and-white typography. Through such radical departures from the printing media, Blake challenged the deadening weight of the social and economic conventions making "typographic fixity" the sole efficient form of communication and authority.

In "Jules Romains, *Unanimisme,* and the Poetics of Urban Systems," Rosalind Williams examines the corpus of Jules Romains (1885–1972), the French novelist and poet who in 1905 proclaimed a new manifesto for literature. Romains's fresh vision drew both upon his scientific training in biology and his perceptions of technological transformation of urban life, specifically in Paris. Romains's movement, *unanimisme,* rendered the rapidly growing Paris, linked by new forms of transportation, as a single organism, an urban system, in which living beings were subsumed in the rhythms generated by traffic ebb and flow. Unlike other movements of the early century, which berated or ennobled technology, *unanimisme* accepted technology as the normal condition of humankind, and sought to treat poetically the quality of human social life in an artificial environment.

Judith Yaross Lee examines an overlooked sector of literature in "The Feminization of Technology: Mechanical Characters in Juvenile Fiction" in terms of what this genre reveals about our attitudes toward technology. Surveying a broad range of twentieth-century children's texts, Lee finds that unlike the representations of machinery in most works written for adults, children's books present technology benevolently. Moreover, the most successful technologies found in these books, she argues, are "feminized," assigned feminine gender and embodying values and attitudes traditionally associated with women. In such tales, power tools and self-propelled vehicles are realized specifically as females, and emerge as heroic by acting selflessly and for the good of the community, while simultaneously eschewing overt claims of physical strength characteristic of young "male" machines. Lee's essay is a valuable corrective to scholarship that has, hitherto, focused almost exclusively upon a narrow range of "classic" literary texts that depict technology as sinister. She also reminds us that children are universally fascinated with mechanical devices, and that children's literature has been the only genre to respond affirmatively to this manifestation of our fascination with technology.

"Technology and the Spy Novel" by Joseph W. Slade considers literature itself as a form of technology, specifically of the technology of information processing. Spy fiction, Slade argues, owes its current popularity to our fascination with information itself, which already in the West (and increasingly in the East) is the commodity most in demand. Spy fiction thus mirrors how we depend on information for survival individually and socially, and how contemporary economies revolve around the exchange of accurate or falsified secrets. Gathering, sorting, and most of all interpreting—attaching value to—unpatterned information is fundamental to the technology of Claude Shannon's communications theory, whose formulations prefigure broader anxieties about information processing in postmodern culture. Yet, as Slade notes, within the contemporary genre the characteristic claims to efficiency of information systems are undercut by the stereotypical spy-hero. The hero of Le Carré and others—often a humanist, amateur, or outsider—employs instinct to triumph over the technology of institutional manipulation.

In "Pynchon and the Civil Wars of Technology," Lance Schachterle argues that the novelist's diverse and often bizarre depictions of technology remind us that if we are victimized by technology, we have willingly created our own predicament. By analyzing particular instances of technologies interacting with characters' "lives," Schachterle opens Pynchon's texts, particularly *Gravity's Rainbow,* to readers who may not have realized fully the philosophical ramifications technology invokes. Building upon the work of theorists such as Lewis Mumford, Jacques Ellul, and especially Martin Heidegger, Schachterle shows that Pynchon's work concerns the inextricable and reciprocal relations between rational technological systems and the contemporary social fabric from which they emerge. The uses to which we put technology, coupled with the psychological dependencies upon technology we develop, reveal the essential nature of Pynchon's depiction of contemporary society and its neuroses. That nature is disclosed in the continuous, tragic struggle between technology's competing claims on us as its makers.

The final essay, David Porush's "Literature as Dissipative Structure: Prigogine's Theory and the Postmodern 'Chaos' Machine," argues for a parallel between postmodern technology and literature. Porush shows that Nobel laureate Prigogine's ideas about order arising from disorder under special thermodynamic conditions offer fruitful parallels to our sense of how postmodern literature functions. In both cases, local islands of order can arise from apparent chaos. Porush substantiates his thesis by examining the development of literature according to Eric Auerbach's well-known mimetic model as elaborated in *Mimesis.* Since Prigogine's work derives from the classic nineteenth-century technology of thermodynamics, "Literature as Dissipative Structure" shows us how a model drawn from technology rather than from science can shed light on the distinctive features of contemporary literature.

A selected bibliography of works devoted to literature and technology concludes the volume. Like the essays that precede it, this scholarship also aims at fostering new work in this emerging area of study.

NOTES

1. Arnold's essay first appeared in *Nineteenth Century* 12 (1882): 216–30, a rejoinder to Thomas Henry Huxley's advocacy of scientific education. For a review of the Arnold-Huxley debate, as well as Arnold's text with convenient annotations, see R. H. Super, ed. *The Complete Prose Works of Matthew Arnold,* 10 (Ann Arbor: University of Michigan Press, 1974), 53–73.

2. "Literature and Science," p. 53. For Aristotle's views on *"techne,"* see the *Nicomachean Ethics,* chapter 4, sections 3 and 4.

3. The scholarship on this discussion is fully documented in *The Relations of Literature and Science: An Annotated Bibliography of Scholarship, 1880–1980,* ed. by Walter Schatzberg, Ronald A. Waite, and Jonathan K. Johnson (New York: Modern Language Association, 1987).

4. Debate on Snow's "Two Culture" thesis has been vigorous. For a summary, see Paul Boytinck, *C. P. Snow: A Reference Guide* (Boston: G. K. Hall, 1980).

5. See "Literature and Science" by George Slusser and George Guffey in Jean-Pierre Barricelli and Joseph Gibaldi, eds., *Interrelations of Literature* (New York: Modern Language Association, 1982).

Some recent collections of essays on Literature and Science include Ludmilla Jordanova, ed., *Languages of Nature* (London: Free Association Books, 1986); Judith Yaross Lee and Joseph W. Slade, eds., *Beyond the Two Cultures: Essays in Science, Technology, and Culture* (Ames: Iowa State Press, 1989); Frederick Amrine, ed., *Literature and Science as Modes of Expression* (Dordrecht: Kluwer, 1989); Stuart Peterfreund, ed., *Literature and Science: Theory & Practice* (Boston: Northeastern University Press, 1990); and George Levine, ed., *One Culture: Essays in Science and Literature* (Madison: University of Wisconsin Press, 1987), announced as the first volume in a series that already has several other volumes in print or in preparation.

G. S. Rousseau has edited two useful collections of essays as special issues of journals: *Annals of Scholarship* 4 (1986) containing essays from the 17th International Congress of History and Philosophy of Science, Symposium on Literature and Science; and *The University of Hartford Studies in Literature* 19 (1987), examining the present state of studies in Literature and Science.

6. One of the present editors (Greenberg) is now president of the Society for Literature and Science; the other (Schachterle) was founding president. SLS is negotiating the transformation of its quarterly newsletter, *PSLS,* into a learned journal, and has established its own literature and science series jointly with The University of Michigan Press.

7. See Kasson's *Civilizing the Machine: Technology and Republican Values in America 1776–1900* (New York: Penguin, 1977).

8. Eric Partridge, *Origins: A Short Etymological Dictionary of Modern English* (New York: Macmillan, 1963), pp. 697–98. Raymond Williams does not consider "Technology" a "key word" in his *Keywords: A Vocabulary of Culture and Society* (New York: Oxford University Press, 1976), though his entries under "Mechanical" and "Science" are of collateral interest.

9. Arnold, "Literature and Science," p. 63.

10. Nicolson's work is reviewed in Schatzberg et al., pp. 108–10. Three of her major studies are *The Breaking of the Circle: Studies in the Effect of the "New Science" on Seventeenth-Century Poetry* (Evanston, Ill.: Northwestern University Press, 1950); *Newton Demands the Muse: Newton's* Opticks *and the Eighteenth*

Century Poets (Princeton, N.J.: Princeton University Press, 1946), and *Science and Imagination* (Ithaca, N.Y.: Cornell University Press, 1956), which includes essays on Donne, Milton, and Swift.

11. On the arts, see Paul Oskar Kristeller's "The Modern System of the Arts," reprinted most recently in his *Renaissance Thought and the Arts: Collected Essays* (Princeton, N.J.: Princeton University Press, 1980), 163–227); on the sciences, see Mark L. Greenberg, "Blake's 'Science,'" *Studies in Eighteenth-Century Culture* 12 (1983), 115–30, especially notes 7, 9, 10, 13, and 20 for other scholarship on the complex changes of "science" over time.

12. R. S. Collingwood, *The Principles of Art* (Oxford: Oxford University Press, 1938), p. 5.

Contributors

TIMOTHY CASEY (Ph.D., Duquesne University, 1986) is Associate Professor of Philosophy and Director of the Center for Science, Technology and Society at the University of Scranton. He is co-editor with Lester Embree of *Lifeworld and Technology* and has published essays on architecture, phenomenology, and the philosophy of technology.

MARK L. GREENBERG has written on eighteenth- and nineteenth-century British literature and on social relations among literature, science, and technology for *Eighteenth-Century Culture, Journal of the History of Ideas, The Library, Annals of Scholarship, Studies in the Literary Imagination, Colby Library Quarterly,* and Stuart Peterfreund's *Literature and Science: Theory and Practice.* He is a contributing editor of *Blake's Poetical Sketches and Criticism* (forthcoming), co-editor of *Approaches to Teaching Blake's* "Songs of Innocence and of Experience," and guest editor for a special issue of *Modern Language Studies* 20 (1990) devoted to "New Models for the Study of Literature and Science." Greenberg has served on the Executive Committee of the Modern Language Association's Division of Literature and Science and is currently President of the Society for Literature and Science and Professor of Humanities at Drexel University.

KENNETH J. KNOESPEL is an Associate Professor and Interim Director of the School of Literature, Culture, and Communication at Georgia Institute of Technology. In addition to his book on scientific aspects of Ovidian commentary, his recent work has appeared in *Literature and Science as Modes of Expression* (Boston Studies in the Philosophy of Science, 1989) and in *Chaos and Order,* ed. N. Katherine Hayles (forthcoming 1991). He has published various articles on the narrative forms used to disseminate science and technology in the Renaissance and other periods. The place of science and technology within the university curriculum has become a central concern in his lectures and writing. His book on *Newton and the Failure of Messianic Science* (with Robert Markley) is forthcoming.

JUDITH YAROSS LEE is Assistant Professor of Journalism in the Scripps School of Journalism and Assistant Professor of Rhetoric in the School of Interpersonal Communication at Ohio University. The Executive Director of the Society for Literature and Science, she has published essays on science, technology, and literature, as well as on American studies in journals as diverse as *American Heritage of Invention and Technology* and *Chicago Review*. She is co-editor (with Joseph Slade) of *Beyond the Two Cultures: Essays on Science, Literature, and Technology*, and author of *Garrison Keillor: A Voice of America*.

ROBERT MARKLEY is Associate Professor of English at the University of Washington and Editor of *The Eighteenth Century: Theory and Interpretation* as well as a new book series, The Series on Science and Culture, affiliated with the Oklahoma Project for Discourse and Theory of the University of Oklahoma Press. He is the author of numerous articles on eighteenth-century studies, literary theory, and cultural studies. His books include *Two Edg'd Weapons: Style and Ideology in the Comedies of Etherege, Wycherley, and Congreve* (1988), *Newton and the Failure of Messianic Science* (coauthored with Kenneth Knoespel, forthcoming), and *Fallen Languages: Representation, Science, and Belief in England, 1660-1740* (forthcoming).

CARL MITCHAM is a member of the philosophy department and of the Science, Technology, Society Program at Penn State University. His publications include *Philosophy and Technology* (1972, 1983), *Bibliography of the Philosophy of Technology*, (1973, 1985), *Theology and Technology* (1984), and most recently *Ethical Issues Associated with Scientific and Technological Research In the Military* (1989).

DAVID PORUSH is the author of *The Soft Machine: Cybernetic Fiction* (1985) and *Rope Dances*, a collection of short stories (1979). He was founding secretary-treasurer of the Society for Literature and Science and is currently an associate professor at Rensselaer Polytechnic Institute where he is Director of Autopoeisis, a laboratory for the investigation of artificial intelligence and literary production. He is at work on a screenplay "Mech Head" and a novel *The Second Coming*.

LANCE SCHACHTERLE is Professor of English and Associate Dean for Undergraduate Studies at WPI. He is author of several critical and biographical essays on Pynchon, and was the Founding President of the Society for Literature and Science. Schachterle has also edited three novels by James Fenimore Cooper, and is a member of the Editorial Board of the Writings of James Fenimore Cooper.

JOSEPH W. SLADE is Professor and Director of the School of Tele-communications at Ohio University. The former editor of *The Markham Review,* he is the author of more than fifty articles and reviews on literature, technology, film, and culture. In 1986–87 he held the Bicentennial Chair of American Studies at the University of Helsinki, a Distinguished Fulbright Award; he has also held NEH, Hagley Museum, and Gannett Institute Fellowships. With Judith Yaross Lee he is co-editor of *Beyond the Two Cultures: Essays on Science, Literature, and Technology* (1990). In 1990, Peter Lang reissued his *Thomas Pynchon* (originally published in 1974); his book *Pornography: A Reference Guide* is forthcoming.

SYLVIA TOMASCH, an assistant professor of English at Carleton College, received her Ph.D. from the City University of New York Graduate School and University Center. This article is part of a larger project on medieval geography, for which she has been awarded fellowships from the Newberry Library, the National Endowment for the Humanities, and the National Humanities Center.

ROSALIND WILLIAMS is an associate professor in The Writing Program, Department of Humanities, Massachusetts Institute of Technology. Her first book was entitled *Dream Worlds: Mass Consumption in Late Nineteenth-Century France* (1982). Her most recent book, *Notes on the Underground: An Essay on Technology, Society, and the Imagination* (1990), assesses the psychological, social, and political implications of living in a predominantly technological environment.

Literature
and Technology

Toward an Archeology of the Philosophy of Technology and Relations with Imaginative Literature

CARL MITCHAM and TIMOTHY CASEY

For most of the history of philosophy, a philosophy of technology is no more than an implicit discipline, scarcely able to be imagined. A history of the philosophy of technology only exists buried within the standard histories of philosophy and of technology, philosophies of science, and allied studies. Discovering the relations between philosophy of technology and imaginative literature about technology must therefore be an archeological task. What the archeological mind uncovers in the remains of its philosophical past may nevertheless provide some orientation among the literary encounters with a world created by modern technological *poiesis*.

PRELIMINARY FIELDWORK AND SITE SELECTION

> There is from of old a quarrel between philosophy and *poiesis*.
> —Plato, *Republic* X (607b)

The relation between technology as a theme in philosophy and in imaginative literature can be read as an instance of the relation between philosophy and poetry. Indeed, given that literature and technology can be viewed as different kinds of *poiesis* or making,

31

what is involved is a tripartite relationship, which may conveniently be diagramed as follows:

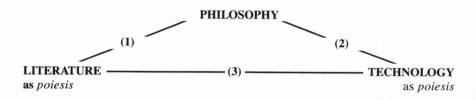

Focusing on relation (1) as diagrammed above, the philosophy-literature relationship, philosophy and poetry, ancient and modern, have held different views of such a relation. Philosophy, from Plato through St. Augustine to Hegel, is likely to argue that although imaginative literature may on occasion give original expression to new ideas or vividly exemplify abstract conceptions, it is not on its own a trustworthy or reliable guide to truth in any comprehensive sense. According to Plato, great poetry depends more on inspiration than *techne* (*Ion* 533e) and thus requires rational or reflective ordering (see *Republic* X, 595a ff.). Separated from its proper role as the handmaid of philosophy, poetry constructs or becomes its own world in competition with reality or being.

Philosophy, according to Aristotle, replaces imaginative or poetic discourse about the gods as extrinsic causes with rational discourse about nature and its intrinsic causes.[1] Poetry, in turn, displaces discourse about nature, that which is in itself, with discourse about making and the made, not to say convention and artifice. St. Augustine describes his conversion as leading from the pursuit of pleasures to the aesthetic life, then to philosophy, and thence to Christianity. The turning from the world of appearance and change, whether hedonistic or aesthetic, to concern with unchanging reality, whether philosophical or theological, constitutes the decisive moment.

Modern philosophy, however, having experienced a certain impotence in the face of the world transforming powers of modern making and scientific artifice, has on occasion exalted the poet if not the novelist. Poetry preceded philosophy, and the best philosophers, such as Plato, are in truth philosopher-poets. Poets have the power to move, to bring about change in their audiences; unlike philosophers, they are effective. It is poetry that has the power to bridge those fissures introduced into culture by modern technology. In the words of poet-philosopher Percy Bysshe Shelley,

> We have more moral, political, and historical wisdom than we know how to reduce to practice; we have more scientific and economical knowledge than can be accommodated to the just distribution of the produce which it multiplies. . . . The cultivation of those sciences which have enlarged . . . the empire or man over the external world, has, for want of the poetical faculty, proportionally circumscribed those of the internal world; and man, having enslaved the elements, remains himself a slave.[2]

More important than what is (the object of philosophy), is what might be (as put forth in poetry), since what is has largely become what is made by science and technology. The poet traditionally criticized philosophy as depriving the world of God or the gods, but in a technological world from which the gods appear to have withdrawn, even thinkers have been known to appeal to the poets for a return of the divine. "On the throne left vacant by the willing abdication of philosophy, poetry comes to sit with its momentary stays against confusion, its acts of finding what will suffice, its supreme fictions."[3] At the same time the poet becomes perforce a philosopher, as when William Wordsworth and Samuel Taylor Coleridge introduce their *Lyrical Ballads* (2d edition, 1800) with a theoretical preface.

From the perspective of imaginative literature—that is, from Aristophanes's "The Clouds" through Voltaire's *Candide* to Tom Stoppard's "Jumpers"—the philosopher is presented as someone lacking in appropriate existential engagement with reality. "Philosopher! a fingering slave," exclaims Wordsworth, "One that would peep and botanize / Upon his mother's grave."[4] Even in fictional memoirs by philosophers, such as *The Education of Henry Adams* or Jean-Paul Sartre's *Nausea,* the protagonist is portrayed in something less than a fully sympathetic light. Perhaps the closest to an exaltation of philosophy that can be found in imaginative literature occurs in Boswell's *Life of Johnson,* where the protagonist is a philosopher in only a very weak sense, or in Herman Hesse's *Siddhartha,* which focuses on a religious, not to say poetic, philosopher.

When imaginative literature undertakes to examine philosophical ideas, it typically places them in dramatic encounters (think of the

theater of George Bernard Shaw). Philosophy, by contrast, regularly uses myths—and those modern myths called novels and their
characters—to illustrate and exemplify arguments and points of
view (as with Socrates's citations from Homer or the philosophical
essays of Albert Camus). Philosophers who also write imaginative
literature (consider Iris Murdoch) generally create less than fully
realized characters. Writers who do philosophy (for example, Leo
Tolstoy) generally lack consistency, depth, and comprehensiveness.
At the very least, then, the relation between philosophy of technology and imaginative literature focused on technology can be
expected to exhibit certain problematic tensions.

These tensions are compounded by a philosophy-*poiesis* opposition present in (2) on the diagram, the philosophy-technology relation. The ancient quarrel between philosophy as discourse about
nature, that which is or comes to be through itself, and *poiesis,*
making or the coming to be through another, certainly implies an
antagonism between philosophy and technology. The irony is that
modern philosophy, first as modern natural philosophy—that is, as
discourse about nature conceived as a kind of cosmic making—and
then as technical philosophy and instrumental reason, would seem
to have prepared the ground for a resolution of this quarrel. But
modern literary *poiesis,* having developed its own epistemological
claims for the imagination and a critique of the social consequences
of technical rationality, reasserts the opposition.

At stake in this complex of historically shifting relations is the
meaning of *poiesis* and its relation to nature—or what is, apart from
convention and artifice. Not only are there at least two distinct
kinds of *poiesis* or making—literary and technological—but there
are various ways in which each can be carried out. Traditionally the
criterion for judging various kinds of making has been nature
(physis). To the extent that *poiesis* mirrors or imitates the fundamental structures of being, construction—whether in language or
material artifacts—is accepted by philosophy. The extent to which
making opposes or even assaults what is natural is the extent to
which philosophers have, until recently, rejected the claims of
poiesis as obstacles to the ultimate comprehension of reality and
the purposes of human life. In the modern world, however, it is
often through poetry that philosophy has been returned to its traditional concerns.

The deformation of philosophy into a kind of technical thinking
parallels the quite recent rise to prominence of the philosophy of
technology as a distinct discipline, a discipline whose basic reference works are listed near the end of this book. Insofar as the

philosophy of technology exhibits its own distinctive (nonfictive) literature, it can be succinctly chronicled:

1877   German-American pioneer Ernst Kapp's *Grundlinien einer Philosophie der Technik: Zur Entstehungsgeschichte der Cultur aus neuen Gesichtspunkten* is published in Germany.

1927   German research engineer Friedrich Dessauer's *Philosophie der Technik* is published. Revised and expanded thirty years later as *Streit um die Technik* (1956).

1933   Spanish philosopher José Ortega y Gasset delivers a series of lectures on technology subsequently published as *Meditación de la técnica* (1939).

1954   German philosopher Martin Heidegger includes "Die Frage nach der Technik" (from a series of lectures originally delivered in 1949) in *Voträge und Aufsätze*. French sociologist Jacques Ellul's *La Technique* published.

1956   Verein Deutscher Ingenieure (VDI, or Association of German Engineers) establishes a special "Mensch und Technik" study group to investigate "Philosophie der Technik" and related topics.

1965   Society for the History of Technology organizes a symposium on "Toward a Philosophy of Technology" at a joint meeting with the American Association for the Advancement of Science in San Francisco; expanded proceedings subsequently appear in *Technology and Culture* (1966).

1972   Philosophy students Carl Mitcham and Robert Mackey edit *Philosophy and Technology: Readings in the Philosophical Problems of Technology,* which is followed the next year by their *Bibliography of the Philosophy of Technology.*

1973   Civil engineer George Bugliarello organizes an international conference at the University of Illinois in Chicago on the "History and Philosophy of Technology," with subsequent proceedings.

1975   American pragmatist Paul T. Durbin hosts the first of two University of Delaware conferences on the philosophy of technology. Durbin also initiates the *Philosophy and Technology Newsletter* and the annual series *Research in Philosophy and Technology* (1978–present).

1976 Civil engineer Samuel Florman's *Existential Pleasures of Engineering* published, followed by *Blaming Technology* (1981) and *The Civilized Engineer* (1987).

1977 Society for Philosophy and Technology (SPT) established. German philosopher Friedrich Rapp's *Analytische Technikphilosophie* published.

1979 German-American philosopher Hans Jonas's *Das Prinzip Verantwortung* published. American phenomenologist Don Ihde's *Technics and Praxis* appears, to be followed by *Existential Technics* (1983) and *Technology and the Lifeworld* (1990).

1981 SPT holds its first biennial meeting in Bad Hamburg, Germany; subsequent meetings: New York (1983); Enschede, The Netherlands (1985); Blacksburg, Virginia (1987); Bordeaux, France (1989); Mayagüez, Puerto Rico (1991); Valencia, Spain (1993).

1988 American philosopher Frederick Ferré's *Philosophy of Technology* published in the Prentice-Hall Foundations of Philosophy series. First Inter-American Congress of Philosophy of Technology, Mayagüez, Puerto Rico. (Second Inter-American Congress, 1991.)

1990 First volume of a new series in Philosophy of Technology published by Indiana University Press.

This cursory chronology nevertheless discloses certain difficulties. What originates in the 1870s in Europe as an isolated work by engineer-philosophers begins to take shape in the late 1970s in the United States as an institutionalized discipline among professional or academic philosophers. One could expect some tensions as a result of these differences between place of birth and current primary residence. There exists, for instance, some diversity of terminology—from German *Technik* and French *technique* to English "technics" and "technology." The root of all these words is the Greek *techne,* which includes the making crafts and art as well as the skills of sport and argument; the English transliteration "technics" is almost but not quite as broad. But the word "technology"—the Greek *technologia* occurs only three times in Aristotle, and means simply grammar—is an early modern neologism for the study of the industrial arts or industrial technics, and in its original restricted meaning indicated only scientific or science-based making.[5] In common parlance it has nevertheless developed a more general connotation of almost any type of the making and using of artifacts, except for the fine arts.

An overview of current discussions in the discipline further reveals an effort to build interdisciplinary bridges between a number of special concerns, from applied ethics (bioethics, environmental ethics, nuclear ethics, engineering ethics, computer ethics) to epistemology and metaphysics. (For example, is technology applied science? Can computers think?)[6] To what extent and in what ways these fields are truly related is not yet completely clear.

Preliminary analysis of the diverse unifying efforts among these various studies discloses at least two different perspectives on such a spectrum of concerns. One of these, in fact the oldest, has been called engineering philosophy of technology, and exhibits tendencies to defend the importance of technology and to extend engineering thinking into other aspects of human affairs. A second approach, humanities philosophy of technology, seeks to interpret technology as only one limited aspect of human affairs and to delimit its practice.[7]

Within this body of literature, however, there are numerous allusions to two other approaches to philosophical reflection on technology. One set of these is to classical philosophical texts—especially those of Plato and Aristotle—which, although they do not contain an explicit philosophy of technology as such, do consider technology within the context of larger philosophical discussions in metaphysics and epistemology or ethics and politics. In such considerations the focus is commonly on technology as craft, with concerns expressed for the ways craft technique can undermine its own foundations.

The second set of allusions is to social science studies and criticism of technology—from proto-sociological texts to Karl Marx and the Marxist tradition (including the Frankfurt School) as well as the work of Max Weber and others. Pragmatist analysis also contributes to this approach, but Jacques Ellul's *La Technique ou l'enjeu du siècle* (1954) with its American edition (*The Technological Society*, 1964) and supplemental studies constitute a *locus classicus* for non-Marxist social criticisms of technology.

Although sociologists of the technological society do not commonly employ the term "philosophy of technology"—except, among East German Marxists, for purposes of derision[8]—such social criticism can nevertheless be identified as a fourth school.

Thus, just as there is no one unified school of imaginative literature dealing with technology, so there is no one philosophy of technology. There are instead various approaches to the philosophy of technology—at least four in number—that also shed some light on different possible imaginative stances as the essays in this book demonstrate. An archeological outline of these four approaches, along with some indications of their imaginative implications and fictive incarnations, follows.

EXCAVATIONS AMONG THE GREEKS: PLATO AND ARISTOTLE— CRAFT AND THE DANGERS OF TECHNIQUE

> Because there are many practices, *technai,* and sciences, there
> are also many ends. [But it belongs to] the principal *techne* . . .
> which appears to be politics [to decide which should be pursued] in the state.
> —Aristotle, *Nicomachean Ethics* I, 1–2 (1094a7–8 and 28–29)

It is sometimes held that the ancient Greeks despised manual work, were indifferent to technological innovation, and were more inclined toward contemplative theory than practical activity. Yet as early as the seventh century B.C.E. Attic and Corinthian pottery was the envy of the Mediterranean world, due mainly to the invention of the flywheel and the introduction of techniques for shaving and contrasting colors. In Ionia, Thales laid the foundations for navigation by the stars, and Anaximander drew up the first world map. Glaucos of Chios discovered a method of welding iron, and Anarcharsis the Scythian and Theodorus of Samos effected improvements in the anchor, the bellows, and the potter's wheel, in addition to inventing the lathe and the key. And the introduction of coins as a guaranteed currency in 700 B.C.E. indicates an advanced state of the art of metallurgy.

Substantiation of respect for technology as craft can readily be found in both literature and philosophy. Aeschylus's hymn to technology in his drama, *Prometheus Bound* (445–508), surveys the development of building, numbering, writing, agriculture, navigation, medicine, prophecy, and metallurgy. In Sophocles's *Antigone*

(335–67), the protagonist repeats the catalog to explain the wondrousness of humanity although acknowledging the limitations of technology in the face of death.

Such technology was not without influence on ancient philosophy. Among the pre-Socratics, Empedocles (Fragment 111) was inspired to propose a kind of crypto-Baconian view of the human relationship with nature, and historian Derek de Solla Price contends that the mechanistic philosophies of Democritus and Leucippus were simply extensions of the construction of automata so prevalent throughout the ancient world.[9] Certainly Theophrastus, in his *Metaphysics,* writes that "generally [matter] is to be explained by analogy with *techne* or by some other similarity."[10] Indeed, "high technology" in Greece was not only directed toward labor-saving devices but toward scientific models and objects of curiosity, for example, Anaximander's mechanical models of the earth and cosmos, automated theaters, and wind-up toys. These latter objects underscore philosopher Robert Brumbaugh's observation that "the everyday world of the ancient Athenians had running through its texture an important strand of interest in mechanism and ingenuity of mechanical design."[11]

According to the account of Socrates's life of interrogation in Plato's *Apology* (21a–22e), the knowledge of skilled craftsmen compares favorably with that of politicians and poets. Indeed, the former are praised as knowing "many and good things" and are thus superior to the poets, not to mention the politicians. Looking at the dialogues as a whole, it is clear that Plato was well acquainted with the day-to-day practice of *techne,* as evidenced by constant references to carpenters, weavers, cobblers, farmers, and the like, and by a rich store of technological analogies and metaphors.

What Plato finds in the practice of every authentic *techne* is the rational implantation of order and harmony through attention to the form or wholeness of a product. As regards this wholeness, Plato also argues that *techne* mirrors the order and moral goodness permeating the cosmos and hence that it points to uses related to virtue and happiness. Built into art, in Plato's view, is a teleological or in-order-to quality that arranges matter, form, and technique into a hierarchy and that bids the artisan to ask: "For what is the sake of my art?"

At the same time, Plato does not naively believe that simply knowing the purpose of an art is sufficient for the production of artifacts. Technical experience *(empeiria)* is needed to enable the expert realization of form in matter. *Emperia* is a term that, as John Wild points out, is used by Plato "in both a good and a bad sense, as the source of true art, or of its characteristic perversion."[12] In the good sense it denotes technique or skill, i.e., a noncognitive capacity that is developed through extensive practice and apprenticeship to accomplished masters. In the bad sense it signifies knackery and/ or mechanical routine or mere technique *(tribe)*.

The danger created by the degeneration of true skill into mechanical routine is twofold. First, there are the inevitably shoddy products resulting from inattentive production. Second, when technique slips into the mechanicalness of routine, it dulls the epistemic side of *techne* and hence the artisan's ability to focus on form.

On its own, mechanical technique maximizes output, and such productivity further opens the door to hedonism and associated social and political ills. A *techne* corrupted in this way aims at mere gratification. Its "success" is measured exclusively in terms of amount of pleasure given or money acquired. Wild refers to it as a "general materialization of *techne*" because it results in a serious disregard for the "real needs of the whole community" by establishing mere production of goods as an end in itself.[13]

Plato is thus concerned with the proper relation between *techne* and the Good. Such a relation, he suggests, depends upon the internal subordination of technique to form because to focus on the form includes attending to the appropriate uses of the product. In a certain sense the form *is* the artifact as best adapted to each kind of use or function, "for each kind of shuttle by nature is fitted for a special kind of weaving, which is true of other instruments in general" (*Cratylus* 389d). An artifact, in other words, is well-formed only when it is harmoniously adapted to its proper use.

Aristotle further develops Plato's insight by relating *techne* and the capacity to produce to the fecundity of nature and its fundamentally teleological character. According to Aristotle, *techne* or art imitates nature. In addition to utilizing the materials of nature, it does so by repeating an in-order-to structure already present in these natural materials. This is not to say that the practice of *techne* is natural in the way that a plant grows or a tree blossoms. *Techne* must be learned and can be forgotten; it is a habit to be cultivated and preserved with effort. Moreover, Aristotle makes it clear that "the deficiencies of nature" are what "art and education aim to make up" (*Politics* VII, 1337a).

Still, Aristotle does not place *techne* in opposition to nature or *physis*. Human needs are not seen as fundamentally at odds with the natural world nor as satisfied only in a technologically controlled environment. Rather, despite its admittedly "artificial" character, *techne* is really a part of nature, for it completes what nature cannot finish regarding human needs and hence again "partly imitated her." Thus the teleology of artifice, though different from the teleology of nature, is in fact continuous with it and dependent upon it as a paradigm. Nature serves as a model for the wholeness artisans seek to implant in their products.

It is through the mimetic character of *techne* that Aristotle clarifies the crucial link in technology between a cooperative stand toward nature and teleological concern for practical life, thus completing the Platonic argument for the subordination of technique to purpose and the good. It is in Aristotle that one finds the most lucid ancient expression of a philosophy of technology that refuses to dissociate a moral concern for humans from a fundamental regard for other living things.

AT THE SURFACE OF MODERNITY: WITH ENGINEERS FROM URE TO DESSAUER— TECHNOLOGY AS EXPANSION OF THE HUMAN

> From the first crude tool . . . to the most highly developed "system" . . . humanity sees and recognizes itself in these external objects.
>
> —Ernest Kapp[14]

Between Plato-Aristotle and the rise of the new technology there is in the history of the philosophy of technology an overriding continuity highlighted by isolated insights and arguments. St. Augustine, for instance, puts forth what might be called an argument for the existence of God from the history of technology,[15] Hugh of St. Victor proposes a classification of several mechanical arts to complement the seven liberal arts, and fifteenth century theologians become fascinated with technologies of logic and casuistry.[16] Traditional philosophy of technology did not, however, undergo fundamental changes until challenged by engineering and social science reflection.

The most dramatic alternative to that classical philosophy of technology that would integrate technology into a teleological or organic view of nature is engineering philosophy of technology, which not incidentally arises in association with the formulation of a new idea of nature as mechanism. The eighteenth and nineteenth centuries witnessed, however, an increasing struggle over the connotations of this basic metaphor of nature as machine—"mechanists" using it with approval and extending its application from nature to society, romantics rejecting its appropriateness in a diversity of contexts.

As an heir to this controversy, the German philosopher Ernst

Kapp (1808–1896) coined the phrase "philosophy of technology." A left-wing German contemporary of Karl Marx, Kapp was also a materialist philosopher who desired to turn Hegel "rightside up." Yet unlike Marx, Ernst Kapp departed Germany not for London and the British Museum to do research, but for the Texas frontier where he became a pioneer settler. There he developed an appreciation for technology as what he called "the externalizing principle as organ projection,"[17] and upon returning to Germany after the Civil War, he wrote the first philosophy of technology, expanding at length on this root metaphor. Basic tools are extensions of the hand (chapter 3), the proportions of the body are the foundations of mathematical measurement (chapter 4), and scientific instruments extend the senses (chapter 5). Moreover, engineered structures repeat structural principles found in the bones (chapter 6), railroads form an external circulatory system (chapter 7), and the telegraph is a projection of the nerves (chapter 8). In the latter instance, especially, "organ projection celebrates . . . a great triumph."[18]

The most outstanding figure in engineering-philosophy discussions, however, both before and immediately after World War II, was Friedrich Dessauer (1881–1963). As a research engineer and entrepreneur who pioneered in the development of X-ray therapy, and a Christian social democrat who openly opposed Nazism, Dessauer not only deepened the engineering analysis of technology, but sought to open up dialogue with existentialists, social theorists, and theologians. It is the work of Dessauer that is most often cited in those instances where philosophers of science mention philosophy of technology.

Contemporary philosophy of science has two dimensions. One focuses on methodological-epistemological questions regarding scientific knowledge (extending the classic analyses of David Hume and Immanuel Kant); the other, more popular, considers the cultural implications of certain scientific theories (as with Thomas H. Huxley's defense of Darwinian evolution). One way to summarize Dessauer's philosophy of technology is to contrast it with such standard approaches to the philosophy of science. For Dessauer, both approaches fail to recognize the power of scientific technical knowledge, which has become, through modern engineering, a new way for humanity to relate to the world. Dessauer attempts to provide a Kantian explanation of the transcendental preconditions not of scientific knowledge but of technological power, as well as to reflect on the ethical implications of its application.

To the three Kantian critiques of scientific knowing, moral doing, and aesthetic feeling, Dessauer proposes to add a fourth—a critique of technological making. Kant of course argued that while scientific knowledge is necessarily limited to the phenomenal world of appearances and can never make unmediated contact with the noumenal "things-in-themselves," moral and aesthetic experience does make contact with a "transcendent" reality beyond appearances. Dessauer contends that making, particularly in the form of invention, does establish positive contact with things-in-themselves. This contact is confirmed by two facts: that the invention, as artifact, is not something previously found in the world of appearance; and that, when it makes its phenomenal appearance, it works. An invention is not something just dreamed up, imagination without power; it derives from a cognitive encounter with the realm of preestablished solutions to technical problems. Technological invention involves "real being from ideas," that is, the engendering of "existence out of essence," the material embodying of a transcendent reality.[19] Thus Dessauer locates the decisive penetration of appearances precisely in a kind of practical experience that Kant failed to recognize as worthy of consideration: modern technology.

In harmony with this metaphysical analysis, Dessauer proposes a theory of the moral, not to say mystical, significance of technology. Most such theories limit themselves to a consideration of practical benefits. For Dessauer, however, the autonomous, world-transforming consequences of modern technology are witness to its transcendent moral value. Human beings create technology, but its power—which resembles, he says, that of "a mountain range, a river, an ice age, or planet"—goes beyond anything man expected; it brings into play more than this worldly forces. Modern technology should not be conceived simply as "the relief of man's estate" (Francis Bacon); it is, instead, a "participating in creation, . . . the greatest earthly experience of mortals."[20] With Dessauer even religious experience is interpreted in technological terms.

ARCHEOLOGY IN THE FUTURE: FROM MARX TO ELLUL— TECHNOLOGY AS SOCIAL ORDER TO BE CRITICIZED

[Our aim is] the union of commercial and manufacturing industry with literary and scientific industry.
—Henri Saint-Simon[21]

If Kapp can be read as father of the philosophical promotion of technology, Karl Marx was parent to a different approach, what could be called social-philosophical criticism of technology. This approach argues that technology can be understood and assessed only by being placed within the social and historical context that both determines and is determined by it. For Marx, of course, this context is fundamentally economic. Thus his contribution to philosophy of technology rests largely in his description of the central role technology plays in economic history, especially as it has progressively enslaved and alienated the worker while paradoxically preparing the conditions for proletarian liberation.

Marx's critique of modern technology, i.e., of the modern division of labor as it culminates in the factory system of industrial capitalism, is in fact a watershed in the history of the philosophy of technology inasmuch as it both looks back to a certain reading of the Platonic ideal of *techne,* across engineering expositions, and ahead to the realization of another ideal in scientific socialism. As a result of this tension, Marx's thought contains two rather distinct evaluations of technology. In his role as critic of modern industrial capitalism, Marx verges on romanticism and even Luddism. At the same time Marx speaks with gratitude of the development of those productive forces necessary for the final eradication of scarcity in a communist utopia.

The Marxist critique of capitalism rests on an interpretation of Platonic-Aristotelian *techne* as what Marx calls the labor process, defined as "human action with a view to the production of use-values, appropriation of natural substances to human requirements."[22] The instrument aided creation of artifacts is *intended* to serve human purposes. Indeed, it is this intention to form a certain matter into a useful object that distinguishes humans from other animals for

> what distinguishes the worst architect from the best bees is this, that the architect raises his structure in imagination before he erects it in reality. At the end of every labor-process, we get a result that already existed in the imagination of the laborer at its commencement.[23]

Technology, in other words, is a purposive activity, and it is in this purposiveness—not in its results—that one identifies its definitively human stamp. Although spiders may spin more intricate and beautiful patterns than most weavers, the least skilled weaver is superior to the spider so far as the weaving process is guided by an intelligence that literally informs the weaving technique.

From this perspective Marx launches his critical analysis of exchange-value and its virtual replacement of use-value in capitalist economic life. The cogency of this analysis is therefore rooted in what Marx borrowed from the Greeks and believes is distinctively human about technology. The ontological priority of use-value over exchange-value is crucial to the Marxist critique of the subjection of labor to capital.

As Marx shows, an exchange-value is measured in terms of the amount of labor-power "congealed" in a particular commodity. Thus the underlying "secret" of exchange-value consists in the amount of labor-time socially necessary for the production of a commodity. Now the level of socially standard labor-time is dependent on diverse factors, for example, the average skill of workers, social organization of production, the state of science and its applicability, sophistication of the instruments of production, etc. all of which are subject to *technical* improvement. It thus follows that any reduction of labor time is mainly possible through the development and improvement of technique. The more use-values recede into the background, the more the preoccupation with exchange-values grows, and with it, a new standard of efficiency that can be augmented through strictly technical measures.

Marx's prediliection for a traditional, ontological justification of technology that emphasizes purpose and imaginative projection is in tension with his distinctly modern admiration for technique and its embodiment in machines, as well as his awe in the face of the power of modern technology to subjugate a hostile nature. It is this Marx who sees in automation the promise of utopian liberation from the capitalist division of labor and who thus has more in common with the engineering philosophy of technology than with Plato and Aristotle.

In short, just as technology plays a crucial role in creating the problem of industrial capitalism, so it will play an equally crucial role in the creation of a socialist utopia. Not only will a socialized technology eliminate scarcity from the face of the planet, but as the "species life" of humanity it will also eradicate the metaphysical alienation that has challenged and baffled philosophers from Parmenides to Hegel. Marxist *techne* will thus accomplish what philosophy and religion have failed to accomplish. By making nature the reflection of essential human powers, it will allow humankind finally to affirm itself in and through the world, and not just in the mind or heaven.

In spite of the obvious moral, political, and material benefits that have resulted from modern technology, it is criticisms of its inhumane dimensions—not utopian visions of technological transcendence—that have multiplied since Marx's day. Many of these criticisms have focused precisely on the growing sphere of the technical. Max Weber's sociological analyses of how modern technique escapes all traditional social delimitations, and of the expansion of bureaucratic technique, are illustrations of such criticisms.[24] The most prominent, contemporary social critic of technology, however, is Jacques Ellul. As Ellul says in an autobiographical reflection on the genesis of his work, he "was certain . . . that if Marx were alive [then] he would no longer study economics or the capitalist structures but technology." He "thus began to study technology using a method as similar as possible to the one Marx used a century earlier to study capitalism."[25] Indeed, Ellul's contention that technology has dislodged itself from traditional and customary restraints and is the dominant force in all human activities today confirms Marx's analysis of the technicization of use-value.

The second great influence on Ellul's work is the Bible, and as a committed Christian he has been inspired to provide his sociological studies with dialectic, theological counterpoints. Against the sociology of *The Technological Society*, there is biblical theory of the city in *The Meaning of the City* (1970); as a companion to *The Political Illusion* (1967), with its description of technique in politics, there is *The Politics of God and the Politics of Man* (1972), a study of II Kings.[26] It is this dialectical, sociological-theological encounter with the many forms of technicization that places Ellul's work on a unique philosophical plane.

Ellul's analysis of the inherent character of this technicization process distinguishes between technical operations and the technical phenomnon (or traditional technical activities and modern technology). With the technical phenomenon, that is, the rational pursuit of efficiency, "technique has taken over all of man's activities, not just his productive activity."[27] The "technical phenonomenon," then, indicates the emergence of technique from its customary restraints and limits.

Ellul identifies in the technical phenomenon many of the characterstics Marx attributes to money alone. It is artificial, self-augmenting, universal, and autonomous. It replaces the natural milieu with one wholly fabricated by human beings that feeds on itself ("The solution to the problems of technology is not less but more technology"), becomes the same everywhere, and seems to grow according to its own laws. It is manifested in economics, government, and even in areas now technicized as "human resources." Medicine, education, sports, entertainment, become increasingly subject to some kind of input-output, cost-benefit analysis in search of "the one best way" to achieve some result.[28] It is a quest for efficiency in means at the expense of goodness of ends. Ellul's indictment of the technological society is similar to the Marxist critique of the capitalist industrial system, but the technical milieu he does not find the human liberation hoped for by Marx. Human subordination to nature has simply been replaced by subordination to technology, but an archeology of this historical development still leaves the future undetermined.

The core of the social science criticism of technology is, however, the search for ways out of such a situation. As Wolf Lepenies has argued, social science arose in response to a special hiatus between science-technology and the literary imagination present in industrial society.[29] Sociology wants to take the insights of the literary critics of technology and bring them to fruition in a new transformation of technology. In the words of sociologist Hans Freyer, "The entire theme of spirit and state, freedom and law, is stretched between these two poles: engineer and poet."[30] Ellul, however, by his critique of the sociologically generated movements of socialism, positivism, and behaviorism precisely for their failures to come anywhere near such a transformation, effectively shifts the hope for transformation back to literature and the arts, which points toward a need to consider that philosophy of technology that is the deepest expression of modern cultural ideals—humanities philosophy of technology.

ANTHROPOLOGY AND ONTOLOGY AS ARCHEOLOGY: MUMFORD AND HEIDEGGER— TECHNOLOGY AS THREAT TO THE HUMAN AND TO BEING

> In self-assertive [technological] production, the humanness of humanity and the thingness of things dissolve.
> —Martin Heidegger[31]

The defense of the humanities as larger and more inclusive than the technological initially comes to the fore in certain voices of the romantic movement. Already in the seventeenth century Blaise Pascal, whose thought often anticipates romantic themes, contrasts *l'esprit géometrique* with *l'esprit de finesse*.[32] Jean Jacques Rousseau, in his *Discourses on the Sciences and Arts* (1750), criticizes the enlightenment theory that scientific-technological progress advances society by unifying wealth and virtue. According to Rousseau, not only have "our souls been corrupted to the extent that our sciences and arts have advanced toward perfection," but "the sciences and arts owe their birth to our vices."[33] "The politicians of the ancient world talked without ceasing of morals and virtue," observes Rousseau; "ours speak only of commerce and money."[34]

Romanticism affirms the significance of aesthetic judgments of appropriateness over mathematical calculations, of spiritual culture over technical civilization. As such it becomes fascinated by the idea of human beings outside the structures of civilization and the possibility of some vital faculty of mind (imagination) with an access to deeper truths about reality than the strictly rational intellect.

The subsequent romantic critique of modern technology as somehow obscuring or covering over essential human and social possibilities is a rich and varied tradition. For present purposes, it is sufficient to concentrate on two contemporary but commonly unassociated representatives of the humanities philosophy of technology—namely, Lewis Mumford (1895–1990) and Martin Heidegger (1889–1976).

Lewis Mumford and the Myth of the Machine

Like Dessauer, Mumford was excited by electronics during his adolescence, did not complete a standard university education, and made his way in philosophy as an outsider. He became, however, not a research engineer and proponent of engineering philosophy, but a writer and a persistent critic of technology. In his criticisms Mumford represents the American tradition of worldly romanticism that extends from Ralph Waldo Emerson to John Dewey. The tradition is worldly in its concern for the natural environment and the organic harmonies of urban life. It is romantic in insisting that material nature is not the final explanation of human activity. The basis of human action is mind and the human aspiration for creative self-realization.

It was in *Technics and Civilization* (1934)—the bibliography of which contains references to Ure, Zschimmer, and Dessauer—that Mumford first employs his theory of human nature to analyze the broad sweep of mechanical civilization and to write, in the process, a classic in the history of technology. But Mumford's interest is not simply historical. The first two chapters of his book describe, in turn, the psychological or cultural origins, then the material and efficient causes, of machine technology; it is only after this that he undertakes a broad-brush linear history of machine technics. The last third of the book then returns to an evaluation of the contemporary social and cultural reactions. As he says in his own summary,

> We have observed the limitations the Western European imposed upon himself in order to create the machine and project it as a body outside his personal will: we have noted the limitations the machine has imposed upon men through the historic accidents that accompanied its development. We have seen the machine arise out of the denial of the organic and the living, and we have in turn marked the reaction of the organic and the living upon the machine.[35]

Much of Mumford's voluminous writing afterward was an expansion and commentary on this pioneering work, culminating three and a half decades later in *The Myth of the Machine* (2 vols., 1967 and 1970). In extended restatement of his case, Mumford argues that although the human being is rightly engaged in worldly activities, he or she is properly understood not as *homo faber* but as *homo sapiens*. As Mumford says in one essay, the human essence is not making but interpreting.

> What we know of the world comes to us mainly by interpretation, not by direct experience, and the very vehicle of interpretation itself is a product of that which must be explained: it implies man's organs and physiological aptitudes, his feelings and curiosities and sensibilities, his organized social relations and his means for transmitting and perfecting that unique agent of interpretation, language.[36]

The importance of this hermeneutic activity can scarcely be overemphasized.

> If all the mechanical inventions of the last five thousand years were suddenly wiped away, there would be a catastrophic loss of life; but man would still be human. But if one took away the function of interpretation, . . . the whole round earth would fade away more swiftly than Prospero's vision [and] man would sink into a more helpless and brutish state than any animal: close to paralysis.[37]

Against what Mumford considers a technological-materialist image of humanity, he maintains that technics in the narrow sense of tool making and using has not been the primary agent in human development, not even of technology. All human technical achievements are "less for the purpose of increasing food supply or controlling nature than for utilizing [and fulfilling] more adequately . . . superorganic demands and aspirations." The elaboration of symbolic culture through language, for instance, "was incomparably more important to further human development than the chipping of a mountain of hand-axes."[38] For Mumford, the human being "is pre-eminently a mind-making, self-mastering, and self-designing animal."[39]

On the basis of this anthropology, Mumford constructs a distinction between two kinds of technology: polytechnics and monotechnics. Poly- or biotechnics is the primordial form of making; at the beginning (logically but probably also historically), technics was "broadly life-oriented, not work-centered or power-centered."[40] This is the kind of technology that is in harmony with the polymorphous needs and aspirations of life, and it functions in a democratic manner to realize a diversity of human possibilities. In contrast, mono- or authoritarian technics is "based upon scientific intelligence and quantified production, directed mainly toward economic expansion, material repletion, and military superiority"[41]—in short, toward power.

The consequence is the "myth of the machine," or the notion that megatechnics is both irresistible and ultimately beneficent. This is a myth and not reality because the megamachine can be resisted, and it is not ultimately beneficial. Mumford's work as a whole is an attempt to demythologize and delimit megatechnics, and thereby to initiate a radical reorientation of mental attitudes that would transform monotechnical civilization. As he says in an earlier essay, "to save technics itself we shall have to place limits on its heretofore unqualified expansion."[42]

Mumford's aim, he says, is not to discard the Promethean myth of man as tool-using animal, but to "supplement" it with that of Orpheus as "man's first teacher and benefactor." Man became human, "not because he made fire his servant, but because he found it possible, by means of his symbols, to express fellowship and love, to enrich his present life with vivid memories of the past and formative impulses toward the future, to expand and intensify those moments of life that had value and significance for him."[43] Technology is to be promoted only when it can contribute to and enhance what Mumford calls this "personal" aspect of life.

Martin Heidegger and the Way of Technology

The theme that animates Heidegger's philosophy is what he calls the question about the meaning of Being, the famous *Seinsfrage*. The question concerning technology, for which Heidegger is also well known, is a more directed posing of the *Seinsfrage*. As commentator Theodore Kisiel notes, the present concretion of the question of Being is nothing less than the question of science and technology, insofar as the institutions and the attitudes they have provoked permeate the fabric of 20th century existence and thus indelibly mark the way we now live, move and have our being. In short, the question of Being now reads: What does it mean to be in a scientific-technological age?[44]

The ontological way Heidegger works out the connection between Being and modern technology is what distinguishes his approach from the anthropological investigations of Mumford. At the same time, Heidegger and Mumford have more in common than at first meets the eye. Both, for instance, develop their ideas in relation to the thought of Plato and Aristotle.[45] And for both, technology is properly understood as part of a larger or more encompassing reality.

But although Plato and Aristotle provide Heidegger with insight into the relation between technology and Being, Heidegger embarks upon a new interpretation of *Dasein*'s productive relationship toward beings in *Being and Time* (1927), inasmuch as ancient ontology "does not get beyond a common conception of the *Dasein* and its comportments" and "remains within the rut of pre-philosophical knowledge."[46] Hence the tool analysis of *Being and Time,* which links the capacity to make with a preconceptual understanding of Being or world, and which again shows that *techne* and its concern *(Besorge)* for this worldly Being transcends the technical concerns for method and efficient production. As Heidegger puts it in *The Basic Problems of Phenonemology:* "Productive comportment of relationship is not limited to the producible and produced but harbors within itself a remarkable breadth of possibility for understanding the Being of beings."[47] It is not until much later, however, that Heidegger directs this ontological analysis toward modern technology itself.

In "The Question Concerning Technology" (1954) Heidegger reaffirms his earlier notion of *techne* as a "way of revealing" by exposing the unique mode of revealment found in modern technology. He also rejects the commonly held theory of the neutrality of technology and argues that to focus on *techne* as merely a means to an end is to miss its true essence. Rather, he says, any technology is a kind of revealing or truth, and modern technology in particular is a revealing that sets up and challenges nature *(physis)* to yield a kind of energy that can be independently stored and transmitted.

This character of "setting upon" nature to "challenge it forth" is what distinguishes modern technology from a *techne* that "brings forth" Being in the artifact after the manner of traditional *poiesis*. To clarify this distinction, Heidegger contrasts the traditional windmill or water wheel with an electric power plant. Each harnesses the energy of nature and puts it to work to serve human ends, yet the windmill and water wheel remain related to nature in a way that allows nature to remain itself even as it serves human needs. They are a kind of *techne* that lets nature *reveal itself as it is* even as it is used in a technological process.

A coal-fired electric power plant, by contrast, unlocks basic physical energies and then stores them up in abstract, nonsensuous form. It does not just transmit motion; it unlocks or releases and transforms it. Thus modern technology puts "unreasonable" demands on nature by aggressively setting upon it and refusing to let it be as *physis*. And like the corrupted *techne* described in Plato, it is driven by efficiency, that is, "toward driving on to the maximum yield at the minimum expense."[48] Not only are the standards that result from this revealing exclusively human standards, but they are mainly economic considerations of the shortsighted variety that tend to undermine ethical and ecological concerns. An electric power plant seldom fits into or conplements the natural landscape. Large dams flood canyons and cover rapids. Nuclear reactors not only contaminate the environment with heat and radiation, but their location is determined by urban utilities. They have a form that is hostage to internal structural calculations, so that they exhibit a univocal character wherever they are set down upon the landscape.

The net result of this aggressive mode of revealing is the transformation of the world into a vast stockroom where everything gains its ontological status in terms of its "availability" and "disposability" for the process of technological production and consumption. Modern technology generates a world of what Heidegger calls *Bestand*—"stock," "standing-reserve," objects that are "in supply," "resources." This is not just because of mass production, but because of the kind of articles that are mass produced. *Bestand* consists of objects with no inherent value apart from human consumption. Like plastic, their whole form is dependent on human decisions about what they will be used for and how they will be decorated or packaged. Whatever is, "is" to the extent that it serves the industrial-technological order.

Yet, as with Platonic *techne,* the mode of revealing in modern technology is not under the control of the technologist. Rather, producers and consumers alike *respond* to this revealing even unbeknown to themselves. Heidegger calls this mode of revealing *Ges-*

tell, or the Enframing that, as a "destiny" of Being, challenges *Dasein* to challenge forth nature as resources (just as Being qua *Idea* evoked ancient Greek *techne*). *Gestell,* in other words, is the essence of modern technology and hence cannot be found through anthropological investigations or instrumental analyses of machines or processes. "To be" now means to be scientifically calculable and technologically controllable, engendering the illusion that humanity is the "master of being," whereas, in point of fact, *Gestell* has released *Dasein* into an exclusive attachment to beings and hence into a neglect of Being as what makes technology possible and meaningful for *Dasein.* This neglect manifests itself in the world *Dasein* creates for itself. It is an increasingly artificial world where pollution and environmental devastation become the norm and where the standardization of mass production applies to consumers as well as to consumables. Nature hides herself and, in so doing, conceals from *Dasein* a *poiesis* on which are based the more restrained and moderate technologies of the past.

Albert Borgmann, whose work has been inspired by Heidegger but moves in more ethical and political directions, summarizes the point at issue here with a distinction between things and devices. "A thing . . . is inseparable from its context."[49] In our engagement with things such as wood stoves we discover the beginning of the morning and the hearth of a household, are gathered around an object that calls forth different responses from different members of the family (children gather kindling, parents wood; mother cooks upon, and father cleans) and contributes its own reality to the experience of life around it. The paradigm of the modern technological object is, by contrast, what Borgmann calls a device. With the device as with a central heating plant there is procurement alienated from the larger world. With the device we are engaged as little as possible; anyone can turn it on or set the temperature, almost without thinking. The world of modern technology can be characterized as the replacement of focal things and practices by devices.

There is about modern technology, in the Heideggerian view, an air of *hubris,* a marked tendency to push both humans and nature beyond their limits. After all, modern technology is so certain about how to construct this or fabricate that. It has an efficient method or procedure that is superior to all other methods or ways of proceeding, and in this it does not recognize its own limits—it does not know itself. As a counterbalance to this arrogance, Heidegger proposes not that we reject or destroy our power plants and computers—actions that in their attempts at control merely reinforce

Gestell—but that we think through modern technology to that which makes it possible, viz., Being.

FROM ARCHEOLOGY TO MODERN LIFE, PHILOSOPHY TO LITERATURE

> Philosophy without poetry, exactly like poetry without philosophy, is immoderate or unmeasured. In the last analysis, there is no quarrel between philosophy and poetry. . . . Even within the limits of the Tenth Book of the *Republic,* it cannot be too strongly emphasized that Socrates begins with the quarrel but ends with the myth of Er.
>
> —Stanley Rosen[50]

At the beginning this study introduces a distinction between three relationships: (1) philosophy-literature (as *poiesis*), (2) philosophy-technology (as *poiesis*), and (3) literature (as *poiesis*)-technology (as *poiesis*). This was followed initially by a sketch of possible versions of relation (1), noting that there exist movements from the sides of both philosophy and literature to subordinate one to the other. With regard to relation (2), it was suggested that the modern period had witnessed a fundamental reversal in the quarrel between philosophy and poetry by means of a reinterpretation of philosophy as itself a kind of instrumental reason, thus handing over to literature the need to be independently philosophical.

The main body of the study, however, provides in the second through the fifth, sections a more detailed consideration of four possible forms of relationship (2), one ancient and three modern: Platonic-Aristotelian, engineering, social science, and humanities philosophies of technology. For Plato and Aristotle, technology as *poiesis* is clearly conceived as the handmaid of philosophy; whereas for engineers, philosophy can be described as the handmaid of technology (reflecting a technical conception and practice of philosophy in modernity). Social science and humanities philosophies of technology are more ambiguous, but can be interpreted as reflecting to some extent these same basic options. In this sense, philosophy-technology relations (2) exhibit patterns from philosophy-literature relations (1).

It nevertheless remains to observe how the four relations in (2) can be themselves found embodied in (3), the literary *poiesis* of technological *poiesis*. Although there exists a broader philosophical literature on technology than is generally known even among philosophers, literature of the fictive or imaginative engagement with technology is much more abundant and widely read. There is even a literature of ideas about technology—for instance, Max Frisch's *Homo Faber* (1957) and Robert Pirsig's *Zen and the Art of Motorcycle Maintenance* (1974) that constitutes a kind of imaginative presentation of philosophical reflection. Indeed, it is not impossible that philosophy of technology should be inspired by and draw upon such literature.

The Platonic and Aristotelian reflection on *techne,* for instance, can be interpreted as an attempt to respond to the conflicting responses to technology presented by the Greek tragedians. As literary critic Arthur D. Kahn describes it, Aeschylus, Sophocles, and Euripides provide successive reactions to Greek technological changes that mirror those of the twentieth century. "Aeschylus, the eldest, reflects the initial confidence in man's unlimited capacity for controlling nature . . . ; Sophocles exemplifies the measured and cautious attitude of the following generation; and Euripides, the doubt and pessimism of intellectuals . . . in face of the increasing exploitation of the new technology by militarists and profiteers."[51]

> Aeschylus has been aware of the danger in the possible misuse of technology, but for him the question had been simple: tyranny perverts and obstructs, democracy fosters science and technology. . . . [But] contrary to Aeschylus's expectations, the technological revolution . . . associated . . . with the glorious repulse of the Persian invader and the triumph of democracy had provoked apparently insoluble social, political, and moral crises. . . . Little more than a decade [later] Sophocles was wondering whether man *would* use his knowledge and intellect wisely. Twenty years later Euripides wondered whether man *could* use it well.[52]

It is this transition from confidence to questioning that the Platonic-Aristotelian analysis of *techne* exhibits and the need to maintain the mastery of form attempts to explain. By contrast, both engineers and social scientists incorporate commentaries on utopian and anti-utopian literature. Samuel Florman's contemporary defense of "the existential pleasures of engineering," for instance, is developed in conscious response to what he views as the anti-technological literary stance of Jacques Ellul and Lewis Mumford, while Marx and Ellul criticize utopian and scientific socialism, respectively, for their rhetorical or literary flourishes. The writings of Mumford and Heidegger, in turn, draw inspiration from the poetic critique of modern technology.

Without doubt the most common literary use of technology, however, is as apparently "neutral" material for imaginative reflection. The imaginative attitude toward technology in such writings neither supports not condemns technology but rather treats it as a source for imagery, setting, tropes, and the like, utilizing technology much as it does nature and society for similar purposes. Many overt references to the crafts in Plato are of this type, since Plato considers technology a given aspect of life and a possible human manifestation of cosmic harmony and goodness.

It is also significant that the word *techne* designates for Plato what is today separated into fine art and technology. In not making a clean distinction between aesthetic and technical sensibility, Plato upheld a sense of technology as an integral part of human existence and the natural world in spite of its "artificiality" and utilitarian character. This integrative imaginative response is one that "humanizes" technology by subordinating it to imaginative expression and, more importantly, by investing it with more meaning and beauty than commonly exhibited by its strictly functional contributions to everyday life. The same could be said for the literary "use" of any other human or natural phenomenon.

Many examples can be found of this nonjudgmental treatment of technology in imaginative literature. In *Ulysses,* for instance, James Joyce incorporates the telephone into a mythological vision. While walking along Sandymount strand, Stephen Daedalus espies two *Frauenzimmer,* one a midwife toting a bag.

> From the Liberties, out for the day. Mrs. Florence MacCabe, relict of the late Patk MacCabe, deeply lamented, of Bride street. One of her sisterhood lugged me into life. Creation from nothing. What has she in the bag? A misbirth with a trailing navelcord, hushed in ruddy wool. The cords of all link back, strandentwining cable of all flesh. That is why mystic monks. Will you be as gods? Gaze in your omphalos. Hello. Kinch here. Put me into Edenville. Aleph, alpha: nought, nought, one.[53]

The wonderful notion of an umbilical telephone that coils its way back through the human race to Eden and our first parents is a funny and ingenious blending of the ancient and modern, natural and technological, information and mythology. Joyce does not attempt to say that the telephone in itself is either beneficial or detrimental. He simply employs a rather common modern device for a rather uncommon literary purpose and, in doing so, quite possibly changes the way we look at telephones and other mundane appurtenances of daily life that tend to go unnoticed.

Another less fantastic example is James Dickey's "Cherrylog Road," a poem about a romantic tryst between two teenagers in a deserted junkyard of old cars—an unlikely setting for love if ever there was one. But the sense of adventure (a '34 Ford "With a seat pulled out to run / Corn whiskey down from the hills") and romance ("Some long Pierce-Arrow / Sending platters of blindness forth / From its nickel hubcaps / And spilling its tender upholstery / On sleeping roaches") Dickey evokes through his use of technological imagery—combined with the double entendre of "Pierce" and "arrow"—creates an atmosphere of eroticism and daring. Again we encounter the telephone, this time a chauffeur's line to the backseat of the old Pierce-Arrow.

> The back-seat phone
> Still on its hook.
> I got in as though to exclaim,
> "Let us go to the orphan asylum,
> John; I have some old toys
> For children who say their prayers"

Then, with the boy on the phone, "Praying for Doris Holbrook / To come from her father's farm," Doris arrives "With a wrench in her hand" and climbs into the "long" Pierce-Arrow:

> I held her and held her and held her,
> Convoyed at terrific speed
> By the stalled, dreaming traffic around us.

Having consummated their love, the two exit the Arrow, the boy returning to his parked motorcycle,

> Restored, a bicycle fleshed
> With power, and tore off
> Up Highway 106, continually
> Drunk on the wind in my mouth,
> Wringing the handlebar for speed,
> Wild to be wreckage forever.

As in the passage from Joyce, there is no attempt to focus on the technology for its own sake. The sexiness and power and youthful abandon Dickey conjures up with the Freudian Pierce-Arrow, the motorcycle, and the wreckage of the yard transform this scene of technological ugliness and squalor into one of charged emotion and vitality. Remarkably, it poetically redeems our throwaway society without justifying or condemning it.

The philosophy of technology, however, invites us to question such apparently neutral poetic uses of artifacts and to wonder at their appropriateness in certain contexts. In philosophical terms, there is no prime or purely neutral matter. All matter brings some form to any imaginative informing process, so that clay is appropriate for making pots but not tables, and wood the reverse. It is not clear that modern poets always adequately appreciate the material with which they deal.

In another category are those writers who take a more direct and admiring approach to their technological world. Carl Sandburg on Chicago architecture, or Emily Dickinson and Walt Whitman on trains, partially reflect the philosophical attitude toward technology found in the engineering tradition of Kapp and Engelmeier. In "To a Locomotive in Winter," Whitman writes:

> Type of the modern—emblem of motion and power—
>   pulse of the continent,
> For once come serve the Muse and merge in verse,
>   even as here I see thee. . . .
> Fierce-throated beauty!
> Roll through my chant with all thy lawless music,
>   thy swinging lamps at night,
> Thy madly-whistled laughter, echoing, rumbling like
>   an earthquake, rousing all,
> Law of thyself complete, thine own track firmly
>   holding.
> (No sweetness debonair of tearful harp or glib
>   piano thine,)
> Thy trills of shrieks by rock and hills return'd,
> Launch'd o'er the prairies wide, across the lakes,
> To the free skies unpent and glad and strong.

Clearly technology is not here a threat to nature or to the literary imagination. Quite the contrary, the locomotive is the servant of Whitman's Muse, embodying a wild kind of beauty that resonates with the natural surroundings as no "tearful harp" or "glib piano" could. In fact, the machine as aesthetic object and poetic inspiration is a theme that runs through much American literature, one to which even a critic such a Mumford grants some validity,[54] although it is a fair subject for sociophilosophical criticism.

It is another large step, however, to the kind of literature that is unreservedly protechnological and that seeks to extend the spirit of the mechanical to all areas of life. The work of literary technology utopians such as Edward Bellamy, King Camp Gillette, and B. F. Skinner falls squarely in the protechnology camp. The confidence invested in technology as the ultimate solution to the problems of life is the thread that unites such thinkers. In general, this solution will mean an end to human history (since humankind will have reached a state of perfection) and the attainment of the "mastery and possession of nature" dreamed of by Descartes at the onset of modernity.

Central to this vision, according to Howard Segal, is the cult of efficiency. Not only does it drive and animate the imagined physical systems of transportation, communication, agriculture, and manufacture in utopia, but it also permeates moral and political judgments and fosters a technical and pragmatic approach to education, work, culture, and religion. As Segal summarizes, "the ethos of technology shapes the values as well as the physical dimensions of utopia, but the intensity of the influence is surprising. The inhabitants of utopia aim to be as efficient as their machinery."[55]

In direct contrast to technological utopianism is an abundant literature that is profoundly suspicious of the modern drift toward technicism and its antihistorical bias. Samuel Butler's *Erewhon* (1872) and Aldous Huxley's *Brave New World* (1932), for example, represent a dystopian look at a world that is immersed in Ellulian technique and the Heideggerian reduction of nature and humans to *Bestand*.

The original antitechnology work of this genre is undoubtedly Mary Shelley's *Frankenstein* (1818). It is, among other things, an imaginative expression of our worst fears concerning technology, most particularly the concern that our technological creations become autonomous and turn on us, their creators, undermining the ideology of human mastery and control. Thus in contemporary philosophy of technology the alleged of technics is typically referred to as "the Frankenstein phenomenon." Other examples expressing this deep-seated fear are Karel Capek's "R.U.R." (Rossum's Universal Robots) and, of course, Hal the computer in the movie *2001: A Space Odyssey*. Langdon Winner's study of *Autonomous Technology* as a theme in post-Romantic political discussions gives this tradition philosophical articulation.

There are, however, more subtle expressions of the unease and displeasure that oddly accompany our feelings of awe and admiration for technology. Take, for example, John Steinbeck's powerful descriptions in *The Grapes of Wrath* (1939) of the effects of mechanized agriculture on land and farmer.

> The tractors came over the roads and into the fields, great crawlers moving like insects, having the incredible strength of insects. . . . Snubnosed monsters. . . . They did not run on the ground but on their own roadbeds. They ignored hills and gulches, water courses, fences, houses.

The man sitting in the iron seat did not look like a man, gloved, goggled, rubber dust mask over nose and mouth, he was a part of the monster, a robot in the seat. . . . The driver could not control it—straight across country it went, cutting through a dozen farms and straight back. A twitch at the controls could swerve the cat', but the driver's hands could not twitch because the monster that built the tractor, the monster that sent the tractor out, had somehow got into the driver's hands, into his brain and muscle, had goggled him and muzzled him—goggled his mind, muzzled his speech, goggled his perception, muzzled his protest. He could not see the land as it was, he could not smell the land as it smelled; his feet did not stamp the clods or feel the warmth and power of the earth.[56]

Like Marx, Steinbeck is ambivalent toward the machine, and it is this ambivalence that is most unsettling. The real monster is not so much technology as the economic system that drives it:

The bank is something more than men, I tell you. It's the monster. Men made it, but they can't control it.

Thus the farmer

loved the land no more than the bank loved the land. He could admire the tractor—its machined surfaces, its surge of power, the roar of its detonating cylinders; but it was not his tractor.[57]

In short, Steinbeck gives us Whitman's vision sullied by the crassness of capitalism. It is only when seen against Whitman's vision that one feels the pain of Steinbeck's more contemporary and very American uncertainty about economic and technological "progress."

The subterranean nature of this American ambivalence toward the modern world is perhaps nowhere more accurately described and dissected than in Sinclair Lewis's *Babbitt* (1922). Here we have a finely detailed account of a successful American businessman whose self-esteem and happiness are to a dangerous extent bound up with the technological wrappings of his world, from the modern skyscrapers of his midwestern city to the gadgets and appliances that define his suburban home. Here emerges a disturbing picture of a thoroughly thoughtless man, one who gets his opinions from newspaper editorials and his attitudes from the Elks and the Republican party. Babbitt is without a center, without a self—someone wholly immersed in what Heidegger calls The Public *(Das Mann).*

He never put on B.V.D.'s without thanking the God of Progress that he didn't wear tight, long, old-fashioned undergarments. . . . But most wonder-working of all was the donning of his spectacles. There is character in spectacles—the pretentious tortoise-shell, the meek pince-nez of the school teacher, the twisted silver-framed glasses of the old villager. Babbitt's spectacles had huge, circular, frameless lenses of the very best glass; the ear-pieces were thin bars of gold. In them he was the modern business man; one who gave orders to clerks and drove a car and played occasional golf and was scholarly in regard to Sales-manship.[58]

Babbitt's identification with technological objects is almost complete. Lewis chronicles this absorption in the world of appearances through a number of seemingly innocuous items Babbitt encounters from rising in the morning ("It was the best of nationally advertised and quantitatively produced alarm-clocks, with all modern attachments") until he arrives at his office ("The Reeves Building was as fireproof as a rock and as efficient as a typewriter"). The picture he paints is of someone who is fascinated and enslaved by—to use Heidegger's phrase—an exclusive attachment to beings.

A sensational event was changing from the brown suit to the gray the contents of his pockets. He was earnest about these objects. They were of eternal importance, like baseball or the Republican Party. . . . Without them he would have felt naked.[59]

Beneath this pride in being modern by having a modern house and living in a modern city there also stirs a vague, amorphous dissatisfaction with family and home, work and colleagues. In spite (because?) of an enviable prosperity that has provided for a life filled with nothing but the most recent inventions excelling in efficiency and convenience, "the Babbitt whose god was Modern Appliances was not pleased" because his was a life, above all else, lacking in love. While dreaming wistfully of his "fairy child, a dream more romantic than scarlet pagodas by a silver sea," Babbitt is roused from his sleep by

the familiar and irritating rattle of some one cranking a Ford: snap-ah-ah, snap-ah-ah, snap-ah-ah. Himself a pious motorist, Babbitt cranked with the unseen driver, with him waited through taut hours for the roar of the starting engine, with him agonized as the roar ceased and again began the infernal patient snap-ah-ah. . . . Not till the rising voice of the motor told him that the Ford was moving was he released from the panting tension.[60]

The sexual transference here underlines both Babbitt's love-affair with his car, which "was poetry and tragedy, love and heroism." and his confusion and despair over the less sanguine side of modern technology and progress. Machines, he dimly perceives, can invade our privacy and exacerbate our anxieties—even as they lessen our toil and provide us with pleasure. At times they can even let us down, can fail to deliver on their transcendent promise.

> Normally he admired the office . . . normally he was stimulated by the clean newness of it and the air of bustle; but today it seemed flat. . . . He hadn't even any satisfaction in the new water-cooler! . . . He looked down the relentless stretch of tiled floor at the water-cooler, and assured himself that no tenant of the Reeves Building had a more expensive one, but he could not recapture the feeling of social superiority it had given him.[61]

Babbitt senses—but never really *knows*—that the god of progress is a fickle god. His moodiness and susceptibility to the least sign of disorder in his carefully arranged world remain a mystery to him, a mystery precisely because this world—the modern world—was supposedly created as a guarantee against disorder, the unexpected, the aporetic.[62]

The critical eye that Sinclair Lewis brings to his imaginative depiction of the technological world is of a piece with the philosophical critiques of Mumford and Heidegger. It is based very simply on the discernment of a kind of *thoughtlessness* that spreads from technology to all of human existence. This discernment does not arise from an antitechnological bias or animus, but is part of a more subtle and complex approach to technology that is thus easily misunderstood and even more easily dismissed as Luddite or romantic.

Whether such dismissals are merely another manifestation of the thoughtlessness exposed by these critiques is a question to be raised. More important is the confluence of these approaches in their feel for the underlying issues of living in a scientific and technological world. Perhaps one way to begin to overcome the fragmentation that seems endemic to this world is to see these philosophical and literary discussions of technology as a discourse whose participants must seek to draw stimulation and insight from one another regardless of orientation, mode of expression, or ultimate purpose. In the words of Albert Borgmann, "the poet in the stillness of writing and in the calm of speaking gathers and presents the world in the comprehensive and intimate ways that distinguish human beings."[63] But "philosophical reflection can hope to clear

the ground for poetry . . . and thereby for focal things and practices."[64]

NOTES

General note: Unless otherwise indicated, all translations are our own.

1. Aristotle, *Metaphysics* III, iv (1000a9); XII, vi (1071b27); XII, x (1075b26); XIV, iv (1091a34 ff.); and *Poetics* 1 (1447b19).

2. Percy Bysshe Shelley, *A Defense of Poetry,* paragraph 37.

3. Carl Rapp, "Philosophy and Poetry: The New Rapprochement," in Donald G. Marshall, ed., *Literature as Philosophy, Philosophy as Literature* (Iowa City: University of Iowa Press, 1987), p. 129.

4. William Wordsworth, "A Poet's Epitaph," lines 18–20.

5. See Carl Mitcham, "Philosophy and the History of Technology," in Bugliarello-Doner, eds., *The History and Philosophy of Technology,* especially pp. 171 ff.

6. For a survey of the field with bibliography, see Carl Mitcham, "Philosophy of Technology," in Paul T. Durbin, ed., *Guide to the Culture of Science, Technology, and Medicine* (New York: Free Press, 1984), pp. 282–363; and Timothy Casey, "Recent Continental Philosophy of Technology in North America," *Phanomenologische Forschungen* 15 (1983), pp. 94–123.

7. Carl Mitcham, "Dos tradiciones de la filosofía de la tecnología," *¿Qué es la filosofía de la tecnología?* (Barcelona: Anthropos, 1989), pp. 19–87.

8. See, e.g., Günter Bohring, "Wesen und Erscheinungsformen der bürgerlichen 'Philosophie der Technik' in der Gegenwart," *Wissenschaftliche Zeitschrift der Technischen Hochschule für Chemie Leuna-Merseburg* (Halle-Saale) 11, no. 3 (1969), pp. 200–9, and Günter Wettstädt, *Ideologie im Zwielicht: Zum Einfluss bürgerlicher Technikphilosophie auf die imperialistische Bildungsideologie* (Berlin: Akademie-Verlag, 1974).

9. Derek de Solla Price, "Automata and the Origins of Mechanism and Mechanistic Philosophy," *Technology and Culture* 5, no. 1 (Winter 1964), pp. 9–23.

10. Theophrastus, *Metaphysics* 17 (Usener 8a, 19–20). See also Jerzy Schnayder, "Technologisches in den Werken des Theophrastos," *EOS* (Commentarii Societatis Philologae Polonorum) 52 (1962), pp. 259–86.

11. Robert S. Brumbaugh, *Ancient Greek Gadgets and Machines* (New York: Crowell, 1966), p. 46. See also Brumbaugh's *Platonic Studies of Greek Philosophy: Form, Arts, Gadgets, and Hemlock* (Albany: State University of New York Press, 1989), especially Part IV, "Ideal Form in a World of Gadgets."

12. John Wild, "Plato's Theory of *Techne:* A Phenomenological Interpretation," *Philosophy and Phenomenological Research* 1, no. 3 (1941), p. 268.

13. Wild, "Plato's Theory of *Techne,*" p. 292.

14. Ernst Kapp, *Grundlinien einer Philosophie der Technik,* p. 25.

15. Augustine, *City of God* XXII, 24, near the middle. Cf. also Xenophon, *Memorabilia* I, iv, 4–8.

16. See, e.g., Walter J. Ong, SJ, *Ramus, Method, and the Decay of Dialogue* (Cambridge, Mass.: Harvard University Press, 1958).

17. Kapp, *Grundlinien einer Philosophie der Technik,* p. vi.

18. Ibid., p. 140.

19. Friedrich Dessauer, *Streit um die Technik,* p. 234.

20. Friedrich Dessauer, *Philosophie der Technik,* p. 66. (English version, p. 331.)

21. Henri Saint-Simon, *Oeuvres complètes,* vol 1, part 2, p. 137. From "Décla-ration de principles, L'Industrie," vol. II, 1817. Quoted from Keith Taylor, ed., *Henri Saint-Simon: Selected Writings on Science, Industry and Social Organiza-tion* (New York: Holmes and Meier, 1975), p. 161.

22. Karl Marx, *Capital* I, part III, chapter VII, section 1. Quoted from Moore-Aveling trans., p. 183.

23. Marx, *Capital* I, part III, chapter VII, section 1. Quoted from Moore-Aveling trans., p. 178.

24. See, e.g., Max Weber, *Economy and Society,* ed. Guenther Roth and Claus Wittich (New York: Bedminster Press, 1968), vol. 1, p. 65.

25. Jacques Ellul, *A Temps et à contretemps,* interviews with Madeleine Gar-rigou-Lagrange (Paris: Le Centurion, 1981), p. 155. English version: *In Season Out of Season: An Introduction to the Thought of Jacques Ellul,* trans. Lani K. Niles (New York: Harper & Row, 1982), p. 176. Another good overview of his work is provided by *Perspectives on Our Age: Jacques Ellul Speaks on His Life and Work,* ed. Willem H. Vanderburg, trans. Joachim Neugroschel (New York: Seabury, 1981).

26. For a comprehensive study of the Ellul corpus, see Joyce Main Hanks, *Jacques Ellul: A Comprehensive Bibliography, Research in Philosophy & Tech-nology,* Supplement 1 (1984).

27. Jacques Ellul, *The Technological Society,* p. 4.

28. Ibid., pp. 79–80 and ff. See also the definition of technology, p. xxv.

29. Wolf Lepenies, *Between Literature and Science: The Rise of Sociology,* trans. R. J. Hollingdale (New York: Cambridge University Press, 1988).

30. Hans Freyer, *Der Staat* (Leipzig: Wiegandt, 1925), p. 178. Quoted from Lepenies, *Between Literature and Science,* p. 341.

31. Martin Heidegger, "What Are Poets For?" in *Poetry, Language, Thought,* trans. Albert Hofstadter (New York: Harper & Row, 1971), pp. 114–15.

32. Blaise Pascal, "De l'esprit géometrique et de l'art de persuader." See also Plato's distinction between arts based on numerical mensuration and those based on judgments with regard to the fitting, the appropriate, the needful (*Statesman* 284e). This reference is elaborated in David Rapport Lachterman, *The Ethics of Geometry: A Genealogy of Modernity* (New York: Routledge, 1989).

33. Jean Jacques Rousseau, *Discours sur les sciences et les arts* (Pléiade edition of the *Oeuvres complètes*), pp. 9 and 17, respectively.

34. Ibid., p. 19.

35. Mumford, *Technics and Civilization,* p. 433.

36. Lewis Mumford, *Man as Interpreter* (New York: Harcourt Brace, 1950), p. 2.

37. Mumford, *Man as Interpreter,* pp. 8–9.

38. Mumford, *Myth of the Machine,* vol. 1, p. 8.

39. Ibid., p. 9.

40. Ibid., p. 9.

41. Mumford, *Myth of the Machine,* vol. 2, p. 155.

42. Lewis Mumford, "Technics and the Future of Western Civilization," in *In the Name of Sanity* (New York: Harcourt Brace, 1954), p. 39.

43. Lewis Mumford, *Art and Technics,* p. 35.

44. Theodore Kisiel, "Heidegger and the New Images of Science," *Research in Phenomenology,* vol. 7 (1977), p. 163.

45. In *Sketches from Life: the Autobiography of Lewis Mumford* New York:

Dial Press, 1982), pp. 142–43, Mumford cautions that "anyone who would seek to appraise the effect of nearer thinkers upon my intellectual outlook would go widely astray if he did not also take account of my lifelong intercourse with both Plato and Aristotle."

46. Martin Heidegger, *The Basic Problems of Phenomenology,* trans. Albert Hofstadter (Bloomington: Indiana University Press, 1979), pp. 20–21.

47. Heidegger, *Basic Problems of Phenomenology,* p. 116.

48. Martin Heidegger, *Question Concerning Technology,* p. 15.

49. Albert Borgmann, *Technology and the Character of Contemporary Life,* p. 41.

50. Stanley Rosen, *The Quarrel Between Philosophy and Poetry: Studies in Ancient Thought* (New York: Routledge, 1988), p. 26.

51. Arthur D. Kahn, " 'Every Art Possessed by Man Comes from Prometheus': The Greek Tragedians and Science and Technology," *Technology and Culture* 11, no. 2 (April 1970), p. 133.

52. Ibid., pp. 161–62.

53. James Joyce, *Ulysses* (New York: Random House, 1961), pp. 37–38.

54. See especially Mumford, *Art and Technics,* pp. 80–84.

55. Howard Segal, *Technological Utopianism in American Culture* (Chicago: University of Chicago Press, 1985), p. 27.

56. John Steinbeck, *The Grapes of Wrath* (New York: Viking Press, 1967), pp. 47–48.

57. Ibid., pp. 45 and 48.

58. Sinclair Lewis, *Babbitt* (New York: Signet Books, 1961), p. 11.

59. Ibid., pp. 11–12.

60. Ibid., pp. 6–7.

61. Ibid., p. 31.

62. Updating Lewis, John Updike's tetrology of *Rabbit Run* (1960), *Rabbit Redux* (1971), *Rabbit Is Rich* (1981) and *Rabbit at Rest* (1990) bring this imaginative insight into the ambiguous character of technological culture in the post–World War II world of high technology.

63. Borgmann, *Technology and the Character of Contemporary Life,* p. 217.

64. Ibid., p. 188.

Mappae Mundi and "The Knight's Tale": The Geography of Power, the Technology of Control

SYLVIA TOMASCH

Like other technological systems, cartography is also strongly and inevitably ideological: it involves not merely the drawing of maps but the making of worlds.[1] Maps are not just colorings in of preset outlines or simple depictions of portions of the physical universe. Maps present entire world views, with all that that phrase implies in terms of philosophical or scientific outlook, theological import, political influence, aesthetic perspective, and artistic choice. The multifarious worlds cartographers draw are far more than merely passive reflectors of particular cultural circumstances or idiosyncratic renderings of some otherwise objective reality; rather, maps are among the most powerful statements of belief in the worlds that they help to create. They are tools, to be sure, but they are inscriptive tools that allow as well as necessitate perspective; they are tools without which we cannot read and without which we cannot see.

Until very recently, maps have been treated by historians of cartography as transparent objects, mediums for the transmission of information, texts needing interpretation but in themselves innocent of creative function. Perhaps it is this assumption of transparency that explains the many unsuccessful attempts to classify maps, medievals maps in particular.[2] For example, Arthur H. Robinson posits "three general functions" of maps: "1. as a record of the location and identity of geographical features[;] 2. As a guide for the traveler[;] 3. As a vehicle for the figurative expression of abstract, hypothetical, or religious concepts."[3] And David Woodward draws upon Geoffrey Page's distinction between three types of scientific illustration: descriptive, interpretive, and imaginative.[4] Both Robinson and Woodward confine medieval *mappae mundi* to their third categories. According to Woodward, descriptive maps "depict as accurately as possible what the scientist sees," and "the interpretive may leave out details that are not necessary for the immediate purpose of the illustration and involves some subjective judgement by the scientist"; naturally, then, a medieval map must be imaginative, for it is used to "interpret . . . ideas, hypotheses, and speculations rather than the structure or functions of the subject."[5] Both geographers present thoughtful considerations of maps that supersede earlier, superficial views that the history of cartography could be divided into two distinct phases, "a decorative phase, in which geographical information was usually portrayed inaccurately, and a scientific phase, in which decoration gave way to scientific accuracy."[6] Neither, however, acknowledges the complexity of maps as ideological constructs. To suggest that a map as a "guide for a traveler" must concern itself solely with physical matters and cannot partake of the "figurative" mode, or to oppose and privilege "structure or functions" over "hypotheses and speculations" is to ignore the inherent biases of any map from any place at any time. Juergen Schulz presents the two poles of the dilemma clearly: "[E]ven in Renaissance Italy," he says, "a map was not always a map. Often it was the vehicle for elaborate non-geographical ideas."[7] This is precisely the point: a map *is* a map even when (or perhaps because) it includes functions other than geographical positioning. In fact, it is the incorporation of such information that makes maps so important and that makes mapping, as graphic and textual recreations of the world, so problematical.[8]

The specific uses to which medieval maps were put were very different from those of modern maps and reflect an understanding of the universe as a unified and orderly creation.[9] That alien vision is reflected in striking differences of form and content between medieval and modern instances, so striking that it is tempting to see modern maps as accurate, objective depictions of the earth and medieval maps as merely metaphorical representations. However, a careful reading of the early maps as well as of the geographical treatises in which many were originally embedded reveals that these maps were understood first as being literally true.[10] All maps, medieval as well as our own, are a means of cultural inscription; maps are declarations that the universe *as presented* is just what and as we say it is. Because they do not simply reflect reality but create it by informing our vision of what the world "really" looks like, maps can be used as instruments to implement, to impose, or to exploit that vision.[11] They serve as tools of conquest and as technologies of control.[12] The use of maps as tools to further the aims of particular individuals or societies is neither natural (i.e., inevitable) nor unnatural (i.e., necessarily deplorable), but in the making of maps we actively read and revise the world. A vision of a better world—or, in the case of medieval maps, of a divine one—is also part of the cartographic process.

In this essay I suggest that a conception of mapmaking as a process of world-creating was as important in the Middle Ages as it is in our own,[13] and I analyze the uses to which one fourteenth-century English writer, Geoffrey Chaucer, put the discourse of medieval cartography.[14] In the following pages I show that not only does Chaucer draw upon map terminology, map lore, and map form in the imagery of his poems, not only is he familiar enough with geographical representations to reproduce them verbally, but certain of his cartographic references indicate an awareness of some of the problems and consequences of vision, perception, and perspective always implicit in map-production.

I

In the Middle Ages, the predominant geographical vision was based on the Ptolemaic system of orderly creation, with the solid orb of the earth imagined as the centerpiece of a series of crystalline spheres in which were embedded the moon, the sun, the planets, and the fixed stars. These spheres were ultimately empowered by the first mover and locally mobilized by angelic spirits. The sublunary earth, consisting of the three known continents and the ocean sea, was thought of as a post-Edenic world inhabited by the descendants of Noah's three sons.[15] One of the most common medieval cartographic representations of the earth is known as the T-O *mappa mundi*. "T-O" is medieval terminology[16] and refers to the lines (the T) dividing the central land mass (the three known continents, Europe, Africa, and Asia) and the circle of the encompassing ocean (the O) (figure 1). The Mediterranean Sea comprises the upward column of the T, while the Don (or the Tanais) and the Nile neatly meet to form the crossbar. The standard T-O map is oriented with East at the top and typically includes such details as the Garden of Eden in the upper central (eastern) portion, Alexander's fortification against the hordes of Gog and Magog in the upper left (northeast), and at the very center, the navel of the world,

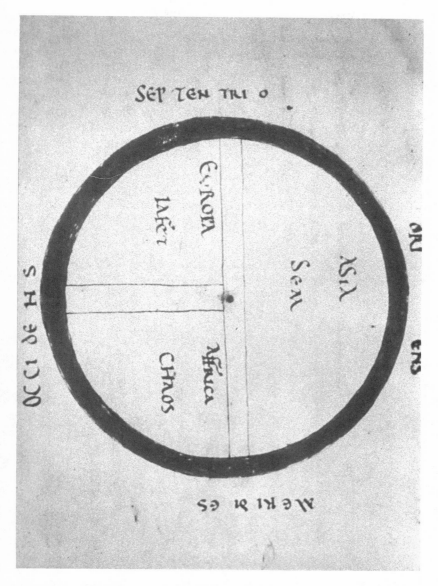

Figure 1. Twelfth-century T-O world map illustrating Isidore of Seville's *Etymologiae*. Reproduced by permission of the Bibliotheque Nationale, Paris.

Jerusalem (figure 2).[17] This form appears as early as the seventh century in illustrations of Isidore of Seville's *Etymologies* and continues to be used through the fifteenth.[18] Important British T-O maps include the rectangular Anglo-Saxon map of the late tenth century, the Psalter map of c.1225, the Matthew Paris world map of c.1250 (another rectangle), the Hereford map of c.1290 (still to be seen today in Hereford Cathedral[19]), and an ovoid T-O illustrating Ranulph Higden's *Polychronicon* (c. 1350), executed in Chaucer's own time.[20]

Possibly conceived in the fifth century B.C. by Ionic philosophers, the T-O idea was adopted by Christian thinkers, and the form was adapted to Christian purposes.[21] In his *Historia adversus paganos*, Orosius follows the authoritative division of all land into three great continents:

> Our elders made a threefold division of the world, which is surrounded on its periphery by the Ocean. Its three parts they named Asia, Europe

Figure 2. Detail from upper portion of thirteenth-century Ebstorf map. Reproduced by permission of the William L. Clements Library, University of Michigan.

and Africa. . . . Asia, surrounded on three sides by the Ocean, stretches across the whole East. Towards the West, on its right, it touches the border of Europe near the North Pole, but on its left it extends as far as Africa, except that near Egypt and Syria it is bounded by Mare Nostrum which we commonly call the Great Sea.[22]

Similarly, Isidore states in his *Etymologies:*

> The ancients did not divide these three parts of the world equally, for Asia stretches right from the south, through the east to the north, but Europe stretches from the north to the west and thence Africa from the west to the south. From this it is quite evident that the two parts of Europe and Africa occupy half the world and that Asia alone occupies the other half. The former were made into two parts because the Great Sea (called the Mediterranean) enters from the Ocean between them and cuts them apart.[23]

In the *De Universo,* Rabanus Maurus provides the important Christian justification for the tripartite structure:

> And most appropriate is this division of the earth into three parts, for it has been endowed with faith in the Holy Trinity and instructed by the Gospels, where we read the words of the Saviour that the world is like unto leaven which the women took and hid in three measures of meal until the whole was leavened.[24]

Rabanus also uses the alternate names for the continents when he states that the earth "has been peopled by the three sons of Noah,"[25] Ham for Africa, Shem for Asia, and Japheth for Europe. This tradition of double naming persists well into the fifteenth century (figure 3). These illustrations and statements reveal a theologically rationalized presentation of the earth that was in no small part also politically based. As Lee Patterson has shown, although the tripartite physical conformation was explained as stemming from divine causation rather than from any human agency, social control was often the aim.[26]

Although our modern American reliance upon empirical data makes it difficult for us to acknowledge how ideologically based our own maps are,[27] we can easily recognize that medieval maps are products of older cultural values analogously manifested in other visual arts as well.[28] For instance, it is commonly recognized that one hallmark of medieval art is the determination of size of persons or objects by allegorical or political importance rather than by any objective physical reality. Such flattening of perspective,[29] along

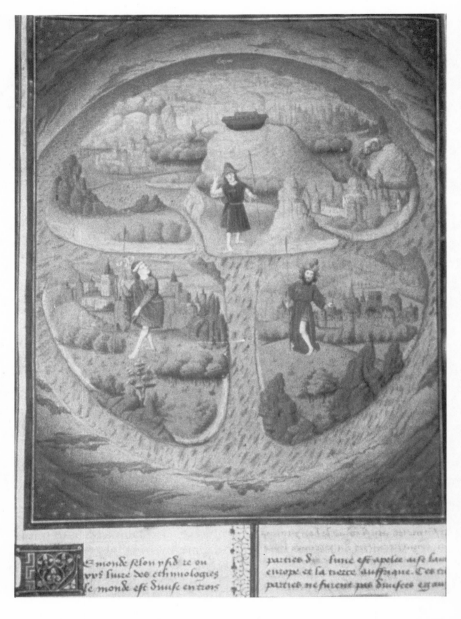

Figure 3. French manuscript, c. 1455, showing Noah's three sons. Bibliotheque Royale Albert Ier, Bruxelles, MS. 9231, fol. 281. Reproduced by permission.

with "the selective magnification of cartographic signs,"[30] suggests
a hierarchizing of value apparent also in literary descriptions of the
physical world. For instance, when Geffrey, in Chaucer's *House of
Fame,*[31] is carried aloft in the eagle's claws, he describes his bird's
eye view:

> . . . y adoun gan loken thoo,
> And beheld feldes and playnes,
> And now hilles, and now mountaynes,
> Now valeyes, now forestes,
> And now unnethes grete bestes,
> Now ryveres, now citees
> Not tounes, and now grete trees,
> Now shippes seyllynge in the see.
>
> (*HF* 896–903)

Although he sees them in passing, Geffrey views animals, mountains, forests, trees, ships, and rivers all from the same lofty
vantage point. This unitary view is that of medieval maps and
paintings as well; they too show a similar imbalance of perspective.
On the Catalan Atlas of 1375, for example, the caravan travelers
appear far larger than the castles along their route to China (figure
4). Foregrounding these figures (rather than natural features or
national boundaries) emphasizes their importance as well as the
fact of their journey. Obviously the opposite emphasis could have
easily been the case, depending upon the purposes of those who
requisition or make any particular map. As the rectangular *mappae
mundi* make clear, medieval cartographers rarely hesitated to
distort size or shape of land mass for reasons of space, as if the T-O
form were not distortion enough (figure 5). Political and religious
beliefs were matters of value that necessarily took precedence over
mere accuracy of geographical fact.

Such subjective imbalance becomes significant when we attempt
to understand certain images in Chaucer's poems. One previously
misunderstood instance of geographical reference occurs in a well-
known passage in *Troilus and Criseyde,* when at the poem's end
Troilus looks down from the eighth sphere to which he has been
transported upon his death and sees

> This litel spot of erthe that with the se
> Embraced is . . .
>
> (*T&C* 5.1815–16)

Concerning these lines, modern commentators, noting parallels

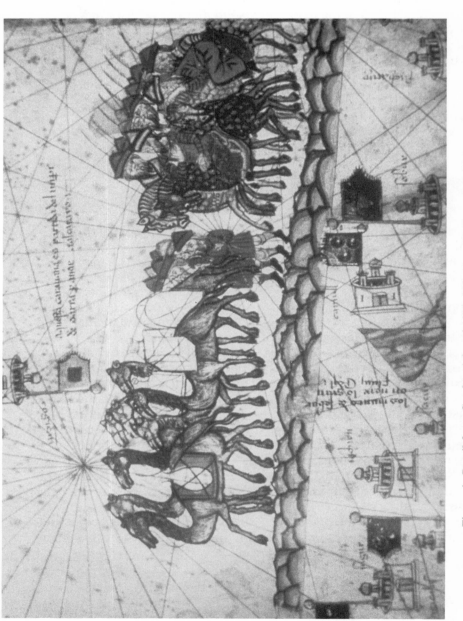

Figure 4. Detail from Catalan Atlas of 1375. MS. Esp. 30. Reproduced by permission of Bibliotheque Nationale, Paris.

Figure 5. Tenth-century "Cottonian" T-O map "squared" to fit the page. British Library MS. Cotton Tiberius B.V., fol. 56v. Reproduced by permission.

with the little earth Cicero and Macrobius mention in connection
with the dream of Scipio, assert that the whole world appears small
simply by virtue of Troilus's great distance.[32] Yet if the desired
effect had been merely to emphasize the hero's physical removal
from the earth and his simultaneous understanding of its insignifi-
cance, Chaucer could have had Troilus say, as Geffrey does in the
House of Fame,

> . . . fro the grounde so hye
> That al the world, as to myn ye,
> No more semed than a prikke. . .
>
> (*HF* 905–7)

In the *Troilus,* however, Chaucer seems to be more deliberately
pictorial, presenting a large, foregrounded Troilus and a small,
distanced earth—an important variation on the usual hierarchical
imbalance. Troilus is no longer on the earth and hence can see it
whole. What he sees accords with standard medieval cartographical
practice: this earth has a central core surrounded ("embraced") by
water; the three massed continents are ringed by the circumfluent
ocean. These verse-lines thus constitute a verbal description of the
circular T-O *mappa mundi.* This depiction does not accord with
modern visualizations of a bright blue marble, but it is a striking
example of Chaucer's very different geographical imagination.

Another important aspect of the medieval geographical imagination is the different understanding of the extent of the world. In the
"Pardoner's Tale," we read of the glutton's chase for dainty bits
through "est and west and north and south, / In erthe, in eir, in
water" ("PardT" 518–19).[33] Similarly, the Monk states about Nero:
"This wyde world hadde [he] in subjeccion, / Bothe est and west,
[south] and septemptrioun" ("MkT" 2466–67, editor's addition).
According to the Wife of Bath, the world ranges "from Denmark
unto Ynde" ("WBPro" 824), "[b]itwix this and the mount of Kau-
kasous" ("WBT" 1140), and "bitwixe the est and eke the west"
("WBT" 1247). More than just poetic synonyms for the ends of the
earth, these phrases refer to the recognized boundaries of the
oikoumene.[34] The ecumene may be defined as "the inhabited
world" or "the habitable world." To the orthodox in the Middle
Ages, these were thought to be the same. Although there were
continual rumors of the Antipodes, authorities such as Lactantius
and Augustine denied the possibility of its human habitation.[35]
Based on Scripture (*Acts* 17:26), the reasoning ran thusly: God
created all nations of one blood; Christ died for all men; therefore
no man can exist except for those here, in this *oikoumene.* The

alternative theory of Crates of Mallos (second century B.C.) that there were four ecumenes "symmetrically distributed over the four quarters of the globe"[36] had its adherents, among them Macrobius in his commentary on the dream of Scipio.[37] More usual, however, was the view that the Antipodes, if they existed, could not hold human life, simply because nothing, including the news of Christ, could pass through the intervening torrid zone (figure 6). Therefore, Christ would have had to die four times or he would have failed to redeem all men. Because both of these options are clearly impossible, there is only one *oikoumene*.[38]

Chaucer presents the limits of this ecumene even more specifically in the description of the Knight in the "General Prologue" to the *Canterbury Tales*. In listing thirteen separate battles in fifteen lines, Chaucer uses these place-names not only to delineate the world of medieval military campaigning but also to delimit the bounds of the known world, which is, in medieval terms, the only world that matters. In traveling from Alisaundre, Pruce, Lettow and Ruce, through Gernade, Algezir, Belmarye, Lyeys, and Satalye, to the Grete See, Tramyssene, Palatys, and Turkye ("GP" 51–66), the Knight touches far and wide in Europe, Africa, and Asia. These references serve as an economical presentation of the *oikoumene*, as an idealized listing that symbolizes the extent of knighthood's range rather than as a reporting of any individual chivalric career.[39] To be sure, Franciscan missionaries, Norse outlaws, and Italian merchants journeyed further (not to mention armchair travelers like Mandeville), but the known world, the habitable world, the Christian world (not the lands of griffins and *sciapodes*), these are the referents of the Knight's travels, these are in the realm of possibility.[40]

Like the maps that attempt to portray it, the Christian *oikoumene* is an incorporative and recuperative model of reality. Understanding it as such helps explain the many urgent attempts to pin down the location of such figures as Prester John and such places as the Terrestial Paradise and the Fortunate Isles, figures and places whose location kept shifting throughout the Middle Ages and well into the Renaissance. Indeed, they had to keep shifting, not merely because explorations pushed the limits of the *oikoumene* outward but because such shifts ensured that the boundaries of the *oikoumene* kept expanding, that anywhere a European traveled would not be outside the limits of the real and the known, and that wayfarers would not find themselves in the dangerous wilderness of truly alien lands. Mapmakers have two choices when faced with undelimited spaces: either dismiss them as unknown (and probably unknowable) bits of *terra incognita,* or incorporate them as territo-

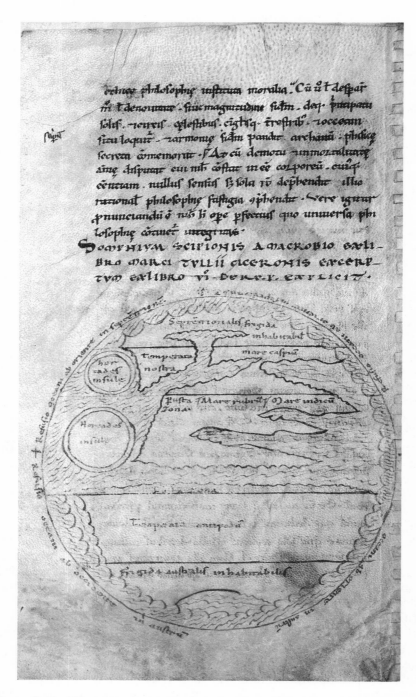

Figure 6. Twelfth-century hemispheric-zonal world illustrating Macrobius's commentary on geography. Walters Art Gallery, Baltimore, MS. W. 22, fol. 64v. Reproduced by permission.

ries not yet known but still definable in their potentiality by inclusion through graphic visualization. In this second way, Orosius's phrase *"Mare Nostrum"* serves, if only on paper, to conquer the Mediterranean. So maps become, in William Boelhower's phrase, "performative scripture."[41] Exclusion and incorporation work simultaneously, though of course neither strategy can ever rest entirely secure. However, in the totalizing system of medieval Christianity, as there were no limits to God's power there could be no rightful bounds to Christendom's geographical sway on the divinely created earth. Ultimately, this is the message of the *mappae mundi*. This is the lesson of the Ebstorf map as well (figure 7).

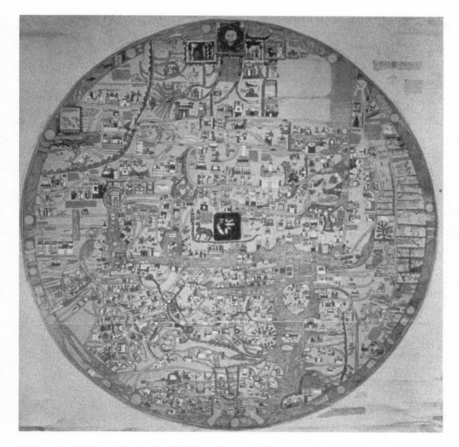

Figure 7. Thirteenth-century Ebstorf map. Reproduced by permission of the William L. Clements Library, University of Michigan.

Cartographic recuperation works temporally as well as spatially; like other contemporary texts, medieval maps are frequently, and deliberately, anachronistic. In the same simultaneous and ahistorical way, Chaucer also presents places from three distinct eras, classical, contemporary, and biblical.[42] From classical sources come Atthenes, Thebes, and Troye ("KnT" 861, 933, 2833), Trace, Parnaso, and Rome (*HF* 391, 521, 1930), and Cartage, Macidonye, and Grece ("FranT" 1400, 1435, 1444), just to mention a few. These places are all commonly found on *mappae mundi,* as is the Strait of Gibraltar, mentioned in these lines from the "Monk's Tale" that describe Hercules's extraordinary strength: "At bothe the worldes endes . . . / In stide of boundes he a pileer sette" ("MkT" 2117–18). Not infrequently, as in figure 5, medieval maps portray a pair of pillars just outside Gibraltar, or, as the Man of Law says, "thurghout the narwe mouth / Of Jubaltare and Septe" ("MLT" 946–47).

From contemporary sources come the actual English towns on the road from London to Canterbury, the places named in the Knight's campaigns, and other locations on the continent, such as Ytaille ("ClT" 57) and Lumbardye ("MerT" 1245). Chaucer mentions the three continents as a trio in the *House of Fame* ("Auffrike, Europe, and Asye," *HF* 1339), as well as that significant body of water, the Mediterranean. Instead of employing that term, however, he uses, in the "General Prologue" ("GP" 59), in the *Romaunt of the Rose* (*RR* 2748), and in the *Book of the Duchess* (*BD* 140), the words "the Grete See," the same terminology employed by Orosius and Isidore. As we have seen, the phrase "Grete See" implies more than just size; aside from the obvious political, economic, religious, and cultural importance of the Mediterranean in the later Middle Ages, this sea was special navigationally as well. It was safe in a way that even the North Sea, much closer to Chaucer's own England, was not. It was not free from pirates or pagans, but very early on it was charted, it was mapped, it was known. Perhaps most importantly from a cartographic perspective, on eastward-oriented *mappae mundi* the Mediterranean serves as the vertical column of the T, rising straight from the surrounding ocean to point like an arrow to the very center of the Christian world: the city of Jerusalem.[43] In Chaucer's works, as on many medieval maps, Jerusalem is also used in three different, and achronic, ways.[44] In the "General Prologue" ("GP" 463), it refers to the contemporary city to which the Wife of Bath went on a previous pilgrimage. In the "Monk's Tale" ("MkT" 2147, 2196), it describes the ancient city of biblical times. In the *Romaunt of the Rose,* it is used generically, as part of a phrase to describe extremes of distance: "Fro Jerusalem unto Bur-goyne" (*RR* 554). Each use recalls the other in a literary conflation of time and space, a move typical of map illustration as well.

From the Bible comes not only Jerusalem but Babilan ("MLPro" 63), Nynyvee ("MLT" 487), the Cane of Galilee ("WBPro" 11), mount Oreb ("SumT" 1891), and Gazan and Chaldeye ("MkT" 2047, 2157). After Jerusalem perhaps the most significant place is the one that exemplifies the unflinching amalgamation of both real and unreal locations on the same surface of the earth: the Terrestial Paradise (figure 2).[45] If we follow the arrow of the Mediterranean upward (that is, eastward), continuing through Jerusalem, we arrive at that most favored spot on earth. Isidore explains that Asia "contains many provinces and districts," of which Paradise is one:

> Paradise is a place lying in the eastern parts. . . . It is planted with every kind of wood and fruitbearing tree, having also the tree of life. There is neither cold nor heat there but a continual spring temperature. In the middle of the Garden, a spring gushes forth to water the whole grove and, dividing up, it provides the sources of four rivers. Approach to this place was barred to man after his sin, for now it is hedged about on all sides by a sword-like flame . . . , that is to say it is surrounded by a wall of fire that reaches almost to the sky.[46]

Most of the aspects Isidore describes, the tree, the rivers, the walls of flames, were typical features of *mappae mundi*. Usually, as in the detail from the Ebstorf map, Adam, Eve, and the serpent were portrayed as well (figure 2). While Chaucer does not enumerate these features, he does appear to acknowledge the actual existence of this place. Twice he briefly tells the story of the expulsion, in the Summoner's and in the Pardoner's tales, the latter explicitly mentioning Adam and the tree ("SumT" 1915–17 and "PardT" 505–11, respectively), and he has the Merchant compare (ironically, I believe) marriage to the "paradys terrestre" ("MerT" 1332).

Given his propensity for irony, it is certainly possible that in making these references Chaucer is using the tradition to toy with his audience, not always intending his instances of cartographical visualization to be taken entirely seriously. For example, in the *House of Fame* Geffrey learns of the palace that stands "[r]yght even in myddes of the weye / Betwixen hevene and erthe and see" (*HF* 713–15). By proposing such an obvious geographical impossibility, perhaps Chaucer is playing on the credulity of an audience that accepted anything or any place as long as it was located cartographically. Well into the fifteenth century, St. Brendan's Island, the Fortunate Isles, Ultima Thule, and Prester John would be

found on maps.[47] While I do not necessarily credit Chaucer with
any greater skepticism than his contemporaries, there were those,
like the Polos and the Franciscan missionaries, who looked for
themselves and reported only what they actually saw.[48] When the
eagle carries Geffrey aloft, he tells his unwilling passenger that he is
now more than twice as high as "Daun Scipio" (916), who saw in his
"drem, at point devys, / Helle and erthye and paradys" (917–18).
While some medieval maps did in fact show hell on the map, more
usual is the representation of the terrestial paradise. Like Mandeville, Chaucer carefully does not say he saw this place with his
own eyes,[49] but, like Mandeville again, his belief in its earthly
existence comes through clearly enough.

II

It is in the "Knight's Tale," in the description of the actions of
Theseus, that we have the strongest evidence of Chaucer's
awareness of some of the implications of medieval geographical
theory and practice. In the first two sections of the poem, Theseus
is seen as a fierce warrior, a compassionate conqueror, and a
righteous ruler. His actions in the third and fourth parts continue
and complement his earlier roles; he appears as a builder for and of
generations, an architect of edifices, a maker of marriages. These
actions reveal his understanding of the importance of consolidation
of power and reestablishment of order when the just rule of the
realm is threatened by the chaos of private vengeance. It is significant that this consolidation and reestablishment take cartographic
form.

In commanding the building of the amphitheater for the tournament between the two suitors of his wife's sister, the Duke of
Thebes exercises his pragmatic understanding of the need to control his subjects and their actions as well as the best means for
doing so. In having every artisan in his domain concentrate all their
skills on the erection of this structure, Theseus illustrates his dominance over men and materials. In shaping this edifice as he so
particularly does, he reveals his belief in his own far-reaching and
infallible power and declares his faith in technological display and
geographical control. However, contrary to Theseus's expectations
and intent, what the tale most clearly illustrates for us is not his
successful control but his ultimate failure. The "Knight's Tale"
discloses the deficiency that Theseus continually tries to conceal:
despite his noble will, no merely human agent can ever truly take

the measure of the earth or make the earth his own. Although, as Kenneth J. Knoespel says, "technology is not a spectacle that momentarily diverts our attention but a medium through which a culture defines itself,"[50] sometimes, as here, such technological definition simply does not work.

The crux of the problem of the amphitheater is its shape: Why is this structure round, when the contemporary pattern for tournament lists was rectangular? Chaucer's source has long been debated. V. A. Kolve, for example, proposes the Roman colisseum as a possible prototype for the circular shape, a form for which there is as yet no evidence earlier than the fifteenth century.[51] I suggest instead that the T-O *mappa mundi* is a far better model; as described by the narrator, the amphitheater matches the typical T-O form in most important respects, from location to configuration to orientation:

> I trowe men wolde deme it necligence
> If I foryete to tellen the dispence
> Of Theseus, that gooth so bisily
> To maken up the lystes roially,
> That swich a noble theatre as it was
> I dar wel seyen in this world ther nas.
> The circuit a myle was aboute,
> Walled of stoon, and dyched al withoute.
> Round was the shap, in manere of compas,
> Ful of degrees, the heighte of sixty pas,
> That whan a man was set on o degree,
> He letted nat his felawe for to see.
> Estward ther stood a gate of marbul whit,
> Westward right swich another in the opposit.
> And shortly to concluden, swich a place
> Was noon in erthe, as in so litel space;
> For in the lond ther was no crafty man
> That geometrie or ars-metrike kan,
> Ne portreyour, ne kervere of ymages,
> That Theseus ne yaf him mete and wages
> The theatre for to maken and devyse.
>
> ("KnT" 1881–1901)

This amphitheater is wide "a myle . . . aboute"), round ("in manere of compas"), encompassed by a "wall [. . .] of stoon," with the emphasis on the east-west axis: the very image, in earth and stone, of the "O" of the typical *mappa mundi*. In effect then, what Theseus commands to be built is not just a tournament round but a world in miniature.

In the creation of this *imago mundi,* Theseus would seem to be
following Mircea Eliade's dictum that "to organize a space is to
repeat the paradigmatic work of the gods."[52] And because he
organizes a space and creates a world, he naturally expects his
creation to follow his rules. Such control may ultimately be illusory,
but technological fiat, especially on a grand scale, impels a movement from resistance to complicity; spectators become participants
and participants become believers. Thus, in the "Knight's Tale," it
is Theseus's own subjects who not only build the structure but
make its meaning as well (just as we, the reading subjects of the
"Knight's Tale," are also active participants in the making of the
meaning of Chaucer's work). In various ways, all under the Theban
lord are subject to the power of this colossal theater, whether
laboring during its construction, painting the decorative images,
fighting in the tournament, cheering on the contestants, or marry-
ing the winner. But what does the power of Theseus's structure
amount to in the end? Countering his (and his subjects') efforts and
best intentions are the deeds of the pagan gods, who have their own
agenda—and the gods themselves are shown to be overpowered by
forces greater than their own. (We learn of Emily's unwilling participation as well as Diana's own inability to undertake independent
action; they make an appropriate pair.) The tale continually insists
that all such endeavors toward order by this pagan prince—by all
pagans—must ultimately be in vain.[53]

Two couplets of the description of the amphitheater become
particularly significant in this regard:

> That swich a noble theatre as it was
> I dar wel seyen *in this world ther nas*
>
> And shortly to concluden, swich a place
> *Was noon in erthe,* as in so litel space
> ("KnT" 1885–86, 1895–96; my emphasis)

In the midst of his elaborate description, the narrator emphasizes
the impossibility of the earthly existence of this structure. At the
very least, these lines imply the failure built into its very conception
(though, as explained below, I believe they do more than this as
well). However much Theseus would position himself as a builder of
worlds (the epitome of the "crafty man" ["KnT" 1897]), in the
terms of this tale, manifested concretely in this amphitheater, he
cannot succeed. He may call upon the gods, he may identify himself with them and even imitate them, but he is only a man, and a
pagan at that. He gets the lists built, he sets the rules of the contest,

he concentrates all the energy of all the members of his society (and of many outsiders as well) on fulfilling his goals. As we learn, however, it is neither the actions nor wishes of lovers, nor those of kings, nor even those of the pagan deities to whom they pray, which finally conquer; rather it is fate in the form of "a furie infernal" ("KnT" 2584) that triumphs in the end.[54]

According to the rules Theseus sets for the tournament, when a contestant is unhorsed he loses the contest, even though, like Palamon (the first of Emily's two suitors), he goes down fighting. If the narrative had ended with Palamon's defeat, it would indeed have served to support Theseus's own view that his judgments result in natural, necessary, and foreseeable consequences—in this case, the enforcement of his rules. But the poem continues, and actions the narrator describes as "a myracle" ("KnT" 2675) lead us, though not Theseus, to the opposite view. Arcite, the second suitor and the momentary winner, is suddenly, unexpectedly, fatally thrown from *his* horse; despite all healing attempts, he dies. The narrator himself despairs:

> Nature hath now no dominacioun.
> And certeinly, ther Nature wol nat wirche,
> Far wel phisik! Go ber the man to chirche!
> This al and som, that Arcita moot dye
>
> ("KnT" 2758–61)

Readers must now ask, what kind of world is it where nature, elsewhere the vicar of God, has no domination? The inevitable answer is that this is a pagan world, under false gods, where only nature exists. Theseus's father, Egeus, states the lesson:

> This world nys but a thurghfare ful of wo,
> And we been pilgrymes, passynge to and fro.
> Deeth is an ende of every worldly soore
>
> ("KnT" 2847–49)

Perhaps because this lesson appears to be accepted by his subjects (just as they, in their earlier participation in the building of the theater, accepted his previous interpretative efforts), Theseus has some justification for his continuing attempts at controlling an unruly world. If there is no higher power, only an end in death, then why not? So we read of still further reorderings of the natural landscape:

> Duc Theseus, with al his bisy cure,
> Caste now wher that the sepulture

> Of goode Arcite may best ymaked be.
> And eek moost honurable in his degree.
> And at the laste he took conclusioun
> That ther as first Arcite and Palamoun
> Hadden for love the bataille hem bitwene,
> That in that selve grove, swoote and grene,
> Ther as he hadde his amorouse desires,
> His compleynte, and for love his hoote fires,
> He wolde make a fyr in which the office
> Funeral he myghte al accomplice.
> And let comande anon. . . .

("KnT" 2853–65)

Where once he attempted topographical interference on the grandest scale, Theseus now commands sepulchers and funeral pyres. In one of Chaucer's neatest puns, Arcite is returned to the site of his "hoote fires," but this is not now the location of lamenting desire nor the triumphant locale of a better love. Now there is only a return to the forest, the undefeated domain of unrulable passion, the place of death.

The Theban duke believes in an original orderly creation of the world by a first mover.[55] But what does this belief add up to in terms of human existence?

> "What maketh this but Juppiter, the kyng,
> That is prince and cause of alle thyng,
> Convertynge al unto his propre welle
> From which it is dirryved, sooth to telle?
> And heer-agayns no creature on lyve,
> Of no degree, availleth for to stryve.
>   "Thanne is it wysdom, as it thynketh me,
> To maken vertu of necessitee,

("KnT" 3035–42)

In raising the amphitheater, Theseus tries to reconstruct the world according to a better, more orderly model, tries to create civilization out of natural wilderness, tries to impose rules of combat on raging passions, tries to change bestial fighters into chivalric heroes. To the best of his ability, using every available means including the cartographic,[56] he indeed tries to turn necessity to virtue. Command as he will, however, in this famous speech he is forced to rationalize his evident powerlessness. Although he identifies himself with Jupiter the omnipotent, the narration serves instead to illustrate Jupiter's impotence as well as Theseus's own.

In addition to the couplets stating the impossibility of the earthly existence of the amphitheater, some of the remaining lines of the description reveal why such such failure is fundamental. In reading this part of the description, we need to be aware that what is omitted, what is so seriously missing, may be of even greater significance than what is included. Although exclusion may sometimes be more difficult to document than inclusion, for that among other reasons it may also be a particularly subtle and powerful force.[57] On maps, modern as well as medieval, omission is frequently as important a strategy as depiction, for, as J. B. Harley says, "silences on maps . . . c[o]me to enshrine self-fulfilling prophecies about the geography of power."[58] We know that Chaucer was familiar with medieval *mappae mundi,* since he referred to them by name in his lyric "To Rosemunde."[59] We know that Chaucer was well acquainted with Macrobius's *Commentary on the Dream of Scipio,* the manuscripts of which contain some of the oldest and most important medieval maps of the world.[60] We should therefore take careful note of what Chaucer leaves out of his description as well as what he so carefully puts in:

> And for to doon his ryte and sacrifise,
> He estward hath, upon the gate above,
> In worshipe of Venus, goddesse of love,
> Doon make an auter and an oratorie;
> And on the gate westward, in memorie
> Of Mars, he maked hath right swich another,
> That coste largely of gold a fother.
> And northward, in a touret on the wal,
> Of alabastre whit and reed coral,
> An oratorie, riche for to see,
> In worshipe of Dyane of chastitee,
> Hath Theseus doon wroght in noble wyse.
>
> ("KnT" 1902–13)

Placing the three temples at the primary compass points around the perimeter emphasizes the structure's circularity and encourages an ongoing visualization of the "O" portion of the T-O form. But this placement also emphasizes omission: in all the many words of the description (204 lines altogether, including lengthy elaborations on the ornamentation of each temple), there is no "T," no intersection of vertical and horizontal lines.[61] As a man-made edifice, Theseus's amphitheater fails to correspond with T-O maps precisely where correspondence is most needed: there is no center here; this map has no Jerusalem.

When listening to a tale told by the Knight, an experienced crusader, a late medieval Christian audience would not be likely to forget Jerusalem. As the most significant spot in mundane creation,

Jerusalem was placed, especially in the later Middle Ages, at the midpoint of the circular world-map, a location befitting its position as the focal point of the Christian religion, as the meeting-place of the three continents, and as the center of the entire *oikoumene*. In this, medieval *mappae mundi* illustrate "a universal feature of early world maps, . . . the way they have been persistently centred on the 'navel of the world.' "[62] The *"omphalos syndrome,"* as Samuel Y. Edgerton, Jr. calls this tendency,[63] is well illustrated in the Ebstorf map, which not only centers the world on Jerusalem but implies a further correspondence of that city with the navel of Christ, making the map of the world a literal re-presentation of Christ's body (figure 7).[64] In contrast, Theseus's cartographic re-creation has three altars but none where it would count the most; on this map, the center is empty. This pagan world embodies the truth of Yeats's lines, but here it is not so much that "things fall apart; the center cannot hold"[65] as that without a center, things *must* fall apart. According to the narrative, everything ordered by humans goes awry, even the best-laid plans of the lovers, of Theseus, and of the gods themselves. When some greater geography of power is at work, human technology is doomed.

Like the teller of the tale, and like the author of the poem, Theseus tries to force his will upon the world in his attempts to impose artificial order upon natural disorder. However, not being and not recognizing a perfect creator, Theseus's grand attempts come to little; he builds an amphitheater but does not succeed in reordering the world. By imitating the greater world, he thinks he has conquered it, but in fact, to borrow Alfred Korzybski's phrase, he confuses the map with the territory.[66] According to Judith Fer-ster, "the First Mover speech is not an attempt to describe the design *of* the world but an indication of Theseus's design *on* the world. . . . Theseus is seeking not to describe or imitate reality, but to control it" [her emphases].[67] I would suggest that Theseus's imitation of the design of the world stands not in contradistinction to domination but is itself a powerful first move in that direction. "Inscription" is a word for the search for permanence, for the immortality of the text, for an ultimate form of control. Inscription is what Theseus tries, and fails, to do.

III

The inscriptive impulse need not be entirely explicit; individual characters need not be as self-conscious as their author. But if some at least did not make the "mistake" of confusing fiction and reality, we would not have the Friar's and Summoner's tales angrily juxtaposed, nor would we have the Parson's rejection of rhymed fictions in favor of a truthful treatise in prose. The rhetorical "japes" Chaucer continually plays remind us of his awareness of the duality of the inscriptive process. Stories have no meaning unless we accept the rules of the storytelling game; but while these rules allow us to see the created worlds, they also remind us that these worlds are creations of the rules themselves. Maps are similarly rule-bound fictions through which we read the worlds they present. Symbol becomes fact, ideology becomes axiom, and maps not only define the landscape but become their own visible interpreters. When the Miller "quytes" the Knight, when in turn the Reeve "quytes" the Miller, and so on throughout the pilgrimage, their tales come to be seen not merely as stories told to pass the time but as cartographic endeavors, contesting visions of reality, individual versions of the greater universe through which they ride. Like medieval maps, the *Canterbury Tales* offers many partial views at once, chorographies as it were, refusing to choose between them, pretending to present them all on the same level of reality. Like a T-O *mappa mundi*, however, it can fashion this seemingly egalitarian display, because in its self-definition as a Christian pilgrimage, ultimate choices have already been made.

The process of alternation of vision culminates not in the long-awaited arrival in Canterbury but in an unforeseen presentation that nonetheless imputes finality. The "Retraction" is the unexpected termination of the *Canterbury Tales*[68] that both warns us of the superfluity of writing and informs us that the world is indeed susceptible to our imaginings. It reminds us that although within the *Tales* the martyr's shrine is never reached, Canterbury, as a type of Jerusalem, nonetheless provides the meaning for the pilgrimage. As sacred space, Canterbury has value within the Christian hierarchy far greater than that of Southwerk or Rochester, those merely temporary stopping places; it thus comes to stand for that for which the pilgrimage—and ultimately the pilgrims—exists. If knowledge of this proper end is either unknown (the pagan's problem) or ignored (the heretic's dilemma), movement in any direction is worthless or, worse, damnable.

Throughout his poetry, Chaucer presents the futility of any human activity (including his own writing) not founded on the proper, preordained order. In the palinode to *Troilus and Criseyde,* Chaucer repudiates the love poem he has just written in favor of a better depiction of the world and suggests that his readers do the same. Note, however, that neither the palinode nor the "Retraction" is an admission of futility. Rather, each is a repudiation of that which is only and entirely human. Like the Ebstorf map (figure 7), the verses that help close the *Troilus* invite a similar move from the dependent earth to the cruciform body of Christ:

> O yonge, fresshe folkes, he or she,
> In whiche that love up groweth with youre age,
> Repeyreth hom fro worldly vanyte,
> And of youre herte up casteth the visage
> To thilke God that after his ymage
> Yow made, and thynketh al nys but a faire,
> This world that passeth soone as floures faire.
> And loveth hym the which that right for love
> Upon a crois, oure soules for to beye,
> First starf, and roos, and sit in hevene above;
> For he nyl falsen no wight, dar I seye,
> That wol his herte al holly on hym leye.
> And syn he best to love is, and most meke,
> What nedeth feynede loves for to seke?

(T&C 1835–48)

Both the graphic and the verbal texts simultaneously connect and distinguish the created world and its creator. In each case the lesson is traditional: while it is right and important to recognize and acknowledge the creator in his works, do not place trust in mundane things. Most importantly, do not mistake the map for the territory, not even the T-O *mappa mundi* imaged during these final moments.[69] These lines make explicit what the creation of the Theban amphitheater (by Theseus, by the Knight, by the pilgrim-narrator, by Chaucer) leaves only implicit: that writing and map-making are both strategies for inscribing a world, giving their audiences no choice but to accept the truth of that inscription. Like Theseus, we today attempt to impose our view of the world on the world by means of maps and globes; from a medieval perspective, however, we can never succeed. We are doomed to mere description. We are limited by our beliefs to imperfect imitation.

Questions of power and human creation are very much at issue here. It is not just that the technologies of mapmaking and writing are analogous in that both are means for creating worlds; this, they assuredly do. More importantly, every technology manipulates its audience by presenting fictions of the world that are simultaneously asserted not to be fictions at all but passive reflections of the thing itself. The better the map, the closer to some prior, knowable reality, the more power (i.e., truth) it is felt to contain. The paradox is that neither maps nor stories can function until and unless we recognize them as both true and false at the same time (even though in any individual case the expectations may not be balanced on both sides; belief may be greater than disbelief, or vice-versa). They gain their power from us, and that is their power over us: this is the duality of inscription.

The force behind spatial and temporal manipulation is not, finally, geographical but imaginative, and cartographic systems and symbols arise out of the imaginations not merely of individuals but of cultures. They are of course ideological constructions, and we think, as Theseus does, that we control them when in fact the opposite is equally true. It may be, as Harley argues, that the "ideological arrows" of cartographic power fly in one direction only (i.e., maps are used for protection or aggrandizement by elite groups),[70] and in fact, this unilateralness is illustrated in the "Knight's Tale": it is the duke, Theseus, who controls the technologies of building, of mapmaking, of war and peace. But Theseus's ultimate impotence illustrates another, more important fact, one that Chaucer appears to know as well: we are all, to some extent, controlled by our creations when we accept the rules that bind them to us. Like the *Canterbury Tales,* medieval maps are valued for their ornamentation and beauty, for their complexity of rhetoric, for their often confusing illusion of completeness. The competing versions of the many tales are matched in the maps by the inclusion of all possible (and some seemingly impossible) elements of the cosmos in one all-encompassing vision of creation. In their incorporative, arbitrary, and anachronistic aspects they are unlike their modern Western counterparts, which pretend to uniformity and objectivity of perspective and sign. On the contrary, these medieval works celebrate the fullness, range, and contradictions of human existence (as seen from a human perspective).

In one sense *mappae mundi* are like modern road maps: they both lead their users on a journey—but in the former case the end of the journey lies off the map. As allegorical devices important beyond the game of verbal or visual decipherment, maps allude to a greater end, and as far as they are able, bring their audiences to their proper terminus. The *oikoumene* is both transitory and meaningful in its transience—is this not why Troilus laughs on seeing "that litle spot of erthe"? Just so, medieval maps, allusive and inaccurate as they must be, indicate the presence of uncharted eternity. By presenting scenes of the visible world, *mappae mundi* intimate the invisible; in this way, they lead pilgrims to the territory beyond. No technology can work without its users' belief in its ultimate efficacy, but, as Theseus refuses to learn, *correct* beliefs are crucial to the *proper* functioning of any technology. Right recognition is the task for which pilgrimage texts are created; without it, order, eternity, wholeness, salvation are lost. This is the lesson of the "Knight's Tale"; this is the lesson of the *mappae mundi*.[71]

NOTES

1. On the relationship of ideology and technology, see Stanley Aronowitz, *Science as Power: Discourse and Ideology in Modern Society* (Minneapolis: Univ. of Minnesota Press, 1988); and Michael Zimmerman, "Heidegger and Marcuse: Technology as Ideology," *Research in Philosophy & Technology* 2 (1979): 245–61. As to a definition of "technology," despite the attempts of Carl Mitcham (among others), we still lack a thoroughly satisfactory one; see "Types of Technology," *Research in Philosophy & Technology* 1 (1978): 229–94. For my purposes here, I follow the editors of this volume in accepting R. G. Collingwood's suggestion that " *'techne'* signifie[s] both art (literature) and craft (technology)" (Mark Greenberg and Lance Schachterle, "Introduction," *Literature and Technology,* ed. Mark Greenberg and Lance Schachterle [Lehigh, Penn.: Lehigh Univ. Press, 1992], p. 17).

2. Recent standard cartographical histories and surveys include J. B. Harley and David Woodward, eds., *The History of Cartography: Cartography in Prehistoric, Ancient, and Medieval Europe and the Mediterannean,* vol. 1 (Chicago: Univ. of Chicago Press, 1987), pt. 3; M. J. Blakemore and J. B. Harley, *Concepts in the History of Cartography: A Review and Perspective, Cartographica* 17 (1980), Monograph 26; W. W. Ristow, *Guide to the History of Cartography* (Washington, D.C.: Geography and Map Division, Library of Congress, 1973); R. A. Skelton, *Maps: A Historical Survey of Their Study and Collecting* (Chicago: Univ. of Chicago Press, 1972); and N. J. Thrower, *Maps and Man* (Englewood Cliffs, N.J.: Prentice-Hall, 1972). In addition, I have not yet been able to see Jorg-Geerd Arentzen, *Imago Mundi Cartographica: Studien zur Bildlichkeit mittelalterlicher Welt- und Okumenikarten unter besonderer Berucksichtigung des Zusammenwirkens von Text und Bild,* Munstersche Mittelalter-Schriften 53 (Munich: Wilhelm Fink, 1984). Woodward argues in favor of retaining a more complex system of classification against Arentzen's suggestions for simplification (*History of Cartography,* 1.296).

3. Robinson, *Early Thematic Mapping in the History of Cartography* (Chicago: Univ. of Chicago Press, 1982), p. 3.

4. LaPage, *Art and the Scientist* (Bristol: Williams & Wilkins, 1961), cited in Woodward, "Introduction," in *Art and Cartography,* ed. David Woodward (Chicago: Univ. of Chicago Press, 1987), p. 7.

5. Woodward, "Introduction," p. 7.

6. Ibid., p. 2.

7. Schulz, "Maps as Metaphors: Mural Map Cycles of the Italian Renaissance," in *Art and Cartography,* p. 122.

8. Recently, some scholars have begun to study early maps as ideological artifacts that inevitably combine functions and defy easy categorization. For example, Richard Helgerson discusses the ironies of representations of power in

Elizabethan maps ("The Land Speaks: Cartography, Chorography, and Subversion in Renaissance England," *Representations* 16 [1986]: 50–85) and J. B. Harley explicitly connects maps and other Tudor cultural forms: "In many contexts maps would have articulated symbolic values as part of the visual languages by which specific interests, doctrines, and even world views were communicated" ("Meaning and Ambiguity in Tudor Cartography," in *English Map-Making, 1500–1800,* ed. Sarah Tyacke [London: British Library, 1983], p. 22). Others are beginning to question the conceptions that rule our understanding of cartography itself. See Denis Wood's review of *Art and Cartography,* "Commentary," *Cartographica* 24 (1987): 76–82; and especially the short essays in the Pompidou Centre exhibition catalog *Cartes et Figures de la Terre* (Paris: Centre Georges Pompidou, 1980).

9. The special character of medieval maps is discussed by David Woodward, "Reality, Symbolism, Time, and Space in Medieval World Maps," *Annals of the Association of American Georgraphers* 75 (1985): 510–21; this article is a preliminary report of research later expanded upon in Harley and Woodward, eds., *The History of Cartography,* vol. 1. Although this special character would seem to be an obvious point, some are still unaware of it. For instance, the recently published *Encyclopedic Dictionary of Semiotics* omits any reference to non-Western or nonmodern maps. See M[artin] K[rampen], "Cartography," *Encyclopedic Dictionary of Semiotics* (Berlin: Mouton de Gruyter, 1986), 1: 98–99.

10. In this way, medieval maps are like other medieval texts in that the literal reading is always primary, the kinds of allegory following; see Hugh of St. Victor, *The Didascalicon,* 1939 ed. C. H. Buttimer, trans. J. Taylor (New York: Columbia Univ. Press, 1961); extracts from books 5 and 6 reprinted in A. J. Minnis and A. B. Scott, eds., *Medieval Literary Theory and Criticism c.1100–c.1375: The Commentary Tradition* (Oxford: Clarendon Press, 1988), pp. 71–86.

11. See J. B. Harley, "Maps, Knowledge, and Power," in *The Iconography of Landscape: Essays on the Symbolic Representation, Design and Use of Past Environments,* ed. Denis Cosgrove and Stephen Daniels (Cambridge, England: Cambridge Univ. Press, 1988), pp. 277–312.

12. William Boelhower, in *Through a Glass Darkly: Ethnic Semiosis in American Literature* (New York: Oxford Univ. Press, 1987), discusses fifteenth- and sixteenth-century European world maps as powerful instruments of colonization that contrast with the weakness of Native American chorographic perspectives; see esp. chap. 2. The bivalent relationship between maps and political and economic power in various periods is discussed in a number of recent works, including Juergen Schulz, "Jacopo de' Barbari's View of Venice: Map Making, City Views, and Moralized Geography Before the Year 1500," *Art Bulletin* 60 (1978): 425–74; Victor Morgan, "The Cartographic Image of 'The Country' in Early Modern England," *Transactions of the Royal Historical Society,* 5th ser., 29 (1979): 129–54; Chandra Mukerji, *From Graven Images: Patterns of Modern Materialism* (New York: Columbia Univ. Press, 1983), pp. 79–130; and Svetlana Alpers, *The Art of Describing: Dutch Art in the Seventeenth Century* (Chicago: Univ. of Chicago Press, 1983), chap. 3. Such relationships have recently been dramatized in Brian Friel's play, *Translations,* in his *Selected Plays* (Washington, D.C.: Catholic Univ. of America Press, 1984), pp. 377–451.

13. The contemporary reluctance to view maps within their political contexts is illustrated by those on both sides of the debate over the Peters Projection. For two contrasting views, see Ward L. Kaiser, *A New View of the World: A Handbook to the World Maps: Peters Projection* (New York: Friendship Press, 1987), and Anngret Simms, "Playing Politics with Maps," *The Irish Times,* 15 April 1989 (a review of Arno Peters, *Peters Atlas of the World* [London: Longman, 1989]).

14. This essay is part of a larger study that considers two basic questions that have not hitherto been brought together: (1) What were the medieval conceptions of the physical world? (2) What were the consequences of these conceptions for artistic discourse of the period? On Chaucer's geographical references and sources, see John A. Hertz, "Chapters toward a Study of Chaucer's Knowledge of Geography," DA 19 (1959), 2600–1; for an annotated list of Chaucerian place names, see Francis P. Magoun, Jr., *A Chaucer Gazetteer* (Chicago: Univ. of Chicago Press, 1961).

15. For a brief but excellent overview of "The Image of the World before the Portolan Charts," see Michel Mollat du Jourdin, "Introduction," in Michel Mollat du Jourdin and Monique de la Ronciere, *Sea Charts of the Early Explorers: 13th to 17th Century,* trans. L. le R. Dethan (Fribourg: Thames & Hudson, 1984), pp. 8–11.

16. References to the T-O form occur in Dati's *La Sfera,* Brunetto Latini's *Livre du Tresor,* and Gervase of Tilbury's *Otia Imperialia,* cited in W. L. Bevan and H. W. Phillott, *Mediaeval Geography: An Essay in Illustration of the Hereford Mappa Mundi* (London: E. Stanford, 1873), p. xv. See also the discussion of T-O maps in C. Raymond Beazley, *The Dawn of Modern Geography: A History of Exploration and Geographical Science from the Conversion of the Roman Empire to A.D. 900,* 3 vols. (London: J. Murray, 1897–1906), 2: 576–79, 2: 627–32.

17. There was a strong scriptural tradition for the central placement of Jerusalem: "This city of Jerusalem I have set among the nations, with the other countries round about her" (*Ezek.* 5:5). On the centrality of Jerusalem, Woodward states that it is only in "the fourteenth and fifteenth centuries [that] the practice of placing Jerusalem at the center became common" (*The History of Cartography,* pp. 341–42), but this is of course the period under scrutiny in this essay.

18. See *History of Cartography,* vol. 1. See also the chronological table of world maps in Leo Bagrow, *History of Cartography,* 1951; 1960 trans. D. L. Paisey, rev. R. A. Skelton (London: Watts, 1964), p. 45.

19. At this writing (August 1989), Richard of Haldingham's map is still owned by Hereford Cathedral, but as it has been advertised for sale that situation may not hold at the time of publication.

20. Bevan lists medieval *mappae mundi* in England (*Mediaeval Geography,* pp. xxxiv–xlvi).

21. Lloyd A. Brown, *The Story of Maps* (Boston: Little, Brown, 1949), p. 96.

22. Trans. George H. T. Kimble, *Geography in the Middle Ages* (New York: Methuen, 1938), p. 20.

23. Ibid., p. 24.

24. Ibid., p. 32.

25. Ibid., p. 32.

26. On the politically repressive connection made in the later Middle Ages between Noah's sons and the three estates, see Lee Patterson " 'No man his reson herde': Peasant Consciousness, Chaucer's Miller, and the Structure of the *Canterbury Tales,*" *South Atlantic Quarterly* 86 (1987): 457–95.

27. See Harley's discussion of accuracy as "a new talisman of authority," in "Maps, Knowledge, and Power," p. 300.

28. Woodward notes the "family of spatial representations and ideas found in architecture as well as in cartography" ("Medieval *Mappaemundi,*" p. 340.)

29. See Samuel Y. Edgerton, *The Renaissance Rediscovery of Linear Perspective* (New York: Harper & Row, 1975), on the medieval "lack" of perspective.

30. Harley, "Maps, Knowledge, and Power," pp. 292–94.

31. All citations and line references are to *The Riverside Chaucer,* 3d ed., ed. Larry D. Benson (Boston: Houghton Mifflin, 1987).

32. For example, Chauncey Wood, *Chaucer and the Country of the Stars: Poetic Uses of Astrological Imagery* (Princeton, N.J.: Princeton Univ. Press, 1970), p. 184. For a recent bibliography of the critical discussion of these lines in context, see the *Riverside Chaucer,* p. 1057.

33. I follow standard usage in abbreviating the titles of Chaucer's works using "PardT" = "Pardoner's Tale", "WBPro" = "Wife of Bath's Prologue", "GP" = "General Prologue", etc. For a complete list of abbreviations, see the *Riverside Chaucer,* p. 779.

34. Boies Penrose discusses classical and medieval conceptions of the *oikoumene* in *Travel and Discovery in the Renaissance 1420–1620* (1952; Cambridge, Mass.: Harvard Univ. Press, 1963), p. 2.

35. Discussed in Bevan, *Mediaeval Geography,* p. 2.

36. Trans. Bevan, *Mediaeval Geography,* p. xvii. See also the discussion of Crates's theory in John Kirtland Wright, *The Geographical Lore of the Time of the Crusades: A Study in the History of Medieval Science and Tradition in Western Europe* (New York: American Geographical Society, 1925), pp. 18–19.

37. On Macrobius's views, see Kimble, *Geography in the Middle Ages,* pp. 8–9.

38. Pierre d'Ailly discusses the size and composition of the *oikoumene* in *Ymago Mundi,* trans. Edward Grant, in *A Source Book in Medieval Science,* ed. Edward Grant (Cambridge, Mass.: Harvard Univ. Press, 1974), pp. 636–38. See also Kimble's discussion, *Geography in the Middle Age,* pp. 209–10.

39. For a bibliography of critical views on the Knight and his campaigns, see the *Riverside Chaucer,* p. 800. In particular, I agree with Maurice Hussey, *Chaucer's World: A Pictorial Companion* (Cambridge: Cambridge Univ. Press, 1967, p. 13) that the "outlying regions [named by Chaucer] are more figures of speech than actual places." For my purposes, recognizing the metaphoric extent of the knight's travels is far more important than identifying any place or actual person who might have served as a model for this character, though numerous readers have attempted to do just that. See William Urban, "When Was Chaucer's Knight in 'Ruce'?" *Chaucer Review* 18 (1984): 347–53, for a typical article of the latter type.

40. Note that the Shipman piloted along the shore, the Merchant traded only across the Channel, the Pardoner had been (he says) to Rome, but only the Wife of Bath journeyed as far as Jerusalem, and that, in terms of travel conditions in the Middle Ages, was far indeed. On travel and literature in the later Middle Ages, see Christian K. Zacher, *Curiosity and Pilgrimage: The Literature of Discovery in Fourteenth-Century England* (Baltimore: Johns Hopkins Press, 1976). On medieval European travel writing, see Mary B. Campbell, *The Witness and the Other World: Exotic European Travel Writing, 400–1600* (Ithaca, N.Y.: Cornell Univ. Press, 1988).

41. Boelhower, *Through a Glass Darkly,* p. 55.

42. These categories are Bevan's in *Mediaeval Geography,* p. xxiii. He adds "legendary" as a fourth source, but I have not found any such references in Chaucer.

43. As Mollat du Jourdin writes, "Predestined to be the site of the spreading of the Gospel, the Mediterranean serves as the axis of the whole [T-O] structure. Everything stems from there, in a convergence of the knowledge of antiquity and biblical traditions" (*Sea Charts,* p. 8).

44. Magoun, *A Chaucer Gazeteer,* also lists three, though different, types of

usage for Jerusalem: the biblical city, the medieval pilgrimage city, and the celestial city (p. 95).

45. Bevan, *Mediaeval Georgraphy,* discusses the understanding of the Terrestial Paradise as an "existing contemporaneous fact" (p. xx) by Higden, Mandeville, Gervase of Tilbury and others, pp. xx–xxi. Kimble, *Geography of the Middle Ages,* adds John of Hesse and John Marignolli, p. 184.

46. Trans. Kimble, *Geography in the Middle Ages,* p. 24.

47. We might note in this context a representative of the race of apple-sniffers, who subsisted entirely on the odor of apples, seated in the lower right-hand portion of the Ebstorf detail (figure 2). Nicholas H. Steneck, *Science and Creation in the Middle Ages: Henry of Langenstein (d. 1397) on Genesis* (Notre Dame: Univ. of Notre Dame Press, 1976), notes the persistence of standard medieval geographical beliefs about the composition and inhabitants of the world into and past Chaucer's own time (p. 83).

48. On Asian travels and travelers, see Campbell, *The Witness and the Other World;* also Kimble, *Geography in the Middle Ages,* chap. 6. On pilgrims and missionaries, ninth through thirteenth centuries, see Beazley, *The Dawn of Modern Geography* 2, chaps. 3–6.

49. *Mandeville's Travels,* ed. M. C. Seymour (London: Oxford Univ. Press, 1969): "Of Paradys ne can I speken propurly, for I was not there. It is fer beyonde, and that forthinketh me, and also I was not worthi. But as I haue herd seye of wyse men beyonde, I schalle telle you with gode wille" (p. 220). After this disclaimer, Mandeville goes on to describe the usual components of paradise, the enclosing wall, the four rivers, etc.

50. Kenneth J. Knoespel, "Gazing on Technology: *Theatrum Mechanorum* and the Assimilation of Renaissance Machinery," in *Literature and Technology,* p. 120.

51. V. A. Kolve, *Chaucer and the Imagery of Narrative: The First Five Canterbury Tales* (Stanford: Stanford Univ. Press, 1984), esp. pp. 105–14. As Kolve notes, Robert A. Pratt, "Chaucer's Use of the *Teseida,*" *PMLA* 62 (1947): 598–621, first suggested the Colisseum as a possible model for Boccaccio (Chaucer's direct source); Kolve explains the importance of Chaucer's elaborations of this image but overlooks the possibility of a connection with the T-O *mappa mundi.* Kolve lacks appropriately dated source images of tournament rounds, but Steven I. Pederson, *The Tournament Tradition and Staging of The Castle of Perseverance* (Ann Arbor, Mich.: UMI Research Press, 1987), presents two fifteenth-century illustrations of circular lists (figures 5 and 6, pp. 105–6). Neither list, however, contains any of the features emphasized by Chaucer. Some earlier critics have noted the problematic nature of the amphitheater, but none has suggested any but a purely metaphorical resolution. See Merle Fifield, "The 'Knight's Tale': Incident, Idea, Incorporation," *Chaucer Review* 3 (1968): 95–106; and Joseph Westlund, "The 'Knight's Tale' as an Impetus for Pilgrimage," *Philological Quarterly* 43 (1964): 526–37.

52. Mircea Eliade, *The Sacred and the Profane: The Nature of Religion.* trans. Willard R. Trask (New York: Harcourt, Brace, 1969), p. 33; quoted by Jesse M. Gellrich, *The Idea of the Book in the Middle Ages: Language Theory, Mythology, and Fiction* (Ithaca, N.Y.: Cornell Univ. Press, 1985), p. 68; Gellrich also discusses medieval maps, pp. 62–64.

53. Some recent discussions of the theme of order in the "Knight's Tale" include Thomas H. Luxon, " 'Sentence' and 'Solaas': Proverbs and Consolation in the 'Knight's Tale,' " *Chaucer Review* 22 (1987): 94–111; T. McAlindon, "Cosmology, Contrariety and the Knight's Tale," *Medium Aevum* 50 (1986): 41–57; Judith Ferster, *Chaucer on Interpretation* (Cambridge, Eng.: Cambridge Univ.

Press, 1985), pp. 23–45; Kolve, *Chaucer and the Imagery of Narrative,* chap. 3; David Aers, *Chaucer, Langland and the Creative Imagination,* (London: Routledge & Kegan Paul, 1980), pp. 174–95, 228–31.

54. Jerold C. Frakes, " 'Ther Nis Namoore to Seye': Closure in the *Knight's Tale,*" *Chaucer Review* 22 (1987): 1–7, suggests *"fortuna* as the controlling *agens* of the events" of this tale (p. 2).

55. Theseus begins by asserting the great chain of being: "with that faire cheyne of love he bond / The fyr, the eyr, the water, and the lond / In certeyn boundes, that they may nat flee" ("KnT" 2991–93). From this orderly creation he derives the existence of the first mover: "Thanne may men by this ordre wel discerne / That thilke Moevere stable is and eterne" ("KnT" 3003–4).

56. Thomas H. Luxon asserts the deliberate quality of Theseus's choices, both of action and of language: "Theseus's proverbial utterances serve much the same purpose of his frequent creation of ceremonies throughout the tale. He choreographs ceremonies as a strategy for containing or resolving the apparent disorder in the world. He does not simply pick from the 'catalogue' of ceremonies or proverbs one that can be applied to a type of situation; he creates the ceremony or sentence he needs out of a hard-won perception of underlying (or overarching) order" (" 'Sentence' and 'Solaas'," p. 105).

57. Harley, "Maps, Knowledge, and Power," pp. 290–92.

58. Ibid., p. 292.

59. Chaucer's use of this word in "To Rosemounde" is noted by Donald R. Howard, *Chaucer: His Life, His Works, His World* (New York: Dutton, 1987), p. 173. I believe that Chaucer's lines here may refer not only to the roundness of the typical T-O map but also (as in the case of the lines of *Troilus and Criseyde* discussed above) to the "embracing" of the continental core by the circumfluent ocean: "Madame, ye ben of al beaute shryne / As fer as cercled is the mapamounde" ("To Rosemounde" 1–2). See note to these lines in the *Riverside Chaucer,* p. 1082.

60. Although it should be noted that Macrobian maps are of the zonal kind, and not the tripartite T-O, so many contemporary examples of the latter existed that Chaucer's familiarity with both sorts is quite likely. See Woodward, *The History of Cartography,* p. 300.

61. On the significance of the T, see Jonathan T. Lanman, "The Religious Symbolism of the T in T-O Maps," *Cartographica* 18 (1981): 18–22.

62. Harley, "Maps, Knowledge, and Power," p. 290.

63. Edgerton, "From Mental Matrix to *Mappamundi* to Christian Empire: The Heritage of Ptolemaic Cartography in the Renaissance," in *Art and Cartography,* p. 26; cited by Harley, "Maps, Knowledge, and Power," p. 290.

64. On a literary analogue to the Ebstorf map, see John B. Friedman, "Medieval Cartography and 'Inferno' xxxiv: Lucifer's Three Faces Reconsidered," *Traditio* 39 (1983): 447–55.

65. William Butler Yeats, "The Second Coming," in *The Variorum Edition of the Poems of W. G. Yeats,* ed. Peter Alt and Russell K. Alspach (New York: Macmillan, 1957), pp. 401–2.

66. Korzybski, *Science and Sanity: An Introduction to Non-Aristotelian Systems and General Semantics* (Lakeville, Conn.: International Non-Aristotelian Library, 1948), p. 58.

67. Ferster, *Chaucer on Interpretation,* p. 35.

68. For some recent views on the "Retraction," see James Dean, "Dismantling the Canterbury Book," *PMLA* 100 (1985): 746–62; David F. Marshall, "Unmask-

ing the Last Pilgrim: How and Why Chaucer Used the Retraction to Close *The Canterbury Tales,*" *Christianity and Literature* 31 (1982): 55–74; Gale C. Schricker, "On the Relation of Fact and Fiction in Chaucer's Poetic Endings," *Philological Quarterly* 60 (1981): 13–27; Douglas Wurtele, "The Penitence of Geoffrey Chaucer," *Viator* 11 (1980): 335–59.

69. In Boccaccio's *Teseida,* Chaucer's source for the "Knight's Tale," it is Arcita's experience after death that is described in terms of a journey into space. Interestingly, Chaucer transfers the passage in presenting Arcite's death from the "Knight's Tale" to the end of the *Troilus.* See the note to lines 1807–27 in Benson, *Riverside Chaucer,* p. 1057.

70. Harley, "Maps, Knowledge, and Power," pp. 300–1.

71. Earlier versions of this essay were presented at meetings of the International Congress of Medieval Studies (1985), the American Library Association (1986), the Rocky Mountain Medieval and Renaissance Society (1987), and the Modern Language Association (1988), and at a lecture at Wake Forest University (1987). I would like to thank Brent Allison for his help in my initial cartographic explorations, Seamus Deane, Heather Dubrow, Duncan Harris, and Gregory Blake Smith for their tough and intelligent readings, and especially Julia Bolton Holloway for originally suggesting the possibility of a connection between *mappae mundi* and Theseus's amphitheater.

Gazing on Technology: *Theatrum Mechanorum* and the Assimilation of Renaissance Machinery

KENNETH J. KNOESPEL

Although Renaissance illustrations of pumps, pulleys, and water mills may catch our eye in history books or on public television, most often we view them as antiquarian curiosities that only hold our attention momentarily, like displays in a museum. When we look more carefully at the iconographic tableaux found in the earliest published illustrations of machinery, we find social codes that tell us much about their assimilation. My intention in the following essay is to identify some of the mechanisms used for the assimilation of Renaissance technology. In particular, I want to emphasize how the narrative responses provoked by Renaissance machines and their graphic representation function as a means for the social absorption of new technology. The theatrical metaphors used in titles and visually displayed in books provide a departure point for asking how we look at machines.

My discussion has three parts. The first introduces early books on machinery and considers specific illustrations and their accompanying explications. The second notices how Renaissance gardens—real and imaginary—provide a narrative setting for staging a broader cultural legitimation of machinery. The third argues that the visual framing of machinery that takes place in pictures or in texts through the use of metaphor may be regarded as a mechanism for transfering authority and the illusion of autonomy to machines or as a means for generating narratives about how they work and how they may be applied.

Several assumptions accompany my discussion and I want to voice them at the outset. One involves an awareness that we cannot expect to approach Renaissance technology unaffected by our own highly technologized culture. Another recognizes that technology does not appear abruptly in the Renaissance but involves a maturation of processes already present in the Middle Ages. Still another assumes that thinking about technology engages one in negotiating between detail and abstraction. In an important book on technology, Langdon Winner suggests that what we need are "inquiries that stand somewhere between the ultimate 'Being of beings' [a reference to Heidegger's work on technology] and the latest squabble on this or that social gadget. One must seek simultaneously to avoid depths without direction and details without meaning."[1] I would situate this inquiry "somewhere between," aware that at times some may find it moving too far in one direction or another. Finally, Winner's comment has a bearing on all the essays in this book inasmuch as literature—understood as not simply the canonical literary genres but texts in that term's broadest meaning—compromises a relay or "somewhere between" the presence of technology in the world and the reflections it provokes.

The theatrical metaphors that abound in Renaissance book titles represent not only the resurgence of drama but the expansion of technology. As Frances Yates and others have shown, theatrical metaphors, grounded in architecture and optics, become encyclopedic devices for bringing order to phenomena as various as memory systems and fishing manuals.[2] Broadly conceived, visual metaphors such as the theater or the mirror permit access to what Christian Metz has called a culture's scopic regimes.[3] What Metz has in mind is simply that our ways of thinking are intimately bound with our sense of sight. In contrast to the medieval metaphor of the mirror, the perspectivalism of the Renaissance theatrical metaphor asserts an even more active and controlling presence of the observer at a distance. The theatre is not casually associated with perspective but architecturally affirms both a practical and theoretical interest in optics.[4] Because of the broad metaphoric extension of *perspectiva* in language and the graphic arts, there is virtually no area of thought in the Renaissance left untouched by the idea of theatrically framing experience. Even a cursory survey of titles in the *Short Title Catalogue of Books Published in England* indicates the popularity of such metaphors.[5] In fact, the very proliferation of such titles in itself is one indication of the very assimilation of the technology of perspective. The books that advertise themselves as theaters for machines and instrumentation—the *theatrum mechanorum*—and the others that represent machines are part of this cultural fascination with the visual staging of knowledge.

VISUAL REPRESENTATION

Although we commonly think of Leonardo da Vinci's drawings of his inventions as the first modern illustrations of mechanical devices, they were virtually unknown during the Renaissance. The first books devoted solely to machinery—influenced by the mechanical studies of Ctesibius, Philo of Byzantium, Hero of Alexandria, the machines in Book 6 of Georgius Agricola's *De re metallica* (1556) and the construction engines included in Book 10 of Vitruvius's *De architectura*—appear in the last half of the sixteenth century.[6] Jacques Besson's *Livre des instruments mathematiques et mechaniques* (1569) introduced and popularized a genre that came to include Agostino Ramelli's *Diverse et artificose machine* (1588), Vittorio Zonca's *Teatro Nuovo di Machine et Edificii* (1607), and Georg Andreas Böckler's *Theatrum machinarum novum* (1662).[7] In the most pragmatic sense, these books circulated as advertisements for their inventors. Besson's book, for example, extended the command performances he put on for nobility and attracted attention not only to machinery but to himself.[8] The illustrations are, however, much more than marketing tools. By placing before the observer an array of machines that illustrate the application of mechanics, the books also fostered the study of mathematics and Archimedes in particular. If we wish, we may think of them as the first modern recruitment literature for civil engineering. Here the mechanical wonders described by practitioners such as John Dee in his Preface to Euclid's *Elements* (1570) are visually demonstrated.[9] "Readers who turned the pages of Jacques Besson's appropriately named *Theatre of Machines* were witnessing a dramatic spectacle that previous scholars had not seen, just as readers of Agricola and Versalius had their eyes opened to 'veins and vessels' that had been less visible before."[10]

Just what kind of spectacle did readers confront in these volumes? To discern more exactly what was portrayed, we must consider further the ways theatrical metaphors function in these books. The titles themselves invite readers to approach the books as collections of views and broadly suggest the way the sixteenth-century theater was regarded as an architectural structure that directed the vision of an audience to particular scenes. *Scenographia,* the Greek word for perspective popularized by Vitruvius in *De architectura,* marks a fascination with visually ordering knowledge. The word literally designates the graphic ordering of sight-lines for the purpose of creating an optical illusion.[11] In practice, *scenographia,* as

Figure 1. Title-page of Georg Andrea Böckler's *Theatrum machinarum novum* (Nurnberg, 1662).

Figure 2. Jacques Besson, *Livres des instruments mathematiques et mechanique* (Vecenza, 1582) (Plate 52).

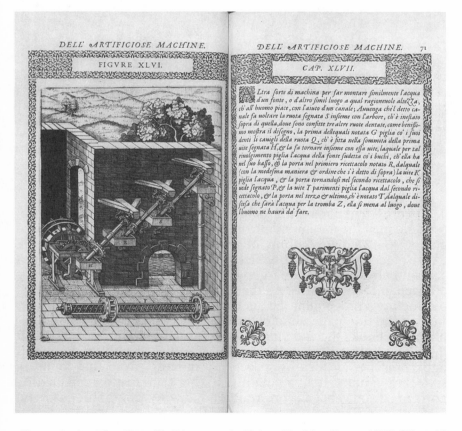

Figure 3. Agostino Ramelli, *Diverse et Artificiose Machine* (Lyon, 1588) (Plate 46).

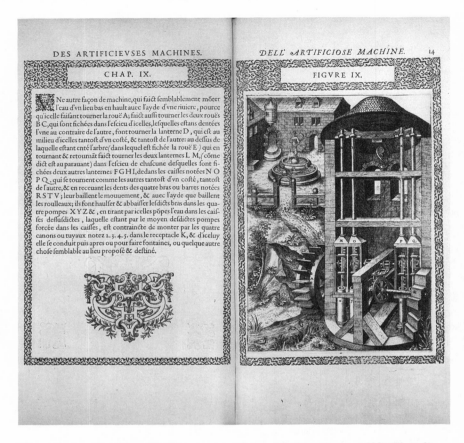

Figure 4. Agostino Ramelli, *Diverse et Artificiose Machine* (Lyon, 1588) (Plate 9).

perspectiva and *cinematographia,* challenges the observer to comprehend how the manipulation of sight becomes a means for manipulating knowledge. A form of *scenographia* is exhibited by the frontispiece to George Böckler's *Theatrum* (figure 1) showing a curtain being drawn aside to reveal a town landscape with an array of mechanical apparatus. As the reader looks into the scene framed by Böckler's procenium, he anticipates an evolving picture theater. Just as the title-page anticipates the collection of views that comprise the book, the individual views promote an expectancy that they may be realized in the world. The theatricality of Böckler's book presents an idea of space very different from that found in sixteenth-century Italian painting. Rather than comprising an allegorized drama based on religious or mythographic stories,

Böckler's illustrations—at once civic and secular—bear the expectation that they may be carried out. By giving a preview of what is to come, the illustrations may be compared to modern architectural drawings or computer-generated images that insert still-imagined buildings within a landscape of familiar structures. By staging machines, these Renaissance folios provide a glimpse of how technology may be assimilated.

The distinction between the narrative mode of Italian Renaissance painting and the descriptive force of northern European painting offers a useful way for approaching the illustrations of machinery and the way they order perception. Compared to Italian painting that used perspective to stage stories drawn from the Bible or from poets such as Ovid, northern painting becomes engaged in descriptive exploration that opens possibilities for more localized narratives.[12] While idealized images from the Bible or classical antiquity become enframed in much Italian painting, in Dutch painting the world extends beyond the frame. The representation of machinery offers an example of a visual mode whose departure point is description rather than narrative. Here we must be careful not to make a simple either-or distinction between description and narrative. While narrative is removed from the portrayal of machinery as the primary vehicle of representation, the illustrations provoke narrative on a different level. As the observer responds to the images—images removed from the metanarrative provided by mythological stories—narratives are formulated that work toward the very assimilation of technology. In fact, the illustrations of machinery function in a manner similar to a variety of new descriptive images such as Galileo's representation of the moon or Leeuwenhoeck's images of microscopic bodies. The narratives are a means for thinking the devices into the world. By provoking assimilating narratives, the illustrations function as relays. Even if a particular machine is rejected as impractical, the technology itself is not rejected, for there may be a setting in which it finds application. Besson includes a plate depicting a mechanical fan that initially appears impractical because of its sheer size. Even though one may reject the application depicted, one recognizes that the mechanism may be applied to a stamping mill as well. Rather than providing grounds for their rejection, the interrogation of machines creates grounds for the machines' incorporation.

The illustrations also invite us to view these machines as visual puzzles. Besson's illustration of a fire engine—the first known published illustration of such a device—supplies an example (figure 2). Response to the image may be tracked by formulating three simple questions: (1) What am I looking at? (2) How does it work? and (3) How does the apparatus apply to the world I live in? The answer to the first question comes by recognizing the burning building and an apparatus used to direct water to the flames. The second follows the observer's inspection of the picture and the association between the cranking mechanism, the water being poured into the engine and the stream of water coming from the nozzle. This answer, however, is only provisional, for the illustration does not supply enough information for the reader to understand the physical workings of the engine. A detailed answer to the second question must await further study, consultation with the author, an actual effort to construct the machine, or a combination of all three. The response to the final question may well determine whether or not the observer decides to learn more about the apparatus before him. In the case of the fire engine, applicability may be self-evident but may also lead to practical questions about efficiency or the proximity of a water source.

The second edition of Besson's work offers an example of how the illustrations provoked commentary. While Besson's first edition of 1569 included the plates with simple descriptive titles, the edition published in 1578 included more detailed explication by Francois Beroald. Each machine is not simply labeled but, following a practice drawn from classical texts on mechanics, referred to as a proposition. Proposition 52—the fire engine—reads: "A kind of new invention useful for casting water on a fire especially when the flames are so intense that they prevent anyone from approaching the burning building."[13] A description of the fire engine—titled "Declarat. de la LII Figure"—follows. The headings used by Beroald are revealing inasmuch as they present the machines as arguments.

Another feature of Beroald's commentary may be mentioned before considering Beroald's description of the fire engine. Besides authorizing each machine within a tradition of mechanics by referring to them as propositions, Beroald maps the machines by including a rudimentary scale for measurement. A special page (fol. a 4 recto), devoted to formulating special terminology, appears at the end of the Preface.[14]

To better understand the machinery you will notice these (figures) on all the illustrations (whether they are configured one way or another). Since the top of the page is called the north, the line at the top edge of the plate is called the northern line. The foot (of the page) is called the south and the edge of the plate that turns in this direction is called the southern line. The side (of the page) facing the binding is called the west and the edge of the plate which faces it is called the western line. The opposing side of the page is called the east and the corresponding line of the plate is the eastern line. In addition, even though letters do not appear on the plates to provide guidance, I would point out that I replace them by using a measure divided into twenty four parts. All of this appears on the following page which is made available for your benefit. (fol. 3 verso)

Beroald has in mind a system of measurement that may be compared to the grid system used by a draftsman or cartographer. Quite simply he uses one form of technology—measurement—to promote the understanding of another. From a sixteenth-century vantage point, the schema is analogous to the compass or wind tables at the beginning of map collections. In effect, Beroald implies that just as one might orient a map relative to a constant table of directions, one may map the layout of measurement of a machine to meet a recognized standard. The references to Septentrion, Septentrionale, Midi, Meridionale, Occident, Occidentale, Orient, and Orientale in his explication refer to such a grid. What is striking is the effort to map the machines within an idealized space that is expected to be shared by the readers.

Beroald assumes the reader has the table of measurements in mind as he studies his description of the fire engine.[15]

The entire machine rests on two wheels; the middle of the machine is 2.m.12.p south and 22.p east. The machine is supported on four feet at the following distance from the above mentioned lines: 2.m.2.p and 4.p for the one pair and 18.p and 18.p for the other, these being the feet which are attached by two hooks. At the northern end there is a strut to break the machine. (fol. E 2 verso)

While Beroald's description provides remarkably detailed measurements for thinking about the engine, it does not supply knowledge sufficient for its construction. At best the information supplied by the illustration and the commentary creates an intermediary space that might entice the reader to develop the additional expertise necessary to realize the engine.

An even more sophisticated visual presentation of machinery appears in Ramelli's staged presentation (figure 3) of an Archimedean screw (1588): We explore the waterworks with our eyes much as a stage set would be investigated in anticipation of action. The illustration is divided into three planes: the background landscape; the apparatus in the middle ground (an archimedean screw driven by an undershot water wheel); and the foreground (a cutaway illustration of the screw with cogs and gears). The force of the illustration comes from the stone wall and floor that draw the planes together and orient our exploration of the picture. Here architecture quite literally stages the machinery and explains its relation to the landscape beyond the wall. The natural scene beyond the wall is being harnessed to run the machine. Just as nature itself draws upon the stream to nourish vegetation, humans may now use the stream to drive a waterwheel and foster their own enterprise. We notice other details as well. While the control of nature appears to be the general purpose of the machine, the machine itself has no specific application in the illustration. We see before us—as in many of Ramelli's machines—an image of perpetual motion that may well remind us of Escher's modern graphics. The water that drives the machine and that is drawn up into the mechanism drops into a pipe to once again return to the stream. The image offers a glimpse of a circuit—an ingenious thought experiment—whose application or extension is left to the audience. Ramelli's machine stands before us as a conceptual blueprint.

The walls in the illustration alert us to a further extension of nature as well. Rather than viewing the pump on an enclosed proscenium stage, we view only a corner of a larger setting. Instead of encircling the machinery, the wall extends beyond the border of the picture. Ramelli stages the machine not within the arches of a proscenium stage but within a fragmentary setting that waits for incorporation into the world. Much as the walls invite extension, the machinery itself waits to be coupled to other devices. By depicting the connection of a waterwheel to a water screw, Ramelli indicates his interest in such complexity. Ramelli is hardly alone in depicting the mechanical elaboration of technology. The manuals do not set forth simple mechanisms but show an attraction to assemblies that may be adapted or interconnected.

That Ramelli is primarily interested in the general principles demonstrated by the machine appears in his commentary. Rather than including engineering specifications for parts of the engine as Besson and Beroald, Ramelli draws attention to a progression of events caused by the water's natural force.[16]

The nature of this machine is no different than the preceding one, as one notices, (except that is is for pumping water) and serves to pump water from a canal, river, well, or similar place to a convenient height. By turning the wheel marked Z by the force of the water in the canal or river mentioned above, the water is taken up by the small paddles (as you see in the drawing) to the first receptacle marked H. At the same time, wheel N makes wheel T turn which is geared to wheel Q connected to the covered screw drive marked A. Wheel N (as one notices) is connected to the same gear. This gear is made in the same way as the others. By its turning it takes the water from the first receptacle to the second marked R, and then to the third marked S by the very movement described above in regard to wheel N which gave it movement taking with its teeth the cogs of lantern-like wheel marked M," which is geared just as was described above. In the same order, gear K takes the water from the third receptacle and as it turns brings the water to the fourth and final receptacle where by means of a pump (as one sees in the figure marked V) one can make the water descend or lead the water wherever it is most useful. (p. 70; Paris, 1588)

To a modern audience, the cumbersome description of the machine—even more evident in the French original—stands in stark contrast to the clarity of the illustration. After noticing that the machine is a variation of the previous one in the collection, Ramelli indicates how the individual parts are connected through a cause-effect relationship set in motion by the power of the water. The conjunctions in the prose actually become a reflection of the machine's own gear work. Even the machine's artifice, which is noted at the very beginning, lies in its ability to use natural force to cause a mechanical chain reaction. By keying the major parts of the machine, the author makes it apparent that he intends the text to be an aid in studying the illustration. Even when combined, however, the image and the text hardly provide sufficient information to construct the machine. Rather, the ensemble sets before the reader a thought experiment that promotes access to underlying principles.

Ramelli's account, like Beroald's, challenges the reader to fill in diverse information. While the machine's purpose is certainly conveyed, the question of its practical construction remains a matter to be supplied by a very different set of narratives. Finally the machinery reminds us that an entire level of practical discourse remains absent from the presentation for the simple reason that it is assumed to be related through spoken instructions. In fact, as we look at these pictures we need to imagine how each marks an entry point of a myriad of narratives that cannot be recalled because they were not written down.

Although I have concentrated on individual scenes, I want to notice that such fragmentary images also contribute to a larger social assembly. As the illustrations provoke the formulation of assimilating narratives—indicated by questions explored above—

they also invite the reader to review the social organization implicated in the operations depicted. Besson's depictions of floating
pile-drivers, cranes, and dredges are not isolated vignettes or fragments but open to express a larger social interest in land reclama-
tion and harbor improvement. We might think of such images as
"postcards" giving us glimpses into the larger civil projects well
underway in the Veneto and in Holland during the later half of the
sixteenth century.[17] In other words, at the same time that the
machinery provokes the observer to devise individual narratives to
explain what is going on, it is already assumed to be part of a larger
social process.

The drama surveyed in the illustrations found in Besson, Ramelli,
and Böckler denotes transformations not only in the status of
nature but in the role of human beings. The illustrations indicate
that a transition has taken place in the idea of the actor, for the focal
point within the illustrations has shifted from the human to the
mechanical. In the Ramelli illustration considered above (figure 2),
the pump dominates the scene and becomes a quasi actor within
the landscape. When humans are included in illustrations such as
Besson's fire engine, their subservient status only strengthens the
central role of machines. Böckler shows a more developed
awareness of how machines alter the status of workers as well as
owners in his seventeenth-century illustrations. In one, a curtain
has been drawn aside to reveal a couple at leisure eating dinner
while the mill, tended by workers, operates on the floor beneath
them (plate 53). Here the machine begins to determine the roles
played by humans. The various illustrations portraying humans
attentively watching a machine's operation indicate even further the
centrality of the apparatus in the drama being portrayed.

Although machinery receives a central position in these illustrations, it would be wrong to view such technology as autonomous in
any way for such machines are invented and operated by human
agents even if such agents are not present. In fact each machine
should be thought of as a separate sculpture-like creation controlled by separate operators. A comparison of the machine illustrations and sixteenth-century emblem books suggests one way these
images conferred authority on their audience. Just as Andrea Alciati's *Emblemata* (1531) requires the reader to puzzle out hidden
morals, Ramelli's illustrations challenge the reader to puzzle out
hidden mechanical relations.[18] For example, in the Ramelli illustration of the fountain system, the cutaway depiction of a pumphouse
indicates that a concealed apparatus supplies water for the fountain
system (figure 4). In effect, Ramelli educates the reader to expect

that machinery exists behind a scene, much like Alciati educates the reader to expect moral significance. The emphasis on concealed pumps, pipework, pulleys, and gearworks—often exhibited through superimposed and cutaway drawings—indicates that the machine illustrations work much like allegorical handbooks in their assumption that knowledge comes only when one has been initiated in an explanatory code. Indeed, such comparisons are actually implied by Ramelli in his Preface. Rather than appealing to an unstated system of moral values, the images in the machine books respond to a body of practical knowledge. While the emblem books direct the reader to a moral superstructure, the books on machinery impell the reader to what we may call a superstructure in mechanics and mathematics. Much like the allegorical superstructure that controls a Botticelli painting, a techno-mathematical code implicitly controls the illustrated machinery.

However, while the mathematical practitioner—one of the many persons literally behind the scene—controls the machinery, human agency also becomes circumscribed by the very apparatus. Once constructed, the machine dictates not only its own maintenance but also its own improvement. Ramelli's pumps illustrate not only his inventiveness but the way that technology begins to determine *where* and *how* invention may take place. To a considerable degree, Ramelli's machines are extension of each other. Just as mythographic handbooks supplied components that could be combined inventively, the mechanical handbooks provided departure points for invention. Just as the cogs and gears of the pump must connect for the engine to work, the machines themselves wait to be applied to new tasks and even to be linked to other machines. The successive portrayal of pumping mechanisms shows a fascination with exploring various applications of the new technology. Just how the new mechanisms could be applied, however, becomes the domain not of the single hero but of the humans required to maintain and manipulate the new codes. While it may be tempting to imagine a single human agent or practitioner in control of the machine, we must be careful not to approach the machine or the human with a singular idealizing narrative that blurs the complex intersection of narratives that accompany and sustain technology.

In *Utopia* (1516), Thomas More refers to the world as a machine: "He has set forth the visible mechanism of the world [mundi huius visendam mechinam] as a spectacle for man."[19] More's simile alludes not only to the many components that must fit together if the social engine is to operate but also to an assumption that the engine should be seen as a whole. If we wish, we may think of his comparison as looking toward urban planning. The books considered above appear a little more than a half-century after *Utopia* and indicate that the broader social narrative associated with urban planning is no longer simply a dream.

PUMPS IN THE BOWER OF BLISS: NARRATIVE RESPONSE TO THE VISUAL REPRESENTATION OF MACHINES

The problems staged in the books by Böckler, Besson, and Ramelli comprise more than isolated thought experiments. Some of the ideas represented in these collections become literally exhibited in Renaissance gardens such as the garden of the Villa d'Este at Tivoli (1565–1575) and in the Pratolino garden (1569–1584) outside Florence.[20] Such Italian gardens and the projects they influenced in the north function not only as beautiful sites but as laboratories or test sites for technology. Besides being physically realized, however, the mechanical ideas are also set within a specific narrative context. As the observer moved through the new Renaissance gardens, he simultaneously undertook an allegorical journey based on established mythographic stories and encountered an array of new technological devices that challenged him to a new awareness of technology. For the Renaissance observer, the movement from moral to mechanism was facilitated by the academic distinction between moral and physical allegory. What *was* new was that the Renaissance observer found that the distinction between physical and moral allegory was no longer simply a conceptual distinction but a physical one as well. Renaissance gardens became at once stages for reviewing traditional narratives, showcases for technology, and sites for their conceptual integration.

When the Elizabethan traveler Fynes Moryson saw the hydraulic automata of the Pratolino garden in the middle of the 1590s he described them with fascination.[21] "There is a Cave, vulgarly called la grotta Maggiore. . . . In the said Cave, a head of marble distilleth water; and two trees by the turning of a cocke shed waters abundantly, and a little globe is turned around by Cupid, where the Images of Duckes dabble in the water, and then looke round about them; and in the middest of a marble table is an instrument, which with great art and force, driveth water into any furthest part of the Cave." In another grotto "certaine images of Nimphes are carried by the water out of the Cave, and in again, as if they had life"; in another he discovers "the image of Fame doth loudly sound a

Trumpet, while the Image of a Clowne putteth a dish into the water, and taking up water, presents it to the Image of a Tyger, which drinketh the same up, and then moves his head and lookes around about with his eyes." Moryson concludes by saying "I know not any place in the World affoords such rare sights in this kind."

The Pratolino garden visited by Moryson was broadly modeled on the earlier Este water garden at Tivoli.[22] In a descriptive catalog of the garden composed for Catherine di Medici, probably in 1571, the author lists sixty-five different marvels to be seen in the garden including the Fountain of the Water Organ. The focal point of this fountain, begun in 1568, was a statue of the many breasted Diana of Ephesus, also referred to as a statue of Nature or Fortune. A water organ behind the statue was set in operation by the rush of water that simultaneously forced air through organ pipes and triggered mechanical controls opening and closing the pipes. "The voices of many animals and sounds of almost all the instruments as beautiful as music are represented in these mechanisms" (145). [In essa si dovevano rappresentarele voci de molti animali et suoni di quasi tutti gl'istrumenti cosi bellici, come musici.] The spectacle so intrigued Pope Gregory XIII, when he visited the garden in 1572, that he requested to meet their inventor, Claude Venard.

Edmund Spenser's contemporary, Thomas Nashe, who visited Italy in the 1580s includes a long account of a Roman garden with automata in *The Unfortunate Traveller*.[23] "Why, you should not come into any man's house of account, but he had fish-ponds and little orchards at the top of his leads. If by rain or any other means those ponds were so full they need to be sluiced or let out, even of their superfluities they made melodious use, for they had great wind instruments instead of leaden spouts, that went duly on consort, only with this water's rumbling descend" (267). Surrounding a banquet house, the traveller observes a "conspiracy of pine trees" (268) that offers a perch for songbirds.

Who though there were bodies without souls, and sweet resembled substances without sense, yet by the mathematical experiments of long silver pipes secretly enrinded in the entrails of the boughs whereon they sat, and undiscernibly conveyed under their bellies into their small throats' sloping, they whistled and freely caroled their natural field note. Neither went those silver pipes straight, but, by many edged unsundered writhings & crankled wanderings aside, strayed from bough to bough into a hundred throats. But into this silver pipe so writed and wandering aside, if any demand how the wind was breathed: Forsooth the tail of the silver pipe stretched itself into the mouth of a great pair of bellows, where it was close soldered, and baled about with iron, it could not stir or have any vent betwixt. Those bellows with the rising and falling of leaden plummets wound up on a wheel, did beat up and down uncessantly, and so gathered in wind, serving with one blast all the snarled pipes to and fro of one tree at once. But so closely were all those organizing implements obscured in the corupulent trunks of the trees, that everyman there present renounced conjectures of art, and said it was done by enchantment. (268–69)

Although the magnificent artifice of the garden described by Nashe is intended as a satire of human efforts to outdo nature, it also conveys an ambivalence concerning the society that has made such urban engineering possible. At the same time that the contrived scene may be read as an indictment of artifice and sterility— an indictment that extends to the Popish religion—it also bears a fascination with the techniques of such fabrication. Consider the ironic comment that closes Nashe's description: "O Rome, if thou hast in thee such soul-exalting objects, what a thing is heaven in comparison of thee, of which Mercator's globe is a perfector model than thou art? Yet this I must say to the shame of us Protestants: if good works may merit heaven, they do them, we talk of them" (270). Following the account of inanimate objects that fill the garden, the "soul-exalting objects" can only be soulless. Nonetheless, as the final comment indicates, such objects are already on the minds of Englishmen.

While the extravagant hydraulic spectacles and mythographic scenes found in late sixteenth-century gardens provided the subject for numerous travel accounts, they also helped promote publications that explained how others could achieve similar effects. Together with the works by Besson and Ramelli, fragments from the work Ctesibius, Philo of Byzantium, and Hero of Alexandria fueled Renaissance curiosity in mechanical marvels. The work of Salomon de Caus is a case in point. Having studied the work of Hero as well as the illustrations of Besson and Ramelli, the Frenchman Solomon de Caus published a detailed book on hydraulics entitled *Les Raisons des forces mouvantes* (1615). Together with its later redactions by his brother Isaac de Caus, the work of Solomon de Caus became one of the most influential seventeenth-century books on the application of machinery to gardens. Besides supplying a remarkably detailed introduction to hydrostatics, Isaac de Caus's *Nouvelle invention de lever l'eau* (1644)—it appeared in English editions in 1645(?) and 1659—included the description of numerous mythographic garden scenes powered by mechanical devices.[24]

By the 1580s such gardens were not simply found in travel reports but were being constructed within the English landscape.

Italianate gardens, influenced by the Este and Pratolino gardens, could be found at Kenilworth, Theobalds, Nonesuch, and Hampton Court.[25] By 1600 Lord Burgley's garden at Theobalds (constructed between 1575 and 1585) had become the subject for a travel description in its own right.[26]

> There is a fountain in the centre of the garden: the water spouts out from a number of concealed pipes and sprays unwary passers-by. . . .

> In the first room there is an overhanging rock of crag (here they call it a "grotto") made of different kinds of semi-transparent stone, and roofed over with pieces of coral, crystal, and all kinds of metallic ore. It is thatched with green grass, and inside can be seen a man and a woman dressed like wild men of the woods, and a number of animals creeping through the bushes.

Another contemporary visitor describes the labyrinths, pools, and entertainment rooms and other visitors noticed "a little wood nearby. At the end you come to small round hill built of earth with a labyrinth around. [It] is called the Venusberg."[27]

The development of technologically landscaped gardens in the sixteenth and seventeenth centuries also corresponds to gardens in Renaissance poetry. The link between technology and the poetic representation of gardens is not surprising, considering that in medieval settings such as the *Roman de la Rose,* the garden was not an artificial structure for some ponderous, moral allegory but offered a setting for developed discussion of physical phenomena. For Jean de Meun, who probably was a professor of natural philosophy at the University of Paris, the fountain becomes a vehicle for an informed discussion of optics.[28] Renaissance literary scholarship has so frequently assumed classical and medieval sources for the gardens in Renaissance pastoral and epic poetry that it tends to overlook how the representation of Renaissance gardens in poetry also registers curiosity regarding science and technology.

Spenser's *Faerie Queene* offers a significant example, for it invites us not only to survey poetic gardens from antiquity to the cinquecento, but also to explore technologically perfected gardens.[29] While the Bower of Bliss portrays a developed allegory of sensuality set off by Guyon's temperance, it includes features similar to the Renaissance gardens being engineered for wealthy nobles during the later half of the sixteenth century. Comprising many acres, the Este and Pratolino gardens and their English counterparts included an array of mythological settings that were intended to be discovered separately. Entry to an outdoor banquet house or

pavillion replete with fountains and mosaics representing mythological themes could be on the culmination of one's progression
through the garden.[30] Guyon's progression through a variety of
visual stations on his way to the intimacy of the Bower of Bliss
describes a movement that would have been familiar to a Renaissance reader aware of the new Italian gardens with their constructed grottos and banquet rooms. The description of rolling
waves without wind (2.12.22), metalic boughs and ivy (2.12.55), a
fountain-lake "three cubits deep" (2.12.62)—all make it appear that
Spenser's garden is shaped with the artifice found real as well as
poetic gardens. Once it even appears that Spenser could be describing not only painted metal but metal that had literally turned green
through oxidation.

> And over all, of purest gold was spred,
>   A trayle of yuie in his native hew:
>   For the rich mettall was so coloured,
>   That wight, who did not well avis'd it vew,
>   Would surely deeme it to be yuie trew.

> (2.12.61)

Within the decorous but unfortified confines of the garden, Guyon
discovers a fountain with "infinit streames" (2.12.62) flowing into a
pool with a mosaic bottom. While such a stream is a common trope
in itself, the figures moving within its rushing water are described
like the mechanical statues in the Pratolino garden.

> Sometimes the one would lift the other quight
>   Above the waters, and then down againe
>   Her plong, as over maistered by might,
>   Where both awhile would covered remaine,
>   And each the other from to rise restraine;
>   The whiles their snowy limbes, as through a vele,
>   So through the Christall waves appeared plaine:
>   Then suddenly both would themselves unhele,
> And th' amarous sweet spoiles to greedy eyes revele.

> (2.12.64)

Rather than being celestial in origin, the pleasing music heard by
Guyon as he progresses further seems to have its source in a water-
organ.

> Eftsoones they heard a most melodious sound,
>   Of all that mote delight a daintie eare,
>   Such as attonce might not on living ground,

Save in ths Paradise, he heard elsewhere:
Right hard it was, for wight, which did it heare,
To read, what manner musicke that mote bere:
For all that pleasing is to living eare,
Was there consorted in one harmonee,
Birdes, voyces, instruments, windes, waters, all agree.

(2.12.70)

The comparison of the Bower of Bliss to mechanical gardens found outside Tivoli, Florence, or London would make much sense to a Renaissance reader. Although we may be more inclined to think of a Renaissance response to technology in Donne or in Jonson's masques designed by Inigo Jones, the new interest in science and technology presents itself in works written by an earlier generation as well.

With a broader awareness of Renaissance technology, we discern that *The Faerie Queene* challenges readers to recognize technological as well as poetic artifice. The presence of technology in the Bower of Bliss finally intensifies Guyon's warning that one cannot trust appearances. When Guyon destroys the Bower at the end of Book III, we can imagine Spenser quite simply turning off the machinery that has kept the garden in animation. Even the representation of a figure like Archimago in Book I may be read as a warning regarding the new mechanistic capacities claimed by late sixteenth-century engineers. Ultimately the artificial schemas and engines that appear in Spenser's poem remind us of how the romance genre could function as a narrative instrument for testing the specific engines that were appearing at the end of the century and for revealing the uncritical manner in which they were being received. The ingenious pumping mechanisms displayed in Besson and Ramelli may contribute more than we expect to the artificially engineered landscapes of the *Faerie Queene*.

Gardens, whether set out in Renaissance poetry or on the estates of the nobility, offer a controlled means for assimilating the new technology. In each case, the audience views the machinery at a privileged distance as it would an entertainer. But something more is at stake as well. By placing automata within the context of traditional mythological narratives, the illusion is created that the comprehension of the mythographic code also entails the control of the technological code. Each time the visitor describes what he or she has seen, narratives are generated that facilitate the continued assimilation of technology. It does not matter whether the mechanics of the machinery is understood. In fact, the garden conceals technology in its mythological narrative. Gardens really become precursors of industrial exhibitions and amusement parks such as Disneyland, where the modern cartoon pantheon shapes the way the visitor views the technological marvels of Tomorrow Land.

The theatricality of the illustrations in Besson, Ramelli, and Böckler remind us how existing modes of representation were used for the assimilation of the new technology. Finally, the theatrical enframing of technology in engravings, in grotto scenes of Renaissance gardens, or in poetry conveys an important tension. Although the staging of technology holds the audience at a distance and idealizes the mechanism, the narratives generated by the representation challenge the visual idealization of the machinery. At the same time that works by Besson, Ramelli, and Böckler idealize machinery, they also promote the aural transmission of the know-how to build the mechanisms. The machine is never simply a spectacle to be framed and viewed at a distance but a social relay that anticipates the physical transformation of nature as well as the alteration of human life. An illustration in Böckler (plate 49) that depicts a man watching a waterwheel suggests fascination with the process as well as entertainment. Above all, it suggests that the process has become entertaining precisely because the machine has taken the place of men and other working animals. Böckler emphasizes this detachment in other illustrations by showing unbridled horses around waterwheels and men and women occupied with tasks separated from the machinery. Ultimately the separation of the audience and machine is momentary because the machine transforms all observers into potential figures for generating assimilating narratives. Because machines cannot speak, the audience is called upon to speak for them.

We may characterize the larger narrative enacted by the audience as it turns from one illustration to the next. As the audience explores the machines and through imagination tests their assimilation into the world, it participates in a romance. Romance characterizes the process of assimilation because it describes the way in which the audience's puzzling over these illustrations enacts a search to understand how the machines may be understood and applied.[31] There is another facet to the romance as well. The path that the romance takes is finally not simply the result of the narrative response to machines. Once constructed, the machines stand outside of the narrative process that facilitated their realization. In effect, when realized, the machinery itself participates in an evolving romance. Although the reader or observer may momentarily believe that he can control the machines by theatrically framing them, such images ultimately serve as a means for their proliferation as much as a means for their control.

VISUAL FRAMING AND MYTHIFICATION

At a rudimentary level the illustrations of Renaissance machines are a means for disseminating ideas. They are not, however, iconographic narratives that may be resolved with allegorical schemas drawn from classical or Biblical texts, but representations that also provoke different forms of response. In the final section, I want to review the narrative responses provoked by such illustrations. Before I do so, however, I want to notice how the illustrations participate in defining a new kind of space.

The illustrations considered in this essay define a new way of seeing. In fact, they have a function similar to Galileo's published illustrations of the heavens or Vesalius's illustration of the human body. The drawings of the human body published by Vesalius in *De fabrica* (1543) or the sketches of the moon published by Galileo in *The Starry Messenger* (1609) do more than share images that had never been seen before. At the same time they tell the audience what it should see, they validate a way of seeing. The drawings by Besson and Ramelli have a similar function for it is ultimately not a question of whether they provide blueprints for the machines but rather a question of the expectation they provoke. Whether they were actually constructed or not does not matter. What matters is their creation of an idealized space for thinking such mechanisms into the world.

The theatrical enframing to which I have drawn attention works as a means for thinking the machines into the world, for it links the visual with the linquistic response. As we study these illustrations we need to be careful not to think of them as theatrical images that distance the viewer from the object, but as images that also provoke local narratives. In his treatise, *The Vision of God* (1453), Nicholas of Cusa describes a carefully constructed portrait (probably by Roger Van der Weyden) whose eyes appear to follow everyone in the room simultaneously.[32] For Cusa, the portrait functions both as a technological exhibition of perspective and as a metaphoric argument for God's ability to see each individual at the same moment in time. The double quality of Cusa's experiment can also be applied to the Renaissance representation of technology. In each case the gaze of the observer is not neutral, for it either authorizes an abstraction subsumed within a broader cultural code or provokes further investigation.

While the theatrical enframing of technology orients the approach to Renaissance machines, it should not delude us by promoting an illusion of control. There is a double-sided quality to such visual framing that we cannot afford to ignore. The metaphoric duplicity accompanying these Renaissance illustrations may be compared to our own propensity to personify the machines or instruments surrounding us. While personifying a computer or car may make us feel that we dominate the machine, our very language only works to integrate the machinery even more into our world. By calling a computer "user-friendly" we do not imply that we understand our computer's circuitry, but instead advertise the benefits of a particular machine. While metaphors may promote a familiarity that allows our coexistence with technology to continue, they also contribute to its mythification. The location of machines in mythological gardens is an early sign of such mythification. Perhaps the most powerful modern manifestations of such mythification is the prevalent perception of technology's autonomy or its characterization as a Frankenstein out of control. To think of technology as a Frankenstein-like creature hardly asserts control but only serves to mystify our technological creations by projecting onto them greater authority. The narratives we bring to technology need to be examined carefully.

Technology is not a spectacle that momentarily diverts our attention but a medium through which a culture defines itself. Unlike the play set off and viewed at a distance, technology installs itself with physical force and becomes an integral part of the space we inhabit. As we think of technology's integration, its theatrical framing bears different implications. While it may transform an audience into passive observers entertained by a distant spectacle, it also provokes narratives for its interrogation. When applied to technology, the theatrical metaphor has the potential of giving an audience the illusion of control or challenging an audience to devise narratives for assimilation and comprehension.

Besides challenging us to think about the way machinery becomes visually framed, the illustrations provoke several kinds of narrative response. On the most basic level, the illustrations generate local narratives for identifying and describing the machinery. For a given illustration there may be a variety of local narratives involving a simple label as well as a sequential explanation of the machine's workings. But as I have suggested in my comments on

Renaissance gardens, narratives operate on a broader level as well as through the metanarratives or conceptual codes used for the cultural assimilation of the machines. The mythographic and romance codes found in Renaissance gardens, the hydrostatic principles implicit in the workings of the machinery, and finally the visual order—the *scenographia*—implicit in illustrations comprise such metanarratives.

Although seldom acknowledged, another level of narrative presents itself as well. The illustrations and written narratives remind us that technology is bound up not only with writing but with a multitude of narratives that remain unacknowledged because they are unwritten. Each illustration may be thought of as provoking oral or psychological responses as well. Such responses cannot be discounted because they comprise the most common response for explaining and relating to technology. Even though we may not recover such narratives, they may be discerned in the written narratives that remain or in the narratives that we ourselves play open as we look at the illustrations. While Ramelli's book sets before the reader a collection of conceptual blueprints for thinking machines into the world, the actual construction of these machines by artisans assumes the presence of skills that are not conveyed through writing but through practice and oral instruction. As we think of the assimilation of technology, we cannot simply think of written narratives but must also acknowledge the spoken narratives that sustain technology.

The earliest published illustrations of machinery challenge us to ask how we have come to gaze on technology. Besides observing some of the mechanisms used to stage machinery, we have noticed how machines provoke narrative responses that promote their assimilation, and we have identified how the very metaphoric devices used to frame and control technology function as relays that bring it greater authority. Another concern has accompanied the discussion as well. As we have surveyed examples of Renaissance technology, we are reminded that technology requires interpretation. Its interpretation, however, cannot be compared to literary hermeneutics because it ultimately transcends ordinary language as well as the mathematical codes that help bring it into being. We may think of technology as another language written within the very horizons in which we live.

There is an irony here as well. Although the Renaissance efforts to construct a universal language are regarded as failures, do we not discover in the ingenious pumps and mills at which we have glanced the rudiments of an unexpected fulfillment of such aspirations? The task that confronts us involves the formulation of a hermeneutics of technology that will permit us to deal with such a language even more effectively. Asking how we look at technology comprises a step within such an effort.

NOTES

I want to thank Mark Greenberg and Lance Schacterle for their careful reading of this essay in an earlier form.

1. Langdon Winner, *Autonomous Technology: Technics-Out-of-Control as a Theme in Political Thought* (Cambridge: MIT Press, 1977), 134.

2. See especially Frances A. Yates, *The Art of Memory* (Chicago: Univ. of Chicago Press, 1969).

3. See Martin Jay, "Scopic Regimes of Modernity" in *Vision and Visuality,* ed. Martin Jay (Seattle: Bay Press [Dia Art Foundation Discussions in Contemporary Culture, 2], 1988), 3–23.

4. For consideration of optical metaphors in Renaissance drama see Ernst B. Gilman, *The Curious Perspective* (New Haven: Yale Univ. Press, 1978).

5. *Short-Title Catalog of Books Published in England, 1475–1640* ed. A. W. Pollard and G. R. Redgrave; 2d ed. W. A. Jackson, F. S. Ferguson, and Katherine Pantzer (London: Bibliography Society [Oxford Univ. Press], 1986)

6. Georg Agricola, *De re metallica,* trans. and ed. H. C. Hoover and L. H. Hoover (New York: Dover, 1950 [1956]); Vitruvius, *On Architecture,* 2 vols. ed. and trans. by Frank Granger (Cambridge: Loeb Classical Library-Harvard Univ. Press, 1970).

7. Original dates of publication are indicated in the text. Besson's work was known as *Theatre des instrumens mathematiques & mechaniques* in all editions appearing after 1578. Editions appeared in 1578, 1579, 1582, 1602, 1594, 1595, 1596, and 1626. I have examined the Lyon edition published in Vicenza in the Price Gilbert Memorial Library of the Georgia Institute of Technology. The following folios were examined at the Newberry Library: Agostino Ramelli *Diverse et Artificiose Machine* (Lyon, 1588); Vittorio Zonca, *Teatro nuovo di machine et edificii per varie et figure operationi* (Padua, 1656), and George Andreas Böckler, *Theatrum machinarum novum exhibens opera molaria et aquatica constructum industria* (Nurnberg, 1662). See also the fine reprint of *Ramelli: The Various Machines of Agostino Ramelli,* tran. Martha Teach Gnudi with technical annotations by Eugene S. Ferguson (New York: Dover Publications, Inc., 1987). A. G. Keller's *A Theatre of Machines* (New York: Macmillan Company, 1964) remains the most available collection of illustrations.

All illustrations and references are to volumes in the Newberry Library. I am grateful to the Newberry Library for permission to reprint the illustrations and, in particular, to Mr. Paul Gehl, Curator of the Newberry's Wing Collection.

8. A. G. Keller describes Besson's career as an engineer in Lausanne, Geneva, Rouen, Paris, and Orleans. As a protestant, Besson fled France after the St. Bartholomew's Day Massacre. According to Keller he moved to London where he died in 1575 (Keller, 7–8). According to Bertrand Gille, *The Renaissance Engineers* (London: Lund Humphries, 1966 [French 1964]), Besson fled to Geneva where he died in about 1576 (Gille, 199).

9. See Frances Yates's discussion of Dee in *Theatre of the World;* see also my

discussion of Dee's *Preface* in "The Narrative Matter of Mathematics: John Dee's Preface to the *Elements* of Euclid of Megara (1570)," *Philological Quarterly* 66:1 (1987), 27–46.

10. Elizabeth L. Eisenstein, *The Printing Press as an Agent of Change* 2 vols. (Cambridge: Cambridge Univ. Press, 1979), II, 556.

11. "Item scaenographia est frontis et laterum abscendentium adumbratio ad circinique centrum omnium linearum responsus." [Scenography (perspective) also is the shading of the front and the retreating sides, and the correspondence of all lines to the vanish point, which is the center of a circle.] Vitruvius, *On Architecture,* [Book 1.2.2] vol. I, 26–27.

12. For the distinction between narratival and descriptive forms of painting see Svetlana Alpers, *The Art of Describing: Dutch Art in the Seventeenth Century* (Chicago: Univ. of Chicago Press, 1983)

13. "Espece d'artifice nouveau, propre a ietter l'eau contre le feu mesmement lors que la flamme empesche que nul ne peut approacher de l'edifice qui ard."

14. Pour laquelle mieux entendre, tu noteras ceci en toutes les figures, (soit qu'elles soyent disposees d'une facon ou d'autre,) que la teste du livre est nommee Septentrion, la ligne du bord de la planche estant pour ceste cause appelee la ligne Septentrionale: la bas, Midi: le bord de la planche tourne vers ce quartier, la ligne Meridionale: la cousture, Occident, & le bord qui la regarde, la ligne Occidentale: l'opposee, Orient, & la ligne, Orientale. Outreplus, pourautant qu'il n'y a point de lettres es planches qui servent a demonstrer, afine que je te meine au lieu qu j'entendray, j'useray souvent d'une mesure divisee en vingtetquartre parties, laquelle avec tout le reste est mise en la prochaine page, a laquelle tu pourras avoir recours. (fol. a 4 verso)

15. Toute la machine est menee sur deux roues, dont le moyen de celle qui se void est loing de la ligne de midi 2.m.12. p. & d'orient 22.p. & sostenue sur quatre pieds, dont deux se voyent loing des lignes susdictes: ascavoir 2.m.2p & 4.p. l0un, & 18.p. & 18 p. l'autre, estans tous deux tenus en raison par deux crochets, qui viennent de la base, en laquelle au bout septentrional est une grille pour arrester la machine.

16. L'Artifice de ceste machine n'est pas different de la machine precedente, comme l'on voit (excepte que pour conduire l'eau) & sert mesement pour faire monter l'eau d'un canal, riviere, fontaine, ou d'autre semblable lieu a une convenable haulteur, en ceste facon car en se tournant la roue notee Z par la force du canal, ou de la riviere susdicte, prende d'icelle l'eau avec ses cassettes, & la porte (comme il appert par le dessein) dedans le premier receptacle marque H, & faict en mesme temps tourner la roue T, qui est dentee de la roue Q qui est fichee dans la vis couverte notee A, la faict tourner en semble avec l'autre roue N, qui (comme l'on void) est fichee dedans la mesme vis; laquelle vis est faicte en la forme que represente les autres; & par tels retournement prend l'eau du premier receptacle avec les troux qu'elle a en bas, & la porte dedans le second marque R, duque] receptacle la vis L prend l'eau, & la porte dedans le troisreme note S, par le moyen de la roue N qui luy donne mouvement, prenant avec ses dent les suseaux de la lanterne M, qui est fichee dedans la susdicte vis; & avec les mesme ordre, la vis K prend l'eau du troisiesme receptacle, & la porte en se tournant dans le quatriesme & dernier, d'ou par une pompe (comme l'on void par celie qui est notee V) l'on la faict puis apres descendre ou l'on la mene de la, ou il est plus commode a qui en veut user.

17. For a discussion of the special significance of technology in the Renaissance see Arnold Pacey, *The Maze of Ingenuity* (Cambridge: MIT Press, 1976), esp. 116–73. For projects in the Veneto see Manfredo Tafuri, *Humanism, Technical Knowl-*

edge and Rhetoric: The Debate in Renaissance Venice, (Cambridge: Harvard Univ. Graduate School of Design [Walter Gropius Lecture]), 1986. For technology in Holland see Joyce Oldham Appleby, *Economic Thought and Ideology in Seventeenth-Century England* (Princeton, N.J.: Princeton Univ. Press, 1978) esp. 73–98.

18. Andrea Alciati, *Emblemata* (1531); I have used a later version, *Emblemata cum commentariis* (Padua, 1621, rpt. New York: Garland, 1976).

19. "Mundi huius visendam machinam homini (quem solum tantae rei capacm fecit) exposuisse spectandam: eoque chariorem habere: curiosum ac sollicitum inspectorem, operisque sui admirationrem: quam eum qui velus animal expers mentis: tantam ac tam mirabile spectaculum, stupidus immotusque neglexerit." [He has set forth the visible mechanism of the world as a spectacle for man, whom alone He has made capable of appreciating such a wonderful thing. Therefore He prefers a careful and diligent beholder and admirer of His work to one who like an unreasoning brute beast passes by so great and so wonderful a spectacle stupidly and stolidly.] *The Complete Works of St. Thomas More,* Vol. 4, *Utopia* ed. Edward Surtz, S.J. and J. H. Hexter (New Haven: Yale Univ. Press, 1965), 182–83.

20. For discussion of Renaissance gardens see Roy Strong, *The Renaissance Garden in England* (London: Thomas and Hudson, 1979) and John Dixon Hunt, *Garden and Grove: The Italian Renaissance Garden in the English Imagination 1600–1750* (Princeton, N.J.: Princeton Univ. Press, 1986)

21. As cited in Strong, *The Renaissance Garden in England,* p. 79.

22. All references included in the text are to the seminal study by David R. Coffin, *The Villa D'Este at Tivoli* (Princeton, N.J.: Princeton Univ. Press, 1960).

23. Thomas Nashe, *The Unfortunate Traveller in Elizabethan Fiction,* ed. Robert Ashley and Edwin M. Moseley (New York: Holt, Rinehart and Winston, 1953), 203–308.

24. Isaac de Caus, *Wilton Garden: New and Rare Inventions of Water-Works* (New York: Garland Publishing Inc, 1982 [London, 1659]).

25. See Hunt, "My Patterne for a Country Seat," *Garden and Grove,* esp. pp. 104–9, and Strong, "The Emblematic Garden," *The Renaissance Garden in England,* pp. 45–75.

26. As cited in Hunt, p. 105.

27. As cited in Strong, p. 53.

28. For physical allegory and discussion of optics in the *Roman de la Rose* see Patricia J. Eberle, "The Lover's Glass: Nature's Discourse on Optics and the Optical Design of the Romance of the Rose," *Univ. of Toronto Quarterly* 46 (1977), 241–62; see also my "Medieval Ovidian Commentary," in *Narcissus and the Invention of Personal History* (New York: Garland Publishing Inc., 1985), 23–58.

29. All references to Spenser are to *The Faerie Queene,* ed. A. C. Hamilton (London: Longman, 1977).

30. See especially John Dixon Hunt, "Ovid in the Garden," in *Garden and Grove,* 42–58.

31. For romance as metanarrative see Frederic Jameson, *The Political Unconscious: Narrative as a Socially Symbolic Act* (Ithaca: Cornell Univ. Press, 1981).

32. Nicholas of Cusa, *The Vision of God,* ed. Evelyn Underhill (New York: Frederick Ungar, 1969); see also Ernst Cassirer, *The Individual and the Cosmos in Renaissance Philosophy,* trans. Mario Domandi (Philadelphia: Univ. of Pennsylvania Press, 1972), 36.

33. Cusa's metaphoric use of the optical phenomena in *The Vision of God* is related to his optical research found in his work *De Beryllo.* Specific examples in *The Vision of God* are related to one of the major medieval optical treatises, Alhazen's *Opticae thesaurus.*

Robert Boyle, Peter Shaw, and the Reinscription of Technology: Inventing and Reinventing the Air Pump

ROBERT MARKLEY

Robert Boyle's description of his air pump in his *New Experiments . . . Touching the Spring and Weight of the Air* (Oxford, 1660) has been recognized by a number of scholars, particularly Steven Shapin and Simon Schaffer, as a seminal contribution to the development of the technical or scientific report.[1] They have emphasized, in particular, what they call Boyle's "literary technology of virtual witnessing," his concerns with reproducing in his experimental reports the "immediacy" of experience and with creating a set of generic expectations for scientific discourse. For Shapin, Schaffer, and Peter Dear, the development of "modern science" is thus a literary as well as experimental process.[2] But "experience"—especially the literary (re)creation of experience in seventeenth-century natural philosophy—is historically as well as theoretically problematic. Charles Bazerman has shown that even the most seemingly objective and precisely written of early scientific reports—Newton's "A New Theory about Light and Colours" (1672)—is an elaborate fictional construct, the result of a literary technology that displaces historical experience for an "experience" that conforms to the generic constraints of experimental description.[3] In Newton's case, and, as I shall argue, in Boyle's works, "experience"—even the most seemingly disinterested and mundane experience of technical description—is a rhetorical postulate, an abstract and generalized construct that is comprised of a number of cultural discourses that traditionally have been assumed to be "nonscientific." In this respect, the "experience" of seventeenth-century natural philosophy can be understood as the site of

125

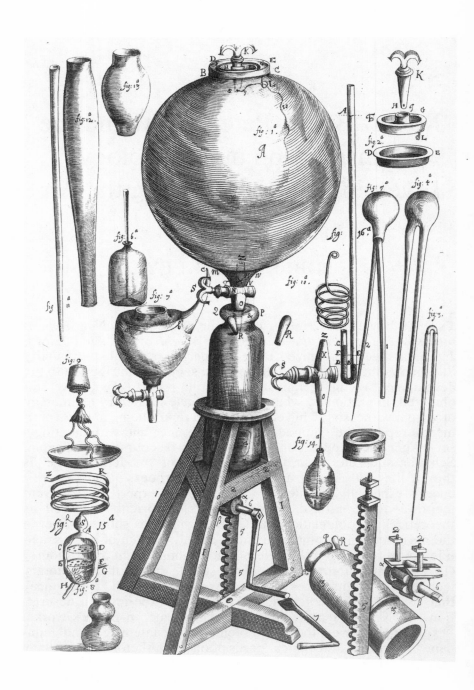

Figure 1. Robert Boyle, *New Experiments* (1660).

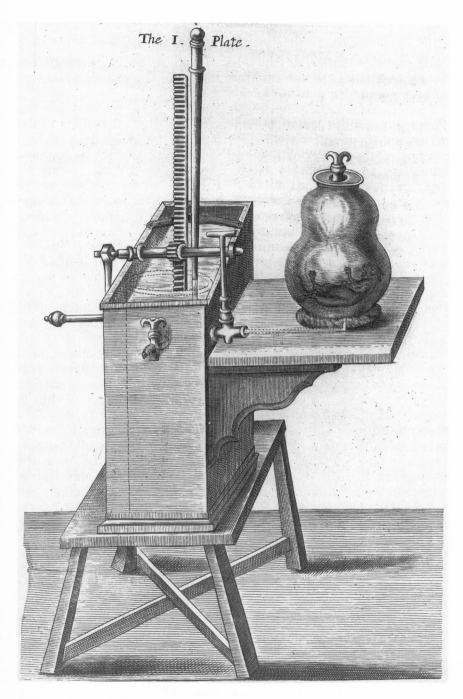

The I. Plate.

Figure 2. Robert Boyle, *Continuation of New Experiments* (1669).

dialogical interactions among what Mikhail Bakhtin calls different
"speech genres," different literary means of constructing and representing what happens in the laboratory.[4]

In this essay, I shall investigate some of the ways in which the
"philosophical" or technical languages that Boyle develops to describe his air pump are interpenetrated by the discourses of contemporary theology, politics, sexual ideology, and socioeconomic
and class structures. My purpose is not to "attack" Boyle by
arguing that he was not a disinterested or "pure" scientist but to
call attention to the "impurity" of all modes of technical description
that surround the air pump and to emphasize the ultimate dependence—in Boyle's own mind—of scientific experimentation on explicitly theological and sociopolitical justifications. Boyle does not,
then, develop a single, monological scientific style but instead de-
ploys a number of rhetorical strategies that work polemically to
explain, defend, and institutionalize his experiments with the air
pump. In this regard, the differences between Boyle's descriptions
of his first air pump in *New Experiments* and his improved version
of it in *A Continuation of New Experiments* (Oxford, 1669) are
historically significant because they indicate how his perception of
the relationship between technological artifact and its literary representation changed in response to "external" factors. Between
these two works, we can chart a rhetorical and ideational shift in
Boyle's emphases from the air pump as a heuristic device, designed
to explore the mysteries of a divinely structured nature, to the air
pump as an emblem of an institutionalized ideology of scientific
progress that must be defended and disseminated. In brief, the
changes in Boyle's "literary technology" of technical description
suggest how his literary construction of experience redefines not
simply what he reports but the assumptions and values that inform
his investigation of the natural world.

This process of institutionalizing the air pump, however, extends
beyond Boyle and beyond the sociohistorical context of the 1660s.
In the early eighteenth century, Peter Shaw, later to become a
prominent physician, produced his three-volume revisions of
Boyle's scientific works, *The Philosophical Works of the Honourable Robert Boyle, Esq.; Abridged, Methodized and Disposed
under the General Heads of Physics, Statics, Pneumatics, Natural
History and Medicine* (London, 1725). As Shaw's subtitle indicates,
this is not an edition of Boyle's essays but a systematic, often line-
by-line recasting in broadly Newtonian terms of both the style and
substance of seventeenth-century natural philosophy. The fact that
Shaw found it necessary to rewrite the works of England's most

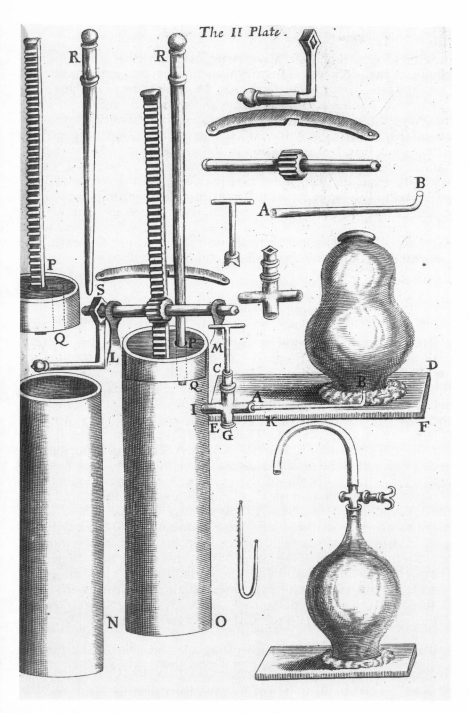

The II Plate.

Figure 3. Robert Boyle, *Continuation of New Experiments* (1699).

prominent experimental chemist suggests something of the complexity of the problems of literary transmission and epistemological
continuity in early modern science. More specifically, Shaw's reinscription of the air pump within the accepted canons of eighteenth-century scientific prose challenges a number of assumptions
about the "rise" of science and the unproblematic "progress" of
technology. A full consideration of the implications of Shaw's revision would carry us far beyond the limits of this study. I would
suggest, however, that Shaw's reinscribing of the "original" air
pump within the context of different historical assumptions about
language, the relationship of experiment and theology, and the role
of the scientist offers us a means to explore the ways in which the
rhetoric of technological description responds to changes in the
cultural discourses that both shape and impinge upon it.

1

Prior to the publication of Boyle's *New Experiments* in 1660,
natural philosophy in England had generally followed the literary
and conceptual models of Aristotelian science, even as it invoked
the methodology of Baconian empiricism. Through much of the
seventeenth century, scientific publications in Great Britain take
the form of treatises that purport to offer encyclopedic treatments
of the topics they discuss. They are frequently concerned with
elaborating taxonomies, describing universal laws, offering general
accounts, and (following Descartes) developing abstract systems
that offer holistic visions of the universe.[5] To a great extent, the
ideal of a "just enumeration" of all things in creation underlies
these utopian projects, like Wilkins's *Essay Towards a Real Character and a Philosophical Language* (London, 1668).[6] What distinguishes Boyle as a scientific writer from his predecessors and, at
least through the mid-1660s, from most of his contemporaries is not
simply his intellectual and financial commitment to laboratory research but his distrust of the systematizing tendencies that had
defined philosophical discourse since Aristotle. In his *Certain
Physiological Essays* (London, 1661), Boyle argues that

> it has long seem'd to me none of the least impediments of the real
> advancement of true Natural Philosophy, that men have been so for-
> ward to write Systems of it, and have thought themselves oblig'd either
> to be altogether silent, or not to write lesse than an entire body of
> Physiology. . . . [W]hen men by having diligently study'd either

Chymistry, Anatomy, Botanicks, or some other particular part of Physiology, or perhaps by having only read Authors on those Subjects, have
thought themselves thereby qualify'd to publish compleat Systems of
Natural Philosophy, they have found themselves by nature of their
undertaking, and the Laws of Method, engag'd to write of several other
things than those wherein they had made themselves Proficients, and
thereby have been reduc'd, either idly to repeat what has been already,
though perhaps but impertinently enough, written by others on the
same Subject, or else to say any thing rather than nothing. (3–4)

Boyle's attack on systematizers is based on their substitution of
generic "laws of Method"—in effect, the rhetorical form of universalizing theories—for hands-on experience. His critique is also
based on his recognition that the language in which these systems
are described is constitutive rather than merely reflective; "what
has been already . . . written" becomes part of traditional natural
philosophy, the "compleat Systems" and received wisdom that
serve as "impediments" to the development of "true" experimental
science.

Boyle's attempts to revolutionize experimental practice, therefore, necessitate his developing a language in which to describe
these "new experiments," as Shapin and Schaffer argue. But the
language of experimental observation that Boyle develops is not the
dispassionate, objective, "modern" discourse that internalist accounts, particularly in the history of chemistry, assume.[7] Boyle's
essays are comprised of a network of discourses that shape—or,
more radically, constitute—his scientific endeavors in complex and
historically specific ways. As James Paradis has demonstrated,
Boyle's experimental essays owe much to the example of Montaigne's moral essays, and as I have argued elsewhere, the metaphors that Boyle uses to describe the natural world as both the
work of God and as the corrupt physical realm of Calvinist tradition
implicate his scientific practice in the discursive traditions of seventeenth-century theology and Restoration politics.[8] In a juxtaposi-
tion of striking images, Boyle offers what we might take as an
emblem of the "Christian virtuoso" whose experiments seek to
reclaim the postlapsarian physical world for theological speculation: "since ev'n the illiterate Husbandman can, with the most
abject Dung it self, give a flourishing growth to the most useful
Grains, to Medicinable herbs, and ev'n to fragrant Flowers, why
may not a wise Man, by the meanest Creatures, and slighted'st
Object, give a considerable Improvement to the noblest Faculties of
the Soul, and the most lovely Qualities of the Mind[?]"[9] Boyle's
metaphors idealize the role of the experimentalist; they describe

not the processes of investigation but the spiritual effects of contemplation.

As Boyle makes clear elsewhere in his works, the endeavors of the experimentalist always verge—and, indeed, depend on—divine revelation. In *The Excellency of Theology, Compar'd with Natural Philosophy* (London, 1674), Boyle first establishes "the Preference I [give] Divine Truths (before Physiological ones)" (A4v), and then goes on to argue that in natural philosophy, as in theology, "bare Reason well improv'd will suffice to make a man behold many glorious Attributes in the Deity; yet the same Reason, when assisted by Revelation, may enable a man to discover far more Excellencies in God, and perceive them, [than] he contemplated before, far greater and more distinctly" (5). Discovery and perception, "the noblest Faculties of the Soul, and the most lovely Qualities of the Mind," are themselves theologically grounded. What sanctions experimental investigation in Boyle's mind is precisely its usefulness in contributing to man's understanding of his role in a divinely ordered universe: "both these Doctrines [Christianity and corpuscularianism] . . . seem to be but members of the Universal Hypothesis, whose Objects, I conceive, to be *the Nature, Counsels, and Works of God, as far as they are discoverable by us* (for I say not *to us*) *in this Life*" (52).

I stress Boyle's privileging of theology over experimental science to emphasize that his rhetorical practice in his experimental essays is not—and is not intended to be—conceptually self-sufficient; it is part of an undifferentiated discourse that conflates the languages of Baconian experimentation, of Renaissance moral reflection, of upper-class apologetics, of latitudinarian theology, of Calvinistic distrust of the physical world, of masculinist constructions of nature, and of ideological moderation in the decades following the Civil War and Commonwealth. For Boyle and his contemporaries, science, theology, and the social structure of Restoration England are part of the same cultural and ideological matrix. Writing to Joseph Glanvill in 1677, Boyle invokes the same kinds of assumptions and values that Shapin and Schaffer identify with his scientific writing to credit the "virtual witnessing" of reports of witchcraft and alchemical transmutation: "I hope . . . that your intended narration will resume the credit of [witchcraft] stories in the opinions of unbiased men, by having its circumstances warranted with testimonies, and authorities, which, the nature of the thing considered, may suffice to satisfy those, that are different, out of cautiousness, not prejudice. . . . [A]ny one relation of a supernatural phenomenon being fully proved, and duly verified, suffices to evince the thing contended for." Boyle goes on in this letter to

illustrate this principle by invoking the "witnessing" of "the illustrious count of *Wallestein*" who has seen "the famous frier
Wencel several times actually [make] transmutations of baser metals into gold, in the presence of the emperor, and divers noblemen,
and good chemists."[10] The criteria for verifying matters of "fact" in
theology and alchemy are those that Shapin and Schaffer identify
as instrumental in the construction of scientific facts. At witchcraft
trials, as at demonstrations of his air pump, Boyle's witnesses are
defined as credible by their social, political, and ecclesiastical
standing. In this respect, the authority of virtual witnessing depends on ideological conceptions of authority extrinsic to the actual
experience of observing experimental phenomena. Similarly, the
reliability of Boyle's experimental essays depends upon his readers'
identifying with the efforts of the "Christian virtuoso" who justifies
his research not by idle speculation or appeals to ancient authority
but by invoking shared sociopolitical values and the supreme authority of a mysterious and omnipresent deity.

My point here is not to demonstrate Boyle's credulity but to
suggest that his scientific practice and the literary technologies he
develops to promote the air pump are part of a larger project—his
celebration of a "Wisdom so Boundlesse" that all his efforts can
yield is an imperfect understanding of *"the Nature, Counsels, and
Works of God."* Science, in short, has neither an ontological nor a
teleological significance independent of theology. In this regard,
Boyle's remarks on the relationships between the physical "laws"
he studies and the divine intentions they represent undermine the
internalist distinctions that have often been imposed on his work to
divide his "actual" scientific practice from its theological "context." Even astute critics like Shapin and Schaffer have tended to
examine Boyle's experimental philosophy in isolation from his theology or, at most, suggested parallels between the endeavors of the
experimentalist and those of the theologian.[11] But particularly in
The Excellency of Theology, Boyle subordinates natural laws—and
by implication the scientific facts that the experimentalist constructs—to divine authority:

> Theology teaches us expressly from Divine Revelation, that the present
> *course of Nature* shall not last always, but that one Day *this world* or at
> least this *Vortex* of ours) shall either be Abolished by Annihilation, or
> (which seems far more probable) be Innovated, and, as it were, Trans-
> figur'd, and that by the Intervention of that Fire, which shall dissolve
> and destroy the present frame of Nature: So that either way, the present
> state of things (as well as Natural as Political) shall have an end. (22)

For Boyle, nature does not exist independently of its divine "Author," and its phenomena can be understood only through the agency of "Divine Revelation." "The Divine Attributes are such fruitful themes, and so worthy of our Admiration," says Boyle, "that the whole Fabrick of the Universe, and all the *Phaenomena* exhibited in it, are but Imperfect Expressions of Gods Wisdom" (64). Therefore, the natural philosopher "contemplates the works of Nature not barely for themselves, but to be the better qualified and excited to admire and praise the Author of Nature" (161). For Boyle, then, scientific writing is not simply the dispassionate recording of phenomena and processes but a morally revealing, epistemologically self-consuming demonstration of the inadequacy of human discourse to comprehend fully the "author of Nature."[12] In this light, his experimental essays must be read not as narrowly technical descriptions but as texts self-consciously participating and embodied in the discourses of latitudinarian theology and the ideological values and assumptions that underlie and inform it.

Because Boyle invests the ultimate authority for his scientific endeavors in his theological beliefs, he has no need for the "compleat Systems of Natural Philosophy" that attract many of his predecessors and contemporaries. They are, at best, presumptive and, at worst, arrogate to themselves the authority to explain nature that in Boyle's mind belongs solely to God. Therefore, his means to understand *"the Nature, Counsels, and Works of God"* becomes in *New Experiments, Certain Physiological Essays* and his other experimental essays of the early 1660s a discursive practice modeled on the moral essay, a "philosophical style" that is heuristic rather than systematic, deliberately incomplete rather than self-aggrandizingly authoritative. In this regard, the form of Boyle's scientific writing serves broadly ideological as well as generic functions. It represents a historically specific effort to demonstrate that the order of the universe, the political order of Restoration England, and the authority of the Bible are effectively one and the same. His experimental essays—although they self-consciously promote the ideals of scientific distinterest and scientific progress—participate in discourses that are irrevocably politicized. It is for this reason that they become important documents for both defenders of the early Royal Society, like Glanville and Sprat, and its antagonists, like Hobbes and Henry Stubbe.[13]

2

Boyle's *New Experiments* begins with an elaborate description (accompanied by an "exploded" diagram) of the air pump (see figure 1) that Robert Hooke had constructed for Boyle in 1658–1659. Faced with the prospect of describing what, in 1658, was perhaps the most elaborate piece of equipment ever built solely for the purposes of scientific inquiry, Boyle seeks to familiarize this new technology by deploying a variety of descriptive strategies. His descriptions are copious, conversational, and unencumbered by either the overt theologizing of his metascientific commentaries or disclaimers about the limitations of experimental philosophy. The treatise takes the form of a letter to his nephew, Lord Dungarvan:

> At the very top of the Vessel, (A) you may observe a round hole, whose Diameter (BC) is of about four inches, and whereof, the Orifice is incircled with a lip of Glass, almost an inch high: For the making of which lip, it was requisite (to mention that upon the by, in case your Lordship should have another Engine made for you) to have a hollow and tapering Pipe of Glass drawn out, whereof the Orifice above mentioned was the Basis, and then to have the cone cut off with an hot Iron, within about an Inch of the Points (BC).
>   The use of the lip, is to sustain the cover delineated in the second Figure; where (DE) points out a brass Ring, so cast, as that it doth cover the lip (BC) of the first Figure, and is cemented on it with a strong and close Cement. To the inward tapering Orifice of the Ring (which is about three Inches over) are exquisitely ground the sides of the Brass stopple (FG;) so that the concave superficies of the one, and the convex of the other, may touch one another in so many places, as may leave as little access, as possible, to the external Air: And in the midst of this cover is left a hole (HI) of about half an inch over, invironed also with a ring or socket of the same mettal, and fitted likewise with a brass stopple (K) made in the form of the Key of a stop-cock, and exactly ground into the hole (HI) it is to fill; so as that though it be turn'd round in the cavity it possesses, it will not let in the Air, and yet may be put in or taken out at pleasure, for uses to be hereafter mentioned. In order to some of which, it is perforated with a little hole, (8) traversing the whole thickness of it at the lower end; through which, and a little brass Ring (L) fastened to one side, (no matter which) of the bottom of the stopple (FG) a string (8, 9, 10) might pass, to be imploy'd to move some things in the capacity of the empty'd Vessel; without any where unstopping it. (9–11)

Shapin and Schaffer are surely correct in arguing that passages like these are designed to mimic the immediacy of pictorial representation, that Boyle's scientific prose, in other words, is experiential. Yet the experience it describes is historically specific. The air pump is the product of gentlemanly leisure as well as philosophical interest for those, like Boyle's nephew, who have the money to "have another [such] engine made for" them. The role that Boyle creates for himself in this passage is less that of an active participant than of an observer orchestrating the assembly of this engine; the verbal constructions—"you may observe," "have another engine made for you," "have the cone cut off," and so on—describe not Boyle's hands-on experience in building the air pump but a recreation of his experience of directing and overseeing someone else (presumably Robert Hooke, his jack-of-all-trades in the late 1650s) assemble its parts.[14] In this respect, Boyle's description of his "engine" is grounded in the class-specific assumptions and class-specific forms of gentlemanly address of a seventeenth-century member of the upper classes who is accustomed to, and can afford, having his menial labor done for him.

The class-specific nature of Boyle's description of the air pump both shapes and is repressed within his prose. If his prose style advertises itself as the product of upper-class sociopolitical values, it also strives to universalize the historically specific discourses of gentlemanly prerogative as disinterested attempts to discover nature's secrets. Boyle's writing, as this passage demonstrates, is synthetic. If the author is creating a new literary technology, he is also concerned to depict the experimentalist as a manager capable of bringing together what had previously been discrete technologies: glassblowing, metal-working, and so on. In an age before the mass production of scientific instruments, Boyle describes the design of his air pump less as an exact science than as an art: virtually all the measurements and tolerances in his description, for example, are prefaced by "about" or "almost." Boyle's "art," however, lies not in the production of the various parts of the air pump but in his directing their assembly into a technologically sophisticated apparatus. In *The Excellency of Theology*, Boyle characterizes "the study of . . . Experimental Philosophy" as "a very troublesome and laborious Employment" because it "will put [the scientist] upon needing, and consequently applying himself to such a Variety of Mechanick People, (as Distillers, Drugsters, Smiths, Turners, &c.) that a great part of his time, and perhaps all his Patience, shall be spent in waiting upon Trades-men, and repairing the losses he sustains by Their disappointments" (117). In effect, Boyle's ability to transcend the "disappointments" of having to deal with "Mechanick People" depends upon his having the economic means to purchase and coordinate their services. Yet in his *New Experiments,* there is little to suggest his "troublesome and laborious Employment," no references to what must have been the painstaking trials necessary to produce (even by others' hands) a vacuum pump. The rhetoric of Boyle's description effectively subsumes the history of constructing the air pump under the studied ease of a gentlemanly prose style that issues decorous and implicit commands to unnamed subordinates who, if we were to judge from the ease with which Boyle moves from describing one part to the next, just as easily comply. In short, the form of Boyle's description—its copiousness, its disinterest, its "objectivity"—is an outgrowth of his class-based assumptions about the role of a gentleman-philosopher. The experience that is rendered by Boyle in *New Experiments,* then, might mimic pictorial representation but only because it is a consciously constructed fiction, an idealized account of a problematic physical world. Its "scientific" detachment is not intended as an accurate portrayal of historial experience but as a polemical rendering of an experimental ideal that is designed, as Boyle repeatedly tells his readers, to promote natural philosophy.

The fictional nature of Boyle's description, however, leads to the kinds of questions about language, ambiguity, and the "traces" of pre- or unscientific understanding in a "scientific" text traditionally proscribed by the "two-cultures" account of the development of modern scientific writing. In seeking to familiarize his "engine," Boyle offers an anthropomorphized description of the air pump that casts its "otherness," its unfamiliar workings, within the rhetorical traditions of seventeenth-century physiology. Described anthropomorphically, the air pump mediates between the external world of "nature" and the internal world of the experimental philosopher who studies natural phenomena in order to reclaim the fallen world of Calvinist theology by demonstrating the "hidden properties" and mystical regularities that can be discerned within the physical universe. In an important sense, Boyle's technological description creates a dialectical relationship between the experimenter and his device; paradoxically they become both implicated in each other's existence, with the air pump functioning as the "other" that inhabits and is inhabited by the constructed experience of scientific observation.

In the past decade or so, discussions of the "otherness" of seventeenth-century natural philosophy have been transformed by feminist intrpretations, such as those of Brian Easlea and Evelyn Fox Keller, that have emphasized the split between the culturally constructed "feminization" of nature and "masculinization" of science.[15] Boyle's air pump represents, I would argue, a crucial transitional moment in the emerging discourses of gender, science, and technology precisely because it seeks to mediate between "nature," figured as feminine, and a theologically based inquiry into her "secrets" that is typed with increasing frequency in the seventeenth century as "masculine."[16] The anthropomorphized terms of description that Boyle employs in describing the air pump are frequently (if seemingly subliminally) sexualized. The vessel has an "Orifice . . . incircled with a lip of glass"; the lip is made by having "a hollow and tapering Pipe of Glass drawn out [of the orifice] and then . . . cut off with an hot Iron"; the orifice is filled by a "Brass stopple . . . so that the concave superficies of the one, and the convex of the other, . . . touch one another in so many places, as may leave [no] access"; this stopple, in turn, has a small hole fitted with its own stopple in the shape of a "stop-cock" that may be "turn'd round in the cavity it possesses, . . . yet may be put in or taken out at pleasure." Vulgar Freudians interpreting Boyle's descriptive strategies might have all sorts of fun with repressed images of castration and intercourse. What is more significant, though, are the ways in which these images supplement Boyle's theocentric view of the physical world in Calvinist terms as both corrupt and corrupting; they are, in this respect, ideologically rather than narrowly psychologically revealing. Boyle's implicit gendering of the air pump can be described as an attempt to represent the complexities of gender ideology during the seventeenth century. What we read in this description is less a conscious suppression of the feminine than a figurative rendering of both a "feminized" nature and the "masculine" machine designed to probe its secrets. In this regard, Boyle is drawing upon sexualized imagery prevalent in the writings of Francis Bacon and other seventeenth-century naturalists, but these images seem to have been both internalized as the "natural" means to describe his technological apparatus and simultaneously defamiliarized by the very act of his seeking to make them concrete rather than figurative, to make them refer directly to a machine constructed to produce scientific "facts." His technical description depends, in this regard, on what we might call the defiguration of figurative language: feminine nature and masculine technology become, for Boyle, both inscriptions of cultural constructions of gender and what he perceives as utilitarian strategies to promote the air pump as a means to validate experimental philosophy and the ideological prerogatives on which it depends.

Having described the individual parts of the air pump in copious detail, Boyle gives an account of how the apparatus works.

All things being thus fitted, and the lower shank (o) of the stop-cock being put into the upper Orifice of the Cylinder (&), into which it was exactly ground; the *Experimenter* is first, by turning the handle, to force the Sucker to the top of the Cylinder, that there may be no Air left in the upper part of it: Then shutting the Value with the Plug, and turning the other way, he is to draw down the Sucker to the bottom of the Cylinder; by which motion of the Sucker, the Air that was formerly in the Cylinder being thrust out, and none being permitted to succeed in its room, 'tis manifest that the cavity of the Cylinder must be empty, in reference to the Air. So that if thereupon the Key of the Stop-cock be so turn'd, as that through the perforation of it, a free passage be opened betwixt the Cylinder and the Receiver, part of the Air formerly con-tain'd in the Receiver, will nimbly descend into the Cylinder. And this Air, being by the turning back of the Key hinder'd from the returning into the Receiver, may, by the opening of the Valve, and forcing up of the Sucker to the top of the Cylinder again, be driven out into the open Air. And thus by the repetition of the motion of the Sucker upward and downward, and by opportunity turning the Key, and stopping the Valve, as occasion requires, more or less Air may be suck'd out of the Re-ceiver, according to the exigency of the Experiment, and the intention of him that makes it. (17–18)

Boyle's description of the operation of the air pump depends upon strategies similar to those he uses in anatomizing its parts. Meta-phorically, the air pump is both part of a "nature" that is con-ventionally figured as feminine, and therefore to be subjected to the pleasure and dominion of man, and a means of intervening in and "forcing" nature into "unnatural" forms—a vacuum—so that she may be made to yield up her secrets. Once again, however, the images of fetishization—stop-cocks, orifices, and suckers—cannot be read simply as Freudian projections of psychological neuroses onto the physical world. Instead they suggest the ambivalent rela-tionship of the experimenter to the natural world, the paradoxes that describe both Boyle's sense of the theological significance of his undertaking and his awareness that his experimental program verges (as his critics like Hobbes and Stubbe charge) on transgress-ing the boundaries between the profane and the sacred, the physical and the spiritual.[17] What we do not find in Boyle, however, are consistently worked out patterns of imagery that reveal specific intentions. Instead, as in the air being thrust out, we find a language that implicitly as well as explicitly encodes the sociopolitical real-ities of 1660 as part of the "natural" order. Although Boyle resists making large theoretical claims for his experimental practice, his language works to validate his ideological and theological con-ceptions of what nature is and how it is to be examined. In an important sense, Boyle's experimentally created vacuum represents the intrusion of the experimenter into nature—the disruption, the

gap—caused by his inquiry into the works of God. It is, in effect,
the space of human attempts to gain a supernatural knowledge of
the "mysteries" of the physical universe. In this regard, the air
pump becomes a tool, an extension of human experience—and
metaphorically of the human body—that helps both to reveal and
constitute the "order" of nature.

As Boyle makes clear in his next paragraph, however, the operation of the air pump that he has described is an idealized version of
how it should—in theory—work. The actual experience of getting
his "engine" to function adequately is far more problematic than
his description initially makes it seem:

> Your Lordship [Boyle's nephew] will, perhaps, think that I have been
> unnecessarily prolix in this first part of my Discourse: But if you had
> seen how many unexpected difficulties we found to keep out the exter-
> nall Air, even for a little while, when some considerable part of the
> internal had been suckt out; You would peradventure allow, that I might
> have set down more circumstances than I have, without setting down
> any, whose knowledge, he that shall try the Experiment may not have
> need of. . . . [U]pon tryal, we found it so exceeding (and scarce imagin-
> able) difficult a matter, to keep the Air from getting at all in at any
> imperceptible hole or flaw whatsoever, in a Vessel immediately sur-
> rounded with the compressed Atmosphere, that in spight of all our care
> and diligence, we never were able totally to exhaust the Receiver, or
> keep it when it was almost empty, any considerable time, from leaking
> more or less: although (as we have lately intimated) by unwearied
> quickness in plying the Pump, the internall Air can be much faster
> drawn out then the external can get in, till the Receiver come to be
> almost quite empty. And that's enough to enable men to discover hith-
> erto unobserved *Phaenomena* of Nature. (17, 18–19)

Boyle's term for the experiments that follow his description of the
air pump is, significantly, "Narratives." The experiments he reports
are not conscious fictions—they are not simply fabricated—but
they constitute a selective and idealized rather than historically
accurate representation of experience. These "Narratives" bracket
the problem of maintaining the vaccum by creating a set of generic
parameters and discursive conventions that idealize the experience
of experimentation in a manner analogous to Boyle's idealized
description of how the air pump should work. In simple terms, the
air pump exists discursively in a realm of "as if"; the experiments
report on "hitherto unobserved *Phaenomena*" "as if" a perfect
vacuum—or a perfect "enough" vacuum—had been achieved.
Boyle does not, as Shapin and Schaffer note, make any theoretical

claims for his course of experimentation; but having indicated that difficulties exist in constructing and operating the air pump, he develops an internal logic within the experimental essays that is designed to forestall questions about the actual conditions of experimentation. Once Boyle acknowledges the difference between what "really" happened and the idealized discourse of experimental reporting (which takes as its warrant the fact that the receiver's being "almost quite empty" is "enough" to discern and report experimental data on the spring and weight of the air), he allows himself to enter the generic territory of "as if." The space of the imperfect vacuum—the space of man's intervening in the natural world—is, in this respect, the space that, once acknowledged, can be displaced by the textual fiction of a perfect vacuum. The vacuum, idealized as though it were absolute, represents metaphorically the fiction of successful technological achievement, the ideal for which experimental philosophy is to strive.

Boyle's acknowledgment of his problems with his air pump in a preface to the "Narratives" of his experiments is thus a double rhetorical gesture: it convinces his readers of the reliability of his account by frankly noting the difficulties he experiences and, by relegating these observations to a preface that is formally distinct from his accounts of the experiments themselves, effectively brackets this experience so that his readers can credit his "Narratives" "as if" they occurred exactly in the way in which they are described. No descriptions of Hooke or other technicians madly "plying the Pump" to maintain the semblance of a vacuum are included in Boyle's accounts of the experiments. Having acknowledged the vagaries of experimental experience in his preface, Boyle asks us to participate in the fictional or narrative representation of laboratory experience in which previously "unobserved *Phaenomena* of Nature" are revealed. Paradoxically, however, Boyle can make this demand on his readers precisely because he offers not an account of universal truths but discrete observations that are intended to be taken heuristically rather than as incontrovertible evidence for the sort of systematizing that characterizes Aristotelian natural philosophy. In current philosophical terms, then, Boyle's idealizing of experimental experience is intended to emphasize that his "Narratives" constitute notes toward a theocentric account of knowledge rather than a conceptually independent theory of scientific truth. The reliability of his experimental essays derives ultimately not from their comprehensiveness but from their carefully limited claims to offer modest insights into "hitherto unobserved *Phaenomena*."

3

Boyle's *Continuation of New Experiments,* published nine years after his first book of experimental essays, exists within different discursive and political contexts from its predecessor. Soon after the publication of *New Experiments,* Boyle found himself involved in both scientific and political controversies with opponents of his and his colleagues at what was soon to be chartered as the Royal Society—most notably, Thomas Hobbes. In 1662 Boyle responded to Hobbes's disparaging of experimental philosophy by launching a brilliantly crafted counterattack, *An Examen of Mr. Hobbes his Dialogus Physicus de Natura Aeris.*[18] Boyle's strategy in his response is five-pronged: he attacks Hobbes "for want of having sufficiently considered the Experiments he would be thought to despise" (a2v); for using this attack on experimental science as a pretext to promote his "dangerous Opinions about some important, if not fundamental Articles of Religion, [of the sort Boyle] had met with in his *Leviathan,* and some other of his Writings" (a2v); for engaging in an unfair and unprovoked personal attack on Boyle; for showing ingratitude to his patron; and for showing disrespect to his social superiors by "causelessly and needlessly . . . fall[ing] upon a Society, whereof, besides many other Persons of Quality and men of Parts, his own great Patron, and my highly Honour'd and Learned Friend, *The Earl of Devonshire* himself, is an Illustrious Member" (2). Boyle portrays himself as a put-upon gentleman, who has "a natural Indispos'dness to Contention," struggling to maintain a proper "Civility" in his reply, that nonetheless "leaves [him] but little hope that [he] can oppose [Hobbes] without angering him" (2–3). The brilliance of Boyle's rhetorical strategy lies in his identifying experimental science with gentlemanly "Civility," national prosperity, a stable sociopolitical order, established religion, and the kind of exemplary disinterestedness that Hobbes, as a "Writer of Politicks" (2), compromises. In brief, by subtle insinuation and strategically deployed buzz-words, Boyle describes Hobbes's attack in terms reminiscent of the radical challenges to ecclesiastical and civil authority during the Civil War. In contrast, experimental philosophy is described in terms that anticipate Thomas Sprat's ideological defense of experimental philosophy in his *History of the Royal Society* (1667): stability, reverence for political and ecclesiastical authority, national prosperity, and scientific progress.[19]

The significance of Boyle's response to Hobbes lies, in part, in his recognition (idealistic disclaimers notwithstanding) that scientific controversy cannot be separated from "personal and extrinsic Matters" (3), from the political and cultural contexts in which it takes place. Boyle is not arguing in bad faith against Hobbes; he believes in the concepts of scientific disinterest and utilitarian progress that his works promote. Yet his yoking of experimental science and ideology in the *Examen of Hobbes* leads him to redirect his subsequent experimental essays toward offering a more sociopolitically engaged vision of scientific research. In one sense, the *Continuation of New Experiments* is less a radical break with his first volume of experimental essays than a more explicit articulation of the ways in which scientific technology in the 1660s is a means for consolidating rather than redistributing political and economic power. Nevertheless, the rhetorical strategies he employs in his *Continuation* differ from those of his earlier "Narratives"; they redefine his view of the relationship between technology and experimental investigation, his conception of his audience, and his description of "experience" itself.

Boyle begins his preface to *A Continuation* with a brief account of how he was prevailed upon to improve the design of his original air pump (which he had donated to the Royal Society) in order to continue his experiments. With "the help of Other work-men then Those [he] had unsuccessfully imploy'd" before, Boyle "procured a new Engine lesse [expensive] than [the earlier model] and differing in some Circumstances from it"; the new version "work[s] as well as the Other, and, as to some purposes, better" ([a3r]). These technological improvements, however, are not described in the detail that Boyle had lavished on his first air pump. The physical design of the new model is relegated to a relative brief (for Boyle) five-page section, entitled *"Some Advertisements touching the Engine it self"* (b4r), which prefaces the reports of his experiments. Boyle begins this description by carefully defining the audience for whom it is intended:

> As for the Construction of the second Engine it self, since tis presumed, that the Readers of this Book have already perused That of which this is a Continuation, and understood the contrivance of the Instrument that belongs to it, it was presumed sufficient to exhibit in the first Plate the delineation of the entire Engine ready to be set at work; and in the second, the figures of the several Metalline parts that compose it, before they are set together. For though these have not verbal and Alphabetical explications annexed to them, yet the sight of them may suffice to make those that have an imagination fitted to conceive

Mechanical contrivances, are acquainted with the former Engine, comprehend the structure of this; which, Alphabetical explications would
scarce make such Readers do, as are not so qualified. (b4r)

A sea change has occurred in Boyle's rhetorical strategies. In place
of the explicit, piece-by-piece description of the original air pump,
Boyle offers in this passage simple allusions to a knowledge that he
presumes already exists. His audience is no longer comprised of
interested amateurs (like his nephew) but those with "imagination[s] fitted to conceive Mechanical contrivances," that is, other
experimentalists and members of the Royal Society. In effect, Boyle
has divided his potential readers into those who can understand the
operation and significance of the improved air pump and those who
cannot; he then dismisses the latter as an unfit audience. By limiting his readers to a select group of virtuosos, he can dispense with
many of the laborious, overexplicit semiotic strategies—"verbal
and Alphabetical explications"—that he had previously employed.
In this sense, Boyle's "advertisements" for his "Engine" both reflect and participate in the institutionalization of a scientific
discourse that, by 1669, has become more or less familiar to readers
who have at least been exposed to the rhetoric of the essays
published in the Royal Society's *Philosophical Transactions,* the
"unadorned" styles of experimentalists such as Hooke and Power,
and the ideological arguments for experimental philosophy advanced by Sprat, Wilkins, Boyle, and other members of the Royal
Society.[20] In one sense, Boyle's *Continuation* depends upon an
exclusionary strategy to distinguish, even "create," an audience
sophisticated enough to comprehend the workings of his new air
pump without the kind of meticulous description that he had employed in 1660. The air pump has become not simply a means to
investigate nature but an object that creates a conceptual, rather
than purely physical, space to which access can and should be
controlled.[21]

This shift in rhetorical strategies signals an important change in
Boyle's depiction and conception of experimental experience. His
difficulties in constructing the original air pump and in getting it to
function properly, which occupied a good deal of his attention in
New Experiments, are downplayed, tucked into a parenthetical
admission that "we did (though not without trouble enough) bring
[the new pump] to work as well . . . [or] better" than its predecessor (a3r). The first plate of the redesigned air pump (see figure 2) is
not, as in the original, an "exploded" diagram but an artistic rendering of the finished product, complete with a dead cat in the receiver.

The technological improvements are reserved for the second plate (see figure 3) and are decorously laid out on the page with (for Boyle) a minimum of accompanying explanation. If the first plate is reasonably accurate in its depiction of detail, the new workmen whom Boyle employed took some pains to make this "engine" look more like a piece of furniture than a utilitarian apparatus. Note, for example, the bevelled edge at the bottom of the water tank, the curve and bevelling of the supporting arm of the higher platform, and the pear shape of the vacuum chamber. In brief, the two plates in *A Continuation* offer less technical information than the single plate in *New Experiments*. They work, like Boyle's brief description, to de-emphasize the historical circumstances of the air pump's construction and operation in favor of visual appeals to a knowledge, a technical expertise, that is presumed already to exist. In this respect, the purpose of Boyle's description and the accompanying plates of the new air pump is not so much to educate readers or convince them of the value of experimental science but to create in them the desire for a kind of knowledge that only this technologically advanced apparatus can satisfy. Boyle's "engine," in other words, becomes less of a heuristic device for probing the kinds of secrets that lead to a heightened religious devotion and more of a fetish, an object that has begun to displace the desire for knowledge by becoming that which is in itself desirable.

4

The changes in Boyle's rhetorical strategies between *New Experiments* and *A Continuation* are indicative of the ways in which the discourses of natural philosophy developed in the late seventeenth and early eighteenth centuries. On the one hand, the ideological and theological bases of experimental science are described in relatively consistent terms between 1660 and 1750. As late as 1748, for example, Colin Mclaurin, in *An Account of Sir Isaac Newton's Philosophical Discoveries,* describes scientific investigation in terms reminiscent of both Boyle's and Newton's overt theologizing: "natural philosophy is subservient to purposes of a high kind, and is chiefly to be valued as it lays a sure foundation for natural religion and moral philosophy; by leading us, in a satisfactory manner, to the knowledge of the Author and Governor of the universe."[22] Yet on the other hand, the teleological certainty with which eighteenth-century natural philosophers pursued their inquiries allowed them to bracket theology as a means of explaining physical phenomena, relegating it to the status of a transcendent guarantee of the value of their efforts, and to focus on anatomizing the structures and "laws" of the physical world. In contrast to Boyle and Newton—both of whom held the voluntaristic position that God's intervention in the natural world was essential to its harmonious functioning—their eighteenth-century followers increasingly, and often only half-consciously, began to sound like the systematizers, particularly Descartes and Leibniz, whom their predecessors had attacked.[23] The systematizing of the universe—the displacement of teleology by an emphasis on the harmony of the natural world and the smooth functioning of its "laws"—is, in effect, also a fetishizing of the technological apparatus that are employed to discover and exploit the workings of nature. In short, the processes that we can begin to see operating in Boyle's description of his redesigned air pump become, by the early eighteenth century, dominant modes of scientific discourse and of figuring the relationships among technology, humankind, and nature.

Peter Shaw's three-volume "revision" of Boyle's works, *The Works of the Honourable Robert Boyle . . . Abridged, Methodized, and Disposed under the General Heads of Physics, Statics, Pneumatics, Natural History, and Medicine . . .* (1725) goes beyond the boiled-down synopsis of the kind published by Richard Boulton in 1699–1700 to reinscribe Boyle's works within what he perceives to be the Newtonian orthodoxy.[24] In rewriting Boyle's works, often line-by-line, Shaw effects radical stylistic and conceptual changes in his efforts to make his predecessor's miscellaneous essays conform to what he considers the bedrock tenets of scientific discourse: objectivity, concision, and clarity. As "the introducer, or, at least, the great restorer of mechanical philosophy among us," Boyle was concerned, according to Shaw, "to deliver himself in the most full and circumstantial manner," even to the point of "immoderate length." Given the "miscellaneous manner" in which they were written, Boyle's works create "a matter of some difficulty to reduce them to an order fit for a ready and commodious perusal" (i). Therefore, to render Boyle accessible to an eighteenth-century audience, Shaw sets himself the task of regularizing Boyle's corpus—cutting, rearranging, rephrasing, and paraphrasing Boyle's original works so that they "should together tend to compose one regular whole" (ii). To improve Boyle's "copious, diffusive, and circumstantial style," Shaw announces that he will "leave out in the abridgment whatever was merely personal, or had no relation to the argument; and to contract [Boyle's] words into as small a compass as appear'd consistent with the perspicuity requisite in philosophical writings" (ii).

Shaw, however, finds himself, as he recognizes, in the awkward position of systematizing a writer who disparaged all forms of systematizing. Boyle, he notes, "never design'd to write a body of philosophy, only to bestow occasional essays on those subjects whereto his genius or inclination led him; 'tis not to be expected, that even the most exquisite arrangement, should ever reduce them to a methodical and uniform system, tho' they afford abundant material for one" (ii). Boyle, then, is to be admired for the breadth and perspicuity of his inquiries into the natural world and regarded as a noble forefather, who "laid the foundations of almost all the improvements which have been made since his time, in natural philosophy," rather than as a systematic natural philosopher. Shaw's effusive praise puts him in the paradoxical position of commending his predecessor for *not* having "work'd up a glorious system, and erected a more pompous, ostentatious, and, perhaps, a more durable structure of natural or chymical philosophy" (xv)—in other words, for *not* having done what Shaw in 1725 must do to his work in order to get people to read it. What Shaw asks his readers to see as an act of homage, of rewriting Boyle in order to restore him to his rightful place as the progenitor of experimental philosophy, may also be read as an act of epistemological violence, of recontextualizing Boyle in a way that dehistoricizes his laboratory experience and subsumes his explicit theological rhetoric within the increasingly institutionalized and commodified world of early eighteenth-century science. In this respect, the purpose of Shaw's methodizing and abridging of Boyle's writings is not to deliver "new" experimental experiences in the form of original essays but to refashion Boyle's past experiences into a commercially profitable form—a three-volume, meticulously printed "system." Natural philosophy has become both a rhetoric—a way of explicating universal "laws"—and a product to be displayed in the most intellectually and financially advantageous way possible.

A detailed study of Shaw's abridgement would literally require a volume in itself. But some idea of the nature of his revisions may be gleaned from his version of Boyle's description of the operation of his first air pump (quoted on pp. 138–39 above):

That no air, also, may remain in the upper part of the cylinder, the handle is to be turn'd till the sucker rises to the top; and then, the valve being shut, it is to be drawn down to the bottom; by which means, the air being driven out of the cylinder, and a succession from without prevented, the cavity of the cylinder must be empty of air; so that, when the stop-cock is turn'd to afford a communication betwixt the receiver and the cylinder, part of the air before lodged in the receiver, will be drawn down into the cylinder; which, by turning back the key, is kept from entering the receiver again, and may, by unstopping the valve, and forcing up the sucker, be driven into the open air; and so, by repeated exsuctions out of the receiver, and expulsions out of the cylinder, the versions may be exhausted as the experiment requires. (2.1: 409)

At the end of this paragraph, Shaw directs his reader's attention to the following footnote: "The air pump has received great improvements since the time of Mr. *Boyle,* and seems brought to its utmost degree of simplicity, and perfection, by the late, and the present [that is, the father and son] Mr. *Hauksbee*" (2.1: 409n). The footnote then provides a detailed seven-hundred word description of Hauksbee's air pump that refers the reader to its own pictorial representation at the end of the volume.[25] This note, in effect, introduces a second order of displacement into Shaw's rewriting of Boyle's description. On the first level lies Shaw's revision. Boyle's *"Experimenter"* literally disappears as passive verb forms replace active ones. The vitalistic "traces" of an anthropomorphized natural world present in Boyle's description are reduced to bare, almost dead, metaphors ("succession" for "none being permitted to succeed in its room"). Shaw edits out of existence any sense of historical immediacy, of the experimenter's "forcing up of the Sucker to the top of the Cylinder," and offers in its place a generalized, impersonal, and transhistorical experience of objective observation. Boyle's account of his experience in the laboratory is further idealized into a seemingly dispassionate rhetoric of scientific investigation. In this respect, Shaw's language does not promote itself as the narrative of an actual, historical experience; it takes as its referent Boyle's "circumstantial" representation of that experience, his "technology of virtual witnessing." In Shaw's version the fiction of the "virtual witness" has disappeared along with that of the experimenter. The laws of the weight and pressure of the air have become part of a systematized knowledge of the world and need only be evoked by scientific allusion rather than supported by a "literary technology" that seeks to convince us of their existence. Boyle's epistemology of discovery has given way to Shaw's comparatively static display of timeless physical "laws."

On the second level, that of Shaw's footnote, the revised version of Boyle's description is itself displaced by the technological superiority of Hauksbee's air pump. The footnote becomes the center of the reader's attention, the primary conveyer of up-to-date scientific information; the text is relegated to the marginal status of a pioneering technique that has been mastered and surpassed. The original air pump is transformed into a historical curiosity. Boyle's complaints about workmen and warnings about the difficulty of creating even a temporary vacuum, in effect, are replaced by a machine "brought to its utmost degree of simplicity, and perfection." Precisely because Shaw views the laws of nature as immutable, the process of discovery—Boyle's concern with the epistemology of which his air pump is both an end and a means—becomes less important than the functioning of technology as a means to verify what is already known. At the risk of simplifying, then, we might say that in moving from Boyle to Shaw we are moving from one concept of the relationship of technology to knowledge to another—from the air pump as a heuristic apparatus that can be given away, set aside while Boyle pursues other avenues of experimental investigation, and redesigned to the air pump as an artifact, a "perfected" commodity, a fetishized representation of humankind's progress in and domestication of scientific knowledge.

The two levels of displacement in Shaw's rewriting of Boyle, then, mark a further development of the process of familiarization that occurs in Boyle's *Continuation*. Throughout his preface, Shaw emphasizes the utilitarian aspects of his predecessor's research:

> [Boyle] shews us trades in a new light, and makes them, what they really are, a part of natural philosophy; and considering them accordingly, reveals some of their mysteries; all along advancing proper means to encourage, promote, and multiply the arts [e.g., industries or trades] themselves. The goldsmith, the lapidary, the jeweller, the refiner, the stone-cutter, the dyer, the glass-maker, artizans of all kinds, will from him receive the best informations, as to the working, managing, and employing to advantage their various commodities, materials, engines, and instruments. The husbandman and the diver are here instructed in their arts; and the mineralist, the miner, and assayer, to find and separate their ore to the greatest profit; to increase the quantity, to meliorate, improve, and enrich their metals; to purify and and [re]fine them, and accurately to distinguish the genuine and pure, from the adulterate, base, or counterfeit. (xiii–xiv)

For Shaw, the value of Boyle's scientific discoveries are—quite literally—inseparable from the material value, the "profit," to which they lead. This view is typical of eighteenth-century natural philosophy in Britain. As Larry Stewart and Margaret C. Jacob, among others, have demonstrated, the institutionalization of scientific research included popularizations, lectures, courses of instruction for the general public, traveling demonstrations of new technologies, and other forms of dissemination that, in effect, treated the investigation of nature as a commodity to be packaged, promoted, and sold to the middle and upper-middle classes, the tradesmen to whom Shaw appeals in depicting Boyle's works as a means to greater monetary as well as intellectual profit.[26] Because the air pump has seemingly little direct connection to the practical "arts" of glassmaking, farming, metallurgy, and so forth, it functions more or less symbolically as a product of scientific investigation, an object to acquire, a status symbol for those who can afford to attend the lectures at which Hauksbeep's apparatus is demonstrated. In this respect, the air pump has become less a state-of-the-art experimental device than an object for the well-to-do and intellectually inquisitive patrons who are willing to pay to see or read about it in action.

As even this necessarily brief account should make clear, Shaw's rewriting of Boyle's works has significant implications for historians of science and of eighteenth-century culture. Traditional accounts in both fields frequently assume as a matter of course that the "rise" of modern science, of "secularization," and of the so-called age of reason are master-narratives that need only to be retold rather than interrogated. Shaw's revision of Boyle's works suggests that the "rise" of science is a complex process that depends, to a great extent, on the repression of historical experience into generic conventions of "objective" scientific discourse that embody and promote a host of nonscientific ideological, socioeconomic, and political values.[27] To make this argument is not, I believe, to suggest that some pristine, unproblematic "experience" exists—whether in Boyle's laboratory or elsewhere—that can be somehow saved from processes of appropriation and mystification and that can be "captured" or "reflected" in a politically neutral language. The issue in Shaw's revision is not the *ethics* of scientific writing—of being "true" to a "real" experience—but the *politics* of science, of investigating how nature and experience are constituted in his "methodizing" of Boyle and how these ideological constructions are then used for scientific and nonscientific purposes. What we witness, then, in moving from Boyle's works to Shaw's is not the linear progress of scientific method, or writing, or experimentation but a discontinuous narrative that marks shifting currents within the cultural and ideological justifications for natural philosophy.

In one respect Shaw's version of Boyle enacts the narrative of technological progress, of a linear development in experimental science, that it seeks to promote. It privileges what I have termed fetishized notions of technological "perfection," objective description, and scientific disinterest, reifying them as properties of the experimental method rather than acknowledging them as discursive, heuristic, and even polemical strategies. Although in Shaw's mind the scientific "facts" or "laws" that Boyle discovered are timeless, his redaction effectively promotes a view of natural philosophy that implicitly subverts many of the principles of Boyle's writings, particularly the dependence of experimentation on theology, even as it extends the process of institutionalization evident in the exclusionary rhetorical strategies that the author adopts in *A Continuation of New Experiments.* Shaw's redaction, in this respect, represents both a rupture and a continuation of Boyle's natural philosophy—a reinscribing of technology as product rather than process, of reifying historical experience as a specific instance of generalized observation. In effect, Shaw's revision represents a continuing displacement of experience into an ideology of "progress." Like Boyle in 1669, Shaw is moving toward a transhistorical view of science, a science of "being" rather than "becoming."[28] The irony, for anyone familiar with the history of science, is that it is Shaw's view of Boyle, if not his actual abridgement, which has generally prevailed over his predecessor's insistence on the asystematic nature of scientific inquiry. To a great extent, we are still trying to recover the ideological complexity of Boyle's experimental and theological inquiries from the literary technology of self-justifying progress that has prevailed since the eighteenth century.

NOTES

1. Steven Shapin and Simon Schaffer, *Leviathan and the Air Pump: Hobbes, Boyle and the Experimental Life* (Princeton, N.J.: Princeton University Press, 1985).

2. In addition to Shapin's and Schaffer's study, see Peter Dear, "*Totius in verba:* Rhetoric and Authority in the Early Royal Society," *Isis* 76 (1985): 145–61.

3. Charles Bazerman, *Shaping Written Knowledge* (Madison: University of Wisconsin Press, 1988), pp. 80–127.

4. See M. M. Bakhtin, "The Problem of Speech Genres," in *Speech Genres and Other Late Essays,* trans. Vern W. McGee; eds. Michael Holquist and Caryl Emerson (Austin: University of Texas Press, 1986). On the importance of literary constructions of laboratory experience, see Bruno Latour and Steve Woolgar, *Laboratory Life: The Construction of Scientific Facts* (1979; rpt. Princeton, N.J.: Princeton University Press, 1986).

5. See, for example, Henry Power, *Experimental Philosophy* (London, 1664), a

compendium of experimental results that preserves, particularly in its preface, the universalizing rhetoric of early seventeenth-century encyclopedic treatises.

6. Wilkins, *Essay,* p. 2. On the roles of taxonomy and the construction of seventeenth-century science, see M. M. Slaughter, *Universal Languages and Scientific Taxonomy in the Seventeenth Century* (Cambridge: Cambridge University Press, 1982), and Tony Davies, "The Ark in Flames: Science, Language, and Education in Seventeenth-Century England," in *The Figural and the Literal: Problems of Language in the History of Science and Philosophy 1630–1800,* eds. Andrew E. Benjamin, Geoffrey N. Cantor, and John R. R. Christie (Manchester: Manchester University Press, 1987), pp. 83–102.

7. For a helpful critique of internalist accounts of Boyle's role in the development of modern chemistry, see Jan V. Golinski, "Robert Boyle: Scepticism and Authority in Seventeenth-Century Chemical Discourse," in *The Figural and the Literal,* pp. 58–82.

8. See James Paradis, "Montaigne, Boyle, and the Essay of Experience," in *One Culture: Essays in Science and Literature,* ed. George Levine (Madison: University of Wisconsin Press, 1987), pp. 59–91, and Robert Markley, "Objectivity as Ideology: Boyle, Newton, and the Languages of Science," *Genre* 16 (1983): 355–72.

9. Boyle, *Occasional Reflections upon Several Subjects* (London, 1665), p. 48.

10. Letter to Glanvill, 18 September 1677 in Thomas Birch, ed., *The Works of the Honourable Robert Boyle,* 5 vols. (London, 1744), 5: 244.

11. Shapin, "The House of Experiment in Seventeenth-Century England," *Isis* 79 (1988): 387–88.

12. See Stanley E. Fish, *Self-Consuming Artifacts: The Experience of Seventeenth-Century Literature* (Berkeley and Los Angeles: University of California Press, 1972). The complexities of the Calvinist heritage of the "scientific revolution" are often ignored in treatments of Boyle, Newton, and their contemporaries. On the implications of this heritage see, Brian Easlea, *Witch-hunting, Magic and the New Philosophy: An Introduction to Debates of the Scientific Revolution* (Brighton, Sussex: Harvester, 1980) and Christopher Hill, *Collected Essays* (Amherst: University of Massachusetts Press, 1985), particularly the essays in volume two.

13. See Shapin and Schaffer, *Leviathan,* especially 283–344; J. R. Jacob, *Henry Stubbe: Radical Protestantism and the Early Enlightenment in England* (Cambridge: Cambridge University Press, 1983); and Brian Vickers, "Restoration Prose Style: A Reassessment," in Vickers and Nancy Struever, *Rhetoric and the Pursuit of Truth: Language Change in the Seventeenth and Eighteenth Centuries* (Los Angeles: Clark Library, 1985), 1–76.

14. On Hooke see Shapin, "The House of Experiment in Seventeenth-Century England," 382.

15. See particularly Easlea, *Witch-hunting* and Evelyn Fox Keller, *Reflections on Gender and Science* (New Haven: Yale University Press, 1985), 67–126.

16. See Susan Bordo, "The Cartesian Masculinization of Thought," *Signs* 11 (1986): 439–56.

17. On Hobbes, see Shapin and Schaffer, *Leviathan,* especially chapters three and four.

18. Hobbes's treatise *Dialogus Physicus* (1661) is translated by Schaffer as an appendix to *Leviathan and the Air Pump,* pp. 346–91. On the second version of the air pump see Shapin and Schaffer, pp. 171–72, 260–64.

19. On Boyle's relationship to the intellectual climate of the 1660s and 1670s, see J. R. Jacob, *Robert Boyle and the English Revolution* (New York: Burt

Franklin, 1977). On the ideology of the restoration, see Nicholas Jose, *Ideas of the Restoration in English Literature 1660–71* (Cambridge: Harvard University Press, 1984).

20. On the institutionalization of scientific discourse during the 1660s, see Dear, *"Totius in verba,"* who argues that the form of scientific discourse was more important than its content; Bazerman, *Shaping Written Knowledge*, 59–79, and Michael Hunter, *Science and Society in Restoration England* (Cambridge: Cambridge University Press, 1981).

21. On the problem of access to experimental sites in the seventeenth century, see Shapin, "House of Experiment," 383–90.

22. Mclaurin, *An Account of Sir Isaac Newton's Philosophical Discoveries* (London, 1748), p. 3.

23. I treat the problem of "order" at greater length in "Representing Order: Natural Philosophy, Mathematics, and Theology in the Newtonian Revolution," in N. Katherine Hayles, ed., *Chaos and Order: Complex Dynamics in Literature and Science* (Chicago: University of Chicago Press, 1991), 125–48.

24. Richard Boulton, *The Works of the Honourable Robert Boyle, Esq. Epitomiz'd*, 4 vols. (London, 1699–1700). In general, Boulton offers a radically pared down version of Boyle's own words and brief paraphrases of his experiments. In 1715 he published an "epitome" of Boyle's theological works. In his preface, Shaw acknowledges the existence of Boulton's epitome but notes that a systematic, comprehensive account of all of Boyle's works (namely his) is needed. Shaw's attempts to fit Boyle into a Newtonian framework are evident in his general preface to his revision and in the numerous footnotes he supplies to update the progress that natural philosophy has made since Boyle's original experiments.

25. Shaw was a sometime collaborator of the younger Francis Hauksbee's, who demonstrated experiments while the former lectured. See F. W. Gibbs, "Peter Shaw and the Revival of Chemistry," *Annals of Science* 7 (1951): 218–20.

26. Larry Stewart, "The Selling of Newton: Science and Technology in Early Eighteenth-Century England," *Journal of British Studies* 25 (1986): 178–92; Margaret J. Jacob, "Scientific Culture in the Early English Enlightenment: Mechanisms, Industry, and Gentlemanly Facts," in Alan Charles Kors and Paul K. Korshin, eds., *Anticipations of the Enlightenment in England, France, and Germany* (Philadelphia: University of Pennsylvania Press, 1987), pp. 134–64.

27. I draw here on Frederic Jameson, *The Political Unconscious: Narrative as a Socially Symbolic Act* (Ithaca, N.Y.: Cornell University Press, 1982). On the displacement of "nature" by "convention" during the period of the scientific revolution, see Lawrence Manley, *Convention 1500–1700* (Cambridge: Harvard University Press, 1980).

28. For efforts to "recover" a science of "becoming" from the modern science of "being," see Gaston Bachelard, *The New Scientific Spirit*, trans. Arthur Goldhammer (Boston: Beacon Press, 1984); Ilya Prigogine, *From Being to Becoming: Time and Complexity in the Physical Sciences* (San Francisco: W. H. Freeman, 1980); Michel Serres, *Hermes: Literature, Science, Philosophy*, trans. Josué V. Harari and David F. Bell (Baltimore: Johns Hopkins University Press, 1982); and Gilles Deleuze and Felix Guattari, *Nomadology: The War Machine* (New York: Semiotext(e), 1986), pp. 17–40.

Romantic Technology: Books, Printing, and Blake's *Marriage of Heaven and Hell*

MARK L. GREENBERG

"William Wordsworth and the Age of Romanticism," a traveling exhibition of paintings, manuscripts, letters, books, and other historically pertinent materials, attracted a great deal of attention when it was assembled at the New York Public Library late in 1987. One viewer, Anatole Broyard, essayist and an editor of the *New York Times Book Review,* was moved by his visit to criticize certain current attitudes toward romanticism. His remarks may strike some as idealized generalizations, which in part they are. They seem to me also to embody a character trait the romantics valued and, at their best, exemplified, and that is courage. "Democracy," he writes, "which is against all sorts of excesses but its own, seems to fear romanticism as a perpetuation of inequalities and a penchant for suffering. Looking back at it, I see romanticism as a time when we thought we were better than we actually are, when we were fonder of ourselves. We loved our fears and believed in believing. Our hunger for absolutes was disarming—even healthy."[1] One of the absolutes of British romanticism commonly assumed by interested readers today—and with some justification—is its apparent opposition to the technological changes that had been sweeping over England since the mid-eighteenth century. Such opposition, most students believe, issued philosophically from the romantics' fundamental antagonism toward the pervasive mechanical worldview espoused most prominently by Newton and Locke, and issued spiritually from their abhorrence of Deism.[2] Doubtless, too, menacing physical manifestations of these complementary systems of belief, apparent everywhere they looked, appalled the romantics for they "lived through the crucial period in which the rise both of democracy and of industry was effecting qualitative changes in society," as Raymond Williams explains. "Of the slower, wider, less observable changes that we call the Industrial Revolution, the life-time of Blake, 1757–1827, is, in general, the decisive period. The changes that we receive as record were experienced, in these years, on the senses: hunger, suffering, conflict, dislocation; hope, energy, vision, dedication. The pattern of change was not background, as we may now be inclined to study it; it was, rather, the mould in which general experience was cast."[3] As a result, Williams goes on, "the romantics consciously cultivated an emphasis on the embodi-ment in art of certain human values, capacities, energies, which the development of society toward an industrial civilization was felt to be threatening or even destroying" (36).

Seen from this cultural perspective, two of the characteristics of romantic poetry that emerge most sharply are, first, its intense involvement with the social events that conditioned poets' experi-ences (and to which much of their poetry refers), and second, the development of written or graphic forms in which adequately to press back against the changes Williams characterizes so power-fully.[4] The topoi of romantic responses to the *effects* of technology are almost too well-known to require rehearsing here: Words-worth's "World too much with us," or his nightmare vision of the young poet as an alien in industrial London, elaborated in the seventh book of *The Prelude;* Coleridge's lifelong attempt to replace the mechanical philosophy with a vitalist alternative; Lamb and Keats's famous toast, at the "immortal dinner" held in Benjamin Haydon's studio, to "Newton's health, and confusion to mathe-matics," followed soon thereafter by Keats's refrain in "Lamia" that "[natural] Philosophy will clip an Angel's wings, / Conquer all mysteries by rule and line, / Empty the haunted air, and gnomed mine— / Unweave a rainbow";[5] Shelley's sonnet "To the Men of England" and his "Mask of Anarchy"; Blake's unremitting struggle with the unholy trinity, "Bacon & Newton & Locke," and against the "dark Satanic Mills," examples of the "mind forg'd manacles" of "London" and of England generally—this dimension of romantic social criticism yields powerful, seemingly inexhaustible articula-tions. It is worth recalling, as well, that the few "canonical" roman-tic poets were not the only people of their age both fascinated by the rapid technological achievements underway and horrified by the cultural changes these achievements wrought; responses, as cap-tured in every variety of writing (itself a technology), were remark-ably widespread.[6]

Indeed, one of the fundamental ironies of romanticism involves authors delivering their criticism of industrial culture through typographically set, mechanically reproduced writing printed upon industrially manufactured paper by laborers, and offered for sale (to a public limited by its rate of literacy and ability to afford the productions of the press) by commercial booksellers. For all the romantic poets save Blake, a sophisticated economic and technological system, fully developed during the eighteenth century, had been operating, in effect, to liberate these writers from patronage. Had the patronage system not been replaced by commercial typography, it is safe to say that most of what we have judged to be the most meaningful expressions of romanticism would not have been produced. Ironically, even the antipictorialism, the pervasive skepticism concerning verbal and visual representations characteristic of Wordsworth, Coleridge, Shelley, and Keats, has to be understood as fostered at least partially by the printing system. Certain fundamental features of the typographical system created the profession of author and also gave authors the freedom to question the implications and limitations of writing and commercial book manufacture.[7] Put most simply, but accurately, the young romantics attacked the Industrial Revolution from a medium created and supported by the very system they abhorred.

"Literature," or "letters" (as the enterprise we now term romanticism was known to its practitioners), had been reconfigured by the time of Blake's birth in 1757. Such change resulted primarily from the broad emergence of printing technology during the eighteenth century. As Alvin Kernan elaborates, "even as print made the works of literature, so it also . . . made authors. . . . Many of the formal properties considered central to romantic and modern literature are also aesthetic expressions of print logic."[8] Moreover, two key features of printing technology, typographic fixity (the preserving power of print and the authority that such power confers upon author and text), and reproducibility on a vast scale, helped foster romanticism. Romantic poets, conscious of these features and of heir effects upon readers, used the logic and spatial organization offered by printing technology deliberately in fashioning intricate arrangements of poems within the volumes they produced.[9] Print technology thus creates a medium through which these poets craft artful volumes whose themes are at least partially antipathetic to technology and its sponsoring ideologies. Such irony continues to this day to characterize virtually all of our relations with the communications technologies we produce.

The irony that printing technology was an important expression of industrial capitalism which made the dominant forms of romanticism possible seems not to have been lost on the only major romantic figure trained as an engraver. The one romantic most conscious of the material conditions of art was also the most bitterly critical of the effects of the commercial production of art in England on the artist and his works, and in responding to the material conditions of art in late eighteenth-century England, he was also the most inventive. William Blake's tangible responses to the prevailing economics and technologies of his time, his composite art of word and image (and of words that are also images), is unique; and for him the creative efforts required to bring about such a form is inseparable from the quest for cultural and psychological health. Although Blake concentrates his "remarks" on printing and books particularly in *The Marriage of Heaven and Hell,* the work on which I shall concentrate, it is worth noting that technology and the conditions of art preoccupied Blake throughout his life, and we find the traces of this concern in many of his other works. For Blake (as for Wordsworth, Coleridge, Shelley, and Keats), questions of scientific method and technological advancement necessarily entail a network of associations that cannot be reduced to simplicities about mechanical versus organic form or explained merely as antinomian rejections of received scientific ideas—or even as principally the repudiation of a social system that was increasingly determined by technology. All the romantic poets consciously employed the possibilities offered by print technology in fashioning their art. Viewed especially from within Blake's project, we can witness technology and prophecy interpenetrate reciprocally and dynamically.

I

For William Blake the network of relationships among producer, meaning, mode of production, and receiver may reach toward the condition of love. "Reader [*lover*] of books! [*lover*] of Heaven / And of that God From whom [*all books are given,*]" commences lines addressed "To the Public" at the beginning of Blake's long work, *Jerusalem*. The passage concludes with "Heaven, Earth & Hell, henceforth" living in "harmony," a consequence for Blake of his own printing.[10]

Blake's *Marriage of Heaven and Hell* has been wed to as many interpretations and approaches as there are interpreters who have committed themselves to the ceremony of print. For the variety of literary and visual modes embodied by the work, the words delivered by a host of generally unspecified and often unstable voices,

and the elusive graphic elements, deliberately arresting and polysemous, have provoked numerous interpretations—all, as Paul
Mann has observed, "true—or at least negotiable" within the community of discourse centered on Blake.[11] Commentators have explored the complex political, sexual, psychological, theological, and
prophetic dimensions of the *Marriage*. Nelson Hilton has suggested that once "we begin to see" Blake's works "in terms of
'levels' (or different orders of levels), possibilities proliferate. We no
longer devour the text, but begin to produce it, to play it."[12] Production and interpretive play seem to me dominant themes and formal
strategies of the *Marriage,* encouraging engagement with it even as
we must honestly admit our being puzzled by much of what we
engage. The work is concerned throughout with its own material
form, with the conditions of writing, printing, and the book, with
the artist's desire to embody imaginative activity within physical
form and to present their confluence as a product that is also the
work's theme. In a number of related formal strategies, the *Marriage* mocks the dominant technology for disseminating ideas—
letterpress—that, in its overwhelming success in the eighteenth
century, seems to Blake to overwhelm the feasibility not only for
the individual artist to body forth and evoke imaginative activity
fully and economically, to identify with and sell his work, but also
by its very success to forestall criticism of the compromises and
limitations inhering in commercial typography. Even as we produce
readings, the work focuses our attention upon production itself by
emphasizing the material conditions of the book and of the reader
of books. In its astonishing diversity of graphic styles, voices,
themes, and startling references to previous books, Blake's volume
also upsets the linear structure (and even the idea of the "central
plot") that, some have argued, result from the logic of print.[13]

II

The self-parody of form in the *Marriage,* its attack upon its own
status as printed book and its exploitation of the commercial and
technological forces that produce works of art, may at first appear
part of the "mock-book" tradition we encounter in Sterne, in
Swift's *Tale of a Tub,* in Pope, and in Byron. William Kinsley has
studied Pope's *Dunciad* as "Mock-Book," illuminating its formal
self-parody while mapping the tradition of the book as an "incarna-
tion of wisdom and a metonym for learning and culture," as well as
a symbol for nature, the "book of nature."[14] It is worth noting as

well that eighteenth-century writers, the first generation to live within a typographical culture, immediately seized upon the world of printing as theme. Blake, like Pope, Swift, and Sterne, satirizes book conventions, but Blake goes beyond such earlier satirists in two ways. First, he anatomizes minutely the very process of printing, exposing the particulars of print technology's mediation between author's ideas or "vision" and reader; and second, he perfects an original, alternate technology in which he embodies the "energetic exertion of [his] talent." Blake delivers his critique of books in a format that, in the late eighteenth century, seemed nontraditional: his illuminated printing in which verbal "text" *as* design along with purely graphic images are printed from copper plates and then hand illustrated and colored, allowing the author to fashion the technology to his purposes rather than the other way around.[15] Instead of mocking print technology from within the form as had Pope, Swift, and Sterne, Blake deliberately satirizes it from without.

Blake perceives a fundamental identity between modes of artistic production and the ideas expressed by the producers. His thinking anticipates and partially prompts ideas about the effects of the medium of communication upon human perception advanced in our century by Marshall McLuhan, Lucien Febvre and Henri-Jean Martin, Walter J. Ong, and others.[16] In the *Marriage* he treats both ideology and representation at once—and as one. The new mode of reproduction he consciously develops as theme in the *Marriage* also is designed to reorient the way we perceive art. It has, in fact, provoked new thinking about art as a social institution and about the relationships among art, technology, and commerce, themes fruitfully studied during the last decade by a number of commentators on Blake and on eighteenth-century culture generally.[17]

III

To assert that *The Marriage of Heaven and Hell* is, at heart, an anatomy of writing, book production, reading, and interpretation is hardly an oversimplification of this protean work. Its themes identify with its form, and both serve perfectly to criticize the subjects and letterpress format of other books while Blake expresses himself by "printing in the informal method," (14; 39) writing with "corroding fires" (6–7; 35). The union implied by the title of this *Marriage* occurs between artist, text, and perceiver; a union lost, according to Blake, partially by our lapse into mechanical letterpress printing.

As if to underscore this point, the dominant subjects of the *Marriage* are books, printing, graphic organization virtually enforced by the use of type, writers as functions of printing, and interpretations of printed texts.

As a professional engraver Blake was intimately familiar with the technology and nomenclature of eighteenth-century printing, book production, and manufacture. He was also attuned to the importance of line, space, form, and other graphic elements that constitute a printed "text." By nature (as his annotations to books reveal), he was a reader who paid attention to the minute particulars of the texts he read and who actively engaged others' writing. Blake was thus by training and inclination particularly conscious of the effects of graphic images and of printing upon readers, of the power extended in space and time of an author's disembodied words, of the authority regularly accorded a bound, typeset volume, and of the aesthetic limitations and economic imperatives behind letterpress. Consider Blake's "Prospectus" to ten engraved works, including the *Marriage,* addressed "To the Public" and issued in 1793. In it, Blake perceives the neglect of most genuine creators in terms of the difficulties of producing and disseminating works of genius at an affordable price:

> The Labours of the Artist, the Poet, the Musician, have been proverbially attended by poverty and obscurity; this was never the fault of the Public, but was owing to a neglect of means to propagate such works as have wholly absorbed the Man of Genius. Even Milton and Shakespeare could not publish their own works.
>
> This difficulty has been obviated by the Author of the following productions now presented to the Public; who has invented a method of Printing both Letter-press and Engraving in a style more ornamental, uniform, and grand, than any before discovered, while it produces works at less than one fourth of the expense. (692)

Blake argues in this passage for a relationship between artists and the technology and economics of art in a commercial culture. He charges that technology has failed to allow the "Man of Genius" himself to disseminate works upon which he has concentrated. But Blake's choice of language—"a neglect of means to propagate *such works as have wholly absorbed the Man of Genius*"—also suggests that the work embodies or becomes, "wholly absorbs," the artist, and that the limited expressive power inherent in letterpress distances producer from product from purchaser-perceiver, obscures the artist's personality or even his identity, while effacing the possibility of contact between the classes of people termed in the *Marriage* as the prolific and the devouring.

In the *Marriage,* Heaven and Hell cannot be wed until ideas communicated by the subjects and physical form of books are challenged and "expunged." Blake perceives an essential unity between philosophy and typography, between ideas and the material construction of books that embody them, as he says on the fourteenth plate of the *Marriage:*

> But first the notion that a man has a body distinct from his soul, is to be expunged; this I shall do, by printing in the infernal method, by corrosives. (39)

As Blake may well have known, the word "expunged" in *his* time, according to the *OED,* was associated with printing, referring specifically to something marked for deletion. For Blake, printing composite form constitutes precisely that achievement of identity between producer, product, and consumer, an overcoming of divisions that Blake expresses, significantly, in terms of his craft. Blake's printing strategies also beckon or even demand an active role for the reader confronting his book. It is for this reason also worth noting that while Blake characteristically inscribed his familiar signature as printer or "Author and Printer" on his other major works in composite art, he omits it, significantly, from *The Marriage of Heaven and Hell,* this book about writing, printing, and books. He suggests thereby that the process of corrective interpretation urged and initiated by the *Marriage* renders authors of us all.

The *Marriage* is, in one important sense, a book about books and printing. The work's success, like that of any satire, depends upon our familiarity with the conventions and contexts invoked; in this case, however, authors, books, and portions of books form both context and theme. In the *Marriage* Blake sensitizes us to the imaginary library books contain and engender. "Thus Swedenborg's writings," says Blake, "are a recapitulation of all superficial opinions, and an analysis of the more sublime, but no further" (22; 43). We find Swedenborg and his writings parodied on plate 3, reduced, in fact, according to the speaker, to the "Contents or Index of already publish'd books"; Milton invoked and corrected on plates 5 and 6; the Bible cited, interpreted, and corrected throughout (with the Book of Job, the Book of Proverbs, the "Jews' code," and the ten commandments specifically mentioned); and a variety of famous authors, ideas associated with them, and specifically "literary" language interpolated throughout the work. Indeed, *The Marriage* specifies and absorbs portions of several books. In it, we encounter references to *Paradise Lost,* and several designs in the *Marriage* allude to events in the first two books of Milton's work. Blake also glancingly refers to Aristotle's "Analytics," and mentions the writings of Paracelsus, "Behmen" (Jacob Boehme), Dante, and Shakespeare.

Blake's book about books particularizes "Isaiah xxxiv & XXXV Chap" (3; 34), in carefully inscribed Roman numerals, typographical icons that evoke printed biblical texts. At the same time he transvalues biblical form (and authority) by displacing scripture from its original context to his "illuminated" book. Intertextuality here becomes theme as context and relative position within the new "host" text produce meaning. Elizabeth Eisenstein has explored the combinatory function of print, the book's joining between its covers diverse disciplines and far-ranging sources, as one of its chief features.[18] By absorbing and "glossing" a range of interacting printed texts and the ideas they disseminate, Blake's often satiric intertextuality emphasizes print's combinatory function and its implicit sanctioning of authority through typographic fixity and repetition. Blake's composite form, in fact, accommodates not only verbal "responses" to books but also offers the added dimension of graphically representing previously published books in order to evoke or parody their physical characteristics. Composite art joins physical form with representation, ideology with its material manifestations. Blake thus encourages his "readers" to reimagine not only existing texts but to associate the material form in which texts are produced and received with their themes and with the particular historical conditions attending their production.

On plate 4, "The *voice* of the Devil" (34; italics mine) inscribes a numbered list of three "Errors" in "All bibles or sacred codes," and then a numbered list of three "Contraries to these." A complex irony is at work involving graphic style and verbal content: the "voice" speaks in carefully enumerated and *printed* words; words printed, that is, in two senses since Blake crafts written characters, which are designed to look like they were produced typographically, and also produces writing literally imprinted on the page by his copper plates. As for "sacred codes," Marshall McLuhan reminds us that "uniformity of codes are the prime marks of literate and civilized societies."[19] Along with ideas committed to writing, "codes" also implies cryptic language, secret symbols, sets of rules or laws, and, as in "codex," books. We are reminded that in Blake's works the principle of repressive and exclusive reason, called

"Urizen," writes most of the books. "Lo!" Urizen declares in *The [First] Book of Urizen* "on / This rock, place with strong hand the Book / Of eternal brass, written in my solitude" (4: 32–33; 72); and in *The Four Zoas,* Urizen "rangd his books around him" (77: 19; 353) and is accused by Orc of sitting "fixd obdurate brooding . . . Writing thy books" (79: 10–11; 354). Indeed Blake is fond of emphasizing the material (and cultural) status of his works *as books* by calling them such: *The Book of Thel; The French Revolution. A Poem in Seven Books; The [First] Book of Urizen; The Book of Ahania; The Book of Los;* and *Milton: a Poem in 2 Books. Jerusalem,* though not labeled a "book," is nevertheless divided into four "chapters." Blake's frequent use of the word "book" extends beyond titles: in all his writings, "book" and its plural appear one hundred thirty times. It is also worth noting that "print" in its various permutations also appears over one hundred thirty times in Blake's writings.[20] Throughout his life, Blake consciously expressed ideas embodied by these words; yet more than any other of his works, the *Marriage* concentrates Blake's fascination with the expressive medium's power.

The *Marriage,* as I have argued, is a book about books. It is also a book against books or at least against received interpretations of existing books. Consider Blake's radical commentary on *Paradise Lost,* the Devil's correction of "Bibles or sacred codes," and the energetic and sometimes deliberately overstated "Proverbs of Hell" as correctives or at least alternatives to traditional proverbs and aphorisms. Writing itself provides the context for much of the writing and for portions of the visual field in Blake's book. Blake reminds us of this within his own context: the words "write," "writing," "wrote," "written," and "printing" appear thirteen times in the *Marriage.* Plates 4 (in minute detail) and 10 graphically depict acts of writing and reading.

The *Marriage of Heaven and Hell* is not only a book about and against books, but a book whose composite form deliberately reproduces certain typographic conventions, the impedimenta of the book, in order to parody them and ultimately to sensitize and perhaps even liberate us from the mental patterns they simultaneously represent and impose. Elizabeth Eisenstein describes this *esprit de systeme* in which "regularly numbered pages, punctuation marks, section breaks, running heads, indexes, and so forth helped reorder the thought of *all* readers."[21] Hence, on plate 21 a voice reduces Swedenborg's texts to the "Contents or Index of already publish'd books," highlighting two of printing technology's organizational features—tables of contents and indexes—that also express the internal logic of books. For Blake, such conventions enforced linear, rational thought, the inexorable logic of mechanical repetition that dulled the senses rather than urging them to participate in the text, a false textual authority, fixity, and deadening order.

IV

Two of the most important books of Blake's time, and works he likely knew, offer examples of just the kind of authority Blake evokes and manipulates in the *Marriage*. In the "Preface" to that great book comprised of portions of other books, the *Dictionary of the English Language* (1755), Samuel Johnson claims to impose order upon the chaos of language even as he wisely recognizes that language constantly undergoes change: "I found our speech copious without order," he writes, "and energetick without rules: wherever I turned my view, there was perplexity to be disentangled, and confusion to be regulated; choice was to be made out of boundless variety, without any established principles of selection."[22] He goes on wistfully, "Language is only the instrument of science, and words are but the signs of ideas: I wish, however, that the instrument might be less apt to decay, and that signs might be permanent, like the things which they denote" (2). In partial fulfillment of this impossible desire, Johnson designates one of the prime functions of lexicographer as "giving longevity" to language whose "own nature forbids to be immortal" (10). Johnson self-consciously acknowledges in the Preface the importance of his crucial decisions regarding orthography, etymologies, pronunciation, definitions, and whether a term is obsolete or current in determining the permanent shape of the English language, yet he never acknowledges the subtle power of his book's typographical form to order the reader's thoughts and affirm the authority of the ideas expressed.

Typographically, Johnson shores language against its ruins, ensuring at least a portion of the congruence between words and things that he desires. His book abstracts, orders, and idealizes language that it reduces to a limited number of words, each with a circumscribed number of "correct" meanings. Moreover, Johnson's *Dictionary* imposes logic on language visually: his book calls forth a panoply of type faces and regular typographic symbols to categorize neatly English words, making the language itself appear rational, orderly, reducible to two nicely arranged, bound volumes, pages ordered into two regular columns, running heads in large, bold capitals atop each page, numerals and indentation guiding the eye—language thus formally ordered and fixed in its meanings, to be pronounced as Johnson sees fit. We should also keep in mind that even as Johnson acknowledged the "boundless chaos of a living speech" as the basis for all language, Johnson's meanings and the lasting power of his exemplary authority derive from other books. As Alvin Kernan observes, the *"Dictionary* was a typical achievement of print, a language book made out of still other books that would determine the language of books still to be written."[23]

A quarter of a century earlier, Ephraim Chambers in his *Cyclopaedia; or, an Universal Dictionary of Arts and Sciences* (London, 1728) used dashes, brackets, superscript numerals referring to some forty-seven footnotes, and an array of type sizes and styles ordered into neat columns and spread across two pages to organize the plan of his work that represents, he claims, all "Knowledge" and by extension all that is knowable.[24] Eighteenth-century printing technology offered its authors new opportunities for codifying and distributing knowledge, and authors quickly took advantage of the medium. As Chambers explains, however, such opportunity was problematic, as he seeks, *de novo,* to elaborate "Knowledge" typographically in a single chart: "the difficulty lay in the form, and oeconomy of it; so to dispose such a multitude of materials, or not to make a confused heap of incoherent Parts, but one consistent Whole—and here it must be confessed there was little assistance to be had" (Preface, 2). Authors like Chambers and Blake are conscious of the dynamic relationships between readers and text engendered by developments in typography. For Chambers, communicating a sense of the organizational plan of his book, a construction itself made possible by typographic fixity and reproducibility, is essential, even if the complications of representing it are, in the end, flawed: "The plan of the work, then, I hope, may be allowed to be good; whatever exceptions be taken to the execution of it" (iii). Arraying categories graphically that purport to represent "knowledge" and then accurately broadcasting that order typographically carried an epistemological burden, for the ultimate purpose of the *Cyclopedia* (and its chart) involved "forming a sound mind, i.e. [readers] acquiring a system of perceptions and notions agreeing to the system of things, or in the relations thereto intended by its author" (xxv). The systematic elaboration of "knowledge" graphically was intended by Chambers to recapitulate itself in the mind of the reader. As passages from Johnson and Chambers show, eighteenth-century authors fashioned typography in deliberate attempts to pattern readers' thoughts. Blake constantly and deliberately frees language from single meaning. For him English is that "stubborn structure, rough basement," upon which he built a multidimensional structure of words, visible images, and words *as* visible images, a polysemous grammar whose minute particulars and overall design urge us to enter into and "play" it."[25]

V

Urging our involvement in the *Marriage,* Blake depicts (and in part parodies) typographic symbols and ritual, specific prompts for the experienced reader of books. A few concrete examples of Blake's evocation and manipulation of certain fundamental elements of print technology at this point may prove helpful. The *Marriage* begins with a richly colored title page upon which a couple embrace below ground level while clouds unfold and flames ascend upward and to the right. Letters appear across this remarkable scene, heralding Blake's illuminated art. The words "THE," "HEAVEN," and "HELL" arrest us in particular: quite evidently written by hand, they parody large block letter type, and contrast markedly with the other words of the title, which are written in flowing script. Calligraphy parodies typography, though Blake's composite form is really neither. This entry into the work, like the ways "into" any plate in composite art, compounds contrary meaning with its material production.

Like *Paradise Lost,* the text begins with an "Argument." But in the *Marriage,* this Miltonic prose form is rendered in verse, a condition signalled typographically. "The Argument" here offers a cryptic, synoptic vision of human life prior to the coming of the prophecy voiced in the *Marriage of Heaven and Hell.* Significantly, the first and last stanzas of "The Argument," as well as the title word "The" are colored red—the printer's conventional "rubric," from which our sense of the word derives. Visual framing and repetition thus communicate the thematic cycles of displacement that the poem presents. The *Marriage* ends with verse headed "A Song of Liberty" followed by lines headed "Chorus." Verses of the "Song," like biblical verse, are conspicuously numbered, another hand-inscribed reference to what had become, by the eighteenth century, purely typographic convention. Throughout the work, audacious and visually distinct section headings, such as "The voice of the Devil" "Proverbs of Hell," and "A Memorable Fancy" (parodies of Swedenborg's "Memorable Relations" that Blake inscribes five times) seem to express conventional functions and form—

chapter headings and other divisions of preexisting books constituting their internal principles of order. Yet in the context created by the *Marriage,* such references often "announce" ideas that clash with the form of the "announcement." Blake's method actively courts paradox and demands interpretation.

Blake's complex technology not only calls attention to itself but also invokes, almost nostalgically, features of the technology with which it competes. On eleven plates (6, 8, 9, 12, 16, 17, 18, 19, 21, 22, and 23) Blake inscribes either complete or abbreviated catchwords. Philip Gaskell has observed that "although the full use of catchwords was general in English and in most continental printing until the late eighteenth century, they were not always considered necessary."[26] Surely Blake, who hand printed and colored every plate on sheets that he then collected into books, would not require them, a fact underscored when we recall that the work was not being mass produced. (Indeed, only nine copies of the *Marriage* are known to exist, and there is no evidence even suggesting that many more were produced.) It is also safe to assume that Blake was not trying to emulate the appearance of typographically produced books for commercial purposes. Rather, I believe these catchwords may constitute a visual spur to readers to read on or perhaps a linguistic device bridging one plate with another or, closer to my argument, a parody of the business of commercial printing. Eighteenth-century print shops apportioned tasks among many different workers, with the result that workers were dissociated from the products of their labor. Consequently, a device built into the text itself was required in order to ensure the proper sequencing of pages in books. The appearance of catchwords in Blake's printing reminds us that all other authors relinquished control over the material production of their work to a commercial enterprise, and the economic imperatives of a profitable publishing operation mitigated against painstaking attention to details by workers who could not possibly identify with the products of their labor.[27] The technology of print organized materials according to its economic requirements and limitations, a condition Blake understood and struggled against. The *Marriage* records the trace of that struggle.

VI

A year before beginning work on the *Marriage,* Blake described three modes of human utterance in the "Introduction" to *Songs of Innocence:* piping, singing, and writing. Along with plate 15 of the

Marriage, with which this essay concludes, the "Introduction" represents Blake's most developed verbal depiction of writing's relation to music and voice and of certain ramifications of writing as a technology. The "introduction" to *Songs of Innocence,* if not also to the "state" of innocence, involves a progression. The poem advances from the Piper "piping down the valleys wild," imposing a kind of order upon the wilderness by his music, to his singing a "song about a Lamb," finally to his writing "In a book that all may read" his "happy songs." The child, who requests the Piper to pipe, sing, and write, disappears, significantly, after ordering the book. The book extends the author's voice in space and time and joins his text to a world of texts, to the real and ideal library of all "books." The price for writing's stability, fixity, and permanence, Blake's Piper unself-consciously acknowledges, is that he must also extend himself into the self-created technology of writing. The results imply a process, a point that Blake emphasizes graphically by repeating the initial words in four successive lines as well as anaphorically and grammatically, by invoking a parallel sequence of active verbs:

> And I pluck'd a hollow reed.
> And I made a rural pen,
> And I stain'd the water clear,
> And I wrote my happy songs
> Every child may joy to hear.
>
> (4:16–20; 7)

Every child "may" joy, but the author, distanced from what was originally a scene of oral communication, will not have this, or any other, response available to him. Breath in the written song has been reduced to individual letters and words, to breathless speech. In printed texts, as Blake knew, a system of repeatable individual letters fragments words even further. Perhaps for this reason so many individual written letters in *Songs* and subsequent works in composite art are joined as if produced calligraphically. They also trail spiralling lines, implying a flow and unity in writing that typography denies, even as it enforces order and linear progression. In this sense, Blake's composite plates represent the human hand's response to the mechanical press. Staining the water also suggests the trading of clarity for fixity and permanence. This trade, of course, need not imply a diminution of joy since safely inscribing the song preserves it. And the final line—"Every child may joy to hear"—in one sense at least promises the possibility of continuing reanimation of the verses as they are sung by others; though the "may," of course, also offers the possibility that although available to future listeners, not all hearing them will "joy." Nevertheless, the author no longer has his audience before him: he thus loses the feedback of immediate responses to his song. Even the most subtle frowns, or quizzical glances, or the facial expressions of boredom or joy that might have led him to adjust his message are no longer present. He also loses the ability to control the communication of variables such as tone, gesture, cadence, repetition—in short, he loses spontaneity and the other elements of reciprocal discourse. Print extends an author's voice abroad, but without the author's "presence." Walter Benjamin, in his classic essay "The Work of Art in the Age of Mechanical Reproduction," terms this presence in an original work of art "aura," and he stresses the fundamental role of mechanical reproduction in its "withering."[28] The art work mechanically reproduced becomes separated from oral tradition, from the traditional relationship between author and listener or perceiver, and, most important for Blake (if not for his "innocent" speaker), works begin to be designed for the agency of reproduction.

Graphic reproduction and its sister trade, print, during the eighteenth century produced a culture that for Blake reduced poetry and vision to discrete, fixed, regular, repeatable letters. The typographical *system* (even down to the forging of the types themselves as we will see Blake explore in the *Marriage*), diminishes the possibility for prophetic utterance. Literally, speech is divided into sense-dulling black marks on white paper whose effect is to distance—indeed, alienate—reader from original utterance and from minute significances that only the hand can inscribe. In reading a typeset work, such as the present text, we have learned not to concentrate upon the actual words (or even, where present, the material form of printed designs) as living embodiments of expression, but only upon the messages "behind" them. The perceiver cannot in any meaningful sense become involved with the material representation of meaning or with materiality *as meaning*. For Blake, who worked intimately with burrin, copper, ink, paint, brushes, and designs, the typographical system itself emphasizes linear movement and the corporeal eye.

In the *Marriage* (and his other composite art works) Blake "rouzes the faculties to act," partially combating the fixity and closure of print. Encountering these works, as Blake's students have argued during the past two decades, one cannot, for example, passively "receive" Blake's deliberately polysemous language networks or reduce to a single meaning the work's richly detailed plates. One cannot profitably or even comfortably "skim" the intricate interlinear and marginal designs or the large graphics and the text as one might a typeset work. Indeed, Blake's art demands a very different kind of "reading" than do works produced in letterpress. Each of the renderings of a work in composite art is unique, requiring us to scrutinize each rendering in order, ideally, to "read" any particular work." In fact, David Erdman and two of his students, who have scrutinized each of the nine extant copies of the *Marriage,* comparing one with another, fill forty-five pages in a large format book describing and interpreting merely their "illuminations" (saying little about rhetorical, discursive, historical, intertextual, contextual, and other pertinent issues).[29] Of course, what we may legitimately assert as thematically significant or true about differences between and among renderings remains problematic.[30]

On the fifteenth plate of the *Marriage* we "enter" the caverns of typographical creation as the printing system, anatomized in its minute particulars, becomes theme. A speaker describes the method of "knowledge transmission" as it occurs in six chambers, in one sense parodying the six days of creation (40). For Blake, the accumulated "knowledge" that fuels his culture takes typographical form. This rich plate has been interpreted variously. Mary Lynn Johnson and John Grant summarize the range of readings succinctly in their note to it: "this allegory on the transmission of knowledge refers both to the conceptual and productive aspects of creativity, to the cleansing of the senses, and to the process of etching."[31] David Erdman has outlined its primary references to Blake's actual process of illuminated printing, observing that "Blake not only sublimated his description of the work processes but departed from their natural order."[32] Without quarrelling with the accuracy of the wide range of previous interpretations Blake's suggestive plate has evoked, another complementary version of the plate emerges from a materialist reading of the *Marriage,* an interpretation whose direction my reader has doubtless anticipated. For Blake, the deadening effects of print, which we have been considering, can be traced to the very process of casting type, to properties that inhere in the most basic elements of the typographical system. I want to suggest that Blake's most profound comments on printing occur on the fifteenth plate of the *Marriage* as Blake anatomizes the casting of the individual type, revealing in the individual casting the forms of error it sponsors.

Blake surely knew that in his day each type piece was described

in human terms—a kind of human anatomy of a cast metal structure
in which types were classified according to "body" (or point) size,
and parts of individual types were called "shoulders," "feet,"
"face," and, significantly for Blake's description of the hoary writer
Urizen, "beard."[33] The typographic system was thus self-legitimiz-
ing and self-reifying. Peopled with inhuman forms, the printshop in
"hell" on plate 15 of the *Marriage* depicts the ways in which such
human features have been imputed to a system that truncates
complete human communication. "I was in a **Printing house** [in-
scribed in bold letters on the plate] in Hell & saw the method in
which knowledge is transmitted from generation to generation," a
"voice" begins. The **"Printing house"** here is enormously powerful,
as it is the locus for the "transmission" of the culture's knowledge
at the same time as its "method"—typography—conditions the
"knowledge" that will be transmitted "from generation to generation." In the biblical sense Blake often invokes, this **"Printing
house"** fuels the *world of generation* with "ideas" delivered in a
particular form; it thus perpetuates and even increases the knowledge that continually reanimates this world. As the remainder of
plate 15 dramatizes, the etching of the individual punch and hand
work "hollowing" the matrix in the "first chamber" ossifies into the
inflexible repetitiveness of the finished matrix into which type is
"cast" in the "fifth chamber." Perhaps Blake is suggesting that
"hollow" matrices produce hollow messages? Similarly, the apocalyptic activity of the "Lions of flaming fire raging around & melt-
ing the metals into living fluids" in the fourth chamber is abruptly
transformed in the next chamber, where "Unnam'd forms"—possibly the printer's "forme" that holds the chases full of type—"cast
the metals into the expanse." Once "cast"—and we may understand this simultaneously as the process of pouring molten metal
and as the distribution, the casting out, of books—the finished
product petrifies: "There they were receiv'd by Men . . . and took
the forms of books & were arranged in libraries." Such arrangement of "received" and determinate works suggests the taming,
perhaps even the imprisonment of living ideas in fixed forms, or
perhaps the "Men" themselves take the "forms of books," becoming what they behold, and are arranged in the libraries—or specialized categories—that print makes possible. Either way, the
point with respect to typographic reproduction remains the same.
Blake signals a direction for this plate by illustrating it with an eagle
clutching a serpent in its talons, a traditional symbol of unity, and
perhaps a vision of the workers in the text above it transformed.

The entire plate becomes, in this sense, illuminated art's answer to the print culture it anatomizes and constantly struggles against.

In introductory verses addressed "To the Public" in *Jerusalem,* (a portion of which I cited earlier in this essay), Blake voices the power of printed communication if only formed by a sufficiently capacious technology. As the *Marriage* may be seen to represent, in Northrop Frye's phrase, the "Beethovenish coda" to eighteenth-century satires on the book and its technology, so the beginning of *Jerusalem* seems the perfect coda to Blake's anatomy of books and writing in the *Marriage* and a fit threshold for the ninety-seven illuminated plates of *Jerusalem* that follow.[34] Blake again invokes the image of the cave, here "awful" and "unfathomd," suggesting a quite different range of associations from those evoked by the Dragons' "cave" of the *Marriage.* Blake's "types" here shall not be "vain" (hollow, fruitless, self-directed), mass-produced, and inter-changeable metal castings or even the alphabetical icons they represent, but types of human life delivered without recourse to the typographical system. The difference is one of attitude toward different kinds of writing and printing and their potential for engendering genuine change:

> Reader! [*lover*] of books! [*lover*] of heaven,
> And of that God from whom [*all books are given,*]
> Who in mysterious Sinais awful cave
> To Man the wond'rous art of writing gave,
> Again he speaks in thunder and in fire!
> Thunder of Thought, & flames of fierce desire:
> Even from the depths of Hell his voice I hear,
> Within the unfathomd caverns of my Ear.
> Therefore I print; nor vain my types shall be:
> Heaven, Earth & Hell, henceforth shall live in harmony.
> (3: 1–10; 145)

In this remarkable passage Blake suggests a union among speech, hearing, and "the wond'rous art" of writing, Blake's own form of printing. For Blake the transmission of aural into visual communication occurs directly, without mediation, from the divine imagination to the prophetic engraving to the reader who is a "[*lover*] of books." Speech is realized directly as hearing: "Therefore," as a consequence of this unity, Blake prints. He creates efficacious "types" of mental figures on plates that formally disavow association with typography. Blake's unique printing, he claims, also has transformative power to bring about universal "harmony."

VII

Blake's grand hymn to his printing method as an agent of progressive change may seem naive from the perspective of the late twentieth century. After all, since the romantics, we have heard time and again practitioners of new art forms (and their attendant technologies) advance often extravagant claims for their art. We have also seen communication technologies usurped by the powerful or by aspirants to power during this century in order to manipulate and deceive. The work of art in the age of electronic reproduction is viewed by many primarily as an extension of ideology and gender, generally triangulating relations among power, language, and meaning; or as language itself, a "text"; or generically related to the historical enterprise of which it forms a part; or as a complex expression of "culture"; or as an expression of a socially constructed institution. Regardless of the "approach" to art one takes, almost no one believes any more, with Blake, that art actually *does* anything. We would do well to remember, however, that Wordsworth, Coleridge, Shelley, Hazlitt, Byron, and Keats, in varying degrees to be sure, understood manifestations of technology as the expression of ideas or systems of belief in physical form, just as they also understood institutions as human constructs: "what is now proved," reads one of the Proverbs of Hell, "was once, only imagin'd." Of all romantic creations, Blake's art most fully represents the artist's struggle to realize in his own technology the intricate network of relationships that exist among powerful institutions, the technologies upon which they are based, and the psychologies—or ideological systems, if you will—that engender and energize them. In these senses, among others, romanticism is very much the precursor, even the foundation or, to borrow an older but perhaps more expressive term, the soul of our own age's preoccupation with relating the manifest forms of human life to patterns of thought that engender them. While we may not attribute to art the transformative power in which Blake believed, recalling an age during which such belief was possible may prove liberating. We may even find ourselves moved to conviction: "The conviction grows on me," writes Anatole Broyard, "—I can already hear the derisive laughter—that it may be the business of art to make the world safe for romanticism."

NOTES

1. "Can Art Make the World Safe for Romanticism?" *New York Times Book Review* (7 February 1988), 13. My reference to Broyard in the final paragraph of this essay also derives from p. 13.

2. See, for example, Thomas L. Hankins, *Science and the Enlightenment,* (Cambridge: Cambridge University Press, 1985), chap. 1 and M. H. Abram's classic studies, *The Mirror and the Lamp: Romantic Theory and the Critical Tradition* (New York: Oxford University Press, 1953) and *Natural Supernaturalism: Tradition and Revolution in Romantic Literature* (New York: W. W. Norton, 1971).

3. Raymond Williams, *Culture and Society 1780–1950* (New York: Columbia University Press, 1958), 31. I note subsequent citations parenthetically in the text.

4. For a remarkably full study of the contexts within which romantic poets' ideas of poetry were conditioned and developed, see Stuart Curran, *Poetic Form and British Romanticism* (New York: Oxford University Press, 1986).

5. For a recreation of the dinner and toast, see Walter Jackson Bate, *John Keats* (Cambridge, Mass.: Harvard University Press, 1963), 270. I quote "Lamia," Part II, from *The Poems of John Keats,* ed. Jack Stillinger (Cambridge, Mass.: Belknap Press of Harvard University Press, 1978), lines 234–37; pp. 472–73.

6. Humphrey Jennings's *Pandaemonium 1660–1886: The Coming of the Machine as Seen by Contemporary Observers,* ed. Mary-Lou Jennings and Charles Madge (New York: The Free Press, 1985), compiles such writings which become, according to Jennings, "a continuous narrative or 'film' on the Industrial Revolution" (xvii). The transvaluation embedded in this description, prompted by our ability now to scan as a single "book" thousands of documents written under various circumstances in widely ranging genres and modes, highlights the complex problems critics face in "understanding" and interpreting the impact of technological change on those who experienced it directly and of attempting to do so in media of communication that are themselves technologies.

7. See W. J. T. Mitchell, "Visible Language: Blake's Wond'rous Art of Writing," in *Romanticism and Contemporary Criticism,* ed. Morris Eaves and Michael Fischer (Ithaca: Cornell University Press, 1986), 46–86; and James K. Chandler, *Wordsworth's Second Nature: A Reading of the Poetry and Politics* (Chicago: University of Chicago Press, 1984), esp. chap. X.

8. *Printing Technology, Letters, and Samuel Johnson* (Princeton, N.J.: Princeton University Press, 1987), 52.

9. On the relations between printing technology and the elaborate construction of books by romantic poets, see Neil Fraistat, *The Poem and the Book: Interpreting Collections of Romantic Poetry* (Chapel Hill: University of North Carolina Press, 1985), 3–23.

10. I quote Blake from David V. Erdman, ed., *The Complete Poetry and Prose of William Blake,* rev. ed., Commentary by Harold Bloom (Berkeley and London: University of California Press, 1982), noted parenthetically in the text by plate and, where appropriate, line numbers, or for *The Four Zoas,* by page and line number, followed by the page location in Erdman. This quotation: 3:1–2 and 10; 145. References to elements on composite plates derive from *The Marriage of Heaven and Hell,* Introduction and Commentary by Sir Geoffrey Keynes (London: Oxford University Press in Association with the Trianon Press, 1975).

The fullest study of Blake's printmaking process is Robert N. Essick, *William Blake Printmaker* (Princeton, N.J.: Princeton University Press, 1980), which should be read in conjunction with Joseph Viscomi, *The Art of William Blake's Illuminated Prints* (Manchester: Manchester Etching Workshop, 1983).

11. Mann offers a "materialist reading" of Blake in which "production is . . . thetic" in "Apocalypse and Recuperation: Blake and the Maw of Commerce," *ELH*, 52 (1985): 1–32; above citation, 2.

12. I quote "Blakean Zen," *Studies in Romanticism*, 24 (1985): 189. Among the many responses provoked by the *Marriage*, the most useful in developing my approach have been those cited specifically in the notes, along with Morton D. Paley, *Energy and the Imagination: A Study of the Development of Blake's Thought* (Oxford: Clarendon Press, 1970), esp. "Appendix A."; David V. Erdman, *Blake: Prophet Against Empire* (Princeton, N.J.: Princeton University Press, 1977), chap. 8, and Erdman, annotator, *The Illuminated Blake* (Garden City, N.Y.: Anchor/Doubleday, 1974); Joseph Anthony Wittreich, Jr., *Angel of Apocalypse: Blake's Idea of Milton* (Madison, Wisc.: University of Wisconsin Press, 1974), esp. chap. 3; John E. Grant's note, "Regeneration in *The Marriage of Heaven and Hell*" in Alvin H. Rosenfeld, ed., *William Blake: Essays for S. Foster Damon* (Providence, R.I.: Brown University Press, 1969), 366–67, and Grant's brief debate with W. J. T. Mitchell in *Visionary Forms Dramatic*, ed. Erdman and Grant (Princeton, N.J.: Princeton University Press, 1970), 63–64; and Lawrence Lipking, *The Life of the Poet: Beginning and Ending Poetic Careers* (Chicago and London: University of Chicago Press, 1981), 34–47.

13. See, for example, chaps. 4 and 5 of Walter J. Ong's *Orality and Literacy: The Technologizing of the Word* (London: Methuen, 1982).

14. "The *Dunciad* as Mock-Book," *Huntington Library Quarterly* 35 (1971–72): 30. For more on the history of the book as trope, see Ernst Robert Curtius, *European Literature and the Latin Middle Ages,* trans. Willard R. Trask (London: Routledge and Kegan Paul, 1953), chap. 16 (302–47). On Blake's satire, see Robert F. Gleckner, "Blake and Satire," *Wordsworth Circle* 8 (1977), 311–26, and specifically on the *Marriage* and satire, consult Leslie Tannenbaum, "Blake's News from Hell: *The Marriage of Heaven and Hell* and the Lucianic Tradition," *ELH* 43 (1976): 74–99.

15. See W. J. T. Mitchell, *Blake's Composite Art* (Princeton, N.J.: Princeton University Press, 1978), esp. 3–39.

16. Despite his often vague and excessively modish language, McLuhan still has much to offer in *The Gutenberg Galaxy: The Making of Tyographical Man* (Toronto: University of Toronto Press, 1962) and in *Understanding Media* (New York: McGraw-Hill, 1964), books informed by McLuhan's study of Blake. See also Lucien Febvre and Henri-Jean Martin, *The Coming of the Book,* trans. David Gerard (London: NLB, 1976), esp. chap. 8 (248–332), and Ong, cited in note 13.

17. On Blake, see the essay by Mann, cited above, n. 2; Morris Eaves, "Blake and the Artistic Machine: An Essay in Decorum and Technology," *PMLA* 92 (1977): 903–27; and Michael Ferber, *The Social Vision of William Blake* (Princeton, N.J.: Princeton University Press, 1985). Two useful collections of essays on the cultural impact of books during Blake's age have appeared during the past decade: *Books and their Readers in Eighteenth-Century England,* ed. Isabel Rivers (Leicester and New York: Leicester University Press and St. Martins Press, 1982); and Raymond Birn, ed., *The Printed Word in the Eighteenth Century:* a special issue of *Eighteenth-Century Studies* 17 (1984).

18. In *The Printing Press as an Agent of Change,* 2 vols. (Cambridge, Eng.: Cambridge University Press, 1979). Many of the ideas elaborated in this two-volume work Eisenstein condenses in her 1983 Cambridge University Press *The*

Printing Revolution in Early Modern Europe. Walter J. Ong's *Orality and Literacy: The Technologizing of the Word* (New York and London: Methuen, 1982) counterpoints differences "between the ways of managing knowledge and verbalization in primary oral cultures . . . and in cultures deeply affected by the use of writing" (1).

19. McLuhan, *Understanding Media,* 87.

20. My source is the 2-vol. *Concordance to the Writings of William Blake,* ed. David V. Erdman, *et al.* (Ithaca: Cornell University Press, 1967).

21. Elizabeth Eisenstein, "Some Conjectures about the Impact of Printing on Western Society and Thought: A Preliminary Report," *Journal of Modern History* 40 (1968): 15.

22. Pages of the "Preface" are unnumbered; here I cite p. 1. Subsequent citations appear parenthetically in my text, for convenience carrying my numeration.

23. Kernan, *Johnson,* 197. See also Kernan's *The Imaginary Library: An Essay on Literature and Society* (Princeton, N.J.: Princeton University Press, 1982). On the literary culture of this period and its often antagonistic or self-consciously detached relationship with society, see Raymond Williams, *Culture and Society: 1780–1950.*

24. I refer to the first edition; in the 2d. ed., 1738, which appeared in folio, the table occupies one page.

25. For the fullest exploration of the dimensions of Blake's language, see Nelson Hilton, *Literal Imagination: Blake's Vision of Words* (Berkeley, Los Angeles, and London: University of California Press, 1983).

26. *A New Introduction to Bibliography* (New York and Oxford: Oxford University Press, 1972), 53.

27. Kernan, *Johnson,* 55ff., explains how, to assure profitability, presses during the eighteenth century were driven to run with as few interruptions as possible. Type, always in short supply, had to be endlessly recycled, so that new jobs awaited the completion of books in press.

28. First published in 1936, the essay appears in *Illuminations,* trans. Harry Zohn (New York: Schocken, 1968), 217–51.

29. See "Reading the Illuminations of Blake's *Marriage of Heaven and Hell,*" by Erdman with Tom Dargan and Marlene Deverell-Van Meter in *William Blake: Essays in Honour of Sir Geoffrey Keynes,* ed. Morton D. Paley and Michael Phillips (Oxford: Clarendon Press, 1973), 162–207.

30. On the problematics, see Robert N. Essick, "William Blake, William Hamilton, and the Materials of Graphic Meaning," *ELH* 52 (1985): 833–72.

31. *Blake's Poetry and Designs* (New York: Norton Critical Editions, 1979), 94.

32. "A Temporary Report on Texts of Blake," in *Blake: Essays for Damon,* 411.

33. Philip Gaskell, in his *New Introduction to Bibliography* (cited in note 26), diagrams the "body parts" of type on p. 9 and discusses them in detail on pp. 9–39.

34. *Fearful Symmetry: A Study of William Blake* (Princeton, N.J.: Princeton University Press, 1947), 201.

Jules Romains, *Unanimisme,* and the Poetics of Urban Systems

ROSALIND WILLIAMS

Over the last century, a human life has become a machine for burning petroleum. . . . It makes no sense to talk about cars and power plants and so on as if they were something apart from our lives—they *are* our lives.
—Bill McKibben
"Reflections (The End of Nature)"
The New Yorker (11 September 1989), p. 92

Since the Industrial Revolution, the contrast between organism and mechanism has been a fundamental theme in Western thought. Ralph Waldo Emerson, Thomas Carlyle, Matthew Arnold, John Ruskin, and William Morris, among many others, repeatedly propose "the organic" and "the mechanical" as opposite poles of knowledge and value.[1] It is also true that since the Industrial Revolution, Western literature has explored the territory between these two poles, discovering that they might not be so far apart after all. Writers like Charles Dickens, Herman Melville, and Émile Zola (to cite three obvious examples) show how human beings can become mechanized and how technological devices can assume organic qualities. We are now beginning to recognize how prophetic such writers are. The merging of organic and mechanical creations is no longer a topic of interest primarily to cultural and literary scholars; this process has earth-altering practical effects, as natural cycles have become progressively interwoven with technological ones.

Historians of technology—whose methods and vocabularies are quite different from those of imaginative writers—are still shaping a conceptual language to describe this process of interpenetration. These historians are more and more often using *systems* rather than *machines* as their basic unit of analysis. In theory, the concept of technological system is certainly broad enough to include both mechanical and organic components. In practice, however, the concept is usually used to describe a mixture of technological and social elements; natural elements tend to be considered "external" factors outside the system.[2]

In *The Myth of the Machine* (1966, 1970) Lewis Mumford proposed a more specific term, the *megamachine,* to describe a system with both technological and organic components. According to Mumford, this system was first devised by the ancient Egyptians to assemble and organize the manpower required to build the great pyramids. This megamachine was, in Mumford's words, "a great labor machine . . . its components, though made of human bone, nerve, and muscle, were reduced to their bare mechanical elements and rigidly standardized for the performance of their limited tasks." The concept is provocative, but its scholarly influence has been limited just because of its strongly ideological overtones. For Mumford, "megamachine" is a term of abuse. The pyramid building megamachine, he asserted, is the earliest working model for all later complex machines including the American "pentagon of power," a nuclear-armed and potentially catastrophic version of the Egyptian system.[3]

This essay will describe and analyze another concept of a system wherein organic and mechanical life have merged. This concept is far more positive than that proposed by Mumford; it was formulated fully a half century earlier than the megamachine (even though its originator was born only ten years before Mumford); and finally, it was first advanced as a literary cause rather than as a mode of historical analysis. The concept is the *unanime,* and the literary movement based on the apprehension of these partly mechanical, partly organic groups is called *unanimisme.* The movement was announced in a 1905 manifesto in the French literary journal *Le Penseur.* The manifesto was written by twenty-year-old Louis Farigoule, who later became famous, at least in France, under the *nom de plume* Jules Romains.

In unfurling the banner of *unanimisme,* Romains proclaimed that writers of his generation should take as their theme the new social groups created by the interaction between human beings and their technologies in contemporary urban life. In his *unanimiste* manifesto he explained

> The current tendency for people to gather in cities; the uninterrupted development of social relationships; the very strong, close ties established among men by duties, occupations, and common pleasures; and

always greater encroachment of the public on the private, of the collective on the individual: these are facts that some may deplore, but that no one denies.

It is impossible that such a way of living would not bring about a corresponding way of feeling.[4]

As we shall see, many writers of Romains's day assumed that their major challenge was to find new literary forms to express new technological forms. Romains defined the challenge somewhat differently. For him, the central literary problem was to express new *social* forms, and for this reason, Romains did not join the aesthetic debate, which engaged so many of his contemporaries, over the compatibility of beauty and utility. Is an automobile beautiful? Romains did not care. His poetry describes not the appearances but the rhythms of modern life; not objects, but environment; not the automobile, but traffic. He is the poet of urban systems. While the technologies of production are nearly absent from Romains's work, he is fascinated by the new ways of living and feeling he saw developing along with new systems of communication and transportation. The dominant technological presence in *unanimiste* poetry is the subtle pattern of city vehicles weaving an ever-changing yet predictable network. In the life of the *unanime* the rhythms of human beings mesh with those of technology; indeed, their common rhythm *is* the *unanime*. Romains expresses these rhythms in the language of fluid dynamics: images of circling and ebbing, of crisscrossing and intersecting, of whirling and dispersing. In the flowing universe of *unanimisme,* the physical and mental cycles of human beings have become intertwined with the cycles of the technologies they have created.

This essay will begin with a brief biographical sketch of Romains, who is not well known on this side of the Atlantic and whose fame has faded even in France since his death in 1972. Next, we shall take a longer look at the technological environment in which he grew up and that was so significant in inspiring *unanimisme*. Since his early poetry—his freshest, sweetest, and most *unanimiste* writing—has not been translated into English, I will then present my own unpretentious rendition of some key passages.[5] Finally, I will analyze *unanimisme* for its assumptions about the interpenetration of organism and mechanism in the landscapes of modern life.

The main purpose of this essay is not so much to describe a writer, or even his poetry (though both are well worth the attention), but rather to explore the theoretical framework, long associated with Marxist cultural analysis, of technological base and literary superstructure.[6] The validity of the base-superstructure formula must be an issue, implicitly or explicitly, in any study of the relationship between technology and literature. This is not so true of studies that attempt to relate literature and science; in that relationship, both elements are often assumed, however uncritically, to be "superstructural." As noted in the introduction to this volume, both literature and science are habitually perceived as text-based, as part of "higher culture" rather than "everyday life," and as aloof from immediate, practical goals. When we are dealing with technology and literature, on the other hand, the differences are far more evident than the similarities. Technology is material, "everyday," practical; literature is verbal, "special," noninstrumental. While these dichotomies are very much open to question, the obvious differences between technological and literary creations challenge us to define the relationship between the very different ways they are produced.

The Marxist formula proposes that we begin with material production and analyze literary production as a dependent variable: a real and given world, an imaginative and contingent response. As we shall see in the earlier biographical sections of this essay, the origins of *unanimisme* are indeed intimately related to technological changes that were transforming Paris so rapidly and markedly. These changes can certainly be understood as the technological basis of Romains's *unanimiste* superstructure. This is not a sufficient reading of *unanimisme,* however. As we shall see later on in the essay, the relationship between mechanical and organic life expressed so eloquently in *unanimisme* is more than a response to technological events. In a far more active way, *unanimisme* affirms and even promotes the same assumptions that inspired the policymakers largely responsible for those events. In other words, the technological environment is not just a material given, which in turn inspires a literary perception. The technological world itself is shaped by imagination and metaphor—in this case, by the visions of a living city and a dead nature. We are dealing here with a single social world, at once conceptual and technological.

*   *   *

Jules Romains (1885–1972) was the only child of *déracinés,* provincials from the region of Velay who moved to the city when Jules's father became an *instituteur* at a lycée on Montmartre. Jules grew up in the family's apartment on the south slope of the butte. He was a brilliant student, first at elementary school on Montmartre and later at the lycée Condorcet in downtown Paris. He was also an aspiring poet, choosing his pen name when he was only a teenager and publishing his first poem under that name when he was seventeen.[7]

When Romains published his 1905 manifesto, it drew no particular attention; dozens of such declarations were appearing in those years.[8] But a few years later, when Romains published *La Vie unanime* (1908), his first volume of *unanimiste* poems, he won both attention and praise. In the first issue of *La Nouvelle Revue Française,* André Gide wrote, "I consider this newcomer's book one of the most remarkable and significant that has been given us by the rising generation." Gustave Kahn, Émile Verhaeren, and Guillaume Apollinaire also praised the volume extravagantly.[9]

Romains's career and that of *unanimisme* were launched together. In later life he marveled how, in the three or four years following the publication of *La Vie unanime,* he managed to do so much: completing two *licenses* (one in literature and one in biology) from the École normale supérieure; achieving his *agrégation* in philosophy from the Sorbonne in 1909 and then embarking upon a teaching career; carrying on an active social life of salons, dinners, and readings in Parisian literary circles, as well as participating in an artistic commune, the Abbaye de Créteil; and all the while continuing to write *unanimiste* poetry [*Premier livre de prières* (1909), *Deux poèmes* and *Un être en marche* (1910), and *Puissances de Paris* (1911)] as well as *unanimiste* theater [*L'Armée dans la ville* (1911)] and prose [*Manuel de déification* (1910) and *Mort de quelqu'un* (1911)].

This happy and productive life collapsed when war broke out in August 1914. Romains, then twenty-nine years old, was called to active duty, but he suffered a nervous collapse and was hospitalized in 1915 from mid-July to September. After being discharged from the army at the end of 1915, Romains convalesced and eventually returned to teaching in Paris in mid-1916. There he wrote the long poem *Europe,* which proclaimed that the Continent was now the supreme *unanime* and which appealed to all Europeans not to let it die. To publish this poem at the height of wartime patriotic fervor, when pacifism was equated with treason, took considerable courage.[10]

In 1919 Romains ended his university career to devote himself exclusively to writing. In 1923 his play *Knock* made its Paris debut; in subsequent years this supremely witty, fast-paced farce was staged countless times around the globe. By the later 1920s Romains had an international reputation and regularly attended writers' conferences in Europe, the United States, and the Middle East. He began to participate in PEN, the international writers' association, and later served as its president for many years. In 1928 Romains purchased an elegant estate in Touraine, where he began work on the first volume of *Les Hommes de bonne volonté* [*Men of Good Will*], which appeared in 1932. Twenty-six more volumes followed, adding up to a jumbo (three million words) series of novels giving a panoramic view of European society in the early twentieth century.

Since World War I Romains had continued to reiterate the theme of an underlying, common European culture. Whatever the virtues of this theme in shaping *Les Hommes de bonne volonté*, it led him into some unfortunate dabbling in diplomacy in the 1930s that more resembled appeasement than pacifism.[11] Only with the fall of France did Romains give up hope in European-wide *unanimisme*. He left the country in June 1940 (with his second wife, who was Jewish), settling first in New York City and later in Mexico City. His actions during the war went far to salvage his reputation. He consistently supported the Free French and General de Gaulle, and as president of PEN, he worked tirelessly to rally writers to the Allied cause.

Returning home after the war, Romains was elected to the Académie française in 1946. The same year saw the publication of the last volume of *Les Hommes de bonne volonté*. From then on, Romains traveled widely and wrote primarily reminiscences and essays on general social themes. Since his death in August 1972, at the age of eighty-six, Romains's memory has been carefully tended by admiring friends and family. In general, however, his reputation has declined. Neither revered nor reviled, Jules Romains now dwells in the purgatory of the ignored.

*   *   *

Romains is to some extent a victim of his own later fame, which has overshadowed his earlier achievements. If he had died in 1911 or 1912, Romains once remarked, his poetry and poetic theories "would have merited more attention."[12] In order to give *unanimisme* the attention it is due, we must leave behind the grand old man of French letters and return to a vanished Paris, Paris of the Belle Époque, to recover the young man in the young century. Romains himself recalled that epoch in his speech accepting his seat in the Académie française:

The great city breathed around us and through us. Its streets were the paths of our promenade. . . . The rumors of its thick quarters, of its distant railroad stations, the distant vibration of its fanlike suburbs, accompanied us with a perpetual music. In the streets of the city, in its swirling intersections, we learned confidence in the multitude—as the fisherman's son learns the sea, and understands it so profoundly that he no longer thinks to fear it.[13]

In the midst of his intensive academic education, Romains received quite another type of schooling—*une leçon des choses,* "a lesson of things," to use an expression popular in that day. To borrow his own metaphor, he grew up swimming in an urban ocean, and he always prided himself on his easy, confident familiarity with its waters. During his lycée years, Romains established close friendships with other students such as Georges Chennevière[14] and André Cuisenier, who shared his passion for Paris. They delighted in improvising new routes between Montmartre and downtown Paris, and they skipped classes or even entire days of school to take extended excursions to distant suburbs, sometimes using a tramway or bâteau-mouche, but more often walking.

Jules's familiarity with the city was encouraged by his father, who also took pride and pleasure in exploring his adopted home (he would challenge Jules to name a street he could not locate). Romains's rapport with the city seems to have even deeper sources, however. As the only child of emotionally distant parents,[15] he appears to have projected onto the urban landscape his yearnings for intimacy and emotional rapport. Consider, for example, the highly charged language of Romains's 1925 preface to *La Vie unanime,* when he asks why "searchers after influences" could not recognize that

> *La Vie unanime* was above all the book of a Parisian child, who was drenched in Paris, inebriated by Paris, for innumerable hours and days, who knew all the quarters, all the suburbs, who had walked in all the streets, who could distinguish, with his eyes closed, the noise of one intersection from the noise of another, who received from the soil, from the walls, from the sky of the great city a thousand secret communications that he held in his heart, that were day and night his treasure and his delight, and who was made to tremble unto tears and put into a state of medium-like lucidity by this lost cry that he alone heard, by this rustling, by this whisper?[16]

A thorough discussion of the origins of *unanimisme* would have to include a wide variety of textual sources, both literary and scientific.[17] As Romains points out, however, the city itself was the

ultimate source of *unanimisme*—in the same sense that Wordsworth's childhood experiences of the natural landscape can be
regarded as the ultimate source of his mature poetry.[18] Romains's
childhood coincided with a sweeping transformation of everyday
material life, the transformation usually referred to as the second
industrial revolution. Individuals do not see an "industrial revolution," however. They see a world transformed, and Romains's boyhood world was Montmartre.

In the late 1800s Montmartre had, in Romains's own words, "a
quite singular character—very contradictory, very temporary."[19]
When he was born in 1885, the butte was a ramshackle jumble of
mills, fields, goats, vineyards, scrubbrush, alleys, gardens, and
cabins—a semirural village still quite isolated from Paris. Each year
his father would ask his students how many of them had seen the
Seine, and regularly well under half of them would raise their
hands.[20] The urbanization of Montmartre began when the butte was
chosen to be the site of the Cathedral of Sacré-Coeur, built to
expiate the collective sins that had supposedly led to France's
humiliating defeat by Prussia in 1871. At the time of Romains's
birth, the cathedral had been under construction for ten years.
Among Romains's earliest memories was the sight of a dozen or so
yoke of oxen hauling a prodigious bell up the slope; he also recalled
hearing the bell rung for the first time.[21] When Sacré-Coeur was
completed in 1891, the Montmartre real estate boom began. Spec-
ulators erected town houses all along the rue Caulaincourt, which
they had laid out to connect Paris with the south slope of
Montmartre. When Romains walked to the lycée Condorcet, half
the time he arrived with plastery mud caked on his shoes. By the
time he was a young man, the advancing edge of the city had
engulfed the village of his boyhood.[22]

In another way, too, the Paris of Romains's youth had a "very
contradictory, very temporary" character: the streets of the city
presented a swarming, bewildering spectacle of vehicular evolution.
While the human population of Paris continued to grow steadily
(the city had two million inhabitants at the outset of the Third
Republic, and just under three million by 1914), this growth was far
outstripped by that of the population of motor vehicles, which
increased ten-fold from 1891 to 1910. During this period, modes of
transportation dating back to the *ancien régime* rubbed fenders
with new and sometime bizarre vehicles. Around 1890 the primary
means of transport were horse-drawn carriages (either privately
owned, or cabs called *fiacres),* horse-drawn omnibuses, and horse-
drawn trams on rails. By 1900 a variety of new and strange vehicles

had begun to appear: a few automobiles (only 1672 in all of France in 1899, the first year they were taxed); safety bicycles; a cable car line, the Belleville funicular; subway cars (the first Métro line opened in 1900); and a variety of trams running on compressed air or on electricity from batteries, from overhead lines, or from live studs transmitting current to a stake mounted under the cars. (Because overhead trolley lines were considered hopelessly ugly— they were nicknamed "trop laid" ["too ugly," pronounced *tro-lay*]—they were usually restricted to areas outside the city's fortifications.)

In the first decade of the twentieth century, the internal combustion engine became increasingly dominant. The number of automobiles doubled from two thousand in 1903 to just over four thousand by 1906. The first automobile taxis appeared in 1905, notably at stands near the Opéra; they cost four times as much as a *fiacre* and consequently were hired only by the very rich and by English tourists. In 1905 the first "autobuses" appeared, clumsy vehicles that chewed up the roadways and emitted so much noise and smoke that people living along their routes kept their apartment windows permanently closed. Sometimes the frame of a horse-drawn omnibus would be outfitted with an internal combustion engine to create a hybrid vehicle, though these proved unstable because the body was too heavy for the chassis.[23]

As Raymond Williams has reminded us, *traffic* is not only a pattern of moving vehicles, but also a dominant pattern of social interaction in modern urban environments: "a form of consciousness and a form of social relations."[24] Thus it is appropriate that Romains's poetic epiphany—the moment he first apprehended a *unanime*—came in the midst of evening rush hour. Late one October afternoon in 1903, Romains and Chennevière emerged from the lycée Condorcet to begin walking home to the Farigoule family apartment. They stepped from the entrance to the lycée, located on a quiet side street, into the busy place du Havre near the Gare St. Lazare, the major railway station connecting Paris with the north. They began walking up the rue d'Amsterdam toward the place Clichy, where the rue Caulaincourt would lead them to Montmartre. As the two schoolboys ambled along the rue d'Amsterdam, they were surrounded by other pedestrians on the sidewalk, by carriages and omnibuses in the roadway, and by shop windows displaying Oriental rugs, perfumes, and jewelry. Suddenly Romains had a vision: to him the street, the shops, the vehicles, and the crowds seemed the unified body of a larger, elemental being of which he himself was the mind. He thought

In the rue d'Amsterdam I am like a cell in the body of a man or in the leaves of a tree. At the moment I am the only one conscious of this. It is for me to suck forth from the street all the life it contains in its dense mass of vehicles and people. It is for me to lead it to the light of consciousness, above and beyond the explosions of its motors, above and beyond the movements and thoughts of each person.[25]

For Romains, the city street would always be the prototypical *unanime*. In *Puissances de Paris,* his collection of prose poems published in 1911, the majority of the twenty-six *unanimes* described in it are streets, passageways, or squares (the rest are assorted gatherings such as a literary salon, cinema and theater audiences, and groups of passengers on an omnibus or bâteau-mouche). The rue Montmartre, for example, is "a unified being" despite its length, because its daily rhythms are as predictable as the tides: "it is the center of reliable whirlpools, and the regular passageway for reliable floods."[26] The first volume of *Les Hommes de bonne volonté*—which Romains considered "a vast *unanimiste* synthesis of our time"[27]—begins with a chapter titled "Paris goes to work on a fine morning" that describes morning rush hour on 6 October 1908. (Romains chose this date because in retrospect it seemed to him the foot of the historical wave that would crest in August 1914.) In the last volume of the series, Romains again uses rush hour to portray his collective hero, Paris, this time going to work in the much more ominous atmosphere of 7 October 1933.[28]

The street-*unanime* is the paradigmatic *unanime* because its "body" so evidently unites human and technological components ("its dense mass of vehicles and people"). Other sorts of *unanimes* also come to life through the interaction of human beings with their immediate material surroundings—pavement, benches, walls, tables, merchandise. In this treatment of the technological objects of everyday life, then, Romains insists that literature should deal with them not simply as material objects, but as parts of a more encompassing social environment. He focuses on the common ground from which both literature and technology arise: the social landscape.

In this respect, Romains differs from most other writers of that postsymbolist age, who were still hotly debating whether utilitarian objects could be considered beautiful.[29] Beginning in the early 1890s, the symbolists and their decadent cousins had proclaimed that beauty was incompatible with utility, and that in modern life *la vie factice*—by which they meant primarily the artifice of art, not that of technology—had triumphed over *la vie naturelle*. (These principles were largely derived from Théophile Gautier's highly influential 1868 preface to Baudelaire's *Fleurs du mal.*) According to the symbolists, then, the goal of art was to create aesthetic objects that would create a counterworld to the ugly, banal world of modern utilitarian society.[30]

A new literary front had begun to blow through in 1897, when St. George de Bouhélier published a *naturiste* manifesto in *Le Figaro* declaring that literature should return to "nature" and "life." Because the *naturistes* tended to identify natural life with rural life— peasants, regional literature, the quiet lanes and fresh air of the countryside, daily labor in the fields, simple pleasures around the hearth—in practice they did little more to incorporate modern technologies into poetry than had the symbolists. To be sure, one wing of *naturisme,* led by Eugène Montfort, did resist this bucolic tendency. Montfort declared that his subject was "the beauty of modern life," and he explicitly included industrial artifacts:

> Art is not in the thing contemplated by the artist, but in the artist who contemplates: it is a movement of his soul. Thus there is nothing ugly. . . . We can build ugly houses, we can fill the streets with factories and machines, but these destroy neither art nor artist; on the contrary, the latter will soon find something new to adore in these spectacles . . . [the artist] will find relationships and marvelous analogies in them that had escaped everyone else.[31]

Montfort, then, celebrated not so much "the beauty of modern life" as the power of the artist to transform even the ugliest materials by discovering aesthetic "relationships and marvelous analogies." Like the symbolists, he emphasized the power of art—in this case not to create a counterworld to ugly utilitarian modernity, but to redeem and transform that world through aesthetic perception.[32] The *naturistes* therefore stayed within the aesthetic polarities established by the symbolists: beauty vs. utility, *la vie factice* vs. *la vie naturelle.*

Romains broke away from those dichotomies. Like the *naturistes,* he wanted to end what he considered poetry's secession from the modern world.[33] Instead of advocating a return to nature, however, Romains was convinced that "in modern man social feeling predominates over feeling for nature."[34] *Unanimisme* proclaims neither *la vie factice* nor *la vie naturelle,* but *la vie sociale*—the social life of the *unanime* that emerges from the ever-increasing interpenetration of mechanical and organic life. Let us see how Romains expressed this interpenetration in *La Vie unanime,* his most complex and ambitious *unanimiste* poetry.

* * *

Romains once commented, "I unreservedly admire critics who discern that the description of an autobus [in *La Vie unanime*] comes from a hand that has been leafing through the Iliad." Like Baudelaire before him, Romains assumed the mantle of antiquity to invest modern life with heroic grandeur. He intended *La Vie unanime* as an epic of modern life.[35] "From the beginning," Romains explained,

> I had conceived the general movement of the work and the large divisions it has retained. . . . Once a poem was completed, I looked for a place for it in my edifice. . . . In its divisions it marked the stages I had come to recognize in the impassioned relationship between the soul and the *unanime* that completely preoccupied me.[36]

The two major divisions of *La Vie unanime* are titled "Les Unanimes" and "L'Individu"; each is subdivided into three parts. The two major divisions, furthermore, are framed between a prefacing and a concluding poem that serve as slender bookends for the volume as a whole. Most poems begin with an epigraph from preceding ones, so that the volume is knit together through self-allusion. *La Vie unanime* is indeed an "edifice" rather than a collection.

The first division, "Les Unanimes," opens with a vivid portrayal of urban anomie in a city where *unanimes* have not yet been born. The noise of rusty, inefficient machinery echoes the cry of lost and disconnected people:

> The axle of the cart grates and the horse stumbles.
> At the corner of the wall a child cries. He is lost.
> He believes that it is over forever; that his father
> Is dying, trapped in the thick swarming
> Of the crowd. . . .
>
> I am searching.
>   The child cries.
>   The cart grates.[37]

But before long "Something begins to exist. . . . Another soul advances."[38] Grating fades, harmony emerges, and soul of the street begins to assume a regular pattern:

> What is it that thus transfigures the boulevard?

The passers-by almost appear not to be physical;
They are no longer movements, they are rhythms.[39]

The narrator gradually loses his sense of isolation. As he lives alone in his room, the supposedly impermeable walls still let in a "lukewarm drizzle" of city noises: the voice of an anxious doctor treating a sick child, the tinkle of a piano. When the narrator later rises and walks through the foggy streets, he notices that the gaslights illuminate the moist air, making the space between people tangible and giving them a sense of interconnection. *Unanimes* are coming to life: "Great beasts are stirring."[40]

The second subsection describes the stirring of these various "beasts"—barracks, theaters, churches, cafés. As the jerking, grinding existence of disconnected individuals begins to yield to harmonious rhythms, the patterns of the *unanimes* are occasionally cross-cut by other rhythms that are reminders of the countryside—the diurnal cycle of sunrise and sunset, for example, or the circling of a flock of sheep, their hooves lightly vibrating as they are driven to the slaughterhouse.[41] As the flock moves out of sight, though, the city as a whole assumes the flowing candence of *unanimisme* triumphant:

> It seems to me that in the depths of my streets
> The passers-by flow in the same direction,
> And, unravelling the neutral intersections,
> Straighten out the twisted boulevards;
> So that, less and less divergent,
> Despite the walls, despite the timbers,
> Innumerable forces flow together
> So that brusquely the entire surge
> Sets all the houses moving.[42]

In "Dynamism," the third and last subsection of "Les Unanimes," the narrator celebrates the new groups that have been born in the city. He emphasizes the technologies that helped bring them to birth. Electricity, for example, recreates a sunlit village in the urban darkness:

> Above the boulevard the manmade twilight
> Crystallizes into an electric arc . . .
>
> . . deep within bodies, cells
> Feel the marvelous waves undulate
> Toward them . . .

> The unity of the flesh begins to crumble; . . .
> The mind surrenders its force to the electrical influx.
> Suddenly the street resolves to enjoy itself.
> At the corners of its intersections it clots into
>   couples;
> Seeds stir. Some men come to sit down at the table,
> Small circular groups in the taverns.
> The crowd dreams of being a village in the sun.

Automobiles too break down isolation. The passengers feel an intoxicating excitement as the city becomes pure movement for them, and onlookers become more aware of their surroundings as they look up to see an automobile roar by:

> The motor lives through obedient explosions;
> The atoms of gas scuffle while they sing;
> The groups die and are born. The metal trembles.
> Each tooth of the gears is a springboard
> From which the force leaps, its legs together . . .
> The people who are in the car, elbow to elbow,
> Bathed by speed, lose their heaviness,
> They exist more ardently than just before . . .
> Along the cold sidewalk, passers-by are shut up
> In a burrow of habits to which they have closed the
>   openings.
> But they have seen the fierce vehicle running;
> They all straighten up, like a trampled lawn
> That is watered.[43]

The second half of *La Vie unanime,* titled "L'Individu," begins with a celebration of the state of blissful unself-consciousness that comes from immersion in a city of *unanimes.* The narrator no longer feels any distinction between the movements of his body, those of nature, and those of the urban environment:

> Being myself no longer, I no longer feel what touches
>   me.
> My skin is the sidewalk of the street, and the sky. . . .
>
> The wheel of the omnibus that makes sparks,
> And the wheel of the sun stuck in the clouds
> Give a rhythm to my impersonal thought;
> I am a majestic wheeling of images. . . .[44]

The city is a continuum where vehicles, buildings, and people all flow together, everything connected to everything else, like the stanzas of the poetry:

> Where the eyes do not see separate forms,
> Where one thinks of nothing that does not seem a
>   totality.
> Each thing prolongs the other. The metal
> Of rails and the dazzling cobblestones; the entryways
>
> Of houses; the pedestrians, the horses, the vehicles
> Are joined to each other and join my body;
> We are indistinct, each of us is dead,
> And *la vie unanime* is our sepulchre.[45]

In the second subsection, titled "Moi en révolte," the plot and the tempo begin to thicken. The narrator becomes restive and begins to rebel against this immersion in collection life. He yearns to reassert his individuality, and he calls upon nature as his accomplice. If modern traffic patterns largely define *unanimes,* the linear railroad track makes possible a quick escape from them: the narrator boards a train and soon finds himself in the countryside. At first he is relieved to be away from the city. Slowly the urban rhythms fade, replaced by the timeless fragrance of fires, leaves, freshness. Initial pleasure, however, is followed by an overwhelming lethargy. The tempo of the poetry slows almost to a halt, as the narrator's refrain becomes, "To sleep under the leaves . . ." He gazes at a sunset, a "yellow ocean" of color, and suddenly panics; he becomes afraid of losing consciousness altogether, of being drowned in the "unfeeling ocean of nature"—in short, of dying. Unlike the trees and fields also enveloped in the yellow light, he suffers in nature's arms. Cold and afraid, he concludes that the dream of merging with nature is, for modern man, an atavistic weakness. Nature is empty; it is "the void between people."[46]

As the narrator begins to look again at the countryside, however, he recognizes that it is not "pure nature" but "fermented nature," not empty but overflowing with evidence of humanity's presence. The soil has been divided by human labor into fields and pastures, and enclosed by hedgerows representing human laws. Man-made roads roll toward the horizon, each mile representing a victory of human communication. The telegraph wires too remind the narrator that "I swim among human vibrations," even in the country. The networks of human society so evident in the city extend even here. The narrator consequently decides that instead of drowning in unfeeling nature, "I prefer to drown myself by throwing myself into men." Wiser and chastened, he returns to the city and once again immerses himself in *la vie unanime*.[47]

The final subsection, "Nous," sings of the reconciliation between the wiser *moi* and the *unanimiste* city. The poet now understands his mission. He will participate in the efficiency and power of the networked city so that he becomes part of the infrastructure, at once technological and social, of modern life:

> . . . I will be
> The man who knows how to steal power from other men,
> A joyous crossroads of *unanimiste* rhythms,
> A condenser of universal energy. . . .
>
> I want to be at least
> In the obscure tangle of cables and wires
> The slender thread of consciousness, through which the
>   fluid
>   Travels with incandescent emotion
>
> And others, here and there, will begin to shine.[48]

La Vie unanime, which began with the image of grinding wheels, concludes with "Un jour," a poem that envisions human beings as efficient and unself-conscious as machines:

> One day we will be wheels
> That only think of doing good;
> We shall exist in copper and iron,
> But not in "soul."
> We will transmit exactly
> The force that is entrusted to us.
>
> What we take from the flywheels
> We will pass on to the transmission belts. . . .
>
> We shall dream of minimizing
> Our grindings, and of softening them
> Into a well-oiled and gliding hum.
> Our bodies will exude
> A silence that is full and saturated with energy. . . .
>
> We shall exist in action and in iron.[49]

* * *

Ezra Pound wrote in 1913, "[Romains] has achieved a form which fully conveys the sense of modern life. He is able to mention any familiar thing, any element of modern life, without its seeming incongruous, and the result is undeniably poetic."[50] In order to understand the sources of this achievement, *La Vie unanime* deserves a much closer reading than it has received here. The purpose of this essay, however, is not to analyze the place of *unanimisme* in the history of French literature, but to show how it illuminates the relationship between literature and technology. This emphasis is justified because Romains—like Mumford—insisted that the organic/mechanical being he had discovered was not just a striking metaphor, but an objective social reality. Romains, indeed, went further than Mumford, insisting that in modern times the *unanime* was the *only* social reality:

> The period of abstractions is going to end. Society, categories, classes, "le monde," "le demi-monde," "le peuple," abstractions; collective words that designate no collective being. Nothing of all that has concrete existence, and therefore nothing of it will last. Social consciousness, class consciousness—abominable metaphors. What exists, what is beginning to exist with a complete, bodily, conscious life, are groups; streets, city squares, meeting halls, theaters. These are the beings that have a future.[51]

Critics then and now have noted striking similarities between Romains's concept of *unanimes* and concepts proposed by contemporary social thinkers such as Gustave Le Bon, Gabriel Trade, and Émile Durkheim. Romains, however, denied any such influence; his respect for the biological sciences was matched by his contempt for the social sciences.[52] Instead, Romains preferred to compare his discovery of the social landscape of *unanimisme* to the romantics' discovery of the natural landscape. "Both causes involved a discovery of a sensibility and a reality which, to be sure, existed already, but of which the human soul was becoming much more attentively and warmly conscious than before."[53] Like mountains, he said, *unanimes* had always existed, but they had not been noticed. "*Unanimisme* means an effort to teach people to perceive the *unanime* as they have learned to perceive landscapes."[54]

Let us pursue this suggestive analogy between romantic and *unanimiste* literature. Both are based on a radical sense of estrangement that leads to a yearning for the reestablishment of connection between oneself and the larger whole. Instead of communing with nature, however, Romains seeks to commune with society.[55] At the moment of his epiphany in the rue d'Amsterdam, he felt he had lost the burden of individuality and had become part of a larger organic life, in this case the life of a social organism: a mountaintop experience in the midst of the city. The paradox of both romanticism and *unanimisme* is that the loss of individuality depends upon a supreme effort of the individual will. The poet must be "strong" (Wordsworth's term) in the sense of having "the power of conferring the visionary quality upon an ordinary sight."[56] While a mega-machine is created by a political authority (whether pharaohs or Pentagon chiefs), Romains's collective being is created by poetic authority. While the organisms' body is made up of vehicles and pedestrians, its mind is that of the poet: "I am the only one conscious of this. . . . It is for me to lead [the *unanime*] to the light of consciousness."

The *unanime* is a chance gathering of people who cohere because their daily routines happen to intersect. Romains claimed that *unanimes* were not mere crowds, though, at least not in the sense that his contemporary Gustave Le Bon was using the term. The *unanime* goes beyond the simple physical unity of the crowd to attain complex self-consciousness, a "soul." Similarly, the *unanimiste* poet is not just a passive *flâneur*—someone who mingles with the crowd but stands aloof from it, a keen but detached observer.[57] The *unanimiste* poet actively *creates* the crowd. He is the one who endows mental unity upon what would otherwise be a merely physical agglomeration. The *unanime* exists only when the self-conscious individual—usually a poet, and sometimes, especially in Romains's plays, a prankster—imposes upon the urban landscape (and here I am deliberately using romantic language) the vital, transforming power of his imagination.[58]

But this is a strangely incomplete community. In the first place, it is *optional:* Romains can leave at any time, either physically (by withdrawing from the city on a train) or psychologically (by withdrawing his imaginative powers). The *unanime* is created by the temporary elevation of individual consciousness, not by enduring social and economic relationships. It provides a resolution of Romains's conflicting desires for individuality and solidarity, but this is only a tenuous and transient compromise. From this community, furthermore, some crucial social and economic relationships are absent, or nearly so. If Romains succeeded in bringing modern technologies into his poetry, they are largely the technologies of transportation and communication; those of production are rarely seen. He returns again and again to the rhythm of commuters, but he rarely describes the rhythm of their labor once they have arrived at work. One poem of *La Vie unanime* does describe the vitality of factories, in order to contrast their vibrancy with a moribund atmosphere of a church:

> . . . now they have arisen, the factories,
> The youthful factories! They live very robustly.
> They send smoke higher than the bells can ring.
> They are not afraid of hiding the sun
> Because they make some sun with their machines.[59]

But while the narrator enters the church and portrays its congregation in careful detail, he never enters the gates of the factories to see the workers. Other poems in *La Vie unanime* describe isolated workers—the shepherd driving the sheep to the slaughterhouse, a sewing machine operator working alone in her apartment—but the only laboring *unanime* portrayed is a group of soldiers in a barracks. Most of the groups in *La Vie unanime* are composed of people taking it easy: lounging at the café, picnicking at a park on a Sunday afternoon, dining, riding the train. The absence of working groups is even more evident in *Puissances de Paris,* where among the twenty-six *unanimes* in the collection only one is a working group—a gang of laborers digging a tunnel for the Métro.[60]

When "technology" is perceived primarily as modes of communication, transportation, and entertainment, class divisions are muted. In a typical *unanime*—whether a movie audience, a queue, or a flood of commuters—people are equalized because they move in a common rhythm. Everyone is slowed down by the traffic jam; everyone is caught up in the cinemagraphic drama. When people go to work or return home or lounge around, when they are seen as part of a crowded street, questions of ownership and power are not so sharply evident as they are in, say, a factory setting—at least in a day when "the democratization of luxury" (a popular contemporary term) was greatly reducing formerly sharp differences in consumption patterns. The technologies associated with street life seem to have no owner. They are the cityscape, a leveling backdrop—the environment of modern life.

At this point we need to recall Raymond Williams's dictum that "environment" is a "bourgeois notion." "By contrast," Williams adds, "the Marxist definition of realism starts talking about society or history."[61] Romains, of course, scorned just these traditional categories of society and history ("Nothing of all that has concrete existence, and therefore nothing of it will last"). It is this attitude that led him into compromising positions during the interwar period, when his vision of a Europe beyond class and nation encouraged him to disregard existing political realities. Romains proclaimed the *unanime* as the fundamental reality of modern collective life, and he wanted to believe (to quote from *Les Hommes de bonne volonté*) that "Collective life, breathing life, is quite another thing than history, and does quite well without it."[62]

The lesson of the twentieth century is that history does not leave collective life alone. Here we begin to glimpse some of the complexities of the relationship between Romains's poetry and historical events, or between the literary superstructure and the technological base, if you will. It is true that the technological restructuring of Paris during Romains's youth is a primary source of repeated, striking, novel sensory experiences—sights, sounds, and rhythms—that he expressed so well in his writing. In their "very contradictory, very temporary" character, furthermore, these sensory experiences impressed Romains as metaphors for more general social changes taking place in French society. But the connection between technology and imagination is reciprocal rather than unidirectional. Romains is not just a passive subject responding to technological change. He is not just someone "influenced by." Instead, in his work he actively affirms and praises an imaginative vision—the vision of the city as an organism including both human beings and the built environment—that motivated those technological developments in the first place.

It is well known that Paris was rebuilt between 1853 and 1869 under the orders of Napoleon III and the management of Baron von Haussmann. This, however, was just one phase in a continuing process of urban renewal, which continued at a brisk pace right up until the first world war. The city continued to extend outward, its traffic increased dramatically, and other major building projects were undertaken (for example, for various international expositions and for the Métro system). From Haussmann on, this "rationalization" of Paris depended, paradoxically enough, upon the assumption that the city should be regarded as a gigantic organism. The most "modern" aspect of Haussmann's accomplishment is that "no one, before him, had considered the city as a single organism, a unit which could be conceptualized, planned as a unified system, and realized through technical, scientific and mechanical means."[63] Haussmann and his successors speak over and over of the city's biological "functions"—digestion, respiration, and above all circulation. (Maxime Du Camp's monumental study of the restructured city, published in six volumes in 1893, is titled *Paris, ses organes, ses fonctions et sa vie dans la second moitié du XIX siècle*.) Haussmann's plan emphasized wide boulevards and straight streets that were to be the "major arteries" of the urban circulatory system.[64] Opening them up eliminated urban "congestion," just as opening up tree-lined, light-filled vistas provided "breathing space" for urban life. In other words, technological values associated with organic movement came to dominate over older technological values associated with stable structures. The values of communication triumphed over those of architecture. Whatever was part of a circulatory system was healthy and vital; anything detached from it was old, diseased, dangerous.[65]

When cities are conceived as superorganisms, the needs of this fictitious being may come to supersede the needs of human beings who live on a far smaller scale. When Napoleon III and Haussmann designed the boulevard system, they paid far more attention to the aesthetic effect of the façade than to the comfort of the people who would live there. As a result, some fine exteriors concealed slumlike interiors. Furthermore, when the streets were laid out on such a grand scale (some of them were three miles long), the vista became lost on the ordinary walker: it could only be imagined from a map, or from a panoramic overview.[66] Finally, of course, the act of constructing the new circulatory system meant the destruction of existing urban settlements. Buildings were demolished and their inhabitants dispersed. Romains's poetic glorification of the temporary, optional community of the *unanime* may be interpreted as an attempt to find a modern dynamic replacement for the more traditional, settled urban communities that were destroyed as Paris became a regional city, as boulevards were laid down through old quarters and open fields, and as villages like Montmartre became integrated into the larger metropolis. If we recall that Paris was rebuilt with highly organized gangs of men wielding the simplest of tools—picks and shovels—we can say that the *unanime* protests the megamachine.

Unanimisme is not just a passive response to often destructive technological changes. The *unanimiste* poet who resists history (in the name of "collective life") simultaneously confirms the worldview of those who are making history. When Romains glorifies superorganic urban beings and urges their supremacy over individuals, he is actively celebrating and promoting the very priorities and values that inspired the rebuilding of Paris. Both Haussmann and Romains seek to impose organic categories upon urban life. While the model of technological base and literary superstructure assumes that imagination is a product of technological change, imagination also played a role in producing that change. To encompass this reciprocal influence—to deal with technology as one element in a wider field of social relationships—the Lukàcsian language of social totality is more helpful than that of base and superstructure.[67]

In another way, too, Romains echoes a reversal of organic and

technological categories characteristic of contemporary policymakers: the more the urban landscape is invested with organic
vitality, the more the natural landscape is perceived as lifeless, inert
matter. This reversal of categories is most apparent in the long
section of *La Vie unanime* where the poet describes an episode of
getting back to nature—or rather of trying to do so. Although the
episode, and the book as a whole, ends on a note of triumphant
reconciliation, this narrative of a failed return to nature—this final
farewell to an old lover, to use Romains's image—is described with
powerful undertones of grief and loss. The price of Romains's rapport with the social landscape, it seems, is the loss of any sense of
connection with the natural landscape. When he gazes upon it, he
sees only blankness and death. What compensates (at least in part)
for this loss of rapport is his newfound perception that the human
presence extends into the natural landscape in the form of telegraph
wires, hedgerows, cultivated fields, and the like. Certainly this
perception is an important and valuable corrective to the sentimental view that would glorify an "unspoiled" natural landscape as a
Holy Other. We should remember, however, that in the urban landscape Romains succumbed to a very similar sentimentalism; in the
countryside he perceived the technological evidence of human
labor that he had scarcely noticed in the city.

I want to invoke Raymond Williams one last time to remind us
that this response to the natural landscape—unreal nature, dead
nature—is common among writers in the late nineteenth century:

> This social character of the city—its transitoriness, its unexpectedness,
> its essential and exciting isolation and procession of men and events—
> was seen as the reality of all human life. . . . City experience was now
> becoming so widespread, and writers, disproportionately, were so
> deeply involved in it, that there seemed little reality in any other mode
> of life; all sources of perception seemed to begin and end in the city, and
> if there was anything beyond it, it was also beyond life.[68]

Once again, we are dealing with more than a literary response to
technological change. Once again, in their assumptions about
nature, writers like Romains actively (if unwittingly) affirm the
ideological assumptions driving technological change. In this case,
I am referring particularly to economic assumptions generally
shared by capitalists and socialists of the late nineteenth century
for whom nature is first a storehouse and second a dump. Both
unanimisme and the dominant economic systems deny independent significance to nonhuman nature; the human world is all that
counts, and nature is unreal except as it bears the imprint of human

intervention. In that case, no element of earthly life transcends or even lies outside human values and purposes. Everything—organism and mechanism alike—becomes part of a human-organized system. *Unanimisme* is part of a social world, a world at once ideological and technological, that celebrates what Francis Bacon called "the human empire."

NOTES

1. Leo Marx, "Lewis Mumford: Prophet of Organicism," in *Lewis Mumford: Public Intellectual,* ed. Thomas P. Hughes and Agatha C. Hughes (Oxford and New York: Oxford University Press, 1990), p. 168.

2. To be sure, the work of Thomas Parke Hughes and others discourages a "rigid demarcation between the system and the environment in which the system develops," but the "environment" is often defined in social rather than in natural terms. (Donald MacKenzie, "Missile Accuracy: A Case Study in the Social Processes of Technological Change," in *The Social Construction of Technological Systems: New Directions in the Sociology and History of Technology,* ed. Wiebe E. Bijker, Thomas P. Hughes, and Trevor J. Pinch [Cambridge, Mass. and London: The MIT Press, 1987], p. 197.) Another favored term in contemporary history of technology is the "seamless web," used to describe an ideal of contextual history. Although this is a metaphor based on an analogy between historical studies and organic life, in practice "the seamless web" more often refers to social networks than to natural ones.

3. Marx, "Prophet of Organicism," p. 177. See also Lewis Mumford, *The Myth of the Machine: Technics and Human Development* (New York: Harcourt, Brace & World, 1966), pp. 189–211 passim.

4. Bonner Mitchell, *Les Manifestes littéraires de le Belle Époque* (Paris: Seghers, 1966), p. 81. The manifesto appeared in *Le Penseur,* 5th year, no. 4 (April 1905), pp. 121–24.

5. Unless otherwise noted, all translations in this essay are mine.

6. For a summary and discussion of the base-superstructure relationship in Marxism, see Raymond Williams, "Base and Superstructure in Marxist Cultural Theory," in *Problems in Materialism and Culture: Selected Essays* (London: Verso, 1980), pp. 31–49.

7. For information on Romains's early poetry and choice of pen name, see Annie Angrémy et al., *Catalogue de l'Exposition Jules Romains* (Paris: Bibliothèque Nationale, 1978), pp. XI–XVI, 3; Michel Décaudin, preface to Romains's *La Vie unanime, poème 1904–1907* (Paris: Gallimard, 1983), p. 7; André Guyon, "Jules Romains avant l'unanimisme," *Cahiers Jules Romains 3, Actes du Colloque Jules Romains,* Bibliothèque Nationale, 17–18 February 1978 (Paris: Flammarion, 1979); and Guyon, "J'entends les portes du lointain . . . ," *Cahiers 4* (Paris: Flammarion, 1981).

For a fairly complete review of Romains studies, see M. Raimond, "État présent des études sur Romains," *L'Information littéraire,* no. 5 (1980), pp. 190–93.

An excellent introduction in English to Romains's life and letters is Denis Boak, *Jules Romains,* gen. ed. Sylvia E. Bowman, ed. Maxwell A. Smith (New York: Twayne, 1974).

8. Many of them are found in Mitchell, *Manifestes.*

9. Romains himself later remarked on the book's reception, "One would have needed a truly insatiable vanity not to be satisfied with the welcome it received. I came to know all the types and degrees of praise that can be bestowed, with a freshness that is tasted only once" Angrémy et al., *Catalogue*, pp. 25–27. See also Romains, "Préface de 1925," in *Vie unanime*, p. 27, and Claude Martin, "Le Dossier de presse de *La Vie unanime*," *Bulletin des Amis de Jules Romains*, 6th year (December 1980), and 7th year (December 1981).

10. Boak, pp. 64–65. See also Georges Bonneville, "Jules Romains et l'Europe," *Cahiers 3*, pp. 253–65. Romains had first been drafted in 1905 and had also suffered a nervous breakdown as a consequence.

11. See Georges Bonneville, "Jules Romains et l'Europe," *Cahiers 3*, pp. 253–65; also Romains's own self-justifying description of his negotiations in *Sept mystères du destin de l'Europe*, written at the request of the *Saturday Evening Post* and published in New York in 1940. (The book was never published in France, for its opinions were deemed too controversial.) See Angrémy et al., *Catalogue*, pp. 70–75, for a brief summary of Romains's interwar diplomatic efforts. Also see Boak, pp. 99–101, for a description of another now-embarrassing publication from the interwar period—Romains's epic of the white race, *L'homme blanc* (1937).

12. Jules Romains, *Ai-je fait ce que j'ai voulu?* in *Les Auteurs jugés de leurs oeuvres*, ed. Philippe Carlier (Paris: Wesmael-Charlier, n.d.), p. 44.

13. Quoted by André Bourin, *Connaissance de Jules Romains, discutée par Jules Romains de l'Académie française. Essai de géographie littéraire* (Paris: Flammarion, 1961), p. 212.

14. Léon Debille, also an aspiring writer, is best known as well by the pseudonym he adopted as a teenager—Georges Chennevière. Louis/Jules and Léon/Georges remained artistic and personal comrades until the latter's untimely death in 1927.

15. Only after his father's death did Romains learn, to his astonishment, that he had been married earlier, briefly, to a woman who died shortly after the wedding. (Boak, *Romains*, p. 19.) There are a number of intriguing biographical parallels between Romains and Mumford. They were both raised in families that did not provide much emotional closeness; in their childhood they both developed a powerful rapport with their native cities; and as adults they both shared a sense of being outside conventional social categories, especially those of social class.

16. Romains, "Préface de 1925," *Vie unanime*, p. 31.

17. Some literary influences will be mentioned later on in this essay, but the influence of Romains's scientific studies is at least as important. At the time he was writing his early poetry, he was also studying for his *diplôme d'études supérieurs* in biology. The interplay between these two pursuits is most evident in the fundamental metaphor of *unanimisme:* the *unanime* is a great beast, a new kind of organism. Such biological analogies were common in the intellectual discourse of the time, but Romains went further, seeking *unanimiste* principles in biology itself. The title of his biology thesis—"L'État 'individu' dans la matière vivante"— echoes one of the prime assertions in *La Vie unanime*, the illusory nature of the "individual state." The purpose of the thesis (that Romains admits was overly ambitious, and that his advisor severely criticized) was to show how simple plant and bacterial colonies exhibit rhythms that can be express in scientific laws. (Bourin, *Connaissance*, pp. 124, 127.)

Even more generally, Romains sought to demonstrate that scientific knowledge could be attained through intuitive apprehension rather than through analysis. In a series of "méditations unanimes," written between 1904 and 1907, he tried to apply *unanimiste* principles to knowledge in general. He proposed that knowledge be sought not in the analytic enumeration of essences, reasons, first causes, and the like, but in the apprehension of "rhythms, *ways of grouping* phenomena" (Décaudin, preface to *Vie unanime,* pp. 16–17). Throughout his life Romains kept returning to the quasi-mystical conviction that fundamental scientific discoveries could be made through intuition and imagination—most notably in his experiments between 1918 and 1923 to demonstrate the possibility of "extraretinal vision," a type of sight through hypothetical minute organs in the skin that can distinguish shapes and colors independently of the eyes. In 1920 Romains produced a monograph on the theory—the only work he published under his given name Louis Farigoule. Other scientists remained unconvinced. (See Boak, *Romains,* pp. 65–68.)

18. See the discussion by Basil Willey, *The Eighteenth-Century Background: Studies on the Idea of Nature in the Thought of the Period* (Boston: Beacon Press, 1961 [1940]), pp. 270–93.

19. Bourin, *Connaissance,* p. 85.

20. *Ibid.,* pp. 112–13.

21. Angrémy et al., *Catalogue,* p. 5.

22. *Ibid.* One should recall that Braque and Picasso were both living in Montmartre at the time Romains was composing *La Vie unanime* (Braque settled there in 1902, Picasso in 1904), and this was the milieu where—beginning in 1908, the year *La Vie unanime* appeared—they collaborated to invent cubism. Cubism too shatters the autonomy of the individual object to integrate it with its environment; it too celebrates instability, indeterminacy, and change.

23. On population growth, see Charles Rearick, *Pleasures of the Belle Époque: Entertainment and Festivity in Turn-of-the-Century France* (New Haven and London: Yale University Press, 1985), p. 169. From 1901 to 1906 alone, the population of Paris increased by about six hundred thousand inhabitants to around 2.5 million. On changing modes of transportation, see Charles S. Dunbar, *Buses, Trolleys & Trams* (London: Paul Hamlyn, 1967); Paul Delay, "La Transformation des moyens de transport à Paris," *Le Correspondent,* vol. 229 (10 October 1907), pp. 69–97; Auguste de Morsier, "Chronique scientifique.—Les tramways éléctriques," *La Semaine littéraire,* no. 149 (7 November 1896), pp. 537–39; Eugène Henard, *Études sur les transformations de Paris* (Paris: Librairier-Imprimerier Réunis, 1903 et seq.); and Louis Mocquant, "Les grands travaux de Paris," *Le Nouvelle Revue,* 3d series, vol. 8, no. 31 (10 October 1907), pp. 323–31.

24. Raymond Williams, *The Country and the City* (New York: Oxford University Press, 1973), p. 296.

25. Romains himself never wrote a description of this awakening, except for an oblique reference in a poem composed a decade later ("En revenant du lycée," in *Le voyage des amants* [1921]). The description given here was paraphrased from Romains's verbal accounts by his good friend André Cuisenier in *Jules Romains et l'unanimisme* (Paris: Flammarion, 1935), p. 17. Romains and Cuisenier had just met at the time of the rue d'Amsterdam experience, but Romains did not mention it to Cuisenier until three years later—and Cuisenier did not record this description until he published this first volume of his two-volume biography (the second volume, published by Flammarion in 1948, is entitled *L'art de Jules Romains*). Evidently Romains said nothing to his companion Chennevière during or immediately after the event. Taken together, these circumstances suggest a good deal of conscious mythologizing by Romains and his *amis.* See André Guyon, "Le Souvenir de la rue d'Amsterdam," *Bulletin des amis de Jules Romains,* 3d year, nos. 8–9 (April–June 1977), pp. 13–29.

26. Jules Romains, *Puissances de Paris,* 7th ed. (Paris: Éditions de la Nouvelle Revue Française, 1919), pp. 24–28.

27. Romains, *Ai-je,* p. 104.

28. Jules Romains, *Men of Good Will,* vol. 1, *The Sixth of October,* trans. Warre B. Wells (New York: Alfred A. Knopf, 1933), esp. pp. 4–7. This chapter should be compared with chapter 18 of the same volume, "Introducing Paris at Five O'Clock in the Evening," and with the opening chapter of *The Seventh of October,* trans. Gerard Hopkins (New York: Alfred A. Knopf, 1946). See the discussion of these works by Josef W. Konvitz in *The Urban Millennium: The City-Building Process from the Early Middle Ages to the Present* (Carbondale and Edwardsville: Southern Illinois University Press, 1985), pp. 140–42. For the choice of October 6 as the foot of the historical wave, see Romains, *Ai-je,* p. 112.

29. Romains also differs in this respect from the futurists. In his view, they never overcame a somewhat infantile fascination with machinery. Moreover, he was much more cerebral in his approach while the futurists praised irrational instincts. While writing *La Vie unanime* Romains became quite friendly with Guillaume Apollinaire, and Apollinaire was one of those who praised the book highly. Romains hoped to forge a literary alliance between Apollinaire and Max Jacob on the one hand and his Abbaye friends on the other. In 1909 Romains proclaimed a united new generation of writers in a much discussed article published that year in *La Nouvelle Revue Française.* There were always strains in the relationship, however, and a rupture came in 1911 when Apollinaire wrote a highly critical review of Romains's play *L'Armée dans la ville.* [Apollinaire's review appeared in *La Nouvelle Revue Française,* no. 28 (1 April 1911), pp. 610–13.] While a reconciliation was effected, Romains's relations with Apollinaire never regained real warmth. See Angrémy et al., *Catalogue,* pp. 31–33; Apollinaire's "La vie anecdotique" in *Mercure de France,* quoted in *Cahiers 1* (1978), p. 44; Guy Taillade, "Unanimisme, Futurisme, Abbaye de Créteil," *Bulletin des Amis de Jules Romains,* 7th year (March 1981); Bourin, *Connaissance,* pp. 149–51; Christian Sénéchal, *L'Abbaye de Créteil* (Paris: André Delpeuch, 1930); and Marc Baroli, *Le Train dans la littérature française* (Paris, 1963), p. 332.

30. See the analysis by Wylie Sypher, *Literature and Technology: The Alien Vision* (New York: Random House, 1968), p. 62. For an overview of the postsymbolist interlude, see Michel Décaudin, *La Crise des valeurs symbolistes: vingt ans de poésie française* (Toulouse: Privat, 1960).

31. Eugène Montfort, "La Beauté Moderne," *La Plume,* 14th year, no. 305 (1 January 1902), pp. 49–50. This is the last of five articles Montfort published in *La Plume* under this collective title; it is dedicated to Jean Jaurès.

32. Some of Bouhélier's fellow *naturistes* were Henri Ghéon, Eugène Montfort, Paul Fort, and Francis Jammes. See Eugène Montfort, *La Beauté moderne, Conférences du Collège d'Esthétique* (Paris: Éditions de la Plume, 1902). See also Baroli, *Train,* p. 331n.

At the beginning of 1901 Montfort established a Collège d'Esthétique moderne on the rue Rochefoucault, where he organized art exhibits, brought in speakers (including Saint George de Bouhélier), and lectured on topics such as "the beauty of the street." The Collège survived only six months. The *naturiste* group as a whole broke up in 1902, as members drifted off in various directions. Montfort went on to become an important literary critic and along with André Gide established the *La Nouvelle Reveue Française* in 1908. After the first issue appeared in February (the issue that contained Gide's laudatory review of *La Vie unanime*), the partnership broke up, and Gide assumed full control of the journal. Décaudin, *Crise,* pp. 115–17.

33. Romains criticized the symbolists for relying upon "accessories borrowed from lost civilizations, things no longer part of human experience." Romains, *Ai-je,* p. 52. In recalling his youth, Romains remarked that "the symbolist storm hardly dampened him at all." *Ibid.,* p. 30.

34. *Ibid.,* p. 48.

35. Romains, "Préface de 1925," *Vie unanime,* p. 31. Romains always down-played—and one suspects underplayed—his debt to modern writers. He admitted to savoring some verses by Mallarmé, Verlaine, and Rimbaud, and of course he had read Verhaeren and Baudelaire. Romains later recalled telling someone around 1903 or 1904 that Baudelaire was the most important influence on his own poetry, but he later confessed that this was "a little lie dictated by fear of not appearing sufficiently advanced." In fact, he said, he found Baudelaire too perverse for his taste (Romains, *Ai-je,* p. 31). Later, in his book *Saints de Notre Calendrier,* Romains referred to Baudelaire as "the first poet of the modern great city, of its murmurings, of its occult powers, of what he calls its 'innumerable rela-tionships.'" (Quoted by P. J. Norrish, *The Drama of the Group* [Cambridge: Cambridge University Press, 1958], p. 101.)

36. Romains, "Préface de 1925," *Vie unanime,* pp. 25–26.

37. Romains, *Vie unanime,* p. 15. I am providing a fairly literal translation of Romains's poetry, which deserves far better.

38. *Ibid.,* p. 46.

39. *Ibid.,* p. 47.

40. *Ibid.,* pp. 23–24, 56.

41. *Ibid.,* pp. 71–72.

42. *Ibid.,* p. 82.

43. *Ibid.,* p. 94.

44. *Ibid.,* p. 133.

45. *Ibid.,* p. 138.

46. *Ibid.,* pp. 167–79.

47. *Ibid.,* 179–82. See the discussion in chap. I, "La Nature," in Cuisenier, *Jules Romains et l'Unanimisme,* pp. 79–82.

48. *Ibid.,* p. 209.

49. *Ibid.,* p. 215.

50. Ezra Pound, "The Approach to Paris," *The New Age,* N.S. vol. 13, no. 21 (18 September 1913), p. 608. This article is the third is a series of seven reports on contemporary French poets. Pound ends with these words: "Whatever we may think of his theories, in whatever paths we may find it useless to follow him, we have here at least the poet, and our best critique is quotation." (The article includes a long quotation from *Puissances de Paris* translated into English by Pound. Other quotations are given in the original French.) In the last article of the series, Pound remarks, "[In England I cannot] see about me any young man whose work is as refreshing as Romains's" (N.S. vol. 13, no. 25 [16 October 1913], p. 727).

51. Quoted by Bancquart, "Langage," *Cahiers,* p. 47.

52. Durkheim was teaching at the École normale while Romains was a student there, but Romains claimed he never heard Durkheim lecture or read his works at that time (he did eventually profess great admiration for Durkheim as "the Des-cartes of *unanimisme*"). Romains spoke of Le Bon even less charitably, saying that the very title of Le Bon's well-known study *La Psychologie des foules* made his skin crawl. Romains explained that he disliked Le Bon's work so intensely because "I suspected it [of] putting its clumsy paws on realities that I wanted to touch only through pure intuition of mystical ecstasy and love." Romains, "Préface de 1925," *Vie unanime,* pp. 28–29. See also P. J. Norrish, "*Unanimiste* elements in the works of Durkheim and Verhaeren," *French Studies,* vol. 11, no. 1 (January 1957), pp. 38–49.

53. Romains, preface to *Death of a Nobody,* trans. Desmond MacCarthy and Sydney Waterlow (New York: Howard Fertig, 1976), pp. iv–v.

54. Romains's response to Lucien Maury's *enquête* in *Revue bleue* (4 September 1909), as quoted in Blancquart, *Cahiers 3*, p. 53.

55. Wordsworth's *The Prelude* can be read as a mirror image of *La Vie unanime*. In Wordsworth's epic, the interlude in London serves the same purpose as Romains's visit to the countryside does in *La Vie unanime*—a journey of temptation and education that ultimately convinces the narrator of the superior virtues of the alternative environment.

56. Willey, *Eighteenth Century Background*, p. 279.

57. The term has been made famous by Walter Benjamin in his analysis of Baudelaire. The *flâneur* (as described by Benjamin) is marginal both to the city and to the bourgeoisie: "Neither of them had yet overwhelmed him. In neither of them was he at home." The fact that he can stroll rather than work shows he is a gentleman of leisure, and yet he is not part of the powerful, decision-making class. He is lucid, but helpless. "As *flâneurs*, the intelligentsia came into the marketplace." (Benjamin, "Paris—the Capital of the Nineteenth Century," *Charles Baudelaire: A Lyric Poet in the Era of High Capitalism*, trans. Harry Zohn [London: NLB, 1973], p. 170. See also pp. 36, 69, 129, 162.) Even more ambivalent than Baudelaire, Romains is no longer so content to stand aloof from the crowd: one part of him still wants to, but another part of him longs to be drowned in the "ocean of humanity." At times he assumes the role of the self-conscious *flâneur*, but at other times the isolation of that role becomes too burdensome. He seems to yearn for (though he never completely gives himself over to) a social role more like that of the unself-conscious *badaud*—the onlooker who loses his individuality as he becomes absorbed by the outside world, forgetting himself under the influence of the intoxicating urban spectacle. See Rearick, *Pleasures*, chap. 7, "The Spectacle of Modern Life," pp. 167–95, on the traditions of the *flâneur* and *badaud* and on Parisian street life in general around the turn of the century.

58. More ominously, Romains sometimes describes the poet as someone who imposes a soul upon an unconscious assembly, who remains outside the group rather than participating in it. For example, in June 1909 Romains's long poem *À la foule qui est ici* was delivered by the actor de Max at the Odéon Theater as part of a poetry competition. With his powerful voice and gestures, de Max recited the words intended to transform the *foule* into a godlike, self-conscious *unanime*. His performance caused a tumult and Romains won second prize. (André Cuisenier, *Souvenirs unanimistes* [Le Celle-Saint-Cloud: J. Cuisenier, 1975], p. 30; also Norrish, *Drama*, pp. 15–16.)

Sometimes the individual who arouses the *unanime* may act less like a poet than like an *agent provocateur*. In Romains's play *Le Bourg régeneré* (1906) and in his novel *Les Copains* (1913), high-spirited young men created *unanimes* in dull provincial towns by staging pranks—writing annoying graffiti in public urinals, or arranging elaborate hoaxes. While at the École normale, Romains himself acquired considerable local fame as a prankster, especially when he orchestrated an elaborate and convincing campaign for a nonexistent candidate—an incident that suggests his contempt for ordinary political processes and activities (Bourin, *Connaissance*, pp. 128–29).

In the *Manuel de déification* Romains is even more outspoken in recommending that individuals create *unanimes* by arousing already existing groups. "Do them violence," he declares at one point, and at another, more benignly, he recommends giving groups "still naive, spontaneous, and childlike, clear consciousness, the concept of their living unity, the revelation of their self." (Quoted by Décaudin in his preface to *Vie unanime*, p. 18; also Norrish, *Drama*, p. 13.) Such groups, in short, are passive audiences prone to manipulation by the superior poet-prankster.

There is a fundamental ambivalence here, as *unanimisme* expresses both complicity with and contempt for the urban crowd.

59. Romains, *Vie unanime,* p. 140.

60. The absence of work and workers in Romains's poetry is by no means unusual among writers of his time. "The literature of the Belle Époque is not at all a literature of labor" (Baroli, *Train,* p. 361).

61. Raymond Williams, *Politics and Letters: Interviews with New Left Review* (London: Verso, 1981 [1979]), p. 205.

62. The remark is made by Jallez, a contemplative, studious, mild Parisian who represents cultural Europe, the continent of daily life, comfort, and happiness that exists in an eternal present—the *unanimiste* ideal. A second character, Jerphanion, is an ambitious, practical man of action from Velay. He represents political Europe, the continent with a past, a future, a history. Romains uses this literary device of "doubling" to express the contradictory sides of his personality. See Bonneville, "Jules Romains et l'Europe," *Cahiers 3,* pp. 257–58.

63. Shelley Rice, "Parisian Views" (*Views Supplement,* September 1986, pp. 7–13), p. 10 of manuscript version. In this discussion I am indebted to this and another fine essay by Rice, "Still Points in a Turning World" (*Afterimage,* May 1987, pp. 10–13).

64. Marshall Berman, *All That Is Solid Melts into Air* (New York: Simon and Schuster, 1982), p. 150.

65. Wolfgang Schivelbusch, *The Railway Journey: The Industrialization of Time and Space in the 19th Century* (Berkeley: University of California Press, 1986 [1977]), p. 195. See also pp. 178–97 passim. In the words of J. B. Jackson, the nineteenth-century rebuilding of Paris is a prime example of the "triumph of the street" by which we "perceive the city less in terms of architecture than in terms of communication." J. B. Jackson, "The Discovery of the Street," in *The Necessity for Ruins, and Other Topics* (Amherst, Mass: University of Massachusetts, 1980), p. 55.

66. Rice, "Parisian Views," pp. 11–14.

67. See the discussion of Lukács in Williams, "Base and Superstructure," pp. 35–37. Note particularly Williams's discussion of the limitations of Lukács's approach on pp. 36–37.

68. Williams, *Country and City,* pp. 234–35.

The Feminization of Technology: Mechanical Characters in Picture Books

JUDITH YAROSS LEE

For many years popular literature has occupied a special place in American studies as a source of insight into cultural concerns and values.[1] The Indian captivity narrative of the eighteenth century, for example, along with the dime western of the nineteenth and the murder mystery of the twentieth centuries, helped reveal our faith in the principle that Richard Slotkin termed "regeneration through violence."[2] From other popular American formulas—not only the Harlequin romance and the Horatio Alger tale, but also television's endless demonstrations that "Father Knows Best" (recently revised in *The Bill Cosby Show*) and the ubiquitous if-at-first-you-don't-succeed chronicles of new products and inventions—we have learned about cultural conflicts over issues as diverse as authority, success, class, race, and gender.[3] Formulas aimed at young children ought to lead the list of popular genres for consideration, considering their role in the process of acculturation, but in fact, scholarship on juvenile formulas has concentrated on books for older readers and overlooked picture books almost entirely.[4]

This neglect reflects historical and technical considerations perhaps more than critics' preferences. After all, children's picture books only recently joined the ranks of mass literature. To reach a mass market, picture books require cheap lithography, preferably cheap color lithography, which became widely available only after 1930.[5] The limitations of nineteenth-century printing technologies, by contrast, kept picture books (as opposed to picture magazines, which aimed at adult readers) beyond the reach of the general public. Few people could afford hand-colored or even woodcut editions for children, especially since they outgrow picture books so quickly. These demographics, in light of the high financial risk involved (one British historian estimated that the high cost of engraved illustrations in the mid-ninteenth century meant that a picture book had to sell *at least* fifty thousand copies to make its publication worthwhile),[6] made publishers reluctant to take on such projects. As a result, the largest market for children's books involved narrative series for older readers. In the United States, these included first the dime novels and Horatio Alger adventures; then Nancy Drew, the Hardy Boys, and the Bobbsey Twins; and more recently Beverly Cleary's Ramona books, Jay Williams's Danny Dunn series, and the Baby Sitters' Club. Compared to the riches of such fully realized novels, the simplicity of picture books offers little of interest to the literary scholar.

Because of their young audience and undisguised didacticism, however, picture books represent a particularly fertile field for exploring values embedded in their narratives. Authors of picture books cannot presume that their audience is familiar with their subject, so they have great freedom in introducing and characterizing it—at least within the general limits of what the adults who produce, buy, and read the book consider appropriate for young children. The result is a body of literature offering interesting insights not only into our culture's official values (the attitudes that we publicly claim and promote), but also, and more importantly, into the ways that the values espoused in children's books differ from those of adult literature with similar subjects and themes. In this context, picture books about machines offer an important case in point. Unlike their adult counterparts, picture books portray technology affectionately and from a feminist point of view.

In contrast to the anti-intellectual conventions of popular adult fiction, which typically portrays technology as the instrument of death and destruction, if not actually the agent of apocalypse, children's picture books assert the essential benevolence of manmade objects.[7] Instead of epic battles between humans and machines, or tragic examples of people destroyed by machines—to cite just two standard adult formulas familiar to readers of science fiction and adventure stories—narratives for children take the form of domestic comedies that climax with *alliances* between people and their tools. In this vein, for example, *Betsy and the Vacuum Cleaner* (1975) initiates children into one mystery of daily life,[8] while stories about quite ordinary fire trucks, tricycles, and bulldozers assure children just discovering their own vulnerability that humans can indeed master the dangers of fire, the difficulties of distance, and the limits of strength. In short, picture books quite literally welcome—even glorify—the *deus ex machina*.

Although picture books about machines vary with age and rhe-

torical purpose in their treatment of gender, the gender values of
any given book hinge less on when it was published than on
whether it dispenses facts or fables. Anyone who has read to
children is painfully familiar with the factual volumes. Most settle
for unadorned description and classification, although a few invent
a narrative frame. Janet Smalley's account of a furnace with a
cheerful face in *How It All Began* (1932) exemplifies the genre at its
simplest: "This is a furnace, down in the cellar. There is one in your
house. It burns coal or oil or gas. It sends heat to every room by
steam, hot water or hot air. (The stove is smiling because it likes to
make people comfortable)."[9] The more complex volumes include
not only the kinetic depictions of Richard Scarry but also miniature
encyclopedias on types of fire trucks and object lessons in tricycle
use and maintenance.[10] Recent books celebrate fathers standing
over hot stoves and women running power rigs, but older books
(still on the shelves of the public library) remain influential, and in
any event the genre of factual books has changed little since Wilfred
Jones published *How the Derrick Works* in 1930.[11] A recent bibliography of Little Golden Books unwittingly demonstrates the
genre's stability: four books spanning almost twenty years have
nearly identical titles.[12] Not surprisingly, the gender values in these
most traditional of texts tend to be as conventional as their plots:
men ride vehicles, operate machines, and fix things; little boys
imitate them while little girls and their mothers merely watch.

Indeed, despite the trend toward less rigid gender models, as
evidenced by titles like *Susan in the Driver's Seat* (1973),[13] feminist
values seem to have had little influence on the structures and
themes of informational tales. A British volume recently republished in the United States, for example, remains rigidly sexist.
Its few exceptions to traditional gender-typing occur in a comic
"what's wrong with the picture?" section, where the incongruities
actually reinforce conventional gender-types. Pictures of a girl
mowing a lawn with a vacuum cleaner and a boy feeding laundry
into a cement mixer imply not very subtly that both girl and boy are
out of their element.[14] Books like this one remind us that not every
children's book available in America today will promote progressive
American values.

Nonetheless, emphasizing the obvious, that children's literature
can attract boys to machines and alienate girls from them, helps to
distinguish these unremarkable informational stories from a group
of tales that we might call *technological fables:* a much more
interesting and much less conventional genre in which machines
are characters. Examples include some of the most familiar and

beloved—even canonized—American picture books, including *The Little Engine That Could* (1930), *Mike Mulligan and His Steam Shovel* (1938), *Scuffy the Tugboat* (1946), and *The Little Red Caboose* 1953). The importance that small children attach to the objects around them easily accounts for the emergence of a distinct class of juvenile stories characterizing machines in human terms, complete with personalities, problems, and genders.[15] It is much more difficult, however, to explain the genre's gender-based narrative formulas. In contrast to the informational texts, which maintain a conventional masculine orientation (or which self-consciously demonstrate opportunities for girls), the fables of personified machines quite literally feminize technology. In this genre, even fairly old stories—that is, those written before heightened consciousness of gender stereotyping—follow a predictable series of feminist formulas. The female machines—those given women's names or referred to by feminine pronouns—are always heroic; the male machines are always humbled.

Technological fables need not rely on these two basic gender plots, which merely mechanize the classic comedies of the *eiron* (the comic inferior who triumphs) and *alazon* (the comic superior who fails). But doing so effectively feminizes technology, allowing female machine-characters to dominate a world usually run (quite literally) by men. The stories rely with remarkable consistency on turning the two gender plots into four basic story lines, used alone or in combination. Tales about female machines commonly assert themes that we might designate "The Best Man for the Job Is a Woman" and "Mild Appearances Belie Great Power," both variations of the *eiron* plot. Stories of male machines, on the other hand, claim "Little Boys Need Taming" or "Mother Knows Best," two versions of the *alazon* plot. Not associated with conventional adult literature about technology, which tends toward the macho formulas of the spy story and the adventure tale, these themes point to the link between children's fiction and women's literature generally. Just as women storytellers shaped the strong female characters of traditional fairy tales,[16] so they continue to mold juvenile literary formulas in the technical age.

The works of Virginia Lee Burton, who built her career on fables of the heroic female machine, offer a series of examples of the feminization of technology. *Mike Mulligan and His Steam Shovel* (1938)[17] exemplifies the prevailing formula, "Mild Appearances Belie Great Power," in which the machine character appears incapable of the heroic acts that she finally accomplishes. (In the same vein is Burton's obscure *Maybelle the Cable Car* [1952],[18] which celebrates the superiority of the cable car over buses and other vehicles in San Francisco.) *Katy and the Big Snow* (1943),[19] by contrast, salutes a long-awaited display of innate heroism, proving that "The Best Man for the Job Is a Woman." Both formulas define the heroic act in terms not conventionally associated with characters named Mary Anne or Katy: outstanding physical strength, courage in the face of great odds, and mastery of nature.

Ostensibly just a fable of loyalty, *Mike Mulligan and His Steam Shovel* not only presents an egalitarian marriage, in which Mary Anne and Mike work and retire side by side, but also demonstrates the value of machines to individuals and society. The opening section of the book celebrates the accomplishments of "Mike Mulligan and Mary Anne and some others," who built our highways, skyscrapers, railroad tunnels, and airports—in short, the creators of modern America. Over the years of their partnership, Mike Mulligan took such good care of his beloved Mary Anne that "she never grew old," yet despite her expertise and condition, she finds herself forced out of work by the newer technologies of the diesel-engine shovels, gas shovels, and electric shovels. Other steamshovel operators have junked or abandoned their rigs, but our narrator tells us, "Mike Mulligan loved Mary Anne. He couldn't do that to her." As in any proper love story, Mary Anne justifies Mike's faith in her when, to get the job digging the foundation for a new town hall in Popperville, he stakes his fee on his favorite brag—that "Mary Anne could dig as much in a day as a hundred men could dig in a week, though he was never quite sure that this was so." Love conquers all, and the end of the book finds them as contented as any other successful old couple: "Mike in his rocking chair smoking his pipe, and Mary Anne beside him, warming up the meetings in the new town hall." Even after retirement, Mike and Mary Anne continue their service to each other and to society, as custodian and furnace, respectively, of Popperville Town Hall.

The pair cannot live happily ever after, however, until they have overcome natural and human obstacles that elevate the love story into an allegory of technological society. Mike's boast about Mary Anne's prowess takes on epic dimensions as Burton measures the steamshovel's work by the position of the sun in the sky—she must finish by sunset. In typical fairy-tale fashion, moreover, the couple's difficulties expand. Despite their ultimate success in the race, Mike and Mary Anne face an obstacle in the mean-spirited, penny-pinching Henry B. Swap, a selectman who had hoped that Mike would fail so the town wouldn't have to pay and who now sneers with pleasure at the sight of Mary Anne and Mike stranded at the bottom of the foundation. They had dug its square corners so speedily and precisely that they no longer had a way to drive out of the hole, and Swap declares that the job remains unfinished and that Mike has lost the challenge. But just when all appears lost, Burton engineers a plot manipulation that allows yet another *eiron* to triumph: Swap accepts a young boy's proposal that Mary Anne stay on in Popperville as the furnace of the new town hall.

In this new role, which allows her to stay in the hole as it evolves from foundation to town hall basement, Mary Anne illustrates at the end of the tale the enduring value of even so-called obsolete technologies like the steam engine. In addition to saving the hard labor of a hundred men, Mary Anne can bring warmth of several kinds to the New England town. Literally she provides the steam heat to keep Popperville's democratic process going in the winter; metaphorically she exudes the personal warmth to convert an adversary like Swap to a friend. John C. Scott misinterprets Mary Anne's obsolescence when he claims that Burton's tales "espouse a return to a simpler way of life"[20] (i.e., that they belong to the genre that Leo Marx called "false pastorals"). On the contrary, every element of *Mike Mulligan* demonstrates that obsolescence is at the very least relative, if not actually in the eye of the beholder. In this deservedly classic tale, everyone benefits from technology—body, soul, and polis—even when symbolized by an apparently antiquated steamshovel.

Nor is the value of technology in *Mike Mulligan* limited to Mary Anne's achievements—either her success in Popperville or the skyscrapers and other worthy projects in which she participated years before. Other technologies also figure in the story, and they likewise contribute to social solidarity. After discovering that Mary Anne works harder and faster as her audience increases, the telephone switchboard operator phones everyone in the surrounding towns to join the crowd. They come in vehicles new and old: horse-and-buggy, bicycle, and automobile. Their contribution to Mary Anne's success extends the technological triumph of the contest with the sun into a victory far more dramatic, illustrating not only human mastery of nature through technology, but also the triumph of American democratic society. Mary Anne's achievement derives from as well as benefits a community that Burton defines as social and political. Technologies of all kind support town government in Popperville, and a female machine paved the way.

As a pattern of plot and character, the feminization of technology in picture books extends beyond displays of unexpected heroism from outdated or otherwise unpromising female machines—even though we should remember that obsolete technologies always seem more friendly and domesticated than new ones. Burton's *Katy and the Big Snow,* for example, chronicles how the "beautiful red tractor" named Katy comes out of her winter retirement to rescue Geoppolis when a blizzard paralyzes the city. Although Geoppolis seldom receives enough snow to warrant hitching up Katy's snow plow, this blizzard proves too powerful for the truck plows, so everyone depends on Katy to clear all the roads and restore the social network—in this instance, represented by police protection, ambulances, and fire trucks. Katy responds to every request for help with a cheerful "Sure. Follow me," and her refrain helps structure the narrative, which continues until, after working through all the points of the compass, Katy has finished plowing out all the side streets and has returned to her garage. "Only then," the narrator points out in the concluding sentence, "did Katy stop." The narrative's geographical structure, like the very name *Geoppolis,* impacts a mythic aspect to Katy's accomplishment, which seems to encompass the whole globe. Without the strong, dependable technology of Katy, as she and everyone knows, her world would have ceased to function. Written in the 1940s, as Americans embraced images of Rosy the Riveter, *Katy and the Big Snow* left no doubt about who was the best person for the job.

The same pride in her work, the same strength of mind and body, the same dedication to public good also motivate other female machine characters—the Little Engine That Could, for instance, who feels sorry for all "the good little boys and girls on the other side of the mountain who would not have any toys [to play with] or good food to eat unless she helped" (165),[21] and the *Columbus,* heroine of "Christopher and the Columbus," a ferryboat on an illicit outing who not only fails to get into trouble herself, but actually rescues three less lucky boys who had become stranded when their raft gave way.[22] Like these exemplary characters, female machines consistently exhibit noble traits that seldom, if ever, characterize their male counterparts, who demonstrate the theme "Little Boys Need Taming." With the overstatement typical of popular literary formulas, the feminization of technology aggrandizes female machines and belittles male machines too.

In contrast to the heroic female machines stand a series of mischievous, selfish, or cocky males cruising for a bruising; the plots of these tchnological fables provide punishments for pride rather than rewards for determination. Gertrude Crampton's *Tootle* (1946) provides the classic—if somewhat extreme—example of this type.[23] *Tootle* tells of a strong and fast young engine destined for a notable career as a great Flyer, who risks losing all he's worked for, as well as all his future promise, through an undisciplined refusal to "[Stay] on the Rails No Matter What." (Along with "Stopping for a Red Flag Waving," this is the primary lesson that Tootle and his companions study at the Lower Trainswitch School for Loco- motives.) The happy ending of the fable depends quite literally on getting Tootle back on the track, on persuading him to forgo the pleasures of freedom and to conform to the rules of his job. Teach- ing this lesson, no easy task, finally engages all the people of the town, and a narrative detail conveys the unhappy image of adults ganging up to impose rigid social goals on children: all the towns- people crouch in the bushes and wave red flags until Tootle gives up, finally realizing that "there is nothing but red flags for loco- motives that get off their tracks" (59). This conclusion underlines how explicitly the structures of technological fables depend on the stereotypes of the good little girl and the unruly little boy, re- gardless of whether the tales focus on male or female machines. Tootle's escapades demonstrate that boys will be boys, while the moral of the story insists that they should not be.

Indeed, the tales of male machine characters send a message that we might phrase (with apologies to Professor Henry Higgins), "Why Can't a Boy Be More Like a Girl?" Technological fables consistently depict male machines in the process of learning to accept social or personal limitations, most often by suppressing macho demonstrations of speed, strength, or independence. The very titles give away the morals of Water Retan's *The Snowplow That Tried to Go South* (1950) and *The Steam Shovel That Wouldn't Eat Dirt* (1948), which may have been influenced by Virginia Lee Burton's *Choo Choo: The Story of a Little Engine Who Ran Away* (1937). But even fables with less obviously moralistic titles, includ- ing Crampton's *Scuffy the Tugboat (and His Adventures Down the River)* (1946) and Marian Potter's *The Little Red Caboose* (1953), insist on domesticating males' unrealistic ambitions. The hero of *Scuffy the Tugboat,* for instance, learns to be satisfied with the small world of the bathtub after many adventures and misadven- tures in the big world represented by the big river; at the end, the cocky toy who had repeatedly insisted, "I was meant for bigger things" (36, 37, 41), contritely concedes, "I was meant for safer things" (48).[24] *The Little Red Caboose* at first seems to violate these patterns because the tale displays a male machine's heroism, but in fact the narrative emphasizes the process by which the caboose comes to accept his limitations. Always last, the little red caboose feels inferior to the other cars on the train because they are bigger, apparently more important, and attract the most attention from the children they pass, attention that has usually waned by the time he passes. One day, when his train begins slipping backwards down a steep mountain, the little red caboose holds the entire train steady on the tracks by gripping tightly with his brakes—and saves the train. Now he gets his proper attention from children wherever he goes, and he tolerates his size and position as the price of success.[25] As these two examples suggest, male machines vary a great deal in their dissatisfaction with the roles assigned them, but their stories consistently represent the technological fables at their most explicitly didactic, equating the mischievous little machines with mischievous little boys.

Together, the humbling of male machines and the glorification of female machines reflect the context in which picture books are written, marketed, and read. Books for young children are written mainly by women,[26] but regardless of their author's gender, they are targeted almost exclusively at women, that is, mothers and children's librarians. In the case of picture books, whose intended audience is pre-literate, the mothers who read the books aloud become the primary readers. These facts of authorship and marketing do not by themselves, of course, explain why the informational texts masculinize technology and the fables feminize it, but they do clarify why writers, when freed from the masculine and realistic conventions of informational narratives, would feminize technology. Picture books function as a subclass of women's literature.

The formulaic gender patterns of the technological fables thus reflect generic convention, not authorial choice. Since English does not require the use of gender-specific pronouns for inanimate objects, the choice is always significant, even more so as traits are repeatedly attributed to fully realized machine characters. In this regard, it is worth noting that although English conventionally uses the feminine pronoun to refer to ships, technological fables almost always characterize ships as male machines and describe their comeuppance. (The odd instance, as in "Christopher and the Columbus," in which the ship has a male name and a female pronoun, portrays the ship as a hero.) The formula's general outlines, however, are clear: the heroic fable of the female machine invites children to link technology to the security and approval of Mom, while the humbling fable of the male machine reminds children (little boys in particular) that other, stronger forces—probably Mom—make the rules.

So strong a formula is the feminization of technology that in cases where the male machine does not undergo a chastening experience, the story nonetheless traces a decline in his status. Jean Horton Berg's *Tuggy the Tug Boat* (1975) illustrates this variation on the theme. After his steam engine renders him outmoded, Tuggy—once the rescuer of mudbound oil tankers and drowning sailors—faces the humiliating prospect of life as a houseboat. But quite fortuitously, he and Captain Larson find a niche for themselves as the operators of "Tuggy's Excursions—Children Only." The resolution has a certain charm as a consolation prize for injured male vanity, since it offers a compromise between the housewife's domesticity and a masculine commercial enterprise, but of course Tuggy's happy ending remains unequivocally his second choice. As a result, his transformation from tough guy to playmate lacks the heroic grandeur of Mary Anne's metamorphosis from steam engine to furnace, and his story presents weaker proof than hers that obsolescence is in the eyes of the beholder. Indeed, *Tuggy*'s tale illustrates once again that in the feminist world of these technological fables, male characters usually come off second best.

Recognizing the technological fable as a women's genre also explains some of the odd elements of Watty Piper's *The Little Engine That Could*,[27] which in this context stands as the purest expression of the wishes and fears implied by the feminization of technology. For those who remember only the immortal words "I think I can," let me point out that this allegory of perseverance contains several train-characters, two female and three male. Compared to their larger male counterparts, appropriately named Shiny New Engine, Big Strong Engine (also known as Freight Engine), and Rusty Old Engine, the two female engines are not only mild and meek, but also markedly unselfish and socially responsible. Quite simply, the female engines care about the fate of children while the males do not.

These gender-based values inform every element of the tale. When, as the story opens, a merry little engine carrying children's toys and food suddenly "stop[s] with a jerk," she worries, "What [are] all those good little boys and girls on the other side of the mountain going to do without the wonderful toys to play with and the good food to eat?" (160). The question could not be more plaintively posed by a new mother kept apart from her nursling, a context that suggests why the tale resolves the problem through another female character, the little blue engine. But gender also informs other contexts of the tale. As the self-satisfied, decidedly macho Shiny New Engine and Big Strong Engine refuse to help because they consider themselves too important to pull a train filled with children's goods, these powerful engines make clear that, whether pulling parlor cars or printing-presses, they belong to the far more important world of grown-ups—and male grown-ups, at that. Their superior status shows in their capitalized names, which contrast with the lower-case attributes of the female engines, who thus remain effectively nameless. This small detail confirms the larger theme equating physical power with status in the adult world, a connection that explains why the Rusty Old Engine chugs off with a defeated "I can not. I can not" (163). In the adult world of *The Little Engine That Could,* here defined as a masculine world, only a female character can resolve anxieties about another woman's inability to nurture. Apparently any female will do, even one so small and naive that she does not even know her limits.

With this resolution, the story repudiates conventional assumptions about gender, status, and power in favor of the feminist values implicit in the tale's portrait of technology. To be sure, one strand of the story simply placates disenfranchised mothers and their children: Mom is strong and important enough for the kids, even if grown-ups do not consider her as strong or as important as Dad (and of course she is certainly stronger than her own worn-out Rusty Old Engine of a father)! Nonetheless, the myth underlying the feminization of technology is quite explicit here, and it offers audiences of women and children some compelling consolations for their lack of prestige. First, the fable distinctly opposes traditional valuations of power by honoring kindness over status and perseverance over strength, that is, honoring children over adults and women over men. In addition, the myth asserts that strength depends less on body than on mind—an arena in which the sexes are equal. That's why the little blue engine insists like a proper Cartesian, "I *think* I can. I *think* I can" as she puffs up the hill, and congratulates herself, "I *thought* I could. I *thought* I could" all the way down (166, my italics). Finally, the story offers feminist wish fulfillment through a nearly pure form of poetic justice: all the conceited men get left behind in the roundhouse while the women and children enjoy the spoils and pride of their victory. In this fable, the meek do inherit the earth.

The Little Engine That Could, like other examples of the feminization of technology, begins by presenting conventional gender roles but ends with the comic reversals of wish fulfillment. Here, as in the other technological fables, individual machines may be naughty, but machines themselves range from the morally neutral to the socially admirable. No machines in the garden, no iron devils, the trains and other machines in children's fables have sufficient neutrality to embody both good folks and bad. Yet the stories make clear that machines exist to serve people, and their basic benevolence makes them—quite literally—the vehicles of health and happiness for the genre's most important people. It is not surprising, then, that these read-aloud stories for mothers should give the source of happiness a female form.

Nor is it surprising that a tale of machine characters written by a man for an audience of adults should disregard these feminist formulas and instead cast "Woman" in the role of villain. In this regard, *The Brave Little Toaster* (1986)[28] by Thomas M. Disch provides a perfect counterexample for the feminist gender-plots of the picture books. Despite many similarities to the technological fables for young children, including a series of heroic machine-characters, *The Brave Little Toaster* could hardly stand further from the feminist values of the picture books. Disch's book makes clear that, as a formula for characterization and plot, the feminization of technology belongs to such women's genres as books for pre-readers and has no place in stories for adult men.

As a fable, *The Brave Little Toaster* is certainly simple enough for children. Five appliances, bewildered at having been abandoned in a country cottage, embark on an epic journey to the city to find their master. As you might expect, each appliance undergoes a test of character, and the group as a whole bonds together for mutual benefit. The vacuum cleaner must endure the mud and dried leaves of the forest; the electric blanket manages to survive its tatters and tears; the tensor lamp replaces its broken bulb with a new one; the clock-radio withstands the piracy of the junk-man; and the toaster warms the hearts (and favorite foods) of every animal and appliance the group meets along the route. The plot continues to twist after the gadgets reach the city, where they find themselves entirely unwanted—indeed, replaced—in their master's apartment. But true to the sentimental values underlying the journey, the end brings the loyal appliances success and satisfaction. Their urban compatriots, the radio and telephone, help the country cousins find love and fulfillment in a new home. The country cousins do not lack resources, *The Brave Little Toaster* thus declares, nor does the loss of one job mean eternal unhappiness to those willing to take their lives under control. Readers of a moralistic bent will find lessons about perseverance and divorce in this story, but except for its unusual characters, it would seem to offer little of compelling interest to most readers.[29]

The problem lies in a conflict between the conception of the book and its audiences. The subtitle, *A Bedtime Story for Small Appliances,* declares the book a children's tale, as in fact Doubleday &

Company marketed it, yet *The Brave Little Toaster* reveals at almost every turn that it aims at an audience of adult males—the very audience addressed by *The Magazine of Fantasy and Science Fiction,* where the tale first appeared in August 1980. Disch's book is not a picture book, to be sure: only nine illustrations punctuate the seventy-eight pages of narrative. Books with such a ratio of pictures to text generally aim at readers ages nine and up, as opposed to the preschool audience of the picture book, but the diction and point of view of *The Brave Little Toaster* would cause difficulties even for most young adolescents. What twelve-year-old would understand, much less appreciate, a toaster's-eye view of a junkyard as populated by "the terrible emblems . . . of its own inevitable obsolescence"? (53). We might excuse such inappropriate narration as the momentary lapse of a writer caught up in his own metaphors, yet a basic inconsistency remains: few children young enough to be interested in the story of an heroic toaster would appreciate why "small appliances who may be listening" should need such advice as "if you are in any doubt about the voltage of the current where you are living, *ask a major appliance*" (21). Such metaphors might simply reveal confusion about what youngsters can interpret, of course, but only a fairly mature audience would appreciate the punning warning, "Never put your plug in a strange socket!" (21). The joke characterizes women as potential sources of danger and therefore calls for an audience of sexually knowledgeable males, revealing in the process that *The Brave Little Toaster,* far from feminizing technology for children, is a maculine tale for grownups.

The conflicts in audience explain why the apparently wholesome juvenile values of the surface yield to an undercurrent of violence and sexuality rare in children's books, if not entirely inappropriate to them. Like the machines in conventional children's fables, the appliances in this tale are heroic underdogs, but in contrast to their feminized counterparts, Disch's unpromising heroes stand at serious risk of victimization—particularly by adults. The dangers here have little in common with the epic tensions of *Mike Mulligan and His Steam-Shovel,* for instance, because the world of *The Brave Little Toaster* teems with threats. To be sure, problems of rust and weather and the physical impediments to the journey belong to the world of the juvenile fantasy, but these comprise the least of the appliances' troubles compared to the dangers represented by people. The so-called "pirate" who kidnaps the toaster and his comrades and imprisons them in the junkyard demonstrates the evils of greed. Worse still, and particularly relevant to the gender issues of technological fables, is the primary villain of the tale: Woman, or—to be absolutely precise—sexuality.

"Gender and the complications it gives rise to simply aren't relevant to the lives appliances lead" (34) the narrator advises, ostensibly explaining the appliances's disinterest in sexual jokes but in fact exposing the story's concern with gender and sex. Indeed, the novella focuses on the ways that sexual relationships violate such gender-neutral issues as friendship and personal fulfillment. The nameless humans in this fable, known only as "the master" and "the mistress," are, if anything, less particularized than their appliances. In the process, the tale acquires an allegorical quality (perhaps self-ridiculing, perhaps not) wherein mistress and master become Adam and Eve in a mechanical "Paradise Lost."

In the distant past before the opening of *The Brave Little Toaster,* the five appliances lived in sexless bliss with their master at his country house. Unable to understand his desertion of them and worried about his well-being, they embark on their journey full of loyal concern. All their suffering on the road proves in vain, however. On reaching his city apartment they discover the reason for their abandonment: the master has gotten married. The mistress has imposed her own choices about home and housekeeping and by implication has achieved mastery over him, as well. The news that she suffers from hay-fever and therefore wants to sell the country house underscores her role as the antagonist in his tale of sexual betrayal. Having first destroyed the camaraderie between the master and his appliance buddies, the mistress now prepares to exile them all from the site of their happy innocence. This sexual crisis requires a resolution in the same terms, and Disch provides it. Thanks to the telephone and radio, the toaster and his pals (all very much the worse for wear after their wasted heroic efforts) find "Paradise Regained": a safe existence with "an elderly, impoverished ballerina who lived all alone in a small room at the back of her ballet studio . . . in the oldest part of the city" (77). This happy ending allows the appliances not only to fulfill their mechanical purposes in life, but also, by taking up residence with a very old woman, to achieve once more a life free from what the narrator delicately calls "the complications" of sex.

The designation of woman as villain and the association of technology with male bonding: these two violations of the feminist formulas of technological picture-book fables would signal Disch's real interest in writing for adults even if his diction did not give him away. What child could love a book in which the ideal world excludes even the possibility of a loving mom and dad? What mother would read her child a book about the dreadful interference of woman in a man's world? Who cares about appliances whose personification lacks the specificity of gender?

Whatever they reveal about *The Brave Little Toaster* itself, such questions help clarify the values underlying technological fables in picture books. Most obvious is how little the feminization of technology, a juvenile formula really aimed at women, informs the *The Brave Little Toaster,* a book written for men by a man. Without several other texts like Disch's we cannot draw conclusions about the generic significance of his choices, but as a counterexample to the picture books, his narrative alone points to the vast difference between the feminist values of technological picture-book fables, on the one hand, and the masculine values of both children's informational texts and adult fiction, on the other.

In the fables, apparently the only technical genre open for feminization, women have recreated the world in their own terms. Here technology participates intimately in human society. *Mike Mulligan, Katy and the Big Snow, The Little Engine That Could,* and the variations of the notion that "The Best Man for the Job Is a Woman" all define a world in which physical power coexists with love, beauty, and noble social goals. Similarly, *Scuffy the Tugboat, The Little Red Caboose, Tuggy the Tug Boat,* and variations on the theme that "Little Boys Need Taming" assert at the very least that Mother knows best, if not actually that girls are superior to boys. But regardless of whether the fables have a male or female machine protagonist, they gratify dreams of success and power more constructively—and, therefore, more realistically—than the familiar aggressive fantasies of Clark Kent or the Br'er Rabbit stories, to cite just two examples of meek or apparently outfoxed figures who ultimately prove themselves superior to their antagonists.

Feminist wish fulfillment ought not, however, overshadow the importance of the genre's most salient feature: *machines* have been invested with these gender formulas. In this genre, technology is no mere scapegoat or plot complication. Rather, machines follow in their creators' images. They have the capacity for great benevolence; selfish disregard for rules or society (rather than outright malevolence) seems to be their worst sin, and it is by no means salient. Although a crude allegory lies just beneath the surface of the male-machine stories, the link between human goals and machines presents children with a wholesome portrait—and a fairly accurate one, at that—of technology as a human tool. Children routinely animate their toys and other objects that have meaning for them, so a story's focus on a personified machine doubtless seems less remarkable to them than to adults, but the machine characters nonetheless offer a few unique features to their young audiences. Machine characters can represent the underdog with particular poignancy, since few fates are more discouraging than being junked or declared obsolete, and even a child too young to understand death can appreciate the finality of a broken toy. On the other hand, through the achievements of machine heroes like Katy and the Little Red Caboose, the fables capture the wonder of mechanical invention, which does seem to give life to the inanimate. Thus the feminization of technology domesticates and enlivens the technical world for children, all the while empowering them and their mothers through fantasy.

Children can turn to informational books about machines if they need to overcome fears of technology; the technological fables serve other, richer needs. The machine characters of *Mike Mulligan and His Steam-Shovel* and *Scuffy the Tugboat,* for instance, become quite human as they take on dilemmas that children can recognize as their own familiar struggles, such as having an apparently impossible task or trying something that proves too hard, but the feminist context of the fables distinguishes them from other tales with similar themes by affirming the power of the mother, on whose strength small children depend. The affirmation amounts to preaching to the converted, since neither the preschool audience nor the mothers who choose the books and read them aloud need such reminders. In a world whose technical power structures continue in the hands of men, however, the formula remains a significant consolation. It not only subverts traditional gender-types, but also, through its divergence from the dominant formulas of adult fiction, offers an alternative view of technology. Adult formula fiction typically represents technology as either an agent of ruin (a staple of dystopian science fiction and the spy novel) or, less frequently, as the *deus ex machina* (the convention for heroic tales of invention). By refusing to carry over those conventions into children's literature, the women writers who have shaped the technological fable have created a literature that characterizes technology in feminist terms. Through the feminization of technology, the picture-book fable presents machines as friends—that is, as thoroughly human presences—whose world reflects a feminist agenda of realigned power and social relations. For the women who write, read, and buy these picture books, the consolation offered by their formulas must, for the time being, suffice.

NOTES

1. The most distinguished scholarship in American studies falls into this category. Such works as Henry Nash Smith's *Virgin Land: The American West as Symbol and Myth* (1950; rpt. Cambridge: Harvard Univ. Press, 1970) and R. W. B. Lewis's *The American Adam: Innocence, Tragedy, and Tradition in the Nineteenth*

222   JUDITH YAROSS LEE

Century (1955: rpt. Chicago: Univ. of Chicago Press, 1971) remain classic investigations treating high and popular culture as a continuum.

2. On the Indian captivity narrative, see Richard Slotkin, *Regeneration Through Violence: The Mythology of the American Frontier, 1600–1860* (Middletown, Conn.: Wesleyan Univ. Press, 1973). On the dime western, see Henry Nash Smith, *The Virgin Land,* and John G. Cawelti, *The Six-Gun Mystique* (Bowling Green, Oh.: Bowling Green Univ. Popular Press, 1975). On the murder mystery, see Cawelti's *Adventure, Mystery, and Romance: Formula Stories as Art and Popular Culture* (Chicago: Univ. of Chicago Press, 1976), which also contains a theoretical analysis of the pleasures of formula literature.

3. On the Horatio Alger story and its variations, see John G. Cawelti, *Apostles of the Self-Made Man: Changing Concepts of Success in America* (Chicago: Univ. of Chicago Press, 1965). A good analysis of television-script formulas is Horace Newcomb, *TV: The Most Popular Art* (Garden City, N.Y.: Anchor Books, 1974). Cawelti's *Adventure, Mystery, and Romance* includes a brief discussion of the romance novel, but the classic study is Janice A. Radway's *Reading the Romance: Women, Patriarchy, and Popular Literature* (Chapel Hill: Univ. of North Carolina Press, 1984).

4. For example, only one of the recent critical works on children's literature focuses exclusively on picture books, and it is more descriptive and appreciative than analytical. See Barbara Bader, *American Picturebooks from "Noah's Ark" to "The Beast Within"* (New York: Macmillan, 1976).

5. Woodcut illustrations gave way to wood-engraving in the 1790s, but etchings on copper plates remained the mainstay of cheap illustration until the refinement of lithography, developed by Alois Senefelder in Munich between 1796–1799, and patented in England in 1800. Until the 1960s, color offset lithography shared the market with color photogravure, a cheaper process first developed for black-and-white illustration in 1890. See S. H. Steinberg, *Five Hundred Years of Printing,* 3d ed. (New York and London: Penguin Books, 1974), 283–85.

6. Alex Ellis, *A History of Children's Reading and Literature* (Oxford: Pergamon Press, 1963), 68.

7. For a general discussion of the values implied by the formulas of adult literature about technology, see Judith Yaross Lee, "Introduction: Scientists and Investors as Literary Heroes," in *Beyond the Two Cultures: Essays in Science, Technology, and Literature,* ed. Joseph W. Slade and Judith Yaross Lee (Ames, Ia.: Iowa State Univ. Press, 1989), 255–258.

8. Gunilla Wolde, *Betsy and the Vacuum Cleaner* (New York: Random House, 1975).

9. Janet Smalley, *How It All Began* (New York City: Morrow, 1932), 18; reproduced in Barbara Bader, *American Picturebooks from Noah's Ark to the Beast Within* (New York: Macmillan Publishing Co., Inc., 1976), 92.

10. See, for example, *Richard Scarry's Cars and Trucks and Things That Go* (New York: Golden Press, 1974) and Pnina Moed-Kass, *Stevie's Tricycle* (New York: A Golden Book, 1982).

11. Wilfred Jones, *How the Derrick Works* (New York: Macmillan, 1930). A less specialized early survey of the made world is Maud and Miska Petersham, *The Story Book of Things We Use* (Philadelphia: John C. Winston Company, 1933).

12. The four are Kathryn Jackson's *Trucks* (1955) and *Cars* (1956), Richard Scarry's *Cars and Trucks* (1959), Bob Ottum's *Cars* (1973). See Dolores B. Jones, comp. *Bibliography of the Little Golden Books* (Westport, Conn.: Greenwood Press, 1987).

13. Kathi Gibeault, *Susan in the Driver's Seat* (New York: Golden Press, 1973); cited in *Bibliography of the Little Golden Books.*

14. Tony Wells, *My First Book of Machines* (New York: Platt & Munk, 1986).

15. Not all personified machines have genders, but genderless machines tend not to be fully realized characters. They are usually paired with a human character for purposes of plot and theme, and their narratives are informational stories rather than fables. The conclusion of Catherine Kenworthy's *Little Squirt, the Fire Engine* (New York: Golden Press, 1983) illustrates that personification alone does not transform an informational tale into a fable: "Back at the fire station, the firefighters hang my hoses out to dry. Then they give me a bath. I like to look my best, for I am Squirt, the little red fire engine, the best fire engine in town!" (23).

16. For discussions of the influence of women storytellers on themes in folk literature, see, for example, Tristram Potter Coffin, *The Female Hero in Folklore and Legend* (New York: The Seabury Press, 1975), and Kay F. Stone, "The Misuses of Enchantment: Controversies on the Significance of Fairy Tales," in *Women's Folklore, Women's Culture,* ed. Rosan A. Jordan and Susan J. Kalcik (Philadelphia: Univ. of Pennsylvania Press, 1985), 125–45.

17. Virginia Lee Burton, *Mike Mulligan and His Steam Shovel* (Boston: Houghton Mifflin Company, 1939). The volume is unpaginated.

18. Virginia Lee Burton, *Maybelle, the Cable Car* (Boston: Houghton Mifflin Co., 1952).

19. Virginia Lee Burton, *Katy and the Big Snow* (Boston: Houghton Mifflin Company, 1943). The volume is unpaginated.

20. Jon C. Scott, "Virginia Lee Burton," *American Writers for Children, 1900–1960,* ed. John Cech, *Dictionary of Literary Biography,* vol. 22 (Detroit: Gale Research, 1983), 93–94.

21. Watty Piper. "The Little Engine That Could," from *The World Treasury of Children's Literature,* introd. Clifton Fadiman, 2 vols. (Boston: Little, Brown and Company, 1984), 1: 158–66; this quotation, 165.

22. Kathryn and Byron Jackson, "Christopher and the Columbus," rpt. in *Tibor Gergely's Great Big Book of Bedtime Stories,* A Golden Book (New York: Western Publishing Company, Inc., 1967), 7–15.

23. *Tootle* has received an unusual amount of attention for a children's tale: David Reisman scorned its emphasis on knee-jerk conformity in *The Lonely Crowd* (New Haven: Yale University Press, 1950; abridged ed., 1964), 105–7; and Bruno Bettelheim criticized its lack of psychological depth in *The Uses of Enchantment: The Meaning and Importance of Fairy Tales* (New York: Vintage Books, 1977), 182–83. See Gertrude Crampton, *Tootle* (New York: Simon and Schuster, 1946); rpt. in *Great Big Book of Bedtime Stories,* 49–59.

24. Gertrude Crampton, *Scuffy the Tugboat (and His Adventures Down the River* (New York: Simon and Schuster, 1946); rpt. in *Great Big Book of Bedtime Stories,* 36–48.

25. Marian Potter, *The Little Red Caboose* (New York: Simon and Schuster, 1953); rpt. in *Great Big Book of Bedtime Stories,* 288–307.

26. Of the twenty-two picture books mentioned in this essay, for instance, fourteen were written by women and only six by men; the gender of one author was unclear from the name, and a second book was written jointly by a man and woman.

27. Watty Piper, *The Little Engine That Could,* illus. George and Doris Hauman (1930); rpt. in *The World Treasury of Children's Literature,* ed. Clifton Fadiman, 2 vols. (Boston: Little, Brown and Company, 1984), 1: 158–66.

28. Thomas M. Disch, *The Brave Little Toaster: A Bedtime Story for Small Appliances,* illus. Karen Lee Schmidt (Garden City, N.Y.: Doubleday & Company, Inc., 1986). Originally published in *The Magazine of Fantasy and Science Fiction,* August 1980, the story was made into an animated film directed by Jerry Rees in

1987. The full-length feature drew praise as "a little masterpiece" when it played at the Film Forum in June 1989 (*New York*, 22 [12 June 1989], 78).

29. Predictably, reviewers found the book more suitable for adults than children. Anna Quindlen, reviewing the volume for the *New York Times Book Review*, 20 April 1986, 29, concluded that children would not care for it, but that "a certain sort of adult" would buy it for his children and read it himself. In the brief review in *School Library Journal*, 32 (August 1986), 91, Lillian N. Gerhardt dismissed the book with an exasperated declaration, "At what point can the pathetic fallacy become lamentable idiocy?"

Technology and the Spy Novel

JOSEPH W. SLADE

> There are so many ways of taking vengeance on the world.
> Sometimes literature is simply not enough.
> —John le Carré, *A Perfect Spy*[1]

Critics ranging from Jacques Barzun to Umberto Eco[2] have fashioned academic "cover stories" of varying degrees of plausibility to explain the popularity of spy novels, whose number has increased explosively in this century. While these disguises have by no means cloaked the genre in respectability, in some cases they do allay suspicion. Some critics discover in espionage a paradigm for the modern political state, a model straightforwardly adopted by some accomplished novelists themselves. As the traitor Bill Hayden says to George Smiley at the end of John le Carré's *Tinker, Tailor, Soldier, Spy,* "I still believe that the secret service is the only real expression of a nation's character." Smiley himself has become one of twentieth century fiction's memorable personalities, a circumstance that adds weight to another argument: that the webs of ideology and intrigue formed by strands of conspiracy, treachery, and betrayal provide ethical and psychological ground for complex character development among the agents operating in the spy genre's covert world. Still other approaches elevate the metaphysical, existential, archetypal, and mythical aspects of the spy narrative. Even so, such ingenious contentions can bewilder students of espionage as a profession. Walter Laqueur complains in *A World of Secrets: The Uses and Limits of Intelligence* that "critics have attempted to transform the spy story from its legitimate function of a vehicle of entertainment into a cultural critique, nothing less than a metaphor for the moral burden of our times."[3] That espionage fiction *can* function as a significant cultural influence, however, is clear from its increasing encroachment on mainstream literature. From a field of examples, two will suffice: Thomas Pynchon's three novels turn on conventions borrowed from the spy genre, and so do many of the tales of Jorge Luis Borges, who confessed an addiction to spy stories.[4]

Because so many readers are addicted in truth, less generous critics take the emphasis on entertainment in the spy novel (and even Graham Greene, perhaps the greatest of all authors in the genre, consistently called his espionage stories "entertainments"[5]) as reason enough to dismiss the form as escape literature or "airport fiction." Adding justification to such snobbery is the formulaic nature of the genre, which is situated—according to a sort of metaphoric division of cloak and dagger—between two other genres: the detective story to one side, the thriller or action plot to the other.[6] At the first extreme, a work like Martin Cruz Smith's *Gorky Park* (1981) combines sleuthing and spying, while at the other, a novel like Robert Ludlum's *The Matarese Circle* (1979) combines paranoia with highly kinetic melodrama. Most spy stories fall somewhere in the middle of this range, but can be further subdivided along a scale stretching from cardboard implausibility to emotional and intellectual authenticity. The typical recipe calls for a good deal of improbable adventure and more modest proportions of exotic sex, seasoned with off-the-shelf ingredients: overwrought deaths, ingenious brutalities, esoteric tradecraft, stereotypical villains, redundant heroics, obvious conspiracies, colorful locations, global quests, cold-war platitudes, and, most titillating of all, nightmare images of apocalyptic, big-power showdowns.

Riveting for some readers, exasperating to others, such clichés nevertheless mask the underlying dynamics of the spy novel. Among their other functions, fictional genres frequently serve as a means for dramatizing historic shifts in cultural priorities.[7] For example, the western novel arose as a medium for processing information about a closing frontier, which forced Americans to deal with the opposed values of the cowboy and the schoolmarm. The detective story flourished as the scientific revolution accelerated because its Sherlocks could at least pretend to emulate on a popular level the scientist's skill in investigation, which in itself represented a different method of processing information. The spy novel, in turn, is even more epochal, for it represents a cultural response to what is sometimes called the Information Age; it is thus a genre devoted to the profound changes in information flow, in the nature of that information, and in the communication systems by which we process that information, all of which may be subsumed under the term technology.

This thesis, however, requires some explanation, if only because the definition of technology on which it rests is itself recent. First of all, technology is to be distinguished from complicated terms like *industrialization* on the one hand, and from relatively simple ones like *tool-making* on the other. Historians have increasingly refined the world *technology* to mean not only "that which can be done, excluding only those capabilities that occur naturally in living systems,"[8] but also the knowledge base that empowers a species to *do:* to invent, to create, to alter.[9] For all its apparent modernity, this comprehensive definition is in fact a legacy from Aristotle, who spoke of technology as the "reasoned state of capacity to make."[10] Such an expanded view of technology makes it possible to characterize as ambiguous technologies not only natural languages (that appear to be partially shaped by the inherent deep structures identified by Noam Chomsky and partially arbitrary in their symbolic functions), but also the capabilities of the human brain itself (whose operations and systemic configurations may well have evolved as a consequence of human reactions to environment, especially in the attempts to impose order by altering that environment, more specifically by making tools and using language). Humans are thus at base a technological species. Language and brain are tools for ordering existence, inventing history, preserving experience, acquiring knowledge, interpreting the world, building culture. Language and brain make possible the manipulation of information, and on these two technologies all others rest.

According to information theorists, the world is made up of matter, energy, and information.[11] All systems, living or artificial, must process matter and energy in order to resist entropy, which, unchecked, will terminate the system through disorder. The key to a system's health is the control it exercises over the hierarchical components of itself, control that is neither too rigid nor too loose. The more complex the system, the more highly organized it must be; the more highly organized, the greater the volume of information it must process. That is as true for a culture or a corporation or an intelligence agency as it is for the organism that processes information not only as the grammatical and syntactical codes of DNA, but also as the chemical messages and electric signals of the immune and nervous systems. Communication is thus crucial to control, for systems operate by processing matter and energy—and information about those elements. The proportion of centralized control to local autonomy may vary, but all systems depend on information. Information is the key to control and to the maintenance of order. Information theory, which grew out of statistics and thermodynamics, has profoundly affected modern molecular biology, but also figures prominently in cybernetics or the study of control. Information theory and cybernetics currently frame our understanding of self-organizing systems, or as the Nobel Laureate Ilya Prigogine calls them, "far from equilibrium systems," i.e., systems capable of resisting entropy through active organization. Such systems exercise control through programming and feedback of information.

Humans maintain control over their lives and institutions through their symbol systems or technologies for encoding information, as carried through various media, or technologies for transmitting information. Most media—or channels—are overt, while some are covert.[12] Manifestly artificial systems like human cultures, which are not only arenas for the exchange of matter and energy but also domains of meaning in which the interpretation of messages and the ranking of ideas are carried out, are thus kept in working order by manipulation of codes and channels. Advanced cultures require massive volumes of information, which can be preserved in data bases ranging from oral folklore to written text to electronic or optical forms of storage. Such storage technologies help organize information hierarchically, and thus function as tools, but in fact any tool, whether a hammer or a dynamo, a corporation or a library, embodies information, i.e., the knowledge or the skill that went into fabricating it. Information is the most essential feature of human technology.

For that reason, some historians construe history as a technological progression involving the communication of larger and larger volumes of information at faster and faster speeds with greater and greater accuracy or integrity. Information, as epiphenomenal to matter and energy, does not drive all life, but it is essential to modern economies or, to be more precise, to the operations of those primarily western postindustrial cultures, sometimes called information societies, whose greater complexity requires greater organization and thus greater control. Cultural systems, like all other highly organized systems, utilize cybernetic technologies like programming and feedback to process messages in order to maintain control. Many factors distinguish postindustrial cultures from agricultural or merely industrialized ones, but two of the most important are (1) an advanced capability for command, control, and communication, and (2) an economy dominated by the exchange of information as a commodity. Countries like the United States, Germany, and Japan are called information societies because the majority of their workers are occupied in information-processing or service sectors, rather than in farming or manufacturing (according to government reports, fewer than 20 percent of American workers manufacture goods, while fewer than 4 percent are engaged in agriculture[13]). In other words, in such societies the processing of material goods, an activity dependent on information, has been eclipsed by the processing of information itself.

This profound shift began in the mid-nineteenth century—a shift that coincides neatly with the early stirrings of the contemporary spy novel—with what James Beniger, using the United States as his example, has called the Control Revolution. Here surges of new information about matter and energy caused successive crises in the economy. Rapid industrialization led to production surpluses that an older distribution system could not process. Advances in transportation and communication swiftly improved distribution but led to attendant problems of insufficient consumption. The successful manipulation of consumption, made possible by the advent of mass media, necessitated more systematic control of entire economies through constant refinements of social, political, and economic programming and techniques of feedback. As Beniger puts it:

> Industrialization became revolutionary when the energy harnessed vastly exceeded that of any naturally occurring or animate source; the resulting throughput and processing speeds greatly exceeded the capability of unaided humans to control. What made the Control Revolution in fact revolutionary was the development of technologies far beyond the capability of any individual, whether in the form of massive bureaucracies of the late nineteenth century or of the microprocessors of the late twentieth century. In all cases it was not the novelty of the commodities processed (whether matter, energy, or information) that proved decisive . . . , but rather the transcendence of the information-processing capabilities of the individual organism by a much greater technological system.[14]

Historically (though Beniger himself gives spying only passing mention), espionage has been an important mechanism for control, almost as important as market research, or the scheduling of railroads, because spying provides additional channels or circuits for the flow of information. Depending on circumstance, these circuits can serve as primary routes of data or redundant backups. Where complex systems—physical, social, political, or any kind—are concerned, maintaining organization requires many alternate routes of information flow. Otherwise, crucial information may be lost or go astray. Alternate channels carry messages that might be degraded in other, noisy channels, and thus ensure feedback necessary for repairs or adjustments. At the very least, surreptitious channels can function as a check on more visible ones; they further control. The notion is explicit in the fiction of John le Carré: the *Rittmeister* of the Cambridge Circus, le Carré's fictionalized version of Britain's Secret Service, is called "Control." Moreover, since World War II, spying has been intimately linked to information-processing: Alan Turing invented the world's first electronic computer, COLOSSUS, while he was a cryptanalyist at Bletchley Park, Britain's principal espionage establishment during World War II. Today, the world's most advanced computers are still those maintained by security agencies.

Well before the advent of the Information Age, in fact, espionage was basic to the industrialization of several nations, including the United States. In 1787, on a European tour, Thomas Jefferson literally stole an improved Italian strain of rice and smuggled it back to America in order to spur agriculture in the Carolinas, despite published warnings by the Piedmontese that the offense was punishable by death. The early textile mills of Rhode Island were built on English models surreptitiously drawn by Samuel Slater, despite strenuous efforts by British mill-owners to prevent the theft.[15] Travelers abroad were expected to report on the technological developments of other countries. So widespread was the practice that historians have begun collecting reports from the eighteenth and nineteenth centuries in volumes with titles like *Mechanical Arts and Merchandise: Industrial Espionage and Travellers' Accounts as a Source for Technical Historians* (1986).[16] Less glamorous perhaps than the more covert and therefore more dramatic military or diplomatic spying, industrial espionage is in nearly all other respects indistinguishable from the latter types. Indeed, Christopher Andrew, the historian of Britain's intelligence service, argues that it was the need for protection of burgeoning English commerce in the nineteenth century that made organized spying imperative.[17]

Today, *most* modern spying is of the industrial variety, a fact that has been less quickly acknowledged by writers of spy novels than by professionals in government agencies.[18] Leaving aside the snooping and theft that are constants among rival domestic companies, the enormous number of illicit technology transfers between countries increasingly occupies the intelligence services of advanced economies like the United States. Appalled by the Soviet theft of American computers, electronic imaging devices, and metallurgical innovations, the Department of Defense's Office of Information Security refers to this kind of espionage as a "hemorrhage of information to hostile nations."[19] Customs officials may in fact be hampered in their efforts by the spy novel's fixation on the KGB rather than on GOSPLAN, the Soviet agency that oversees industrial espionage,[20] a circumstance that has tended to focus the attention of the public on fantasies of cloak and dagger rather than on the real threat. Hardly a business quarter goes by without the United States government announcing yet another tightening of its technology export regulations, which are promptly circumvented. If espionage was part of the historical process by which the nineteenth century industrial world of machines mutated into the modern, postindustrial world of information, it is even more a factor now. Behind both process and reality, however, is the recognition that information is property. That concept, too, is a relatively recent phenomenon.

In oral cultures, information was shared as essential for survival to the tribe or clan. The real check on the spread of information in preliterate cultures was not the barrier of ownership so much as the inability to store and transmit it with accuracy. Before writing was invented, father or mother verbally handled down information gleaned in turn from *their* parents or from personal experience to their children: how to throw a pot, for example, or when to plant. Even after the invention of writing, which empowered those who could read and write, masters continued to transmit information to apprentices using the technology of speech. Though such information conferred a certain degree of privilege, masters were willing to share it because professional communities were still small. Since information is degraded in proportion to the number of oral transmissions, such groups were limited until more precise technologies of communication developed.

New methods of distributing information to larger populations revised both cultural and economic agendas. Although in many respects the advent of mass media technologies like printing fostered democracy, by ensuring the preservation of information through multiple copies, and making those copies available to large audiences cheaply, producing books was principally an economic activity. Inevitably, as information was thus objectified into a commodity, categories of value made certain kinds of information worth more than others. Entrepreneurs traded in specialized information as a form of commerce. Assuming that the information had specialized utility, then the more secret it was, the higher its value. As John Ferguson's *Bibliographical Notes on Histories of Inventions and Books of Secrets* makes clear, people with special knowledge went to extraordinary lengths to safeguard their secrets.[21] Espionage became an industry only when it was possible to traffic in secrets: there had to be something to steal, and there had to be enough of it to make stealing it a steady occupation.

Students of spy fiction have not yet explored the economics of espionage, in part, one suspects, because they assume that there have always been secrets and that humans have always been fascinated with them—after all, Dante long ago consigned spies and traitors to the Ninth Circle of Hell. And, to be sure, espionage is not only one of the world's largest growth industries, but also one of the oldest, a fact made clear by Philip Knightley, who calls his recent examination of modern spying *The Second Oldest Profession*.[22] Spy narratives have similarly ancient antecedents. In *The Spy Story,* the exceptionally fine and easily most comprehensive of several serious treatments of what used to be a subliterary genre, John Cawelti and Bruce Rosenberg point out that espionage can be said to figure as plot and theme in *The Iliad* (the Trojan Horse) and the *Bible* (Joshua's reconnoitering of Canaan). Cawelti and Rosenberg nonetheless assert that the form did not begin to mature until the nineteenth century, and they link that maturity to pressures associated with the onset of industrialization. They do not, however, discuss the informational aspects of industrialization outlined here.

The industrial era generated more information than had ever existed before, if only because industrial societies had to be more rationalized, more specialized, more organized, and more complex than their predecessors. Rationalization, specialization, organization, and complexity are functions of communication, and of the information that flows through communications media. As James Beniger puts it, "because the activities of information processing, programming, decision, and communication are inseparable components of the control function, a society's ability to maintain control at all levels—from interpersonal to international relations—will be directly proportional to the development of its information technologies."[23] Since all these activities were also inherent in capitalism, the economic system dominant in the West, information in western societies began to seem more and more like property.

Literary historians are just beginning to realize that even mainstream writers of the nineteenth century were aware of the changing nature of information. In his brilliant *George Eliot and Blackmail,* Alexander Welsh points out that George Eliot was conscious of the massive shift in her time from shared to *proprietary* information, and that a major theme of her novels is the concept of secrets.[24] Since secrets lose their value unless they can be put to use, a major challenge to a capitalist economy is to find a way to safeguard the proprietary aspects of information by allowing the owner to retain control, at least for a time. In America, Article I of the Constitution institutionalized the principle of intellectual property, by providing for both patents and copyrights. Thomas Jefferson regarded with ambivalence the ownership of ideas. As the nation's first patent commissioner, a duty of his office as the first Secretary of State, Jefferson was reluctant to grant patents on the grounds that they gave privilege to those who owned the information contained in a new invention, and thus undermined the free circulation of ideas by allowing the owners to profit at the expense of others. He seems to have had fewer reservations about the concept of copyright, perhaps because literary rights seemed less substantial. César Graña has pointed out that the imaginative writer's trade is founded on the notion of originality, on the conviction that originality is unique, that it constitutes property, that it represents economic advantage, that it is what makes a writer a professional.[25] His originality is what the writer copyrights. Derek de Solla Price has noted that by 1850 scholars as well as writers of imaginative literature also assumed that what they wrote was property, even if they merely collected information from other sources and then added their own bit of "original interpretation."[26]

Ironically, espionage is part of this tradition, because it too calls for the gathering of data that must then be interpreted. According to Christopher Andrew, when Americans were trying to build an intelligence service after World War I, they were advised by their British counterparts to recruit nonscientists and cryptographers of "an active, well trained and scholarly mind, not mathematical but classical,"[27] i.e., researchers skilled at humanistic information processing. As a veteran spy remarks in *Convergence,* an otherwise unremarkable spy novel: "Intelligence is a form of scholarship, you know."[28] In fact, scholars as spies abound in the genre. My own favorite is Anthony Price's David Audley, an authority on medieval fortifications, among other arcane areas of expertise.[29] But while scholars are apt to think that the appeal of their work is limited to academics, intelligence services quite rightly put a higher value on the sophisticated processing of data.

In the twentieth century, it is clear that information rivals "traditional" capital as an embodiment of wealth. In other words, information is not just a resource or tool, but a form of currency, a portable commodity that can be exchanged. A witticism popular among communication specialists is that if Karl Marx were writing *Das Kapital* today he would title it *Die Information.* Numerous critics have observed that the hegemony of modern communication technologies has undermined Marx's approach to nineteenth-century economics (if only because Marxism ultimately rests on an outmoded positivism) by altering his mechanical concepts of production, distribution, and consumption. In the most fundamental sense, Marx's machine metaphors have been superseded by informational models. As Marshall McLuhan put it, "Marx based his analysis most untimely on the machine, just as the telegraph and other implosive forms began to reverse the machine dynamic."[30] The spy novel as a literary form is a postindustrial and post-Marxist genre because it implicitly acknowledges that classical capitalism has been superseded by systems of command and control. Information is the capital of military, political, and commercial systems, whose lines of demarcation have blurred.

What makes espionage so fascinating, as a real phenomenon and as a literary metaphor, is that it constitutes a shadow economy in which information of varying degrees of secrecy is the commodity bought and sold. It is not just that the commerce in information has increased so dramatically, of course, but also that the commerce has steadily become more closely aligned with national policy among industrialized nations. For that reason, the clandestine agencies of fiction wonderfully mimic the bureaucratic control and feedback mechanisms both of the corporate world and of the communist state.

No more telling indication of this circumstance is the emergence of the Soviet spy novel, which reflects the recent shift in priorities among the Eastern Bloc nations toward *perestroika* and *glasnost*. Such policy shifts have less to do with ideology than with the belated recognition in the East that information is the basis of postindustrial societies. Although we are accustomed to thinking of the spy novel as a *western* phenomenon, i.e., as a form of entertainment indigenous to information economies like those of the United States, Great Britain, Germany, France, and so on, we can expect Soviet examples to multiply. *Perestroika* and *glasnost* are terms associated with the emergence of Mikhail Gorbachev, the charismatic present leader of the U.S.S.R. It is hardly an accident that Gorbachev rose to power in part because he was the protégé of Yuri Andropov, his predecessor as General Secretary of the Communist party, nor was it accidental that Andropov was both a keen student of American economics and (as the Soviet Union's chief spy) an information specialist. Andropov's power base was the KGB, the security agency of the Soviet Union, which he headed for many years. If Andropov was less successful than Gorbachev in his drive to emulate Western expertise and cultural styles, he can be credited with sponsoring the Soviet spy novel. Andropov provided the writer Julian Semyonov with material on an actual CIA spy ring run in the heart of Moscow and suggested that he fictionalize it. Thus far, Semyonov's *Tass Is Authorized to Announce . . .* (1979, translated 1987), has sold more than two and a half million copies in the U.S.S.R. In this espionage novel, stalwart KGB agents, who exhibit the characteristics common to their cunning American counterparts in Western tales, battle evil CIA operatives, who have the earmarks normally found in villains imagined by Western authors in a plot identical to those covert dramas that engage readers in the United States, except that in these pages the United States is allied with China, a Chinese-American conspiracy being the Soviet spy nightmare of choice. The subtext is that information flow erodes ideologies. As one of the KGB supergrades (the equivalent of the CIA employee with a high GS number) puts it in Semyonov's novel: "In our century of the information explosion you can't afford to be egocentric: the very air is saturated with ideas."[31]

Still, Soviet recognition of the capitalistic implications of information notwithstanding, information is not like other commodities. Unlike land and machinery, two of the historically more common embodiments of capital, modern information is as portable as money, but it is also more ephemeral. If one can sell it and still have it, the converse is also true. As the sociologist Erving Goffmann encapsulates this difficulty in terms relevant to espionage, "Among all the things of this world, information is the hardest to guard, since it can be stolen without removing it."[32] Once a secret is stored outside a human mind, preventing its theft may be impossible. That is one reason that spy novels frequently deal with plots to contact or abduct a scientist who holds a key to some plan or process in his head. The greatest secret of our age, the information necessary to build a nuclear weapon, probably remained a secret for as long as it did, as Richard Rhodes suggests in *The Making of the Atomic Bomb*, not simply because so many scientists voluntarily agreed not to publish news of vital discoveries but also because the institution of apprenticeship was still important in physics in the first half of the twentieth century.[33] Since much of the expertise required for understanding nuclear physics was passed along from individual mentor to individual protégé, wider dissemination was effectively slowed. Once the volume of information swelled to the point that it required extensive storage, once the teams of the Manhattan Project began writing things down and coordinating their knowledge with others, however, it became inevitable that Klaus Fuchs and others would steal the secrets.

Anecdotes aside, however, the spy novel represents a serious response to the problematic nature of the value of information in the modern world. Considered as a commodity, information in the form of knowledge, expertise, skill, or merely raw data possesses value that cannot always be precisely quantified.[34] One *can* quantify the degree of redundancy required to ensure the accuracy of a message in transmission, or the exact number of bits of information in a data stream, as do information engineers, who rely on the mathematical formulae of Claude Shannon, the founder of information theory. One can also employ various protocols, or calibrate value in terms of elapsed time of transmission, after the manner of telephone companies, who charge a fee based on the number of minutes a circuit remains open. Since *meaning* is not a factor in these assessments, however, it is obvious that the question of value is extremely complicated.

Ultimately, value must be equated with meaning. Meaning can only be established by interpretation, which is a function of the cultural environment in which humans live. As teachers of freshmen English have insisted for decades, the gathering of information may be a mechanical process, but only humans can assign meaning to the ensemble. It is here that the similarities between espionage and scholarship emerge most clearly: both are ways of assigning value to information by interpreting it. Determining meaning is the central activity of culture, which ceaselessly processes information as its quotidian dialectic; it is also the irreducible premise of the spy novel. For that reason, the finest spy novels, like those of Ambler, Greene, or le Carré, are those that embed the spy's role in the larger context of his culture. A culture processes information in endlessly complicated ways, through filters such as institutions, customs, traditions, laws, and symbol systems, including language itself. Meaning accrues as information passes through systems of programming and feedback, moving from hierarchy to hierarchy of control. The different levels alter the meaning of a message, says Thomas L. Hughes in a pamphlet on espionage, because they affect interpretation:

Cruise missiles or commodity agreements, Kurds or Palestinians: the subject may be the same and the conversation disquietingly different if it is held on the State Department's 7th floor, or the 6th, or the 5th—among high ranking generalists, medium ranking supervisors, or low ranking specialists—among authorities without expertise, or experts without authority, or the brokers in between. The hierarchical factor—

where a man sits—affects timing, choice of colleagues and number of institutionalized hurdles remaining.[35]

It is not mere possession that gives value to information, but its interpretation. Once that is clear, then the gathering of information—the traditional function of the individual spy—becomes less important than its processing through hierarchies—the role of the spy's masters—and the kind of scholarship they use. A real intelligence service, whether located at CIA headquarters at Langley or KGB nerve-centers in Dzerzhinsky Square, collates most of its information from conventional, nonsecret, even pedestrian sources: newspapers and popular magazines, scientific and technological journals, census reports, encyclopedias and almanacs, credit files, farm statistics, meterological analyses, production output predictions, computer manuals, advertising brochures for military hardware, annual reports of corporations, freely available government documents, and other public or quasi-public data. To those sources will be added material gleaned by more obviously technological means: Signals Intelligence (SIGINT), principally code-breaking, Communication Intelligence (COMINT), primarily the interception of radio communication, Electronic Intelligence (ELINT), or the interception of other forms of electronic transmission, Radar Intelligence (RADINT), Photographic Intelligence (PHOTINT), whether based on images shot by satellite or other types of cameras, and so on. According to Herbert E. Meyer, former vice chairman of the National Intelligence Council (an arm of the CIA devoted to analysis), such technological intelligence-collecting is not to be equated with spying, i.e., on-the-spot snooping by undercover agents. Only 5 percent of the intelligence budget of the United States goes toward covert operations in which humans gather intelligence, called HUMINT; the remaining 95 percent funds SIGINT, COMINT, ELINT, and clerical activity.[36] Given these statistics, many intelligence experts discount the importance of the individual agent.[37] Naturally, this debate spills over into the pages of the spy novel:

"I run an analytical shop, not a spy shop," Cole said finally. "We collect electronic intercepts from Soviet space launches, lists of dignitaries at the opening of a new factory near Leningrad, the signature cavitations from the propellers of Russian submarines"—he unconsciously ticked off the items on his fingers—"marriage announcements and rumors on who wasn't invited to the wedding, weather reports, production statistics, pictures of the Politburo members at the Bolshoi, photographs of launching pads taken from sixteen nautical miles up in the sky by planes flying at three times the speed of sound. That's the sort of thing we do. We pool information, we collect and codify it and then pore over it for months in the absolutely religious conviction that if you look at something long enough a pattern will emerge and the pieces will fall into place. . . . The days of clandestine ops, of spies, are drawing to a close."[38]

And they may be. The spy may be popular precisely because he is becoming superfluous, a status not unlike that of the cowboy hero of the western, who flourished as a fictional figure only after the frontier began to close. If literal snooping accounts for only a fraction of the espionage activities of a real intelligence agency, it accounts for nearly all of the action in the agencies of fiction. The central focus of the modern spy novel is the place of the human being in a society defined by its ability to process information on a vast scale, or, to use Beniger's terminology, a society characterized by "the transcendence of the information-processing capabilities of the individual organism by a much greater technological system." The forces arrayed against the typical protagonist are thus not so much our era's ideologies as its technologies.

The least of these technologies are the gadgets common to so many novels. In *The Spy Story,* Cawelti and Rosenberg rank technology fairly low in their list of explanations for the spy novel's appeal, primarily because they construe technology in conventional terms, like the marvelous novelties that Ian Fleming's James Bond carries into his battles with SPECTRE. *The Spy Story* quite correctly observes that Bond and the many clones he has inspired typically exhaust the futuristic weapons quickly in order that the struggle against opponents will devolve into hand-to-hand combat between humans rather than machines. That is true of most genres, of course, even science fiction; viewers of the television series *Star Trek* will know that the phasers and warp drives of the Starship Enterprise usually fail at a critical moment in order for Captain Kirk to settle matters in more "human" ways, using strength or cunning. Specific examples of science fiction may give precedence to artifacts of physical invention, but spy novels are usually closer in spirit to mainstream literature in that they assume a social, political, and economic context for technology.

Nonetheless, many readers prize the technological gimmicks in spy stories, and authors can be obliging. Quiller, the protagonist of Adam Hall's *The Scorpion Signal* (and of many other novels in this series), laments the threat to a spy ring operated by the British. The ring has justified itself by stealing large quantities of Soviet technology:

> The Leningrad cell had taken eleven years to build up, and once established and running it had given us the Sholokoff Project and the submarine dispersal pattern and the tactical analysis for the buried-weapons system for transmission to NATO and the CIA, plus satellite scanning, plus laser progress in the military application laboratories, plus the whole of the missile-testing program including the ultra-classified global-range ICBMs from X-9 to the city-heat guidance marathon 1000. That was the Leningrad cell.[39]

Details of these marvels—which are scarcely comprehensible— would probably detract from the passage; their purpose is to *sound* important.

Similarly, on the most prosaic plane, a particular invention or innovation can function as what Alfred Hitchcock, a master of the espionage film, once called the *MacGuffin,* i.e., an enabling device that sets a plot in motion.[40] This might be a secret formula, a new missile guidance system, a revised order of battle—some advantage that threatens to destabilize the balance of power between hostile nations. These are generally rendered in broad strokes, to forestall excessive scrutiny. Nevertheless, in other contexts, technological specifics are often helpful in establishing authenticity, especially when reproduced with academic accuracy: the weight in ounces of the Soviet Makarov pistol, the suppression required to silence a Heckler and Koch MP5 9mm submachine gun, the precise frequencies monitored by a Vortex spy satellite or an E-3A AWACS (Airborne Warning and Control System) aircraft, the exact resolution of a pair of AN/PAS-5 Infrared Night Vision Binoculars. That this kind of data is there mostly for show is apparent when authors cannot resist providing information that an air traveler can easily pluck from the seat-back pocket in front of him, as in Gordon Stevens's *Do Not Go Gentle:* "The Boeing 727 has three Pratt and Whitney engines each capable of producing 14,500 lbs. of thrust. It carries a payload of forty tons, normally comprising one hundred and forty-four passengers, plus cargo."[41]

In other words, "you can look it up." Such esoterica is essential to some books, like those of Tom Clancy, for example, whose *The Hunt for Red October* seems authentic because of the research that went into submarine warfare. Whether Clancy is a writer of thrillers rather than spy stories is a matter of genre dispute; separating the two types is often difficult. The greater the orientation toward action—as opposed to the gathering of intelligence—the more technological the protagonists become, as if they were themselves machines. In the novels of Gavin Lyall (*Midnight Plus One* [1965]) and Trevanian (*The Eiger Sanction* [1972]), for example, the heroes continuously monitor their alpha-waves and reflexes. They survive back-street encounters with enemy spies by honing their bodies to perfection, sharpening their senses to hard edges. In a genre that dotes on violence, the most satisfying tortures are those that reduce the hero's ability to process information, like the monstrous sensory-deprivation techniques inflicted upon the protagonist of Len Deighton's *The Ipcress File* (1963).

In such cases, the assumption is that spies have to compete with high-tech information-gathering devices. That kind of technology has been developing steadily since World War I, when the British first cut Germany's Atlantic Cable in order to compel the enemy to use wireless messages that could be intercepted and decoded. Everyone has heard the story of how the British anticipated German movements during World War II by analyzing the workings of a German ENIGMA code-machine stolen by Polish patriots. (The ENIGMA machine, code-breaking, and intelligence activities during that war have generated a host of nonfiction works intended to compete in the market for espionage fiction.[42]) The onset of the Cold War triggered still more sophisticated methods. The United States recovered the first film canisters from a spy satellite (Discover 13) only a few months after the Soviets shot down Gary Powers in his U-2 over Sverdlovsk.[43] Since then, both sides have lofted dozens of surveillance satellites, electronically bugged each other's embassies, monitored each other's frequencies, collected messages quite literally by the carload, and spread "disinformation," i.e., fraudulent data, in enormous profusion. Not surprisingly, those who operate such technological systems regard the human spy as obsolete.

Increasingly, however, the technologies that frame the action of the spy novel are far more likely to be those of managerial bureaucracy, the hierarchical elements that control the military-industrial (and academic) complex. By common consent, John le Carré (the pseudonym of David Cornwell) is first among the contemporary craftsmen of the genre, a status he has attained by foregrounding the human in a world of corporate technology. David Monaghan sums up critical comment: "The central problem in all le Carré's novels is how to be fully human in a society whose institutions have lost all connection with individual feeling."[44] Le Carré's metaphors for those bureaucratic institutions are the intelligence services of

Cold War antagonists. Le Carré's hero (if the term can be applied to so unheroic a person), George Smiley, must protect his agents not only from the machinations of Karla, his opposite number on the other side, but also from the bureaucratic stupidities that constantly threaten to subvert the British intelligence service for which he works. The British "Circus" is threatened by entropy; its professionals cannot recognize that not all information is statistical, not all personnel problems managerial, and not all interpretation mechanical. It is a question of knowledge. Fueling le Carré's novels, says Michael Denning, is the opposition between Smiley's donnish and ethical skills that produce a knowledge that is "amateur, humane, and totalizing," as much the product of the man's study of paintings and poems as of his love for and sympathy with others, and "the arcane secrets that are the currency of the spy trade . . . [a] knowledge [that] is professional, technical, and fragmentary."[45] Smiley's strength, in other words, derives from his humanity. Because he understands that information must be interpreted by humans who understand the ways other humans think, he and Karla—who shares that understanding—are superior to the technologies that make up their environments. He is a humanist, a classically cultivated scholar, in a technological world. Unlike the boffins, he measures motives and reactions on a human scale. He refuses to cede to institutions the interpretation of reality.

Most modern spy novels deal with the bureaucratic command technologies identified by Max Weber as essential to the rise of rationalized capitalism. Like Smiley, the protagonists of narratives less accomplished than le Carré's must also deal with the intelligence hierarchies of both sides in their efforts to interpret information. Equally invariably, they will construe the levels of bureaucracy in Weberian terms, and as individuals, they will chafe against their restrictions. The American spy will be just as aware as his British counterpart that those who occupy the top levels of the intelligence hierarchy will be of a different class than the underlings they command. George Smiley must suffer foolish Harrovians and snobbish Old Etonians; American spies sneer at the fatuous graduates from Harvard and Yale who occupy elegant offices at Langley or Foggy Bottom. The typical spy of fiction will be a practical person of action, capable of assessing the worth of a piece of intelligence on the spot, long before his intellectually pretentious superiors can fathom the true situation. And yet, because the upper-class desk jockeys control the lines of communication and command, they have power where he does not. The sin of such intellectual aristocrats is that they treat their agents and pawns as mere bits of information, or so says the narrator of *Agents of Innocence,* a novel based on the CIA's operations in Beirut:

> Lenin had understood that such people make ideal recuits for a secret organization. They think in abstractions and turn the mundane stuff of politics—land, statehood, the exercise of power—into idealized images. Soon these images become so pure and fine, so embued with romance, that the death of mere mortals seems like nothing if it advances the sacred cause.[46]

That is why the hero of a spy novel must so often be an amateur, and why hostility to the technology of bureaucracy is so powerful a theme in spy fiction. An invention refined to efficiency in the nineteenth century, bureaucracy processes information through communication hierarchies in order to exercise control. The structures of a given bureaucracy are subject to the Second Law of Thermodynamics, i.e., vulnerable to the imbalances caused by either too little control or too much. When powerful bureaucracies like espionage agencies grow too rigid, their indifference to the individual threatens citizens. When such agencies grow slack, information is lost, and again people get hurt. Members of an espionage bureaucracy are just as much professional information processors as people who work for corporations or universities, and their professionalism can blind them to failures in the system. The romantic conventions of the spy genre call for a charismatic outsider—the amateur—to deal with espionage organizations suffering from improper rationalization.

The tradition of the amateur as unwilling hero has endured at least since 1900 when Erskine Childers wrote *The Riddle of the Sands.* The classic *The Thirty-Nine Steps* (1913), and subsequent books by John Buchan, enshrined an amateur's adolescent masculinity that at times seemed borrowed from the effusions of Robert Baden-Powell, the founder of the Boy Scouts, who was an amateur spy for Britain in the Mediterranean in the 1880s. Baden-Powell published *Reconnaissance and Scouting* in 1884, and later, in 1915, *My Adventures as a Spy,* in which he spoke of the sporting aspects of espionage:

> For anyone who is tired of life, the thrilling life of the spy should be the very finest recuperation. When one recognizes also that it may have valuable results for one's country in time of war, one feels that even though it is a time spent largely in enjoyment, it is not by any means time thrown away; and though the "agent," if caught, may "go under,"

unhonoured and unsung, he knows in his heart of hearts that he has done his "bit" for his country as fully as his comrade who falls in battle.[47]

Modern readers are apt to laugh at this sort of thing, but as Cawelti and Rosenberg point out in a different context, the amateur's status can be essential to his function as a hero.

Because he is an amateur, he has not lost his humanity to soulless bureaucracy; because he is a nonprofessional, he can treat others as human. The amateur's morality is less important than the assumption behind his effectiveness. We assume that the command and control mechanisms of modern organizations are so pervasive that the spy must operate outside corporate structures—"out in the cold," in the phrase popularized by le Carré; otherwise his "freedom" to act is unconvincing. In contrast to amateurs, professionals regard information as merely a commodity, a conviction subtly asserted in so many spy novels in the expression, "The Company," as shorthand for the Central Intelligence Agency. Amid everyday treachery and deceit, some of it directed against one's own agents, as in James Grady's *Six Days of the Condor* (1974), neither side can claim moral superiority, but the amateur can at least cling to his own freedom of choice and his conviction that information directly affects the lives of human beings. The "amateur" can of course be an ex-professional ejected from his own organization, or victimized by it, as in *Condor,* and thus equally free to move. The amateur spy is a rogue information-processor, and often this role is emphasized by his chosen profession, as in Tony Chiu's splendid *Port Arthur Chicken* (1979), whose protagonist, Raymond Huang, is a Chinese-American journalist caught up in a vast plot.[48] His "amateur's" journalistic ability to collect and interpret information both subverts the established order and "proves" that the individual is a match for a sinister organization, despite the latter's duplicity, power, and brutality.

It is not so much that the amateur reasons or interprets differently from the professionals he opposes (though he usually exhibits more imagination); it is a matter of scale. His scale is small, primitive, and romantic, therefore human. "Theirs" is vast, complex, and sophisticated, therefore mechanical. The amateur is a Jeffersonian, a figurative yeoman who wants to counter the monstrous technologies of agribusiness with the ecological simplicity of the plow. To the amateur spy, less technology is usually more. Free-flowing data flexibly routed, not huge volumes of information under total control, make for healthy systems. To him, espionage is a

shield for freedom, not an instrument of oppression—or so the spy
novel's rhetoric claims.

This demotic theme is apparent in Robert Littell's *The Amateur,*
which most critics include on lists of fine spy novels. While the
protagonist of *The Amateur* is not a spy, Charles Heller does work
for the CIA as a cryptanalyst. He devises codes by using computers, since only computers can encrypt codes of virtually un-
breakable difficulty. But Heller is a humanist, not just a cryptanalyst: he is a Shakespearian scholar. In other words, he is a
super-information-processor: a mathematician familiar with artificial languages, and a literary specialist expert in natural languages and traditional texts. The story begins when Heller's fian-
cée, taken hostage by terrorists who storm an American Embassy
in London, is murdered by them in a scene captured by the world's
media. When the CIA waffles, strangely reluctant to pursue the
terrorists, Heller starts his own quest to track them down. Using his
skills as a researcher, he finds and kills the terrorists one by one,
actually going behind the Iron Curtain, in the process discovering
layer upon layer of conspiracy, until he realizes that the terrorists
have been the creatures of the CIA all along. The climax takes place
in a mirrored room, as if to give form to a famous description of
espionage as a "wilderness of mirrors."[49] Heller succeeds because
as a lover he cares about other people, because as a humanist he is
an expert information-processor, because as an outsider he is free
of institutional corruption, because as an average person he lacks
the contemptuousness of the upper-class professional, and because
as a democrat he despises secrets.

The real secret of the spy novel's appeal, of course, is that there
may be no secrets; although we may be obsessed with secrets
because in an information age there are so few of them. In the
United States, Joshua Meyrowitz observes,

> the general sense of openness of situations that has resulted from the
> widespread use of electronic media has given all closed social systems a
> bad name. Closed meetings are now suspicious, and membership in a
> club that excludes members on the basis of any social category—sex,
> race, or religion—can be the undoing of a political aspirant. . . . Not
> only has the law begun to come into social situations that were once
> independent, but the law has also begun to eat away at the right of
> people to have a segregated sphere of interaction in the first place.[50]

To those legal attacks on privacy can be added the Freedom of
Information Act, which allows individuals at least some access to
information on them collected by government and security agen-

cies. The emphasis on secrecy in the spy scenario may thus be as much a response to the technological onslaught on privacy as an expression of the more cherished forms of paranoia that attribute control of our lives to "them," i.e., bankers, or bureaucrats, or assorted maniacs. The latter scenarios are particularly appealing, to judge from the enormous success of Robert Ludlum, all of whose novels are predicated on ultra-secret global conspiracies, and that is equally true of a great many others, from David Morrell's *The Brotherhood of the Rose* (1984) to the assorted works of Erik Van Lustbader (*The Ninja* [1985], *The Sunset Warrior* [1983]).

As literary elements, global conspiracies rank just above vampires in terms of plausibility, since modern information technology militates against such fantasies. Meyrowitz is explicit:

> By giving everyone greater access to other places, electronic media also remove people socially and psychologically from their physical situations. The ease of "leaving" a place via electronic media has made it easier for children, employees, prisoners, government officials, and others to bypass the information channels and hierarchies of their physical environments. Anyone can use a telephone booth to make an anonymous call to alert authorities about some wrongdoing or problem. Because insiders no longer have to "go" somewhere to speak with an outsider, it is now much more common for information about private group interactions or problems to "leak" into the public forum. Members can "defect" without ever leaving the group's territory, and both amateur and professional investigators can "penetrate" the perimeter of an institution without ever going near it.[51]

That is not to say that plots and cabals do not exist, nor to deny that power can be corrupted. But the spy novelist, like Karl Marx and the rest of us, tends to measure corruption in terms of the older structures of economic and political power rather than the newer ones of information flow. That vast conspiracies are so common in the spy novel indicates, however, that they serve a psychic need on the part of an audience that finds it hard to accept the notion that control of society is actually distributed in complex communication structures rather than vested in powerful individuals. Paranoids, we prefer to believe that somebody is in charge, even if that somebody is evil, and that power resides in secrets.

As indicated earlier, secrets are hard to preserve. On the other hand, information successfully safeguarded by keeping it secret can degrade. The best-kept secrets will eventually lose their utility, if only because no one will be aware of them until their optimum effectiveness has passed. Like radioactive elements, secrets decay according to half-life schedules that point up their essential meta-physical absurdity. In *George Eliot and Blackmail,* Alexander Welsh quotes a reviewer of Victorian sensational novels—the an-cestors of modern spy novels—as observing: "the most completely preserved secret is, of course, that whose existence is least sus-pected; and if ten thousand such secrets existed, the world, simply because they are preserved, could not possibly know them to exist. . . . The marrow of all this wordly wisdom is contained in the self-evident proposition, that a secret, so long as it is a secret, is a secret."[52] To be effective in the real world, or as a plot device in a spy novel, of course, a secret must be known to be a secret.

Obviously, then, that something is secret is less important than what the secrecy represents. In *Cover Stories: Narrative and Ide-ology in the British Spy Thriller,* Michael Denning maintains that the ownership of such information is

> clearly a relation of power; every reader of spy thrillers knows that the interest is not in the secret information itself—how many missiles, or what secret treaty—but in the distribution of knowledge. Power is knowing what they know without their knowing that you know it. If they know you know, you've lost it. And in fact, if you don't know they know you know it, then they've got the power. And it is that "simple" relation that is at the heart of many of the spy thrillers of the le Carré/Greene generation.[53]

In other words, just as imaginative literature generally sidesteps any question of the economic value of information by placing data in a personal or cultural context, so the spy novel avoids assessing the precise worth of a secret by dramatizing it instead, sometimes in apocalyptic terms (a secret weapon capable of destroying all life on the North American continent, say).

In the final analysis, secrets can only be dramatized, given mean-ing in a cultural sense, and that is what the spy novel does. More-over, the spy novelist knows that power derives not so much from holding secrets as from managing information flow. The flow—in all control systems—is critical. Information must be accurate, but it must also reach the right people, those charged with decision making at various levels of hierarchy. It is on this point that para-noia is justified. Even the spy expert Walter Laqueur worries about the transmission routes through the complex levels of espionage bureaucracies: "The stream of paper never subsides, but as the distance between the source and the consumer has grown, so has the danger that important information may be lost."[54] In a world of information, where information moves at great speed, in enormous volume, over vast distances, humans fear that some crucial piece of data may be lost, the code or key that will make it possible to decipher the rest. Thomas Pynchon, the supreme novelist of the information age, has placed that anxiety at the core of his novels, which is why all of them employ plots borrowed from espionage fiction. A similar anxiety may well lie at the base of postmodernist literary criticism, given voice by Jacques Derrida, who reminds us in a famous phrase that "A letter does not always arrive at its destination."[55]

Other anxieties stimulated by the dynamics of an information age also figure in the spy novel. Some of these have been touched on by critics like Cawelti and Rosenberg, but not in informational terms. One is that as ideologies have waned and patriotism curdled under the cynicism of the cold war, intelligence is now a game played for its own sake or simply for money, along the lines of eighteenth-century mercantilism. Still another worry is more common: that the systems of social and political control are so delicate that a single betrayal will threaten to destroy them. "Moles," or traitors in positions of responsibility in the decision-making hierarchy of a nation, especially in the upper levels of the nation's espionage service itself, are constants in spy fiction, including that of le Carré. If one stimulus to modern paranoia is the fear that human life is subject to virtually total control, another is that systems are out of control and that the command structures have been subverted. In N. J. Crisp's *The Ninth Circle,* the menace arises from a conspiracy to bypass normal intelligence channels: " 'The CIA is a vast apparatus,' Haden went on. 'Bits of it operate in secret and as if they were independent.' "[56] In such a situation, the solution usually resides with an agent who is himself out of control, free of programming and assumptions, free to act and to interpret.

The espionage novel, then, may be the literary genre most appropriate to a postindustrial age and to a postmodernist sensibility. Viewed from another perspective, however, the themes of the spy novel may seem anachronistic, and the spy story itself may seem a romantic, not to say reactionary response to contemporary concerns. This is hardly the case with the more thoughtfully conceived examples, such as those by le Carré, but becomes more likely as the spy novel shades into the thriller, where adrenalin drives the narrative. The most obvious of these themes is that a single individual can save the world, by uncovering a plot, discovering a secret formula, preventing the deployment of a doomsday weapon, or simply decimating the opposition by physical violence. In a world of information, action becomes an appealing option. American examples in this vein are apt to be xenophobic and isolationist. The terrain of the spy novel may be a landscape of the mind, as Cawelti and Rosenberg assert, but it can also be geographically symbolic: conspiracies burst into malignancy abroad, on foreign shores, from whence they threaten to infect the United States. Against this disease the agent must function as an antibody. Worse, such thrillers deny the efficacy of politics; diplomacy, where it exists, always fails, precipitating a crisis that requires a romantic hero. The imperatives of adventure then overshadow reasons of state. The thriller is often retrograde also because it asserts simple polarities between good and evil. To the aficionado Ralph Harper, the moral and political ambiguities of the cold-war espionage novel can never hold the same appeal as the "sickness and menace" stressed in earlier World War II thrillers,[57] and a good many readers, to judge by the list of spy best-sellers at any given moment, seem still to prefer precisely those kind of simple Manichean oppositions between good guys and bad guys.

Already the massive upheavals overtaking the Soviet Union in the wake of *perestroika* and *glasnost* are causing mutations in the Western spy genre. Aware that the edges of opposing ideologies lack sharpness, novelists reach back to the World War era for evil conspiracies. German writers like Johannes Mario Simmel, whose books have sold over sixty million copies, are fond of this strategy. Simmel's *The Secret Protocol* (1985) turns on a Nazi scheme buried in 1943 to surface menacingly in the present. Similarly, Ira Levin's *The Boys from Brazil* (1976) features clones of Hitler, while William Goldman's *Marathon Man* (1974) and Ronald Neame's *The Odessa File* (1974) draw on conspiracies mounted by Nazis still in hiding. The veteran James Carroll's latest, *Firebird* (1989), harkens back to the activities of Fuchs and the Rosenbergs. A glance at current best-seller lists indicates also that the thriller, the more weapon-conscious the better, is outpacing the espionage novel of more traditional orientation.

In the most fundamental sense, however, the spy novel puts a human face on anonymous mechanisms of information flow, the reason we praise most highly those examples that foreground character. In this regard, the protagonist of an espionage novel must embody those virtues we associate with any champion of individuality in an increasingly collective society, and must oppose his own inner worth against instruments of corporate or ideological policy. The hero's requirements have been outlined by Stanley Cavell:

Our conviction in the strength of the hero depends upon our conviction in the strength and purity of character he has formed to keep his fires banked. Otherwise he is merely physically indomitable, and no man is; in that case, his success over evil would be arbitrary, an aesthetic and moral cheat. He does not *know* he will succeed; what he knows is himself, his readiness. The private hero must be a hero of privacy.[58]

Private labyrinths are the best training grounds for the more dangerous corridors of intrigue. If the spy novel is ultimately concerned with the traffic in information in impersonal systems, it is also concerned with the human responsibility for the technology implicit in those systems, and for interpreting the messages that flow through them.

Obviously, human endeavor offers greater opportunity for glamor, romance, and drama than the operations of technological surrogates like satellites and computers, and the vicarious pleasures the genre provides are not to be denied. Who would not wish to pocket a false passport and slip across a secular border in a world all too mystified by clouds of information, to pit one's own prowess against inhuman bureaucracies, to champion redistribution of the wealth of data, to recapture meaning in a universe of confusion? But mostly, readers of spy novels want to be assured—in this amorphous, anonymous era of information—that individual messages matter, that urgent signals get through, that communication is real. Behind all spy novels is that hope, never better expressed than in John Trenhaile's *The Man Called Kyril* (1981), in whose pages a spymaster reminds an agent of his mission: "Somewhere out there in your world, the world beyond the seas, there's a man listening for that transmitter."[59]

NOTES

1. John Le Carré, *A Perfect Spy* (New York: Alfred A. Knopf, 1986), 393.

2. Jacques Barzun, "Meditations on the Literature of Spying," *American Scholar* 34 (Spring 1965): 167–78; Umberto Eco, "The Narrative Structure in Fleming," *The Bond Affair,* ed. Oreste de Bueno and Umberto Eco (London: MacDonald, 1966), 35–75; probably the most complete bibliography of comment on espionage fiction has been compiled by Myron Smith, Jr., *Cloak and Dagger Fiction: An Annotated Guide to Spy Thrillers,* 2d ed. (Santa Barbara: ABC-Clio, 1982); see also John G. Cawelti and Bruce A. Rosenberg, *The Spy Story* (Chicago: University of Chicago Press, 1987).

3. Walter Laqueur, *A World of Secrets: The Uses and Limits of Intelligence* (New York: Basic Books, 1985), 6.

4. For brief discussion of espionage themes in the work of Pynchon and Borges, see Thomas Moore, *The Style of Connectedness: Gravity's Rainbow and Thomas Pynchon* (Columbia: University of Missouri Press, 1987), p. 84.

5. Quoted by Cawelti and Rosenberg, *The Spy Story,* 29.

6. Cawelti and Rosenberg break the plots of the espionage novel down into three basic formulas in *The Spy Story.*

7. The criticism on genre functions is vast. For some disparate views on genres as forms for processing information about historical change, see John G. Cawelti, *Adventure, Mystery, and Romance* (Chicago: University of Chicago Press, 1976); Robert Warshow, *The Immediate Experience* (Garden City: Doubleday Anchor, 1964), especially the chapters on gangster and Western movies; Joseph W. Slade, "The Pornographic Film Market and Pornographic Formulas," *The Journal of Popular Film* 6 (1978): 168–86; Thomas Kent, *Interpretation and Genre: The Role of Generic Perception in the Study of Narrative Texts* (Lewisburg, Penn.: Bucknell University Press, 1986). The latter study in particular discusses genre itself in terms of information theory.

8. James R. Beniger, *The Control Revolution: Technological and Economic Origins of the Information Society* (Cambridge, Mass.: Harvard University Press, 1986), 9.

9. Edwin T. Layton, "Technology as Knowledge," *Technology and Culture* 15 (1974): 31–41.

10. Quoted by Hugh G. J. Aitken, *The Continuous Wave: Technology and American Radio, 1900–1932* (Princeton, N.J.: Princeton University Press, 1985), 14.

11. See, for example, Jeremy Campbell, *Grammatical Man: Information, Entropy, Language, and Life* (New York: Simon and Schuster, 1982), which provides an excellent overview of information theory.

12. See "Literature, Technology, and Covert Culture," in Leo Marx, *The Pilot and the Passenger: Essays on Literature, Technology, and Culture in the United States* (New York: Oxford University Press, 1988), 127–38.

13. Marc U. Porat, et al., *The Information Economy,* OT Special Publication 77–12, Department of Commerce, Washington, D.C., 1977.

14. Beniger, *The Control Revolution,* 185.

15. Edwin T. Martin, *Thomas Jefferson: Scientist* (New York: Henry Schuman, 1952), 59; Dirk J. Struik, *Yankee Science in the Making* (Boston: Little Brown, 1948), 141–42.

16. A. P. Woolrich, *Mechanical Arts and Merchandise: Industrial Espionage and Travellers' Accounts as a Source for Technical Historians* (Eindhoven: De Archaeologische Pers, 1986); see also A. P. Woolrich, ed., *Ferrner's Journal 1759/1760: An Industrial Spy in Bath and Bristol.* trans A. den Ouden (Eindhoven: De Archaeologische Pers, 1986).

17. Christopher Andrew, *Her Majesty's Secret Service: The Making of the British Intelligence Community* (New York: Viking Penguin, 1987), 12.

18. For example, when a group of West German computer hackers approached a Soviet intelligence agent in East Berlin with offers to break into United States military computers several years ago, the agent was more interested in obtaining something with commercial value. He gave the hackers $15,000 to search through computers made by the Digital Equipment Corporation for a software program used in computer-aided design, more appropriate for building industrial equipment than Star Wars weapons (John Markoff, "Reassessing U.S. Controls on Computer Exports," *New York Times,* 16 April 1989, E7).

19. Senate Testimony of Arthur van Cook, quoted in Linda Melvern, David Hebditch, and Nick Anning, *Techno-Bandits: How the Soviets Are Stealing America's High-Tech Future* (Boston: Houghton Mifflin, 1984), 271.

20. Melvern, et al., *Techno-Bandits,* 56.

21. John Ferguson, *Bibliographical Notes on Histories of Inventions and Books of Secrets* (London: Holland Press, 1981).

22. Philip Knightly, *The Second Oldest Profession: Spies and Spying in the Twentieth Century* (New York: Norton, 1986).

23. Beniger, *The Control Revolution*, 287.

24. Alexander Welsh, *George Eliot and Blackmail* (Cambridge, Mass.: Harvard University Press, 1985).

25. César Graña, *Modernity and Its Discontents* (Glencoe, Ill.: Free Press, 1967), 41–42.

26. Derek de Solla Price, *Little Science, Big Science* (New York: Columbia University Press, 1963), 65.

27. Andrew, *Her Majesty's Secret Service*, 96. The American unit was called, romantically, the Black Chamber; the British were Room 40, later to metamorphose into the Bletchley Park group.

28. Jack Fuller, *Convergence* (New York: Ballantine Books, 1984), 71.

29. Among Price's novels featuring this protagonist are *Sion Crossing* (1985), *The Alamut Ambush* (1986), *Here Be Monsters* (1987), and *For the Good of the State* (1988).

30. Marshall McLuhan, *Understanding Media: The Extensions of Man,* 2d ed. (New York: New American Library), 49.

31. Julian Semyonov, *Tass Is Authorized to Announce . . . ,* trans. Charles Buxton (Moscow: Druzhba Narodov, 1979; rpt. New York: Avon Books, 1988), 27. The circulation figures appear on the cover of the Avon edition. The information on Andropov appears in a page of blurbs reprinted from London reviews.

32. Erving Goffmann, quoted in Joshua Meyrowitz, *No Sense of Place: The Impact of Electronic Media on Social Behavior* (New York: Oxford University Press, 1985), v.

33. Richard Rhodes, *The Making of the Atomic Bomb* (New York: Simon and Schuster, 1986), chaps. 1 and 2.

34. One way of calculating value is to use the "multiplier" effect pioneered by Lord Keynes, who pointed out that capital, as it percolated through an economy's structures, actually increased in value depending on the uses to which it was put and the additional activity it generated. Information might be said to function in similar fashion.

35. Thomas L. Hughes, *The Fate of Facts in a World of Men: Foreign Policy and Intelligence-Making,* Headline Series no. 233, Foreign Policy Association (New York: Foreign Policy Association, 1976), 13.

36. Herbert E. Meyer, *Real-World Intelligence* (New York: Weidenfeld and Nicholson, 1988), 80–95.

37. Andrew, *Her Majesty's Secret Service,* 85.

38. Robert Littell, *The Amateur* (New York: Dell, 1981), 74.

39. Adam Hall, *The Scorpion Signal* (New York: Playboy Paperbacks, 1981), 32.

40. See Cawelti and Rosenberg, *The Spy Story,* for more discussion of MacGuffins, 56–57.

41. Gordon Stevens, *Do Not Go Gentle* (New York: St. Martin's Press, 1987), 144.

42. See for example William Stevenson, *A Man Called Intrepid* (New York: Ballantine, 1976); F. W. Winterbotham, *The Ultra Secret* (New York: Dell, 1974); David Kahn, *The Codebreakers: The Story of Secret Writing* (New York: Macmillan, 1967).

43. Laqueur, *A World of Secrets,* 29.

44. David Monaghan, *The Novels of John le Carré* (New York: Basil Blackwell,

1985), 11.

45. Michael Denning, *Cover Stories: Narrative and Ideology in the British Spy Thriller* (New York: Routledge, Chapman and Hall, 1987), 136.

46. David Ignatius, *Agents of Innocence* (New York: Norton, 1987), 283.

47. Robert Baden-Powell, *My Adventures as a Spy* (London: C. A. Pearson, 1915), 159.

48. Tony Chiu, *Port Arthur Chicken* (New York: William Morrow, 1979); republished under the title *Onyxx* (New York: Berkley, 1981).

49. The phrase is that of James Jesus Angleton, director of counter-intelligence (1954–1974) for the CIA, and author of the belief that the CIA was subverted by "moles."

50. Meyrowitz, *No Sense of Place,* 183.

51. *Ibid.,* 182.

52. H. L. Mansel in a review of 1863, quoted by Welsh, *George Eliot and Blackmail,* 103–4.

53. Denning, *Cover Stories,* 136–137.

54. Laqueur, *A World of Secrets,* 9.

55. Jacques Derrida, "Le Facteur de la vérité," *La Carte postale* (Paris: Aubier-Flammarion, 1980), 517.

56. N. J. Crisp, *The Ninth Circle* (New York: Viking, 1988), 178.

57. Ralph Harper, *The World of the Thriller* (Baltimore: Johns Hopkins University Press, 1974), viii.

58. Stanley Cavell, *The World Viewed: Reflections on the Ontology of Film* (New York; Viking, 1971), 56.

59. John Trenhaile, *The Man Called Kyril* (New York: Congdon and Weed, 1981), 33.

Pynchon and the Civil Wars of Technology

LANCE SCHACHTERLE

Thomas Pynchon shares with other contemporary novelists a passion to reckon the burdens distinctive to our technologically dependent society. Like Don DeLillo in *White Noise,* Pynchon depicts how technology can place us in jeopardy before "airborne toxic events"; like John Updike in *Roger's Version,* Pynchon can also entertain the vision of technology literally storming the heavens; and like Kurt Vonnegut—with whom he shares a Cornell education in science and an early career in a major technology firm—the attempt to encompass technology conjures up texts whose promiscuous mixing of tragedy, slapstick, satire, and black humor can puzzle and offend the traditional humanist almost as much as technology itself.[1]

But when compared to other writers, Pynchon's concern with technology runs deeper, seems more part of the essential fabric. Technology shaping, beautifying, or invading the human body informs his first novel *V.* (1963). Technology rampant exemplifies the life-style of Southern California developments laid out like a "printed circuit" in *The Crying of Lot 49* (1966). From Oedipa Maas's encounter with a falling can of hairspray becoming sinister projectile through the technique practiced by her dead lover to encapsulate her in his "will," technology assumes the role of coercion of choice. And in *Gravity's Rainbow* (1973), the entire technology of the rocket itself figures the basic metaphor of the novel: the attempt to escape the gravity of death by flying out on a rainbow-parabola of transcendence.

In Pynchon's works, technology threatens because it confers power upon the "elect," enabling them to render the "preterite" powerless. Preterition, as Joseph Slade suggests, is the state of feeling marginalized, unable to change the status quo, not knowing how the big decisions affecting us all are made.[2] From losing sleep over a dripping faucet (an unconquerable technological barrier to

253

Sylvia and John in Pirsig's *Zen and the Art of Motorcycle Maintenance*) through the threat of losing our lives from nuclear war, a technology beyond understanding or mastery dispossesses the Preterite.

Yet for Pynchon, as for philosophers like Heidegger, technology is not intrinsically foreign or anti-human. Technology, rightly apprehended, can create an environment within which the Heideggerian "Sorge" or "Care" focusing Being can operate. And Pynchon never forgets that humans make technology, not the other way round. As Lewis Mumford has argued, our humanity can be defined by our capacity to extend our bodies and minds, our very selves, into the creation of our technology. For Pynchon, the threat of technology is not us versus them, humans versus technology. Technology is not only part of what we make, it is part of what we are. Any antagonism toward it is a civil war, part of what is human in us against ourselves. And, as Pynchon's stories show us, even the "Elect" are human.

1

We create technology because technology creates the things we love. Yet these material products of our techniques often outlast our interest in them, and we become surrounded with the "solid waste" of our technological triumphs. The theme of Pynchon's early story "Low-lands" (1960) is a common one. Dennis Flange's income as a lawyer affords ample access to a consumer society, but cannot bring the happiness or children he senses he really wants. After Dennis abandons his house and wife for the company of Pig Bodine (here as through Pynchon's work a sea-salt realist and survivor), Dennis's fantasy encounter with a nymph takes place in a junk yard filled with the detritus of our times. "[H]alf an acre of abandoned refrigerators, bicycles, baby carriages, washing machines, sinks, toilets, bedsprings, TV sets, pots and pans and stoves and air-conditioners"[3] provides the material backdrop to the waste in the marriage of Dennis and Cindy Flange. In "Low-lands," the only Pynchon work so far set in the Long Island where he grew up, his vision of his birth right is captured by the warring images of a midden heap thrown up by consumerist technology, surrounded by the life-giving ocean.

The power of our technology to flood the world with "goods" appears forcefully again in *The Crying of Lot 49*, the sole Pynchon novel entirely set in contemporary time. To frustrate the importunate Metzger in a game of "strip Botticelli," Oedipa Maas clads herself with everything she has brought along on her impromptu trip to San Narciso to begin sorting out the legacy of Pierce Inverarity, a former lover. She puts on "six pairs of panties in assorted colors, girdle, three pairs of nylons, three brassieres, two pairs of stretch slacks, four half-slips, one black sheath, two summer dresses, half dozen A-line skirts, three sweaters, two blouses, quilted wrapper, baby blue peignoir and old Orlon muu-muu. Bracelets then, scatterpins, earrings, a pendant."

Who would have thought the young woman to have had so much clothes about her? Looking at herself, thus arrayed, in the mirror, she:

> saw a beach ball with feet, and laughed so violently she fell over, taking a can of hair spray on the sink with her. The can hit the floor, something broke, and with a great outsurge of pressure the stuff commenced atomizing, propelling the can swiftly about the bathroom. Metzger rushed in to find Oedipa rolling around, trying to get back on her feet, amid a great sticky miasma of fragrant lacquer [. . .] . The can, hissing malignantly, bounced off the toilet and whizzed by Metzger's right ear, missing by maybe a quarter of an inch. Metzger hit the deck and cowered with Oedipa as the can continued its high-speed caroming [. . .] . She looked up past his eyelids, into the staring ceiling light, her field of vision cut across by wild, flashing overflights of the can, whose pressure seemed inexhaustible. She was scared but nowhere near sober. The can knew where it was going, she sensed, or something fast enough, God or a digital machine, might have computed in advance the complex web of its travel; but she wasn't fast enough, and knew only that it might hit them at any moment, at whatever clip it was doing, a hundred miles an hour[. . .] . The can collided with a mirror and bounced away, leaving a silvery, reticulated bloom of glass to hang a second before it all fell jingling into the sink; zoomed over to the enclosed shower, where it crashed into and totally destroyed a panel of frosted glass; thence around the three tile walls, up to the ceiling, past the light, over the two prostrate bodies, amid its own whoosh and the buzzing, distorted uproar from the TV set. She could imagine no end to it; yet presently the can did give up in midflight, and fall to the floor, about a foot from Oedipa's nose. She lay watching it.[4]

Does one laugh more here with the gusto of the comedy, or cringe with the victims of the peculiarly mindless manifestation of technology?

Readers attuned to science will recognize Oedipa's reference to the Newtonian clockwork universe, where as Laplace claimed, the future could be predicted if technology produced the computational powers needed to extrapolate the movement of all ensembles of objects from present observed positions. "God or a digital machine" might predict the future movements of the spray can, but in her befuddlement, she can only duck. Oedipa and Metzger are the prostrate victims of escaping molecules of gas whose complex interactions under pressure obey those very laws of statistical mechanics, formulated as entropy, that inform Pynchon's fiction from the 1960 shory story "Entropy" on. The complex technology of entropy, which was developed to inquire into the efficiency of steam engines and later served as a model for modern information theory, is harnassed here to provide "efficient" delivery of a technical wonder, hair spray.

Besides weakening Oedipa's resolution not to succumb to Metzger, the scene leads to other consequences. Three pages later, contemplating the shivered mirror, she remarks "Seven years' bad luck [. . .] I'll be 35."[5] Seven years then to thirty-five, the half way point of life in the Dantean formulation, halfway through her generation. The spray can incident also establishes her current age as twenty-eight, allowing the inquisitive reader of the first edition to estimate her year of birth as twenty-eight years before the first copyright date given in the book. The resulting date of birth is 1937, coincident with that of her author. Thus the errant spray can, miracle of consumer technology, points to a congruency in the life pattern of author and heroine. Like her author, Oedipa's "so temperate youth" was "mothered over" by "Secretaries James and Foster and Senator Joseph."[6]

The simple, misguided missile of goopy hair spray yields up other hints to the reader. Why hair spray? Certainly, with the other paraphernalia of wardrope Oedipa deems necessary to bring on her adventure to disentangle the Inverarity estate, the hair spray bespeaks the conventionality at the outset of the tale of its user, whose earliest recorded act in the text is to return home from a suburban Tupperware party "whose hostess had put perhaps too much kirsch in the fondue".[7] Hair spray, by definition, fixes hair into place: it's a technological fix to render permanently in place that which naturally wanders. (The tendency of technology to employ artifice to freeze the natural in place will be noted subsequently.) Why does this young California woman initially living so conventional a life fear change?

2

Reflecting on this question can lead us to considering the wider meaning of technology in the novel. For Pynchon, "technology" signifies more than just a collection of objects, or of ways of making them. Like Jacques Ellul and Lewis Mumford, Pynchon sees technology as rules for manipulating more than just material objects; technology extends as well to principles for organizing whole societies along certain lines. The obsession in his novels with central characters stumbling upon evidences of far-reaching plots constituting the hidden structure of society resembles Ellul's distinctive generalizing of "technology" in *The Technological Society.*[8]

For Ellul, it will be recalled, technology is the pursuit of maximum efficiency through universal applications of rationally contrived rules that determine all behavior within a system. The hallmarks of technology are artifice (as contrasted to nature), standardization (as opposed to individuality), and orderliness (as opposed to mystery):

> Technique is a means of apprehending reality, of acting on the world, which allows us to neglect all individual differences, all subjectivity. Technique alone is rigorously objective. It blots out all personal opinions. It effaces all individual, and even all collective, modes of experience.[9]

What Oedipa comes to confront in *The Crying of Lot 49* is the possibility that her former lover, the fabulously wealthy real estate mogul Pierce Inverarity, may have used his influence to weave around her a web of clues suggesting that a mysterious alternative communication system named W.A.S.T.E. exists. If the clues she encounters sustain the conclusion W.A.S.T.E. is a monumental pratfall engineered by a spiteful ex-lover, then Inverarity's technique is awesome indeed:

> OK, Oedipa told herself, stalking around the room, her viscera hollow, waiting on something truly terrible, OK. It's unavoidable, isn't it? Every access route to the Tristero [the league of malcontents who presumably created W.A.S.T.E.] could be traced also back to the Inverarity estate. Even Emory Bortz, with his copy of Blobb's *Peregrinations,* (bought, she had no doubt he'd tell her in the event she asked, also at Zapf's), taught now at San Narciso College, heavily endowed by the dead man.[10]

Inverarity's technique appears to have been relentlessly efficient indeed.

But Oedipa entertains three other possible hypotheses regarding the mass of clues adumbrating this secret communications network. She may have hallucinated it, victim of drugs she is not aware

of; she may be fantasizing to the point of madness; or the counter-
cultural network might really exist, a product of the collective
frustrations of all those who seek to reject the pursuit of efficiency
Inverarity's estate symbolizes.[11]

The novel, of course, ends with Oedipa suspended at the beginning of the auction of stamp lot 49 that she hopes will decide among
these alternatives. But it is the possibility of W.A.S.T.E. really
existing that intrigues most, for such a league provides an escape
from the crushing weight of Inverarity's testiment to efficiency. The
sequence announcing the four possible hypotheses before Oedipa
begins with:

> She had dedicated herself, weeks ago, to making sense of what Inver-
> arity had left behind, never suspecting that the legacy was America.[12]

and concludes with:

> For there either was some Tristero beyond the appearance of the legacy
> America, or there was just America and if there was just America then it
> seemed the only way she could continue, and manage to be at all
> relevant to it, was as an alien, unfurrowed, assumed full circle into some
> paranoia.[13]

Replace "paranoia" with "care" and Oedipa's prescription for
continuing in America sounds remarkably close to that offered by
Martin Heidegger. Here and elsewhere, Heidegger's late writings on
technology parallel Pynchon's perceptions, and his early work,
Being and Time (1927), seems to inform Oedipa and Inverarity's
thoughts on technology. *Being and Time* stresses the need for the
individual to lay claim to personal self by rescuing it from the mass
of inert society and meaningless material goods. Such a recovery is
accomplished by recognizing the problematic relation of the individual to mass society, by accepting a Kierkegaardian challenge to
open oneself to uncertainties and tentativeness. Heidegger's formulation of this acceptance of vulnerability to Being is "Sorge" or
"care."

Heideggerian "care" is the root of Sartre's famous trio of "Despair," "Anguish", and "Forlornness" in Sartre's "Existentialism"
essay.[14] Despite the apparent cheerlessness of the nouns invoked,
for both authors "Care" and its associated cluster designate concepts that bring freedom to the individual to engage actively in
disclosing personal Being. Individual coming-to-Being, the famous
Heideggerian "Da-sein," can be authentic only as "Being-for-

death," as acknowledging that life exists only in time, not beyond it. The authentic person, acknowledging the finiteness of human control over Being, thus cultivates an openness to the vicissitudes natural to life—a life that ends in death, the greatest, most inescapable and unshareable vicissitude possible.[15]

In this context, we see both Oedipa's growth and Pierce Inverarity's radical dishonesty. Oedipa's fear of change was noted earlier, and the greatest change in death. In the novel she comes to show "Care" for both life and death. While pursuing an apparent W.A.S.T.E. messenger, she comes upon a derelict and deserted sailor in a flophouse under a San Francisco freeway. Rather than ignore the ancient mariner, she remains to comfort him, cradling him in her arms and meditating on the time of his inevitable death. Her meditation, too long to quote here,[16] weaves together her memories of collegiate loves, of freshman calculus with its DT's that come to signify the delirium tremens of the old man and the Delta Time of shrinking to zero in death. Her reflection captures for her for the first time a sense of a world of suffering that she, insulated in suburban Kinneret-among-the Pines, has largely evaded. This scene has often been noted as a secular "pieta"; it might also serve as an emblem of "care."

In contrast, Inverarity uses all his powers to escape "Care." His technique, in the Ellulian sense, struggles to manage all around him in the most efficient way. The America he personifies is one of Big Deals. his dazzling entrepreneurial skills amass and lose him fortunes, and he glories in the complexities of wheeling and dealing across the face of the land. His craft leads Oedipa to suspect that if he arranged all the W.A.S.T.E. hints to mislead her, the colossal joke might be Pierce's slap from across the grave—perhaps even a machination that he hoped would enable him to escape death itself. "Had something slipped through and Inverarity by that much beaten death?"[17] she wonders.

Inverarity embodies that very will to alter the land that aroused Heidegger's ire in his late essays on technology. For Heidegger, man opens consciousness to being through relating to the world around; if this relationship is caring and directed, the disclosing of Being can take the form of art, of poiesis. In true poiesis, if coming-into-Being involves craftsmanship or techne, the emphasis falls on the discovering of Being itself, as in art. Heidegger laments, however, that contemporary techne has displaced Being in favor of the objects with which techne works. Heidegger cites two examples of techne, old and new: the peasant farmer working the land, letting the seed sprout, root, and grow with minimal interference, and the modern technologist-farmer, forcing the land to bear more with chemical and mechanical interventions.[18] Inverarity, with his land dealings, goes one step further than Heidegger's engineer-agriculturalist, by shaping and dividing the land to bear Southern California culture.

Techne, with its stress on challenging or provoking things rather than letting Being speak through them, has two consequences. Because the individual will enters into determining how things are to be used, the individual is caught up within the technological system of "challenging-revealing." This entrapment and ultimate limiting of the individual Heidegger calls "Gestell," or "Enframing." "The essence of modern technology is Enframing,"[19] for Enframing encloses coming-into Being within the boundaries set by the will that determines how things are to be used. "Enframing conceals that revealing which, in the sense of poiesis, lets what presences [here used as a verb] come forth into appearance."[20]

Not only is the consciousness thus bounded and demeaned, but so are objects. Objects regarded as fixed and dead, as tools to serve technological purposes, no longer disclose Being by standing against the individual consciousness and thus letting Being in. Objects thus called upon to "stand by" for future use become the "Standing-Reserve" (Bestand), means not to the pursuit of Being through caring, but to "regulating and securing."[21] What Heidegger here is saying is that ideally objects should challenge us to open ourselves to Being by admitting our own vulnerability and emptiness. Such a relation lets Being in and can take the form, say, of the poetry of Hölderlin that Heidegger so loved. But objects shorn of their innate mystery of otherness, challenged to "stand by, or to be on call for a further ordering,"[22] give us a false sense of security and fullness.

Heidegger is arguing, through his sometimes clotted neologisms, that modern technology's greatest threat is its sense that all man's questions about the world have been answered, that man can be secure in his possession of the power to alter things as the will dictates. To the humanist tradition nothing is more distressing than the assumption—especially among Americans—that technology confers an escape from contingency.[23] So potent does modern technology appear, especially in and to America, that Heidegger's key terms, "regulating and securing," have become routinized into the fabric of our experience. We expect things to work as they are engineered. Chance has no role. Though Laplace had not the calculating machine to predict the future, we think we have. Thus when NASA's attempt to make routine the chanciness of space travel failed with the Challenger explosion of January 1986, our shock is all the greater. No techne, Heidegger might say, exists to domesticate death, to secure us against it.

3

To most people reading this nearly nine hundred page behemoth for the first time, *Gravity's Rainbow* seems to involve an enormously elaborate plot concerning the pursuit of information about the German V-2 project right after the fighting in World War II ended. Most first readers scratch earnestly for the details of a vast plot, hints of which are strewn about with a prodigality anticipated only in the late Dickens of *Little Dorrit* or *Our Mutual Friend*. In the end, this apparent narrative thread proves illusory. Indeed, for the reader raised on the "technique" of the comparably complex and variegated Victorian novel, Pynchon's displacement of that genre's anticipated technology of construction comes as quite a shock.

The relationships of the main characters, Captain Weissmann (known as "Blicero") and Tyrone Slothrop, to the rocket program articulate Pynchon's meaning beyond the ultimate irony of a plot that collapses under its own weight. Slothrop, scion of a Western Massachusetts family rooted in radical Puritanism, appears by some kind of perverse psychological conditioning technique to have developed a sexual anticipation of where V-2s will fall on London. Blicero, an exemplar of German imperial culture, uses his position as officer in the rocket corps to act out his own fantasies about the exhaustion of the European tradition of high culture he so loves. Much of the "action" of the novel involves Slothrop and Blicero's attempts to use the V-2 for their own ends, as well as the counterplots of others to use them as vehicles for gaining control of this new technology in anticipation of the oncoming cold war.

Blicero had served with German forces subduing the Herero revolt in the colony of South-West Africa in the second decade of the century—a campaign, Pynchon darkly warns us, in which German technology was for the first time pressed into the service of genocide. There he met and fell in love with a young half-breed Herero whom he named Enzian, honoring his favorite poet Rilke. This homosexual coupling of German intellectual and African boy close to the primitive instincts of his nearly exterminated tribe seems one of the few instances of meaningful love in the book. Though Blicero feels guilt for accepting the advances of the trusting boy,[24] their love seems genuine: Enzian, always presented with respect in the story, never loses his love or care for his "slender white adventurer, grown twenty years sick and old."[25]

Perhaps had Weissmann, like Kurt Mondaugen in *V.*, disappeared into African desert in disgust with the barbarity of his people, he could have come to terms with the heart of darkness that for Pynchon beats with a healthier energy than the deracinated pulse of Europe. But he returns to Germany, ultimately to the rocket program. Thwarted by his perversions from seeking any love requiring "care," Weissmann adopts the name "Dominus Blicero," Lord of a Whiteness that suggests his enchantment with death. His energies are sublimated into making the German rocket program successful, a commitment he teaches Enzian to accept as the ultimate knowledge about masculine love.

> It began when Weissmann brought him [Enzian] to Europe: a discovery that love, among these men, once past the simple feel and orgasming of it, had to do with masculine technologies, with contracts, with winning and losing. Demanded, in his own case, that he enter the service of the Rocket. . . . Beyond simple steel erection, the Rocket was an entire system *won,* away from the feminine darkness, held against the entropies of lovable but scatterbrained Mother Nature.[26]

In Blicero's exasperated case, technology becomes identified with a masculine victory over what he fears: women, nature, chance. The history of the German rocket illustrates Heidegger's argument for Gestell or Enframing. For Blicero, the rocket becomes an instrument of fulfilling his personal vengeance on Mother Nature. The V-2 breeds a technology whose perfecting—described in some detail through the novel—presses chance out of the system. The fantasy object of the cinema becomes a vehicle to propel a ton of high explosives on London citizens, a warhead whose supersonic and hence unannounced arrival proves to be the only weapon Londoners cannot get used to. "But then last September the rockets came. Them fucking rockets. You couldn't adjust to the bastards. No way," as Slothrop says.[27] Heidegger's argument of technology as "Challenging-Revealing," of imposing will upon Nature to yield up power at the cost of cutting self off from growth into new Being, could be no better illustrated.

And death results. Not only of nameless Londoners, of occasional minor characters introduced to us by name, but of the disillusion if not physical death of a Blicero and all he loves. In a climax surely inspired by the *Götterdämmerung*, Blicero reserves a last rocket, specially insulated with a new erotic polymer, to launch his young lover Gottfried into the heavens. Blicero's romantic, death-sodden rhetoric compels a terminal vision of the bitterness of postwar Europe about to be reinfected with a new virulence of technology. (The principal source of the new technology is an America eager to forfeit its own chances for a free life by grasping for empire.) Blicero's invocation to Gottfried to escape to the heavens, perhaps to a new life on the moon free of earthly gravity, takes on such power and weight that the reader may be swept up by its very potency.[28]

Blicero is clearly mad, probably impotent. His love for Gottfried has been "waste, yes, futility."[29] His projection of Gottfried into the heavens creates not a Rilkean Angel, but a sacrifice of an innocent last seen with "the first star hang[ing] between his feet"[30] as the rocket inevitably reaches its high point and begins its fatal return to earth in inevitable submission to gravity.

In Heidegger's terms, the attempt through technology to submit Being to the "Challenging-Revealing" of total domination not only fails to create a system immune to chance, but closes off that openness to experience that, as a young man, he seemed to demonstrate in his love of poetry and Enzian. Making of the magic of early rocketry the quite literal "standing reserve" of a weaponry stockpile routinizes the charisma of discovery (to use a phrase from Weber Pynchon enjoys). Or—if you prefer a pithier Pynchonesque formulation, the failure of Weissmann's attempt to turn the parabola of descent into an arc of escape may be summarized as:

> Lovable but scatterbrained Mother Nature . . . 1
> Masculine technologies . . . 0.

It remains for Enzian, leader of a small band of Hereros in the undefined Zone between German conquerors, to see the rocket differently. For him, the Black Rocket—throughout paralleled to Blicero's deathly 00000—embodies the strength of his beleaguered people to master a European technology in the face of their oppressors. The rocket they shepherd through the last pages gives them a quest, an identity, an opening to Being, which serves as a counterforce to the death wish of some of their compatriots. The novel does not record their launch, success or failure—but their rocket shows a racial poiesis that is creative. Perhaps they survive.

4

Blicero reads Rilke, especially the Tenth Elegy. Tyrone Slothrop reads Plasticman comic books. In that contrast they prefigure European and American sensibilities—the grand rhetoric of European high culture versus the malleability of American experience. But as readers of the novel know, Slothrop more than reads Plasticman, he may be plasticman. Clues and discoveries suggest that as a young man, Slothrop may have been sold to the omnipresent technological genius, Lazlo Jamf, whose expertise in organic chemistry—and his fascist power politics—combine to make him the novel's arch-technologist. Jamf's vision of the ionic bound as a seizing of power (in contrast to the insipid sharing of covalency,) accords with his politics, and enables him to conquer new areas for technology. Plastics, emulsions for movie film, rocket propellants, synthetic dopes, and the sensuous insulation that proves to be Gottfried's shroud all result from Jamf's enframing of the original (literal) dream of Kekule's organic molecular benzene ring.

While Jamf was at Harvard, he seems to have been working on yet another technology to seize power—a synthetic organic substance to condition humans. The system Jamf explored would have won the admiration of Ellul's efficiency seeking technocrats. Abandoning the expensive measuring apparatus and monitoring of the pioneering student of conditioning, the Russian Pavlov (another gray eminence among the novel's technologists), Jamf hit upon conditioning an infant, Tyrone, to contract an erection upon stimulation with his mysterious substance. Why an erection? "[A] hardon, that's either there, or it isn't. Binary, elegant. The job of observing it can even be done by a *student*."[31]

Jamf, it is hinted, failed in his responsibilities to extinguish Tyrone's conditioning after ending the experiments, and some lingering affinity between Tyrone's cock and the Jamf-chemistry of the V-2 makes Tyrone anticipate where V-2's will hit by making love to various London pickups at locations subsequently struck by the revenge weapon. The discovery that Tyrone's record-grid of conquests overlaps the grid of rocket hits throws into convulsions conventional scientific wisdom, as somehow Tyrone seems to abrogate cause-and-effect by responding to the rockets *before* they explode.

Though Slothrop only haltingly grasps why British intelligence becomes so interested in him, others quickly take an interest in his curious condition. In particular, he is pursued throughout by the

Pavlovian psychologist Edward Pointsman, whose professional dedication to binary thinking—on or off, 1 or 0—is prefigured in his name, which in British parlance signifies a switchman who shunts railcars from one line to another. Slothrop's pre-vision so affronts Pointsman's dedication to cause and effect that Pointsman vows "I will find [how his mind works] if I have to open up his damned skull."[32] To this end, Pointsman's dedication to the technology of behavioral conditoning enlists the support of a diversity of spies and agents monitoring Slothrop's actions—even an obliging octopus named Grigori.

In the end, all who seek Slothrop's secret—including Slothrop himself—fail. Slothrop, ostensibly on a secret mission to gather intelligence about the V-2 program, becomes actor in and progressively victim of a remarkable succession of misadventures. His failure differs from Blicero's. Rather than try to dominate the rocket, Slothrop simply loses interest in it. He has made a "Standing-Reserve" not of things, but of women, especially in his endless and increasingly perverse sexuality. Appropriately the last female we see with him for any length of time is a friendly sow.

As he pursues the mysteries of the rocket through the Zone, he himself becomes a mystery. He assembles hint after hint about the plots pullulating about the rocket, only to have his own consciousness unravel in the face of increasing complexity. The paranoia that drives him to affix the dark hints of his own sale to Jamf to the German rocket finally yields to the opposite—an antiparanoia where nothing connects with nothing.

Though many readers have reviewed this "anti-paranoid part of his cycle"[33] as his demise, he may, in Heideggerian terms, be escaping from the Enframing that hitherto has trapped everybody in the story itself. The latest point chronologically in which we see him sounds like a Heideggerian opening-into Being, an escape through rejection of the "Challening-Revealing" that has conditioned him before. After puzzling over a graffiti he finally identifies as a schematic of the V-2 guidance system, he recalls his past up to this point. The rich memories of a country childhood in Western Massachusetts flood him, providing a personal pattern of order that dissolves the vain quest to order the political empire-building of the Zone. "Slothrop sees a very thick rainbow here, a stout rainbow cock driven down out of pubic clouds into Earth, green wet valleying Earth, and his chest fills and he stands crying, not a thing in his head, just feeling natural. . . ."[34] In possessing the Rocket, Blicero has rejected "feeling natural." In contrast, by here accepting Being for itself without imposing his will on it, Slothrop escapes the rocket's technology. Rather than die, he simply drops out of a book in which all the others continue to hide in self-deceit their inevitable vulnerability to chance, to Earth.

Technology embraces more in *Gravity's Rainbow* than just the stories of Blicero and Slothrop. In the sense given by Ellul, technology as the pursuit of maximum efficiency through systemization of effort controls the war itself. The narrator throughout stresses the dominance of cartels of industries that stretch across even the battlelines of the conflict. As Enzian and his friends discover "In the Zone," the bombs dropped to level a German refinery have instead, by design of the cartel, completed the construction of the very facility they were presumably targeted to destroy:

> the bombing was the exact industrial process of conversion, each re-lease of energy placed exactly in space and time, each shockwave plotted in advance to bring *precisely tonight's wreck* into being thus decoding the Text [. . .]. If it is in working order, what is it meant to do? The engineers who built is as a refinery never knew there were any further steps to be taken [. . .].
>
> It means this War was never political at all, the politics was all theatre, all just to keep the people distracted . . . secretly, it was being dictated instead by the needs of technology . . . by a conspiracy between human beings and techniques, by something that needed the energy-burst of war, crying, "Money be damned, the very life of [insert name of Nation] is at stake," but meaning, most likely, *dawn is nearly here, I need my night's blood, my funding, funding, ahh more, more* . . . The real crises were crises of allocation and priority, not among firms—it was only staged to look that way—but among the different Technologies, Plastics, Electronics, Aircraft, and their needs which are understood only by the ruling elite. . . .[35]

Nothing in the book counters the paranoia repeatedly expressed that the war itself is simply an instrument to maximize efficient use of resources in the service of expanding new technologies. "Don't forget the real business of the War," Pynchon writes, "is buying and selling. The murdering and the violence are self-policing, and can be entrusted to non-professionals."[36] True Technology (Pynchon uses the capital T in the long description above) fears only the cessation of funding that may come with war's end. And true Technology renders the individual impotent: "Once the technical means of control have reached a certain size, a certain degree of being *connected* one to another, the chances for freedom are over for good."[37]

5

Against such monolithic power, what chance does the individual have? Not much, but some. There is genuine love in the book, even moments of the religious peace that passes all understanding; and these moments do show that some chances for freedom remain. These chances, Pynchon shows, emerge from the same creative drives toward freedom and self-expression that inspire technology as well as love.

The best-known lovers in the book are Roger Mexico and Jessica Swanlake. To Jessica the affair with Roger is a passionate fling while she is separated from her earlier love, Jeremy, to whom she knows she will return someday. To his anxious rival Roger, Jeremy, scornfully called the "Beaver," represents the "muddling through" efficiency of the British in the war. "Damned Beaver / Jeremy *is* the War, he is every assertion the fucking War has ever made—that we are all meant for work and government, for austerity; and these shall take priority over love, dreams, and spirit[. . .]"[38]

For Roger, Jessica is everything. Roger is a D.H. Lawrence figure filled with passionate personal love but the blackest hate for the "System." His role in the novel as the most committed love is related directly to his attitudes about technology. A statistician, he serves Pynchon's purposes by reminding us of the uncertainties of nature and of technology. In explaining to Jessica the random distribution of V-2 hits throughout London, he stresses that the Poisson distribution can do no more than define the probability of hits clustering around the target bull's-eye. No science or technology can determine in advance the crucial question: where will the next Vengeance weapon fall.

Throughout the novel Roger engages in a dialectic debate with Ned Pointsman, his opposite by virtue of Pointsman's insistence that science reduces all phenomena to cause and effect. As the student of probabilities, not absolutes, Roger can live between Pointsman's binary opposites, 0 and 1. He hates the System that dominates their lives, and struggles against it. His love for Jessica is so powerful because she represents all the System cannot take away. More significant, her infinite variety mirrors the unpredictability of the mathematical probabilities he studies. For him she is always new, always changing, not pinned down. Her wondrous novelty rests on her unpredicability, her refusal to succumb to any kind of conditioning or pattern:

His life had been tied to the past. He'd seen himself a point on a moving wavefront, propagating through sterile history—a known past, a projectable future. But Jessica was the breaking of the wave. Suddenly there was a beach, the unpredictable . . . new life [. . . .] nothing was fixed, everything could be changed and she could always deny the dark sea at his back, love it away.[39]

In Heideggerian terms, what Pynchon is saying is that for Roger his love opens him to new Being, reveals his vulnerability to another in a way that helps him define his own nature. Jessica is a genuine Other against whom he comes into fuller being, not just an object (or Standing-Reserve) for sexual convenience. The fixedness that comes with being an efficient unit within a mass technological society is dissolved into fluid life.

Pynchon points to the magic of love to dissolve the Enframing of Technology by quite literally making the woman in his other pair of lovers a witch. Geli Tripping, who comes complete with a trained owl and a proclivity to lurk in the Harz Mountains, determines to win the Russian intelligence officer Vaclav Tchitcherine away from the war. To prepare the appropriate love potion she consults an old woman, who assures her "[Y]ou're in love. Technique is just a substitute for when you get older."[40]

Thus emboldened, Geli succeeds in winning her love away from his pursuit of the Black rocket commandoes, and in so doing saves him from fratricide as well (since Enzian whom he is pursuing is his half-brother). In a scene as powerfully written as anything in the amazingly diverse prose of this novel, Geli's presence fills Tchitcherine with a sense of Pan coming to bring him new life, away from the System to which his loyalties were earlier fixed:

This is the World just before men. Too violently pitched alive in constant flow ever to be seen by men directly. They are meant only to look at it dead, in still strata, transputrefied to oil or coal [the bases of modern organic chemistry and hence of much technology]. Alive, it was a threat: it was Titans, was an overpeaking of life so clangorous and mad, such a green corona about Earth's body that some spoiler *had* to be brought in before it blew the Creation apart.[41]

Heidegger argued that the greatest threat of technology is its tendency to make the future appear routine, predictable, dead. Things became means to achieving objectives, to imposing the will over nature—not ends to be valued as providing, in their mysterious apartness, access to a greater sense of Being. Blicero's pursuit of the rocket-technology progressively deadens him to all that had made him attractive before. While preparing to fire Gottfried beyond the realm of an earthly death, he rarely recalls or expresses care for Enzian, the one possible source of his salvation. And the managers of the System, the Lyle Blands and Pierce Inveraritys, use their command of its efficiencies to try to escape from death itself.

Technology, with its pursuit of efficiency, sameness, and predictability, robs us of the chance to take a chance, to open up to the nature of Being. Roger Mexico, who can live with the probabilities between Zero and One, emerges as technology's chief opponent. He can live with risk, risking an affair with Jessica. His final fantasies of disrupting the victory parties of "the Firm" depict his challenge to those, like Pointman, who would manage his life. And recall Tyrone Slothrop himself, who we are told in the end is "just feeling natural."

6

"Feeling natural" appears to be the novel's prescription for avoiding the siren call of technology to pretending certainty. Yet Pynchon's reckoning of technology does not fail to remind us that our love of technology is part of our nature, as natural as Slothrop's Wordsworthian vision of the stout cock-rainbow. The central technology in the novel is the V-2, "an entire system *won,* away from the feminine darkness, held against the entropies of lovable but scatterbrained Mother Nature."[42] That very masculine conquest, however, Pynchon envisions as rooted in the quintessential human drive of techne, the art of playful imitation and natural craft, and the quintessential natural craftsman is the engineer Franz Pökler.

Drawing no doubt from standard sources like Willi Ley, Pynchon depicts the early work on the German rocket as the play of exuberant boys escaping from the dreariness of the Weimar Republic into fantasies of voyages to the moon and planets. Such unchallenging fantasy is Heidegger's poiesis at its best: discovering the other and confronting Being. Indeed, as Pynchon notes, the earliest organized support for the rocketeers came from the German cinema, which supported their work in return for help on the fantasy movie *Die Frau im Mond.*

An early test of the rocket brings Pökler home late to report to his wife Leni:

> "It was a failure," Franz weaving under their electric bulb at three or four in the morning, a loose grin on his face, "it failed, Leni, but they

talk only of success! Twenty kilograms of thrust and only for a few seconds, but *no one's ever done it before*. I couldn't believe it Leni I saw something that, that no one ever did before."[43]

Though Leni does not share Franz's enthusiasm (she soon leaves him, throwing him into such despair that he is ripe for recruitment into full-time rocket work), nothing in her life can equal the thrill of discovery he tries, however lamely, to communicate here.

Pökler's "loose grin" (a sign of his "feeling natural"?) does not soon desert him. But unlike most characters in the novel, he does grow. At first Leni's political consciousness escapes him. During the war, he recalls prewar debates with her about how the rocket will be used. She recognizes its military value, while he clings to the notion that "[w]e'll all use *it,* someday, to leave the earth. To transcend."[44] While much in the text mocks such transcendence, Pökler's hope is never extinguished entirely. His mastery of his craft—of the ΔT equations that integrate the rockets's motion—turns the cinematic plaything into Slothrop's "fucking rockets."

Yet Pökler does not lose hope, even in the succession of daughter-surrogate Ilses that the ΔT's of time bring. We last see him at the end of the war discovering "a random woman" in the Dora concentration camp next to the Nordhausen rocket works where he labored assembling V-2's. "Before he left, he took off his gold wedding ring [momento of the lost Leni] and put it on the woman's thin finger, curling her hand to keep it from sliding off. If she lived, the ring would be good for a few meals, or a blanket, or a night indoors, or a ride home."[45] Such acts of kindness are rare in *Gravity's Rainbow*. (Slothrop performs no comparable act of generosity.)

Pökler's magnaminity emerges from his naive but good nature, which (whatever his rocket does) transcends the war and his temptations. Further, his vision of technology creating a rocket that will fly "[w]herever we tell it to [. . . .] Perhaps someday to the Moon"[46] cannot be gainsaid in the novel. What else but such a sense that technology will go "wherever we tell it to" can prevent the termination on the last page of "the last delta-t" as nuclear war is delivered by the V-2's successors? As the last word of *Gravity's Rainbow* beckons, unless "everybody" joins the singing of William Slothrop's hymn, we all lose "a Hand to turn the time."[47] Such singing can be only the creativity of a Pökler, for whom (as with Yeats)

Soul clap its hands and sing, and louder sing
For every tatter in its mortal dress.

The final testament to the power of technology to thrill (as well as destroy) comes from an unlikely source, Miklos Thanatz, whose views on S and M earn him the by-line "This is Sado-Anarchism and Thanatz is its leading theoretician in the Zone these days."[48] Precisely this extreme distancing from the System enables Thanatz to see the generative power of the Rocket in its early days. When Slothrop first meets Thanatz, he has:

> no problem steering him onto the subject of the Rocket—"I think of the A4," sez he, "as a baby Jesus, with endless committees of Herods out to destroy it in infancy—Prussians, some of whom in their innermost hearts still felt artillery to be a dangerous innovation. If you'd been out there . . . inside the first minute, you saw, you grew docile under its . . . it really did possess a Max Weber charisma . . . something joyful—and *deeply* irrational—force the State bureaucracy could never routinize, against which it could not prevail [. . .]."[49]

Thanatz searches for words to describe the joy creating the rocket unleashed, and haltingly hits upon Max Weber's idea of the power charisma has to explode the stasis of routine. "[S]omething joyful—and *deeply* irrational" is as much a part, a natural part, of technology as is any other successful human enterprise. Such joy is part of the achievement of techne that Heidegger celebrates.

But the novel shows too that the Heideggerian entrapment within the certainties of technique, with the routinization Thanatz regrets, is inevitable. Pynchon leaves us with a Manichaean struggle, a civil war indeed, between "two Rockets, good and evil, who speak together in the sacred idiolalia of the Primal Twins (some say their names are Enzian and Blicero) of a good Rocket to take us to the stars, an evil Rocket for the World's suicide, the two perpetually in struggle."[50]

Heidegger ends "The Question of Technology" so: "The closer we come to the danger, the more brightly do the ways into the saving power begin to shine and the more questioning we become. For questioning is the piety of thought." This questioning establishes the piety of Enzian, of Roger Mexico, of Franz Pökler. Even Blicero himself probes the rocket-technology he has helped to create, and in some mad way sees through it a transcendence to a utopian world beyond pain and war. Their questioning reflects how the human use of technology mirrors, like the Primal Twins above, the radical dislocations of our nature, as Heidegger and Mumford have reminded us.[51]

Not questioning is the most frightening thing about our attitudes toward technology. Roger Mexico inquires from his rival Jeremy why the British are embarking on a program to test fire captured German rockets:

> "Why?" Roger keeps asking, trying to piss Jeremy off. "Why *do* you want to put them together and fire them?"
> [Jeremy] "We've captured them, haven't we. What does one *do* with a rocket?"
> [Roger] "But why?"
> [Jeremy] "Why? Damn it, to *see,* obviously."[52]

But Jeremy, the eager Beaver who "*is* the War[. . .] is every assertion the fucking War has ever made" will of course *not* see. To him the rocket will simply extend his belief "that we are meant for work and government, for austerity; and these shall take priority over love, dreams, the spirit[. . .]."[53] The Beaver will never know charisma. In his hands the rocket will become the coercion of choice for the Cold War. In his austerity—an attitude necessary for insuring the efficiency of technological advance—we see Pynchon's view of the tragedy of our technology, at war with ourselves.

NOTES

1. At Cornell Pynchon studied engineering physics and Vonnegut biochemistry. Both worked for major technological corporations after graduation—experiences that provide the basis for the satire of corporate life in *Player Piano* and *The Crying of Lot 49*. Though Pynchon switched to literature as a major after his first year, what he learned about engineering physics enabled him subsequently to use engineering, science, and mathematics references with sophistication. What biographical facts are known about this notoriously reticent author are gathered in Mathew Winston's "The Quest for Pynchon" in *Mindful Pleasures: Essays on Thomas Pynchon,* edited by George Levine and David Leverenz (Boston: Little, Brown, 1976), pp. 251–63.

2. See Joseph W. Slade, *Thomas Pynchon,* rev. ed. (New York: Peter Lang, 1990), pp. 225–26.

3. "Low-lands," reprinted in *Slow Learner* (Boston: Little, Brown, 1984), p. 66.

4. Thomas Pynchon, *The Crying of Lot 49* (Philadelphia: Lippincott, 1966), pp. 36–38. Here and in subsequent citations to Pynchon's texts, unless noted otherwise square brackets call attention to punctuation or explanatory material I have added.

5. *Ibid.,* p. 41.

6. *Ibid.,* p. 104. Pynchon's "Introduction" to *Slow Learner,* the most revealing disclosure of his personal sense of self in print, stresses vividly a sense of what coming to intellectual maturity was like in the 1950s.

7. *Ibid.,* p. 9.

8. Ellul's 1954 book made its impact on English audiences after its translation as *The Technological Society* (New York: Knopt, 1964). The author's "Note to the

Reader" stressed the breadth of the references to technique and technology: "technique is the totality of methods rationally arrived at and having absolute efficiency . . . in every field of human activity" (xxv). "Technique is not an isolated fact in society (as the term technology would lead us to believe) but is related to every factor in the life of modern man; it affects social facts as well as all others" (xxvi). The references here are to the Vintage paperback edition (1964).

9. *Ibid.*, p. 131.

10. Pynchon, *The Crying of Lot 49*, pp. 169–70.

11. The well-known description of Oedipa's four alternatives occur on pp. 170–71.

12. Pynchon, *The Crying of Lot 49*, p. 178.

13. *Ibid.*, p. 182.

14. See Sartre's essay "Existentialism" in *Existentialism and Human Emotions* (New York: Philosophical Library, 1957), pp. 18–32.

15. These general comments on Heidegger draw upon George Steiner's *Martin Heidegger* (New York: Viking, 1978), especially the second chapter on *Being and Time*.

16. Pynchon, *The Crying of Lot 49*, pp. 125–30.

17. *Ibid.*, p. 179.

18. References to Heidegger's essay "Die Frage nach der Technik" are from the translation by William Lovitt in *The Question Concerning Technology* (New York: Harper and Row, 1977), pp. 14–15. Lovitt's introduction and notes are helpful in establishing the chronology and wordplay of the essay, and the volume contains several important related essays.

19. *Ibid.*, p. 25.

20. *Ibid.*, p. 27.

21. *Ibid.*, p. 16.

22. *Ibid.*, p. 13.

23. The distinction between American and European expectations regarding technology was made by Jean-Claude Lejosne, Chair, Applied Languages, University of Metz, at the "Bridges II" conference, Maine Maritime Academy, Castine, Maine, 19 May 1984.

24. Thomas Pynchon, *Gravity's Rainbow* (New York: Viking, 1973), pp. 322–23.

25. *Ibid.*, p. 660.

26. *Ibid.*, p. 324.

27. *Ibid.*, p. 21.

28. See Blicero's climactic description at pp. 722–24.

29. Pynchon, *Gravity's Rainbow*, p. 722.

30. *Ibid.*, p. 760.

31. *Ibid.*, p. 84.

32. *Ibid.*, p. 90.

33. *Ibid.*, p. 434.

34. *Ibid.*, p. 626.

35. *Ibid.*, pp. 520–21. Here the material in square brackets is Pynchon's.

36. *Ibid.*, p. 105.

37. *Ibid.*, p. 539.

38. *Ibid.*, p. 177.

39. *Ibid.*, p. 126.

40. *Ibid.*, p. 718.

41. *Ibid.*, p. 720.

42. *Ibid.*, p. 324.

43. *Ibid.*, p. 162.

44. *Ibid.*, p. 400.

45. *Ibid.*, p. 433.

46. *Ibid.*, p. 410.

47. *Ibid.*, p. 760. For a useful further discussion of delta-T in the context of Pynchon's use of mathematics, see Lance W. Ozier, "The Calculus of Transformation: More Mathematical Imagery in *Gravity's Rainbow*," *Twentieth Century Literature* 21 (1975): 193–210.

48. Pynchon, *Gravity's Rainbow*, p. 737.

49. *Ibid.*, p. 464.

50. *Ibid.*, p. 727.

51. Heidegger, "The Question Concerning Technology," p. 35. Mumford balances eloquently the progress of technology with its power to unleash the irrational and hateful in man. The "immense gains in valuable knowledge and useful productivity were cancelled out by equally great increase in ostentatious waste, paranoid hostility, insensate destructiveness, hideous random exterminations." Lewis Mumford, *The Myth of the Machine: Technics and Human Development* (New York: Harcourt Brace, 1967), p. 13. So close is this and other passages in Mumford to *Gravity's Rainbow* that one wonders if Pynchon has read Mumford.

52. Pynchon, *Gravity's Rainbow*, p. 709.

53. *Ibid.*, p. 177.

Literature as Dissipative Structure: Prigogine's Theory and the Postmodern "Chaos" Machine

DAVID PORUSH

> Our physics was never capable of truly understanding the Liebnizian harmony of the thousands of voices translating each other in a universal code.
> —Ilya Prigogine and Isabelle Stengers[1]

PRETEXT

The Symbolist poet Paul Valéry wrote, "The poem is a kind of machine for producing the poetic state of mind by means of words."[2] The metaphor challenges us to think about the literary text in an unusual light—as a form of technology. If anything, as our sense of machinery has grown more complex in the intervening century, Valéry's metaphor has come to seem less like a poet's fancy and more like an equation. Certainly, as the concept of *machine* has come to embrace, at least in theory, thinking machines and autonomous cybernetic devices, it has become easier to think of the literary text as a hyper-evolved cybernetic technology: if not a machine in the usual sense, then perhaps a technology in its broader sense, the application and embodiment of scientific principles for the accomplishment of specific tasks through regular operations. William Barrett offers an even more rarefied, but for our purposes more useful, definition; in his view, a machine is "an embodied decision procedure."[3]

Indeed, several postmodern writers—Thomas Pynchon, Samuel Beckett, Joseph McElroy, Donald Barthelme, William Burroughs, Kurt Vonnegut Jr., and Italo Calvino among others—invite us to consider their literary texts quite literally as embodiments of cybernetic decision procedures in words, literal cybernetic systems. It is clear that for these authors the cybernetic metaphor holds an irresistible attraction (or in some cases, a perverse fascination), since it begs a version of systematic authorship, of spontaneous creation within the structures of grammar and the machinery of the text at the same time that it responds to the myths and images of a growing cybernetic age. So it is not surprising therefore that these authors construct fictions that display cybernetic techniques directly in their structure and stylistic choices as well as in their stories.[4] Furthermore, though these authors vary widely in their particular subjects and styles and humor, their purpose in treating their own literary texts as cybernetic devices seems to be the same. Each uses the literary text to achieve a new collaboration and collision between technological models for communication and the values that literature exemplifies and preserves. In their hands, the literary text becomes what William Burroughs called a "soft machine": an organically grown but artifical extension of the ongoing technical evolution of culture.

The hallmark of these "cybernetic fictions" is an explicit and self-conscious dance on a tightrope between mechanism/control and artistic freedom/indeterminacy. Not surprisingly, it is a genre dominated by oxymoronic images of soft machines[5] that in turn (and in typically postmodern fashion) self-reflexively "generate" texts both soft (indeterminate) and mechanical (systematic): a brain linked to an orbiting computer invents its own highly-charged natural language in McElroy's *PLUS* (1977). In Thomas Pynchon's *The Crying of Lot 49* (1967) a young woman gets caught up in a secret communications system, which may be a product of her own imagination, to the point that she feels "trapped between the zeroes and ones of an enormous computer," while the author telling us the tale constructs his novel to maximize its informational entropy. Naked bodies roam in a giant cylinder-machine that is the tenuous construction of Samuel Beckett's self-deconstructing technical language in *The Lost Ones,* (1973). A man drives along a night road imagining he and his words have become messages in a cybernetic system created by a lover's triangle in Italo Calvino's "Night Driver," *T-Zero* (1972).

Yet, at the same time that it strikes this peculiar synthesis between literature and technology, cybernetic fiction is united by a sort of artistic guerrilla action to resist the synthesis it proposes—to refute, by its own demonstration, the mechanistic challenges to human intelligence posed by early cybernetics and its various daughter sciences like artificial intelligence, behaviorism, information theory, and computer modeling. In other words, these authors clearly present their texts as cybernetic devices in order to *defeat* mechanistic classical cybernetic analysis and lay to rest the notion that human expression could be duplicated by deterministic models or algorithms for information exchange. Each in their own way seeks to preserve a sense of mystery and meaning in literary expression that lies outside the mere codes and formalisms of language and information in the text. That is why so many of these cybernetic fictions have a wicked humor and are apocalyptic comedies. They turn upon a wry, typically postmodern irony: cybernetic fictions define themselves, and by implication postmodern literature generally, as *an anti-mechanistic technology.*

The essay that follows extends this postmodern view of the literary text as an anti-mechanistic technology even further. It uses the theory of Ilya Prigogine—about how systems of order spontaneously arise from chaotic situations—to suggest that we can view the literary text as a chaos machine, or more properly, *a dissipative structure*. My purpose is to further elucidate how we can understand the literary text as a postmodern technology—a machine in words, as Paul Valéry suggested—by showing how it applies and demonstrates scientific principles in order to accomplish specific tasks: specifically, dissipative structure technology is applied to rendering the most potent possible description of reality and for the excitation of the human mind to recapitulate and achieve a spontaneously self-organized higher state of order.

The reader should be warned that this essay adopts two tactics that might seem peculiar to a literary audience. First, it engages a rather detailed review of Prigogine's scientific theories. Second, it takes a certain liberty with the notion of a literary text by speaking of it in the abstract rather than concentrating on particular examples. In another essay, I have explored one novel, William Marshall's *Roadshow,* in great detail, showing how it activates principles of the science of chaos in its style, structure, and subject.[6] However, since this essay is framed as a prolegomena, a preliminary exploration of theory, I conveniently lump together the infinitely broad range of human behaviors in language that we call *literature*. I assume that literary discourse generally shares an understanding of language as an extraordinary and specialized means of expression, description, invention, amusement and discovery. Or to put in postmodern terms, I assume that literary language, whatever else it pretends to describe, always includes itself as its subject as well.

INVENTING A REALITY-DESCRIBING MACHINE
(RDM)

If you wanted to invent a machine that would do the best possible job of describing reality in words, how would you go about doing it? Well first, you would be guided by your best understanding of the three most problematic terms in the task you've defined for yourself. You would have to figure out what was meant by *machine,* by *describe,* and by *reality.* If you understood *machine* to mean an orderly arrangement of parts, built according to some scientific principles for the accomplishment of specific tasks, then undoubtedly you would try to choose—or maybe even invent—a language that was most orderly and logical. In short, you would be led to try a project such as that engaged by the early members of the Royal Society, John Wilkins and Thomas Sprat,[7] who, in the seventeenth century, sought to design a perfect language of objects, unencumbered by embellishment or words of fancy, a style that would match word to thing, *verba* to *res.* In fact, having chosen such a language, you have already have solved the problem of defining *description* and *reality,* for a logical language presumes a certain kind of discourse and also presumes that reality can be completely described by logic.

Wilkins and Sprat's project was effectively mocked and vanquished by Jonathan Swift in his satire on the Royal Society (the "Academy of Lagado") in the Third Book of *Gulliver's Travels.* There he portrays the sort of reality describing machine their theories might lead to: a large wooden computer, on which dice are arranged, each face of each die having a word or morpheme inscribed on it. Workers laboriously crank this machine to produce new and surprising but utterly contingent and often meaningless arrays of combinations—while scribes copy down those that seem to make sense. In this way, the natural philosopher during this experiment hopes to accumulate all possible knowledge, an early variation on the thousand monkeys typing. Although Wilkins and Sprat's projects were doomed to magnificent and laborious trivality, in some senses science has always presumed that it does indeed have a language machine for the accurate and complete description of reality. On the one hand, it has evolved an incredibly complex mathematical code; on the other, it has also evolved genres for scientific discourse that are rigorously logical, that scrupulously eschew embellishment, and that cling to what passes for strictly literal/empirical description.

In short, if you believe that the universe is mechanical, then the wild element in your assignment to build an RDM is not *reality* or *machine,* but *description.* The real problem for you is to find a language restrictive enough to be as rational and predictable, as mathematical and logical, as you believe the universe to be. In fact, if you have a language like mathematics that is sufficiently potent, you will soon come to believe that any utterance in that language will have a correlate in reality; that your machine for describing really is so good that not only does it describe what you've already observed, but that anything it can describe must also be part of reality somewhere, even though you haven't observed it yet. Your reality-*describing* machine has in some senses become a reality-*generating* machine.

However, quantum physics has brought us to confront the limits on our knowing and describing of reality, at least at the subatomic level. We cannot know—and therefore cannot describe in words— where an electron will be in its orbit at any given moment. Reality is *definitely fuzzy* at some fundamental level so that we are unable to build a logical machine to describe it. Similarly, Gödel's theorem has brought us to confront the inherent limits of logical descriptions: no nontrivial logical system of description can completely describe the universe and still preserve its internal consistency. The formalist's path to building an RDM has led, in the twentieth century at least, to certain frustrations.

But what if you conclude that reality is not mechanical, in the sense that it is ultimate simple, regular, predictable, and deterministic, but rather it is complex, irregular, unpredictable, and indeterminate (as in the sense of probabilistic)? In such a case, you would set about building an RDM that has a very different understanding not only of reality, but of machinery and of discourse or description as well. For one, you would have to revise completely your notion of mechanics to include unpredictability, noise, and apparently chaotic-seeming wild elements. You would be doomed to trying to build a very unmechanical, irregular-seeming machine. But even more strikingly, you would not be likely to choose a language limited by logic because logic, as it has proven to itself via Gödel, is ultimately insufficient for the task. Rather, you would try to find a language as complex and unpredictable-seeming as reality appears to be.

In short, the project of building an RDM boils down to questions of matching literary style with epistemological presumptions. For instance, to take the example of the discourse problem in physics, following Eric Auerbach we would call the stance of most physicists "mimetic." That is, most physicists must practice what Ilya

Prigogine and Isabelle Stengers in their book *Order Out of Chaos,* call *"naive realism"*—despite the assaults made on their cosmology by quantum mechanics and the Copenhagen Interpretation of reality.[8] Physicists must, at the very least in order to get grants and pursue research (if not to avoid going crazy), believe that mathematical descriptions are realistic, that the universe is always causal everywhere, and that it is essentially simple, reducible to laws of mechanics and logic. As Prigogine and Stengers put it, the scientist as naive realist must believe that the laws of rational thought are the laws of universal mechanics. That is why, they note, the French call classical dynamics, *les mechaniques rationnel,* "implying that the laws of classical mechanics are the very laws of reason."[9]

Questions about the style of representing reality have traditionally been the proper subject of literary inquiry, and the classic in the field is Eric Auerbach's *Mimesis: The Representation of Reality in Western Literature,* which charts the evolution of literary reflections of reality through changing styles. Auerbach's familiar discussion has particular relevance to our view of the hypothetical RDM Project.[10] Clearly, the idea of reality in Western culture, as reflected in its evolving literary styles, has grown more complex and richer as time goes on. Elements have been added, sometimes following deep cultural assumptions about the nature of reality, sometimes (perhaps) limited by technical skill or materials in rendering, occasionally enriched by individual innovations that alter the way reality is perceived wholecloth by an entire culture. (In fact, it is this latter capacity for discourse in culture—the communication of a new vision by individual genius—that provides the common ground for most interesting investigations of literature and science.)

An analogy from visual arts helps us to see this dynamic interplay between discourse and the perception of reality. The stylized two-dimensional figures of Egyptian hieroglyphics partly represent the simple linearity of progression that is deeply rooted in their cosmology, partly the conventions of the hieroglyphic narrative form, partly the technical (physical) limitations of inscribing figures in stone, and partly the technical (artistic) questions of their own rather primitive conventions for the representation of depth or perspective. Altogether, however, these represent now obsolete styles of rendering reality. Undoubtedly, the technical limitations that produced conventions also influenced ways of seeing, just as ways of seeing force-feed conventions. The Chinese really *do* tend to see landscapes shrouded in mists, simple in line, with immutable relations between water, mountains, and sky expressed consistently throughout nature, where we Occidentals see ever-changing variations of particular elements unique to time and place.[11] The English landscape artist's goal is to capture that climactic individualized moment on canvas. The Oriental watercolorist is compelled to discover the idealized, eternal forms lurking beneath the play of surface signs and express those on his canvas. Natives of either culture, when viewing the canvases side-by-side, undoubtedly deem their own as realistic and the other as highly stylized. Take this multiplicity of "realistic styles" to its logical extreme, and you arrive at a notion that has most recently been implicated in quantum physics: every point of view implies a different vista, every observer experiences a different observed.

The two notions that Auerbach develops in *Mimesis* are *(1) that the style of representing reality evolves;* and *(2) styles of representing reality differ between historical moments and between cultures.*

I would argue that the first notion clearly is not limited to literary discourse but can expand to embrace scientific discourse as well. Each successive scientific revolution has altered and complicated our picture of and our discourses about reality in both literature and science. Equally clearly, now that we have introduced the question, the difference in the styles of discourse between the culture of literature and the culture of science has traditionally represented two different ways of viewing the world, two very different RDMs.

Again, Auerbach gives us a way of understanding the differences between these two RDMs by his analysis of two distinct styles in early literature. The first, associated with Homeric epic, relies on "fully externalized description, uniform illumination, uninterrupted connection, free expression [i.e., nothing can't be said], foregrounding of events, displaying unmistakable meanings, few elements of historical development and of psychological perspective." If we add to Auerbach's description aspects of the composing process brought to our attention by Albert Lord in *The Singer of Tales,* then we know that Homeric epics were also composed with mechanical rules governing the arrangements of words and phrases in the line (rhyme and meter), sequences of lines in the stanza, and the use of epithets, themata, and formulae generally.[12] Furthermore, "The Homeric poem presents a definite complex of events whose boundaries in space and time are clearly delimited; before it, beside it, and after it, other complexes of events, which do not depend on it, can be conceived without conflict and without difficulty."[3] The second distinct style, which Auerbach traces to the Old Testament and calls the "Elohist," has "certain parts brought into relief, others left obscure, abruptness, suggestive influence of the

unexpressed 'background' quality, multiplicity of meanings and the
need for interpretation, universal historical claims, development of
the concept of the historically becoming, and preoccupation with
the problematic."[14]

With one important exception, we see that *modern literature has
generally taken the route of the Old Testamental style and science
has generally taken the Homeric*. That important exception is the
claim on veracity, what Auerbach calls "universal historical
claims." In fact, scientific and literary discourses have switched
places in this regard. Whereas the New Elohist style of mimesis, the
literary, has abdicated its claim to represent universal truth and
absolute authority, the New Homeric has laid claim to it. Between
Francis Bacon and our recent post-Kuhnian critique of science,
science has striven for the Homeric style: descriptions are externalized, everything is illuminated equally, the prose is literal and
transparent, everything is causally and continuously connected,
and historical development and psychological perspectives are ir-
relevant. Furthermore, Auerbach's view of the perceptual and analytical nature of Homeric narrative sounds much like a general
description of modern, analytical science method: each "complex
of events" is viewed in laboratory isolation. When we add to this
stylistic characterization an Old Testament style claim on ultimate
validity or authority, we get a very clear view of the popular ideal of
scientific discourse.

By contrast, it is clear that with the exception of its claim on
validity, the literary text has followed the path of Elohist style: both
the New Elohist and the New Homeric styles of discourse are
"preoccupied with the problematic," but in very different ways.
Science is preoccupied with the problematic as urgently needing
solution. Literature is preoccupied with preserving—and multiplying—the problematic as mysterious, as the source of ambiguity,
paradox, metaphor, and silence, the provocateurs of interpretation.
Literature generally multiplies difficulties and interpretations, relies on silence, creates background and foreground characters,
events, relations, symbols, images. Of the two styles, the Elohist—
minus its claim on absolute authority—has proven itself over time
to be better adapted to reflect the evolving complexities of civilization, a literary style devoted to a narrative of human and symbolic
affairs. The Elohist style, as we know, gives rise to Midrash (literally
"seeking"), to the Talmud, to a two-millennium-old living system of
exfoliating and enfolding commentaries that seem inexhaustible
and that generate new problems even as they attempt to resolve old
ones. By contrast, the Homeric style falls away for literary applica-

tions. Its particular and potent brand of naive realism resolves into the monolithic styles of Euclid and Aristotle and Pythagoras and Lucretius and later in the weightless and transparent delivery of data to which contemporary scientific discourse pretends.

So which of these two styles is better suited for the construction of our RDM?

EVOLUTION, ENTROPY AND THE NEW SYNTHESIS: BEING VS. BECOMING

Auerbach says the Elohist style develops "the concept of the historically becoming." This phrase is especially tantalizing in light of Ilya Prigogine's recent scientific theory about the complexity and richness of reality. Curiously enough, Prigogine's work also provides a strong argument in favor of the potency of the New Elohist style.

In 1977, Ilya Prigogine received the Nobel Prize for Chemistry for his elucidation of the spontaneous emergence of what he calls "dissipative structures"—self-organizing systems—from complex and apparently complex natural conditions. In his more technical exposition of these theories for a general audience, *From Being to Becoming: Time and Complexity in the Physical Sciences*[15] Prigogine identifies classical science with its belief that the universe is a simple mechanism as the *science of being*. In its place he offers a more complex version of the universe in which order arises spontaneously and unpredictably out of complex, unstable, apparently chaotic situations. He calls this *the science of becoming*. His work actually gives us the tools to understand and justify features of the literary discourse that are otherwise hard to explain from a scientific perspective: its evolving style of representing reality, its complexity, its unique ability to excite the imagination, its sense of nondeterministic, unpredictable complexity and organization, its narrative of the unruly and chaotic as the grounds for higher insight. This type of order and complexity arising out of chaos is precisely what classical science has had so much trouble defining, up to now, and what Prigogine's model now gives us the tools to understand on a rational basis. Furthermore, Prigogine's work has considerable consequences for our perception of where reality is and thus, what discourses are better suited to describe it. Prigogine's work lends support for what I maintain is a universal feature of the postmodern literary text: a tacit claim to reflect reality "better" than science— what I call its "epistemological potency"—while using a method of discourse entirely opposed to science's constrained, logical, and naively realistic one.

Prigogine's explication of his own work, co-authored with philosopher of science Isabelle Stengers, is written in a self-conscious mode. Prigogine is clearly alert to the way scientific theories can influence the mood of a culture, as well as be influenced by them. Indeed, in *Order Out of Chaos*, he highlights the sources of his own theory in and its potential impact on culture. In the past, this influence of scientific theories on culture have been entirely unreasonable, or can come into conflict with contrary moods created by other scientific theories. For instance, even while social Darwinism was given vigorous encouragement to rampant capitalism and imperialism in the nineteenth century, the Second Law of Thermodynamics presented a gloomy view of our entire universe doomed to flow toward heatless, lifeless extinction. While Darwinism seemed to warrant an outlandish optimism, especially for those who already had reasons for optimism, the notion of an universal entropic death put a damper on the Victorian party.

Evolution and Entropy seem to contradict each other not only in the cosmological moods but in their irreconcilable versions of how the universal machine actually operates. If Rudolf Clausius and Clerk Maxwell were right, then any machine will grind to a halt inexorably when left to its own devices. The combination of ever-present forces—like friction—will degrade mechanical operation as part wears against part, leaking valuable energy and organization out into the universal soup where it joins the larger tide toward randomness and absolute cold. Furthermore, once molecules have vibrated themselves into an effete state of equilibrium—analogous to hot and cold water mixing into one large lukewarm volume—no natural force can retrieve that leaked heat or lost differentiation. The process of degradation toward entropy is irreversible; nature will not reheat the water again.

But if Darwin's vision of nature was correct, then somehow the biosphere has been arranged to give rise to ever more complex and organized structures, biological organisms. One-celled organisms gave rise to multicellular organisms, which diverged, differentiated, grew more complex, more organized, and more needy of energy and information to sustain their growth. Even individual organisms rehearse this flagrant disregard for the Second Law. Trees began as unicellular seeds to sprout into cascades of complex interactions and branching growths, spreading their organized system for the transfer of matter and energy through the soil and sky. The biosphere is an island in the entropic stream, or better, a raft swimming autonomously, inexplicably upstream, gathering flotsam and organizing it into its flotilla, *against* the intractable laws of physics.

For a century this quite apparent paradox gave rise to many speculations but no clear resolutions. Then in the 1960s and 1970s, Prigogine developed a mathematical model that would explain how, under very specialized circumstances, order could arise spontaneously from disorder. His work was quickly recognized as having profound consquences for the way we view the cosmos. For Prigogine the central problem was one of reconciling the two contradictory worlds of microscopic things and macroscopic things. The solution to this contradiction lay in the different views of *time* our culture adopted when examining those two worlds. Physicists still viewed the microcosm as an idealized space where simple particles interacted in well-behaved ways according to the laws of dynamics. Even while the discoveries of quantum physics and the proliferation of subatomic particles throughout our century challenged the classical view of dynamics as deterministic, physicists still clung to a view of interactions as essentially reversible, much as Newton did. That is, interactions at this scale were time-neutral: they could go forward and backward equally. Large particles split into smaller particles and under the proper circumstances those smaller particles should reunite into larger ones. At this level, even entropy was an inconvenience of the macroscopic world. If a jar of black marbles and white marbles chose to arrange themselves randomly when mixed, or hot (fast-moving) molecules and cold (slow-moving) molecules moved at an average speed (equilibrium temperature) some time after being introduced to each other, then that was no concern of the quantum mechanist, who was studying the idealized behavior—or trajectories—of the particles by themselves. As Prigogine notes in his exposition of his theories, in *les mechanicques rationnel*, strict determinism and reversibility hold throughout, statistics and irreversibility are forbidden. Prigogine, adopting consciously the terminology of existential phenomenology, calls this naive realism the science of "being."

The macrocosmic world, by contrast, seems decidedly unruly to a classical dynamicist. First, macroscopic interactions are more vulnerable to entropy. Things move at slower speeds and in massive arrays that rub against other things, degrading the purity of their trajectories. Second, entropy is irreversible: it moves things along in one direction only. Once you're on that entropic road you can't go home again. Clearly, all biological things carry in them what Prigogine calls "the arrow of time." The heart ticks toward the moment it will eventually stop. We grow old and die. Interactions follow trajectories that are rarely simple, and when they are, remain irreversible. Third, the macrocosm is complex. The problem of two bodies interacting in pure Euclidean space follows strict Newtonian laws, but the problem of solving the trajectories of three bodies interacting becomes extraordinarily difficult. Yet, our world is constituted by large numbers of bodies and forces interacting all at once. Conditions change and through feedback processes a system can alter itself as it goes and grows. While individual phenomena remain relatively coherent (my son remains recognizably himself, even though he changes minute to minute, year to year) they are also dynamic, grow in sudden spurts, and alter their own environment that alters them. The macroscopic world is always in process. Any study of this world, Prigogine asserts, requires a science of *becoming*.

Far from being a mere problem of mechanics, this poses a set of philosophical problems as well. For instance, how can we reconcile the idealized version of the human mind (which investigates nature only through reason itself, sprung from classical dynamical assumptions about logic, conservation, and reversibility) with the biological basis for that mind (imbued with an "arrow of time")?

PARADIGM (Theorist)	TIME	CAUSALITY
CLASSICAL MECHANICS (Newton)	reversible	deterministic
QUANTUM MECHANICS (Boltzmann, Heisenberg)	reversible	probabilistic
DISSIPATIVE MECHANICS (Prigogine)	irreversible	probabilistic

We need not even introduce *mind* as anything special in order to see the problem. We can view mind, as many physicists do, free from its cultural trappings and humanist associations. For the purpose of a scientific experiment, the mind of the scientist is merely a perceptual instrument, an elaborate measuring device.[16]

Quantum mechanics was introduced as an attempt to reconcile certain odd behaviors of subatomic particles like the electron. But in fact, in Prigogine's construction of the history of physics of this century, quantum mechanics introduced even odder fundamental challenges to science's reign, one being an apparent contradiction: How do you measure subatomic events that supposedly obey laws of classical dynamics (and are thus free from time's arrow) with macroscopic interventions that are subject to irreversible processes? All the puzzles of modern physics, which have in turn spawned many competing metaphysical explanations, stem from this irreconcilable and paradoxical relationship that arises at the interface between the microscopic and macroscopic realms. Prigogine puts the problem this way:

> How can dynamics, which treats time as a parameter that has no preferential direction, lead to the element of irreversibility inseparable from measurement? This problem currently attracts a great deal of attention. It is perhaps one of the hottest problems of our time, one in which science and philosophy merge: Can we understand the microscopic world "in isolation"? In fact, we know matter, especially its microscopic properties, only by means of measuring devices, which themselves are macroscopic objects consisting of a large number of atoms or molecules. In a way these devices extend our sense organs. The apparatus can be said to be the mediator between the world that we explore and ourselves.[17]

As Nick Herbert points out in his book *Quantum Reality,* such paradoxes have given rise in the scientific community to at least eight distinct versions of reality current.[18] It has invited speculations about a synthesis between Western physics and Eastern mysticism that are at best highly suggestive,[19] and it has encouraged an even more ardent search for unifying theories. The most current one posits a multidimensional universe through which "superstrings" connect, explaining the odd synchronized behaviors of subatomic particles in our mere four-dimensional matrix. By "odd behaviors" I mean particles that wink in and out of existence inexplicably, the need for an electron to rotate 720° in order to complete one revolution, and Bell's Theorem, which predicts that two positrons separated in space act as if they are connected, violating classical assumptions about causality.

While these theories are not to be disdained, it is clear that they arise from deep motivations to preserve a simple universe about which knowledge can be induced forcibly. Thus, with little physical evidence, physicists induced forcibly from mathematics the "superstring" theory, which at first suggested twenty-two dimensions, and in later incarnations 9, 14, 11, and now 10 needed to explain these strange behaviors. Western science has always had a strong compulsion to proceed from large assumptions to finite conclusions granted the force of law, and superstring theory is no less liable to that compulsion.

Nonetheless, this compulsion to induce simplicity stands in direct contrast with the evidence of how reality proceeds in the macroscopic world. Everything in the world around us, our senses tell us, is complicated, seething with multiplying forms and interactions. Furthermore, we have trouble describing this reality in the strictly simple and logical way scientific discourse demands. Things in the macroscopic world—including *measurements* of things in the microscopic world—outstrip anything we can say about them. Gordon Pask, a noted cyberneticist, formulated it after reading similar remarks by Henri Poincaré, Ernst Mach, and Michel Duhem in the following fashion:

> All empirical phenomena are underdetermined by data and therefore permit the construction of an indefinite number of theories.[20]

It would be nice to reduce everything to a few simple universal rules, just as our eye habitually abstracts a simple pure line from the chaotic tangle of color and edges and motion around us, but these are idealizations as well as compulsions. Undoubtedly, we could not function without the ability to abstract, to formulate heuristics, to leap to conclusions, to induce hypotheses and predictions. But to found an entire epistemology on this naive intellectual habit brings us into conflict with the obvious nature of things around us.

Prigogine's achievement is to reconcile the impulse to simplicity (that leads us down the road of what he calls "naive realism in physics") with the seething complexity and dynamic instability of the world presented to our senses (and reflected so well in literature). His model proves how order can arise from chaos, and how that order in turn presents a world of ever-growing complexity and change to our senses.

In terms of our search for the principles of constructing an RDM, Prigogine's work underscores the efficacy of a discourse that captures or recapitulates the complexity and timebound qualities of our experience in the macroscopic world. Indeed, one of Prigogine's original inspirations came from the work of Henri Bergson, the French philosopher who in turn drew on his deep literary resources and first noted the obvious contradiction between the reality implied by the Second Law of Thermodynamics and the reality of our human experience. Consequently, Prigogine's work directly suggest that the discourse of literature somehow more accurately captures the realism suggested by his work as opposed to the naive realism to which the mere logic of classical scientific discourse is confined.

But we are only halfway home to proving our tacit claim that the literary text is the ideal RDM for Prigogine's work also describes in mathematical terms the actual mechanics of chaos, mechanics based on nonlinear partial differential equations as opposed to a mechanics based on simple linear algebra. It seems impossibly farfetched to suggest that such a mathematics could possibly describe the literary text, and I am not suggesting that it is either possible or desirable. Nonetheless, in the next section I consider in just what way the literary text might be viewed as a chaos machine, or to be more accurate, a dissipative structure.

DISSIPATIVE STRUCTURES: A MODEL FOR SELF-ORGANIZING COMPLEXITY

Actually, the word "chaos" is a misnomer, which is why it takes scare quotes in the title to this essay. Though highly dramatic, to call the phenomena described by the mathematics of chaos *chaotic* is oxymoronic, for the revolution ushered in by the science of so-called Chaos is precisely to show that systems that behave in what seemed like random or disordered fashion actually could be described by mathematics. Thus, to call the entire science that flows from this revision of scientific understanding "Chaos" is tantamount to calling astronomy since Copernicus "The New Science of Geocentrism" or quantum physics "the New Physics of Certainty." In its simplest terms, the new understanding of chaos revealed that a hidden order lurks in these complex, apparently chaotic systems. Even James Gleick betrays the extent to which the word is a misnomer in his book that popularized the term and the science for the public imagination:

> either deterministic mathematics produced steady behavior, or random external noise produced random behavior. That was the choice.
> In the context of that debate, chaos brought an astonishing message: simple deterministic models could produce what looked like random behavior. The behavior actually had an exquisite fine structure, yet any piece of it seemed indistinguishable from noise.[21]

Although Prigogine's term "dissipative structures" hasn't sold as well, it is in most senses much more accurate. First, it focuses on the dynamic system that undergoes the sudden transformation from *apparently chaotic* to *increasingly ordered* on the other side of the bifurcation point. Second, it points to the fact that Prigogine's mathematical model specifies certain structures in which such orderliness is not only possible, but even likely to arise. In other words, Prigogine's work proves that under certain conditions, a system can arise that not only *might* begin organizing itself, but is actually *most likely* to do so. This spontaneous emergence of order is called "self-organization," a term that already hints where such a theory might impact literary studies.

Dissipative structures have some remarkable features. They arise spontaneously, continue to survive as coherent entities despite instability (in fact they thrive on it), and when they fall apart, as they may do, *they are likely to reorganize themselves at a higher level of complexity!* Prigogine specifies the following conditions for this remarkable event, the spontaneous formation of a dissipative structure:

- The system must be open. That is, it must be engaged in some ongoing exchange of energy, matter, and/or information with its environment. This is where the term *dissipative,* which is somewhat misleading, comes from. Dissipative structures are not really dissipative in the sense that they evaporate into degraded homogeneity and entropy. Rather, they are islands of antidissipation that must dissipate certain energies in order to maintain the direction of their evolution.

- The system must exist in a condition *far from equilibrium*. That is, it must be highly unstable. The term "far from equilibrium" has special meaning in thermodynamics, and there is a complex branch of statistical thermodynamics devised just to describe such systems. For our prosaic purposes, it is sufficient to describe such systems as being just what they sound like they are: highly unbalanced and prone to erratic, even catastrophic, swings in behavior. This also means that they are highly sensitive to initial conditions, i.e., that small changes in the beginning can have system-altering and global changes at the outset. In chaos theory, this is called "the butterfly effect." As James Gleick describes it, "Tiny differences in input could quickly become overwhelming differences in output—a phenomenon given the name 'sensitive dependence on initial conditions.' In weather, for example, this translates into what is only half-jokingly known as 'The Butterfly Effect'—the notion that a butterfly stirring the air today in Peking can transform storm systems next month in New York."[22]

- The system must *fluctuate nonlinearly*. That is, the amount of energy, matter, and information they contain at any future moment will be unpredictable (they follow nonlinear differential equations that are usually difficult to solve and which describe behaviors impossible to predict).

- The origin of the dissipative structure is the *bifurcation point—*

a system-shattering moment when the previous, simpler organization can no longer support the intensity or frequency of its own fluctuations, and either disintegrates, or jumps to a new level of order and integration. Given a certain set of known starting conditions, you cannot stipulate what the future state of the system will be. And although you can predict that a system with all these attributes will begin to organize itself spontaneously, you cannot predict the shape of that organization. This feature becomes important in making a distinction, often lost on popular thinkers, between mechanism/determinism and organization/indeterminacy. Just because something is organized and systematic does not mean it is mechanical and has lost its freedom. In short, dissipative stuctures are deterministic (their initial conditions can be stipulated in mathematics) but unpredictable (you literally cannot stipulate what they will look like down the road, or across the bifurcation point). This distinction will play a role in our view of the literary text as a dissipative structure technology.

- The dynamic coherence of the system relies on *feedback mechanisms:* negative feedback that suppresses the production of noise, positive feedback that encourages the incorporation of innovations that change the global complexity of the system in ever-broadening orbits. If the dissipative structure is primarily devoted to organizing information, it will capitalize on the noise. (Abraham Moles quipped that noise "appears as a backdrop of the universe due to the nature of things," i.e., a form of entropy.[23])
- The system must be *large enough.* Dissipative structures are scale-dependent. They are a function of size, having to be relatively large with respect to their environment in order to come into being. Below a certain scale, phenomena tend to behave themselves better and more classically, i.e., more in accordance with Newtonian mechanics.

Rather than being an idle, purely abstract model built on mathematics, Prigogine's description actually fits a wide assortment of phenomena, cutting across disciplines and realms, including fluid dynamics, urban planning, chemistry, biology, ecology, and sociology. For instance, the spontaneous appearance of certain kinds of vortices in fluids that have been flowing smoothly (laminar flow) is described by the mathematics of dissipative structures. Perhaps the best-known examples of such vortices are cyclones. More recently, earthlings have become familiar with the large, coherent, centuries-old storm system known as Jupiter's red spot. A well-studied chemical reaction involving citric acid, potassium bromate, and the ceric-cerous ion couple, the Belousov-Zhabotinskii reaction, follows the predictive model of dissipative structures by producing an oscillating reaction of three compounds that continue to produce each other in cycling reactions. The mechanism of the reaction has been elucidated by Richard Noyes, who called it an *Oregonator,* a kind of chemical clock.[24]

Similarly, biology is long familiar with the tendency of enzymes like ATP to increase the organization of energy during metabolism, and of course of DNA to increase the structural organization of organisms generally. Some of these cycles of increasing order and regulation are quite well-elucidated and fit the design for dissipative structures nicely (Prigogine cites regulation of the lactose operon in *E. coli*). From the welter of evidence generally and from fairly obvious patterns of behavior in the global evolution of organisms, Prigogine takes the next step cautiously.

> It seems that most biological mechanisms of action show that life involves far-from-equilibrium conditions beyond the stability of the threshold of the thermodynamic branch. It is therefore very tempting to suggest that the origin of life may be related to successive instabilities somewhat analogous to the successive bifurcations that have led to a state of matter of increasing coherence.[25]

Ecology has found enormous use in the dissipative structure model to describe the fluctuations of populations given the varying conditions of food supply, weather, "economy," and competitive populations. Interestingly enough, computer simulations of urbanization give very convincing portraits of what actually happens in the world,[26] just as fractal geometry has generated very convincing simulacra of landscapes for use in Hollywood films by George Lucas.[27] Even social forms may satisfy the general requirements of dissipative structures. Prigogine himself suggests, somewhat archly, that the progress of scientific revolution itself may be modeled in the cycles of fluctuations-reconstitution he finds in dissipative structures.[28] His presence at his eponymous Center for Statistical Dynamics and Thermodynamics at the University of Texas, Austin has stimulated quite a bit of interdisciplinary research along these lines from sociologists. As Prigogine and Stengers note, "We know now that societies are immensely complex systems involving a potentially enormous number of bifurcations . . . highly sensitive to fluctuations."[29]

Automobile traffic gives us a very good example of how sociological forms can give rise to other dissipative structures. Prigogine's colleagues have found that there is good evidence that his mathematics describes the spontaneous emergence of traffic jams under certain conditions. Ironically, where the human experience of traffic is one of disturbance and disruption, from the Olympian perspective of a statistical thermodynamicist, traffic jams represent the emergence of organization.[30]

What emerges from these bits of evidence and cautious claims is an elaborate network of dissipative structures giving rise to each other at different levels of description and different orders of magnitude. Molecular dynamics supports chemical reactions that behave like dissipative structures; chemistry supports biological processes that fit the bill; biology supports population fluctuations, and masses of population create traffic, communications systems, and cultural systems, such as literary texts.

Though our culture typically privileges the text as an artistic enterprise immune to such contexts, it is nonetheless possible in these terms to view literature as an *artifact of cultural information processing*. After all, if we overcome customary repugnance to the suggestion, what is it that intrinsically distinguishes the literary text from other hyper-evolved expressions of organized behavior that relies on specialized techniques, like a skyscraper or electron-spin spectroscope or an integrated circuit on a silicon chip? From this view, is it possible that some literary texts behave like dissipative structures? Is the text a dissipative structure machine shuttling between an author's imagination/intention and language (in which case we might want to consider both intelligence and language as dissipative structures)? Does the literary text mediate between the author's private imagination-intelligence and the culture or another individual (in which cases we also might want to consider culture and other individuals as dissipative structures, too)?

Whether or not the answers to these questions are affirmative, viewing the text in this light yields interesting speculations. For while it is clear that the literary text is at once an extraordinary device, quite literally a specialized machine, it is possible that it is also a naturalistic phenomenon that fits Prigogine's description of a dissipative structure. As a cybernetic machine, it purposely takes noise from the cultural environment or the author's experience of his/her own mind and language and organizes it, instituting a process of "meaning-making" and of spontaneous self-organization. By contrast, as a dissipative structure, a naturalistic phenomenon, we can describe the literary text as arising from the unstable fluctuations of information spontaneously giving rise to this complex phenomenon we readers experience as meaning just as population creates the ground for traffic jams or turbulence in the flow of fluids create vortices.

In short dissipative structures produced by culture—like literary texts and traffic jams—are both natural and artificial at the same time depending upon how you choose to view them. It is also possible that certain aspects of the complex phenomena of culture, in all their richness, are best elucidated in terms given us by Prigogine's model. Or, in other words, that *describing cultural productions as dissipative structures is more than metaphorical.* While such an assertion immediately sets alarms off among most humanists, this is a very different claim from the one we generally fear. The difference hinges around the distinction between open and closed systems and determinism and predictability. Closed systems are mechanistic. Because they exist (or are viewed) in isolation as self-contained, they are generally compliant to full description in mechanistic terms. However, as Alvin Toffler puts it in his Foreword to *Order Out of Chaos,* "most phenomena of interest to us are, in fact, *open* systems, exchanging energy or matter (and, one might add, in information) with their environment. Surely biological and social systems are open, which means that the attempt to under-stand them in mechanistic terms is doomed to failure."[31] In fact, I suggest that we collapse the terms of the argument—mechanistic versus complex, open systems—to at once grant that certain com-plex open systems can be described deterministically, but that our notion of mechanics must be made more complex to include kinds of machines that we don't yet build. So while mechanistic descrip-tions of biological, social, and cultural phenomena are doomed to failure as long as we understand "machine" in a classical sense, Prigogine has ushered in a new version of mechanics that permits them. In a Prigoginean machine, initial conditions are simple and deterministic but future states of the system are indeterminate, complex, and unpredictable.

Describing the literary text as a dissipative structure thus col-lapses the distinctions between artificial and natural, between "technological" and "human," and between mechanical artifact and cultural artifact. If organic life arose from some chemical soup it was probably as the sort of chemical self-organizing system described by dissipative structures. If self-awareness arose spon-taneously from some less complex system of intellection or sensa-tion, it probably occurred as a consequence of the dissipative structuration of the nerve net, a growingly self-organizing system designed to exchange information with the environment. As intelligence grew, so did expressions of intelligence, which took on a life of their own. For instance, imagine a time-lapse photograph from the upper atmosphere of the growth of road systems in America. It would show that a complex feedback interaction between geography, weather conditions, population size, energy use, material load, habit, and information exchange grew a network of ever-more-complex roads and interconnections not only within a given domain (say the geographical area between New York and Boston), but that the area itself encompassed by the system grows, spreading westward. Furthermore, more microscopie analysis of the photographs would show that the technology of those roads also grows more complex, with changes in material from natural to composite to artificial; with innovations of overpasses, bypasses, cloverleafs, skyways, tunnels, breakdown lanes, etc. We would see that the density of traffic on a given road tends to fluctuate everywhere. And finally, we might look at what travels on those roads and note that interactive change between vehicular technology, road technology, and, perhaps the driver's consciousness that drives and is driven by the other two. Is the road system of the United States a machine? Is it artificial-technological? Or is it "natural," in the sense that it is a product of the imperialism of the human nerve-net itself, part of a continuing process of dissipative structuration of an open, fluctuant system?

This description of traffic is a parable for the evolution of literary discourse. If we treat the literary text as a specialized example of natural technology, then its creative tension between system and spontaneity, between control and chance becomes easier to understand.

The origin of the dissipative structure is the "bifurcation point"—a system-shattering moment when the previous, simpler organization can no longer support the intensity or frequency of its own fluctuations, and either disintegrates, or jumps to a new level of order and integration. At this new level of order, the particulars of change are nondeterministic. One cannot tell where the system will be at any given moment, given certain prior conditions. (This is a feature of nonlinear—partial differential—equations). In essence, dissipative structuration illustrates, is exemplary of, the very values intrinsic to literature, values that have been brought into relief by the postmodern dialectic between scientific and literary discourse exemplified in cybernetic fiction. Even the moment of insight to which great texts bring us can be viewed as an explosively meaningful reorganization and addition of information in the reader's mind, much like the activity of a dissipative structure.[32]

At first glance, these claims may have a certain attractiveness because of the superficial similarities between dissipative structures and certain aspects of some literary texts. It is easy to say that literary texts are "open systems" of information, that they are highly "unstable," and they "fluctuate non-linearly", that they are coherent, rely on feedback loops for change, and when they break down tend to re-organize at a higher level of complexity. But what do these terms mean? They seem attractive as intimations, tantalizing metaphors that seem to reveal something important, perhaps, about the nature of reading and expression, but how exactly could we prove these claims, short of developing a meaningful measure of information (and of meaning!) flow in and between the literary text and the reader's mind, absurd suggestions at best, harmful at worst—as cybernetic fiction shows.

POSTMODERNISM AND THE FUTURE OF LITERARY DISCOURSE

But failing such measurements, we can at least test some of these ideas in a tentative fashion in the laboratory of literary history by observing the more macroscopic behavior of literature. For this, we can return to Auerbach's Olympian survey of stylistic change, since he seems in many ways to have anticipated the problems of style in constructing an RDM with which Prigogine has grappled. In his discussion of early modernism, Auerbach describes both modern consciousness and culture as interactive phenomena that now make refractory sense in terms of dissipative structures. In his view (but not his terms), they are open, fluctuating nonequilibrium systems that grow toward crises, which in turn produce even wider orbits of organization and complexity with each convulsion:

> For Europe there began [after the French Revolution] that process of temporal concentration, both of historical events themselves and of everyone's knowledge of them, which has since made tremendous progress and which not only permits us to prophesy a unification of human life throughout the world but has in a certain sense already achieved it. Such a development abrogates or renders powerless the entire social structure of order or categories previously held valid; the tempo of the changes demands a perpetual and extremely difficult effort toward inner adaptation and produces intense concomitant crises. He would account to himself for his real life and his place in human society is obliged to do

so upon a far wider practical foundation and in a far larger context than before, and to be continually conscious that the social base upon which he lives is not constant for a moment but is perpetually changing though convulsions of the most various kind.[33]

Auerbach has put his finger on the pressure point of literature, the point where it also finds its greatest strength: as social processes speed up and grow more organized through positive feedback looping, consciousness and artistic forms that reflect it feed on a perpetual series of "crisis" and "convulsions" to grow more organized.

However, where Auerbach throws up his hands in dismay is where literature's behavior as a dissipative structure begins to grow most interesting: with late modernism, after Flaubert, after World War I, in short, in Auerbach's own generation. Auerbach views late modernist literature as a willful embrace of anarchy, a threat to what he views as the humanizing impulse to render versions of reality. One can even detect that Auerbach, writing in exile from Nazi Germany in Istanbul, views modernism as part and parcel of the moral abysm that produced the Nazi horror. But in fact, the literature of Joyce and Pound and Eliot that distressed Auerbach are turns of the mimetic screw, next steps in the development of literature's RDM technology. These texts attempt to reflect a newer, more disorienting version of reality. They show a "predilection for ruthlessly subjectivist perspectives" and have hit upon a "method which dissolves reality into multiple and multivalent reflections of consciousness." He singles out *Ulysses* as a hodgepodge of European tradition, "uninterpretable symbolism" filled with "multiple enmeshments" but no "purpose and meaning." "There is often something confusing, something hazy about them, something hostile to the reality they represent. . . . There is a hatred of culture and civilization, brought about by means of the subtlest stylistic devices that culture and civilization have developed, and often a radical and fanatical urge to destroy."[34] (As counterpoint, in the same concluding pages Auerbach praises Virginia Woolf's stream of consciousness technique in *To the Lighthouse* for preserving positive feeling by stressing the random and minute fluctuations of experience and perception.) What Auerbach foretells in apocalyptic language, and what he fears, is a coming "unification and simplification," Modernism, Auerbach is literary fascism for him.

Auerbach seems now in retrospect to have been both correct and incorrect. What is coming, in fact what has happened in postmodernism, is growing organization and complication, not unification and simplification. Organization means multiplying differences and specializations within a coherent structure, not making everything (and everyone) look and act the same. This fundamental misunderstanding of the confusing forces around him, especially in light of his calamitous experiences with Nazism, is easy to understand and forgive.

On the other hand, Auerbach seems to be responding to the hidden mechanistic agenda of late modernism. Again, we can take the visual arts as an analog. The apparent chaos of cubism and expressionism presented on the canvas hide deeper formalist assumptions about vision and color and the representation of motion. In the same way, the unreadability of Joyce's *Ulysses* resolves, with the application of decades of scholarship, into an elaborate algorithmic palimpsest of language, symbol, theme, allusion, and narrative time as rigorous as any blueprint. What Auerbach responds to hostilely, I believe, is that *Ulysses* is imaginatively a closed system, a sort of machine. It does not so much elude interpretation as make interpretation unnecessary; for a while, it multiplies cross-referencing and the completion of a matrix of allusions, but this process is finite. At its end, the reader does indeed get a sense of exhausted possibilities. *Ulysses* invites mapping, not metaphor-making, deduction rather than intimation, and blueprinting rather than interpretation. Indeed, throughout modernism, authors place their stress on the technicalisms of language and form, part of the larger fascination (and identification) of modernist art with the machine.[35] For instance we see a similar equation expressed in the curious assemblages and paintings of Max Ernst such as "1 Copper Plate 1 Zinc Plate 1 Rubber Cloth . . ." (1920), Paul Klee's, "Twittering Machine" (1922), and Marcel Duchamp's "The Bride" (1922).

We find similar technological feats elsewhere in modernism and in Vorticism. The extreme of this movement to identify the literary text with a machine finds its culmination in Raymond Roussel, another great—if even more idiosyncratic—modernist obsessed with mechanisms of language and with creating closed systems of formal inscriptions. In the end, as Robbe-Grillet noted of Roussel's work, he invites us into the room, shows us the desk, asks us to open the drawer, "but the drawer is empty."[36] One artist and critic called Roussel's fictions "*les machines celibataire*"—"autonomous (bachelor) machines."[37]

The trouble, of course, is that Roussel chose the wrong paradigm to express his desire to control all aspects of the text. (Not to mention that such a desire is probably misguided.) Were Roussel correct, then natural languages are merely codes, and consequently artificial intelligence (AI) researchers would be making much more progress toward getting computers to speak to us intelligently than they have. Recently, the artificial intelligence community has begun to realize that the problem hinges around the deep metaphorical resources of natural language and other incalculables (like silence, ambiguity, paradox, etc.) Some have even attempted to formulate computable algorithms for metaphor use.[38] Others have realized that the computer would have to become a very different sort of animal, not only a parallel-processing device with enormous megabyte capacity, but a leaky, more randomizing, self-organizing, growing sort of creature: in short, a very unmechanical sort of machine.[39]

Postmodernism adds important elements to modernism. Where modernism apparently holds faith in the machinery of language and forms, in the grammar of signs, to yield some picture of reality and experience, postmodernism abandons the assurances of method, of certainty, and of meaning itself: in short, of closure. Where modernist texts most often strive to create a closed system of interrelated meanings that ensure certainties of interpretation, postmodernism creates open systems that simultaneously invite interpretation and defeat *certain* interpretation. And where modernist literature still seems to embrace, for the most part, a classical view of the relationship between perception and reality or causality, postmodern literature thrives on instabilities and self-consciousness. What is most important about the evolution of style between the modernist and postmodernist is that in developing a discourse that would block mechanism rather than promote it, literature found its way to a superior form of validity. Science, with the new theory of dissipative structures, has just caught up. The road is paved to a reconciliation between the two by understanding discourse as a technology and the cultural project we call literature as an evolving, organically grown artifice, an RDM.

THE METAPHYSICAL SYNTHESIS: PRIGOGINIAN REALITY

Prigogine's work reconciles the hitherto irreconcilable philosophical bases and assumptions from which two distinct ways of knowing and two distinct styles of discourse—the scientific and the literary—proceed. In the view of most chemists and physicists, the world is still simple, and theory in these disciplines yearn for some grand unifying theory that will banish the confusions introduced by probabilism, Heisenberg's uncertainty relations, and irreversibility. "Science progresses by reducing the complexity of reality to a hidden simplicity."[40] In contrast stand ways of knowing that begin with assumptions tied to the biological world. These ways of knowing are presented in their most graspable forms in cultural expressions: music, dance, art, and literature. Of these, the genre that has best access to expressing epistemological questions is the verbal one, literature. Furthermore, literature incarnates, like many other artistic forms, the time-bound but evanescent movements that dominate our macroscopic human experience.[41]

If we accept some of Prigogine's fundamental assertions, at the very least literature appears to have an advantage over science in describing macroscopic processes, including human behavior, as it really occurs. The discourse of literature fundamentally multiplies problems and interpretations, describes details in contexts, grows plots and themes and symbols and language through a naturalistic feedback process between words and the author's imagination. Prigogine suggests that "the simplicity of . . . physics and chemistry was due to the fact that attention was paid mainly to some very simplified situations, to heaps of bricks in contrast with the cathedral. . . ."[42] Literature has access to tools that reflect how the cathedral *actually* grows and looks. The biosphere, the culture to which it gave rise, and the literature to which that culture gave rise are all dissipative structures, or at least seem to obey the same laws. Literature's evolution along with culture is a study in dissipative structure: it has evolved techniques as culture has evolved.

Prigogine and Stenger's intention is not to privilege literature, but to move scientific understanding into the same realm to which literature has long held the bragging rights. Thus, *Order Out of Chaos* was originally published in France under the title *La Nouvelle alliance*. The authors in their English translation state that their intention in this title was to show how Prigogine's theories point to a resolution of the Two Cultures problems by erasing the scientific assumptions that were the source of irreconcilable differences.[43] As Prigogine's theory reconciles the austerity and time-idealizations of Newtonian mechanics with the indeterminacy and chaotic growth of the macroscopic world, it also puts science back in the realm of language, which abides by macroscopic (social or biological), not microscopic (mechanical) rules. "The natural sciences have thus rid themselves of a conception of objective reality that implied that novelty and diversity had to be denied in the name of immutable universal laws."[44] And in return literature, having the advantage of never having saddled itself with the prime directives of simplicity, transparency, and absolute authority, can now lay some claim to superior epistemological potency, or at least to a sort of veracity that science, until Prigogine, has denied itself: the veracity of hyper-evolved discourse that reflects the time-bound, fluctuant, unstable growth of human activity and imaginings.

Finally, however, this also lays some distinctly unfashionable claims at the doorstep of the literary community. Literary criticism has grown radically specialized and grandiose, at the same time that it has grown alien from its own resources and origins as commentary on and analysis of culture's discourse. Many of the newer breeds of critical theory, most notably deconstruction, have adopted the extreme position of erasing the discourse of reality altogether, or at least, of denying the connection between literary representation and reality. In the view of poststructuralists, the literary text is an interactive web of *mere* formalisms, stuck in and bounded by language, a creation *of* language. Paul DeMan's stance is paradigmatic of the entire school, which persists in portraying language as sheerly rhetorical and autonomous, a resource for combinations that produce effects that having no referent other than those produced in the reader. The goal of reading, for DeMan, is to uncover "negative knowledge about the reliability of linguistic utterance." For him, language, and consequently literature, is "epistemologically highly suspect," a polite way of saying epistemologically impotent.[45]

Perhaps we can forgive deconstruction's stance in an historical light. Since the notion of "reliability" was determined by scientific canons, then deconstruction was simply reacting, underscoring the roots of all discourse in indeterminacy. But with a revised scientific understanding of reliable utterances in which *reliable* does not mean *predictive,* then both literary and scientific language alike opens to a reconstruction of the epistemological potency of discourse. At the very least, we need no longer view literature as inhabiting *only* language, for there is no such thing as "only language." Instead, language is opened by a theory of dissipative structures. The text of our expressions can now be understood as open rather than sterile and self-referential systems of signs, reliant upon input from other sources to make it go and on a process of dissipating entropy (analogous to interpretation) to make it grow. We can now reconceptualize the literary text and language as necessarily open to the world and to culture. The imagination of the author and his/her command of language feed on each other, yes, but also on the world's information and culture's input to grow structures of the literary text.

Michel Serres has already pointed to this reconnection between literature and reality in his works on literature, science, and philosophy, some of which have been strongly influenced by Prigogine's work.[46] Serres maps a truly interdisciplinary study of discourse, rooted in the concepts offered us by cybernetics and the alternative physics that begins with the pre-Socratics, is pursued by Leibniz, and reaches its present state of sophistication with Prigogine. He urges literature and literary theory to enlarge its embrace beyond the domain of philosophy and language, to include the world. From his perspective, Serres at least provides a context in which we can understand the connection between literature and the phenomenal world.

I would go even further than Serres in this direction to confront the very notion of a "formalism." Prigogine has expanded our notion of the richness that can be produced by mere formalisms (such as statistical thermodynamics). By doing so, he has even removed the need for us to qualify *formalism* with *mere*. Formalisms of language, of chemistry, of biology, of cars moving through a city, of the organization of nerves in the cortex, of people organizing themselves in kinship systems all are sufficiently rich to account for reality, which is both formal and indeterminate. As humanists, we have a strong bias that formalisms imply positivistic blueprints for behavior, but as Prigogine and Stengers note, "We can no longer allow ourselves, as far as the physical world is concerned, the privileged point of view which, when pushed to its limit, we once could have identified as that of God."[47] Prigogine's work justifies our ceasing to associate formalism with reductive mechanism. We can turn now to a scientific discourse that is more Elohist than Homeric. In this blueprint for a new RDM, a postmodern linguistic technology, deterministic formalisms now become the starting place for us to generate the origins, but not the future states, of the undetermined, complex, irreversible, fertile processes that dominate our experience of the world. Literary language commands techniques that scientific discourse must adopt if it is going to succeed.

NOTES

1. "Postface: Dynamics from Leibniz to Lucretius," in Michel Serres's *HERMES: Literature, Science, Philosophy* (Baltimore: Johns Hopkins University Press, 1982). Edited by Josué V. Harari and David F. Bell.

2. Paul Valéry, "Literature," in *Selected Writings,* trans. by Louise Varése (New York: New Directions, 1950), p. 152.

3. William Barrett, *The Illusion of Technique* (New York Doubleday/Anchor, 1979), p. 23.

4. See especially Italo Calvino's "Cybernetics and Ghosts" in *The Uses of Literature,* trans. by Patrick Creagh (New York: Harcourt, Brace Jovanovich, 1986), pp. 3–27.

5. In some cases even the titles of these works alone reflect the oxymoronic collisions: *soft machine, gravity's rainbow, player piano, clockwork orange,* etc.

6. See "Fiction as Dissipative Structure: Prigogine and Postmodernism's *Roadsbow*" in *Chaos and Order: Complex Dynamics in Literature and Science,* edited by N. Katherine Hayles (Chicago: University of Chicago Press, 1991).

7. See Hans Aarsleff, "John Wilkins," in *From Locke to Saussure: Essays on the Study of Language and Intellectual History* (Minneapolis: Univ. of Minnesota Press, 1982), pp. 239–77.

8. Ilya Prigogine and Isabelle Stengers, *Order Out of Chaos: Man's New Dialogue with Nature* (New York: Bantam, 1984), p. 22.

9. Prigogine, *From Being to Becoming: Time and Complexity in the Physical Sciences* (San Francisco: W. H. Freeman and Company, 1980), p. 20.

10. Eric Auerbach, *Mimesis: The Representation of Reality in Western Literature,* trans. by Willard Trask (Princeton, N.J.: Princeton University Press, 1953).

11. See David Ward Chambers, "Reading the Hieroglyphics of Nature," in *Essays on Perceiving Nature,* edited by Diana Macintyre DeLuca (Honolulu, 1988), pp. 3–12.

12. Albert B. Lord, *The Singer of Tales* (Cambridge, Mass.: Harvard University Press, 1960).

13. Auerbach, *Mimesis,* p. 23.

14. *Ibid.*

15. Prigogine, *From Being to Becoming,* p. 20.

16. If we wander down the pathway pointed to by Prigogine's theories, we might consider the human mind itself as one of the most fertile dissipative structures, a product of the dissipative structuration of biological evolution and in turn a great progenitor of other dissipative structures, like technology and literature that extend its power and promulgate information. Indeed, this essay relies on just such a definition. For an interesting parallel exploration of the second order cybernetic view of the evolution of the mind, see Humberto Maturana and Francisco Varela, *The Tree of Knowledge: The Biological Roots of Human Understanding* (Boston & London: New Science Library, 1987).

17. Prigogine, *From Being to Becoming,* p. 48.

18. Nick Herbert, *Quantum Reality: Beyond the New Physics* (New York: Anchor Press/Doubleday: 1985), pp. 240–45.

19. These works range from quite unconventional books—which claim that the mysteries of quantum physics in some sense prove or dovetail or are best understood through zen metaphysics—to more sober books that make claims that some other practicing physicists still discount as irresponsible, distorted, or mystical. Collectively, these books illustrate how the popular imagination tends to leap to or seize on metaphysical explanations when confronted by contradictions to common sense of normative views of the universe by emergent paradigms:

The Tao of Physics, Fritjof Capra. Berkeley, Calif.: Shabhala, 1975.
Fabric of the Universe, Denis Postle. New York: Crown, 1976.
The Dancing Wu Li Masters, Gary Zukav. New York: Morrow, 1979.

Dismantling the Universe, Richard Morris. New York: Simon & Schuster, 1983.
Other Worlds. Paul Davies. New York: Simon & Schuster, 1980.
Physics and Beyond, Werner Heisenberg. New York: Harper & Row, 1971.
Quantum Reality, Nick Herbert. New York: Doubleday, 1985.
Taking the Quantum Leap, Fred Alan Wolf. New York: Harper & Row, 1981.
The Cosmic Code, Heinz R. Pagel. Simon & Schuster, 1982.
The Sense of Reality, Bernard D'Espagnat. Berlin: Springer-Verlag, 1983.
In Search of Schrodinger's Cat, John Gribbin. New York: Bantam, 1984.

20. Gordon Pask, "The meaning of cybernetics in the behavioral sciences," in J. Rose, editor, *Progress in Cybernetics* vol. 14 (New York: Gordon & Breach, 1969), pp. 15–44.

21. James Gleick, *Chaos: Making a New Science* (New York: Viking, 1987) pp. 78–79. In this context, it is hard to understand why Gleick's book contains no mention of Prigogine. The omission seems willful. The scientists (like Mitchell Feigenbaum) whom Gleick credits with discovering this new science of chaos are investigating the same phenomena as Prigogine: far-from-equilibrium systems that leap to new orders of complexity and organization on the other side of bifurcation points. The *New York Times* reported extensively on Prigogine during and after his reception of the Nobel Prize in 1977, and Gleick has been an editor and reporter there since 1978. (See *NYT* Wednesday, 12 October, 1977, D19.) Both authors appeal to Mandelbrot's mathematics of fractal geometry to explain certain concepts in self-organization and complexity. Both authors are aware of the paradigm-changing impact of this branch of statistical dynamics and its influence on other disciplines, including population ecology, fluid dynamics, etc. In fact, both appeal strongly to Kuhn, with some important differences: Gleick obviously wrote his book to confirm the model of paradigm change that Kuhn explicates in *The Structure of Scientific Revolutions.* Prigogine entertains the notion that scientific change and evolution is a sort of dissipative process, and takes Kuhn to task, a bit, for not recognizing the extent to which scientific change can come from the normal processes of science, and that no "revelation" is necessary. He and Stengers cite the communal process by which a theory of dissipative structures came into being: "On the contrary, this development clearly reflects the internal logic of science and the cultural and social context of our time" (*Order Out of Chaos,* 309). What is even stranger is that Gleick recently wrote a long article for the *New York Times Sunday Magazine* devoted to systems analysis of traffic flow in several United States cities (see March 1988) without mentioning the impact of chaos studies on it, particularly Prigogine's and his collaborator, Robert Herman (*op. cit,* note 29 below).

22. Gleick, *Chaos,* p. 8.

23. Abraham Moles, *Information Theory and Esthetic Perception,* trans. by Joel E. Cohen (Urbana, Ill.: University of Illinois Press, 1968).

24. Richard M. Noyes and R. J. Field, *Annual Rev, Phys. Chem* 25 (1974): p. 95.

25. Prigogine, *From Being to Becoming,* p. 123.

26. *Ibid.,* pp. 124–26.

27. Gleick, *Chaos,* p. 114.

28. "Because classical dynamics is the oldest of all theoretical sciences, its development illustrates, in many ways, dynamics of the evolution of science." *From Being to Becoming,* p. 20. See also the concluding pages of Prigogine and Stengers, *Order Out of Chaos,* and their discussion of the role of the scientist and of Kuhn's view of scientific change, pp. 307 *et seq.*

29. Prigogine and Stengers, *Order Out of Chaos,* p. 313.

30. See Robert Herman and Ilya Prigogine, "A Two-Fluid Approach to Town Traffic," *Science* 204, 13 (13 April 1979) pp. 148–51.

31. Alvin Toffler, Foreword to *Order Out of Chaos*, xv.

32. The notion that the human mind—or at least its information processing capacities—is itself as a dissipative structure is not as farfetched as it may sound. Very recent theories of neural action, and its integration into the general schema of biological development and human behavior, suggest that these activities operate according to "central mathematical concepts of self-organization in non-equilibrium systems." In short, the model Prigogine proposes "provides a language and a strategy accompanied by new observables, that may afford an understanding of dynamical patterns at several scales of analysis (including behavioral patterns, neural networks, and individual neurons)." G. Schoner and J. A. S. Kelso, "Dynamic Pattern Generation in Behavioral and Neural Systems," *Science* 239 (25 March, 1988), p. 1513.

33. Auerbach, *Mimesis* p. 459. Later, Auerbach describes Stendahl's unique sense of time-bound processes: "Temporal perspective is a factor of which he never loses sight, the concept of incessantly changing forms and manners of life dominates his thoughts" (p. 462).

34. Auerbach, *Mimesis,* p. 551.

35. For a more elaborate discussion of this mechanical trend in modernism, see Hugh Kenner, *The Counterfeiters* (New York: Doubleday/Anchor, 1973).

36. Alain Robbe-Grillet, *"Éigme et transparence chez Raymond Roussel,"* *Critique* December 1963. See my discussion of Roussel as exemplar of this mechanical trend in modernism in "Roussel's Device for the Perfection of Fiction," *The Soft Machine,* pp. 24–44.

37. Michel Carrouges, *Les Machines célibataire de Raymond Roussel* (Paris: Editions Arcane, 1955).

38. Bipin Indurkhya, "A Constrained Semantic Transference: A Formal Theory of Metaphors," *Synthese* 68 (1986): 515–51.

39. See David Porush, "Cybernetic Fiction, Nerves, Metaphors: Working Paper #17," *Studies in Communication and Information Technologies* (Kingston, Ontario: Queens University, 1988).

40. Prigogine and Stengers, *Order Out of Chaos*, p. 21.

41. Perhaps music equals or even exceeds literature's inherently time-bound structure.

42. Prigogine and Stengers, *Order Out of Chaos*, p. 11.

43. The primary obstacle was the clinging by physics to the notion of time as an independent, reversible operator at the microscopic level and consequently, as the tacit position that natural truth flowed from the microscopic level. By showing the ineluctable connection between microscopic and macroscopic, Prigogine's theory forces an alliance between philosophy, history, and language on the one hand, and time-independent physics on the other.

44. Prigogine and Stengers, *Order Out of Chaos,* 306.

45. Paul deMan, "The Resistance to Theory" *Yale French Studies* 63 (1982): 7. In view of recent discoveries about deMan's activities as an active Nazi collaborator and eloquent anti-Semitic propagandist urging deportation of Jews during World War II in Belgium, perhaps we can understand this austere philosophical position proceeding from some deeper, more personal urgency to erase the connection between text and fact, between literary effect and action in the world.

46. Serres addresses this question, of literature abandoning or losing its connection to "the world" in his review of Prigogine and Stenger's work in "Commencements," *Le Monde,* 4 January, 1980, p. 13. See also the special issue of *Critique,*

380 (1979) entitled *"Turbulence et interference"* in which Prigogine, among others, comments on the importance and implications of Serres's work. See also Serres's several books on an interdisciplinary culture, especially *Hermes: Literature, Science, Philosophy,* eds. D. Bell and J. V. Harari (Baltimore: Johns Hopkins University Press, 1982) for which Prigogine and Stengers wrote a postface that, in turn, was adapted as a chapter of *La Nouvelle alliance;* and *Le Parasite* (Paris: Grasset, 1980). Translated as *The Parasite* by L. Scher (Baltimore: Johns Hopkins University Press, 1982).

47. "Postface: Dynamics from Liebniz to Lucretius," *HERMES,* p. 147.

Selected Basic References in the Philosophy of Technology

CARL MITCHAM
TIMOTHY CASEY

Borgmann, Albert, *Technology and the Character of Contemporary Life*. Chicago: University of Chicago Press, 1984. Pp. vii, 302.

Bugliarello, George, and Dean B. Doner, eds. *The History and Philosophy of Technology*. Urbana: University of Illinois Press, 1979. Pp. xxxi, 384.

Dessauer, Friedrich. *Philosophie der Technik: Das Problem der Realisierung* [Philosophy of technology: The problem of its realization]. Bonn: F. Cohen, 1927. P. 180. An English translation of three key chapters from this work can be found under the title "Technology in Its Proper Sphere," in Mitcham-Mackey, eds., *Philosophy and Technology, pp. 317–34.*

————. *Streit um die Technik* [Controversy over Technology]. Frankfurt: J. Knecht, 1956. P. 480. Abridged edition, Freiburg: Herder, 1958. Pp. 205. Described as a "revised edition" of *Philosophie der Technik,* this is actually a completely rewritten and much enlarged volume. Chapter 2 restates and elaborates the basic argument of 1927.

Ellul, Jacques. *La Technique ou l'enjeu du siècle* [Technology or the bet of the century]. Paris: A. Colin, 1954. P. 401. "American edition": *The Technological Society,* trans. John Wilkinson (New York: Knopf, 1964).

————. *Le Systeme technicienne.* Paris: Calmann-Levy, 1977. P. 361. English version: *The Technological System,* trans. Joachim Neugroschel (New York: Continuum, 1980). Updates the first two chapters of *La Technique* (1954). For further update, see *Le Bluff technologique* (Paris: Hachette, 1987).

Ferré, Frederick. *Philosophy of Technology*. Englewood Cliffs, N.J.: Prentice Hall, 1988. Pp. x, 147.

Florman, Samuel. *The Existential Pleasures of Engineering*. New York: St. Martin's Press, 1976. Pp. 160.

————. *Blaming Technology: The Irrational Search or Scapegoats*. New York: St. Martin's Press, 1981. Pp. xi, 207.

————. *The Civilized Engineer*. New York: St. Martin's Press, 1987. Pp. xii, 258.

Heidegger, Martin. *The Question Concerning Technology and Other Essays*. Trans. David Farrell Krell. San Francisco: Harper & Row, 1977. Pp. xxxix, 182. Contents: "The Question Concerning Technology," "The Turning," "The Word of Nietzsche: 'God Is Dead,'" "The Age of the World Picture," and "Science and Reflection."

————. *Nietzsche I: The Will to Power as Art*. Trans. David Farrell Krell. San Francisco: Harper & Row, 1979. Pp. xvi, 263.

Ihde, Don. *Technics and Praxis*. Boston: D. Reidel, 1979. Pp. xxvii, 151.

————. *Existential Technics*. Albany: State University of New York Press, 1983. Pp. ix, 190.

————. *Technology and the Lifeworld: From Garden to Earth*. Bloomington: Indiana University Press, 1990. Pp. xiv, 226.

Jonas, Hans. *Das Prinzip Verantwortung: Versuch einer Ethik für die technologische Zivilisation*. Frankfurt: Insel, 1979. P. 426. English version, incorporating *Macht oder Ohnmacht der Subjektivität? Das Leib-Seele-Problem im Vorfeld des Prinzips Verantwortung* (Frankfurt: Insel, 1981): *The Imperative of Responsibility: In Search of an Ethics for the Technological Age,* trans. Hans Jonas and David Herr (Chicago: University of Chicago Press, 1984). Pp. xii, 255.

Kapp, Ernst. *Grundlinien einer Philosophie der Technik: Zur Entstehungsgeschichte der Kultur aus neuen Gesichtspunkten* [Foundations of a philosophy of technology: Toward an understanding of culture from a new perspective]. Braunschweig: Westermann, 1877. P. 351. Reprinted, Düsseldorf: Stern-Verlag Janssen, 1978.

Mitcham, Carl, and Robert Mackey. *Bibliography of the Philosophy of Technology*. Chicago: University of Chicago Press, 1973. Pp. xvii, 205.

Mitcham, Carl, and Robert Mackey, eds. *Philosophy and Technology: Readings in the Philosophical Problems of Technology*.

New York: Free Press, 1972. Pp. ix, 399. Paperback edition New York: Free Press, 1983. Pp. xii, 403.

Mumford, Lewis. *Technics and Civilization*. New York: Harcourt, Brace and World, 1934. Pp. 495.

———. *Art and Technics*. New York: Columbia University Press, 1952. Pp. 162.

———. *The Myth of the Machine*. Vol. 1: *Technics and Human Development*. New York: Harcourt Brace Jovanovich, 1967. Pp. viii, 342. Vol. 2: *The Pentagon of Power*. New York: Harcourt Brace Jovanovich, 1970. Pp. v, 496.

Ortega y Gasset, José. "Meditación de la técnica," in *Ensimismamiento y alteración* (1939). Included in *Obras completas,* vol. V (Madrid: Revista de Occidente, 1947), pp. 317–75. English version: "Thoughts on Technology," in Mitcham-Mackey, eds., *Philosophy and Technology,* pp. 290–313.

Rapp, Friedrich. *Analytische Technikphilosophie*. Freiburg: Karl Alber, 1978. Pp. 226. English version: *Analytical Philosophy of Technology,* trans. Stanley R. Carpenter and Theodor Langenbruch (Boston: D. Reidel, 1981). Pp. xiv, 199.

"Toward a Philosophy of Technology." *Technology and Culture* 7, no. 3 (Summer 1966), pp. 301–90. Contents: Lewis Mumford's "Technics and the Nature of Man," James K. Feibleman's "Technology as Skills," Mario Bunge's "Technology as Applied Science," Joseph Agassi's "The Confusion between Science and Technology in the Standard Philosophies of Science," J. O. Wisdom's "The Need for Corroboration: Comments on Agassi's Paper," Henryk Skolimowski's "The structure of Thinking in Technology," and I. C. Jarvie's "The Social Character of Technological problems: Comments on Skolimowski's Paper."

Winner, Langdon. *Autonomous Technology: Technics-Out-of-Control as a Theme in Political Thought*. Cambridge: MIT Press, 1977. Pp. x, 386.

Select Bibliography of Works Devoted to Literature and Technology

MARK L. GREENBERG
LANCE SCHACHTERLE

The following list hardly exhausts the thousands of studies that contribute to our understanding of this multidisciplinary field. Rather, in this bibliography we offer interested scholars a necessarily idiosyncratic selection of works that we believe are "classic" or "important" or that have been published recently (and thus may be of current interest)—or that simply suggest possible directions in this emerging area of study. The bibliography includes some general treatments of literature and technology cited in the endnotes to the essays in this volume (and does so in order to highlight such studies and also to put them before readers who may have chosen to skip a particular essay). It also gathers materials not cited in the essays above, thus rendering it an independent tool for research.

Altick, Richard D. *The English Common Reader, A Social History of the Mass Reading Public 1800–1900*. Chicago: University of Chicago Press, 1957.

Amrine, Frederick, ed. *Literature and Science as Modes of Expression*. Dordrecht: Kluwer, 1989.

Aronowitz, Stanley. *Science as Power: Discourse and Ideology in Modern Society*. Minneapolis: University of Minnesota Press, 1988.

Barthes, Roland. *Image, Music, Text*. Trans. Stephen Heath. Glasgow: Fontana/Collins, 1977.

Beniger, James R. *The Control Revolution: Technological and Economic Origins of the Information Society*. Cambridge: Harvard University Press, 1986.

Benjamin, Walter. "The Work of Art in the Age of Mechanical Reproduction" (1936). Pp. 217–51 of Benjamin's *Illuminations*. Trans. Harry Zohn. New York: Schocken, 1968.

Birn, Raymond, ed. *The Printed Word in the Eighteenth Century*. A special issue of *Eighteenth-Century Studies*, 17 (1984).

Bismarck, Klaus v., et al. *Industrialisierung des Bewußtseins*. München: Piper, 1985.

Bolter, J. David. *Turing's Man: Western Culture in the Computer Age*. Chapel Hill: University of North Carolina Press, 1984.

Borgmann, Albert. *Technology and the Character of Contemporary Life*. Chicago: University of Chicago Press, 1984.

Bugliarello, George, and Dean B. Doner, eds. *The History and Philosophy of Technology*. Urbana: University of Illinois Press, 1979.

Campbell, Jeremy. *Grammatical Man: Information, Entropy, Language, and Life*. New York: Simon and Schuster, 1982.

Cavell, Stanley. *The World Viewed: Reflections on the Ontology of Film*. New York: Viking, 1977.

Charbon, Rémy. *Die Naturwissenschaften im modernen deutschen Drama*. Zurich: Artemis, 1974.

Choe, Wolhee. *Toward an Aesthetic Criticism of Technology*. Worcester Polytechnic Institute Studies in Science, Technology, and Culture. New York: Peter Lang, 1989.

Cutcliffe, Stephen H., and Robert C. Post, eds. *In Context: History and the History of Technology*. Bethlehem: Lehigh University Press, 1989.

Davis, Natalie Zemon. "Printing and the People." Pp. 189–226 of her *Society and Culture in Early Modern France*. Stanford: Stanford University Press, 1975.

Dessauer, Friedrich. *Philosophie der Technik: Das Problem der Realisierung*. Bonn: F. Cohen, 1927.

————. *Streit um die Technik*. Frankfurt: J. Knecht, 1956.

Dyson, Freeman. *Disturbing the Universe*. New York: Harper and Row, 1979.

Eaves, Morris. "Blake and the Artistic Machine: An Essay in Decorum and Technology." *PMLA*, 92 (1977): 903–27.

Eisenstein, Elizabeth. *The Printing Press as an Agent of Change*. 2 vols. Cambridge: Cambridge University Press, 1979.

Ellul, Jacques. *The Technological Society*. Trans. John Wilkinson. New York: Knopf, 1964.

————. *The Technological System*. Trans. Joachim Neugroschel. New York: Continuum, 1980.

Febvre, Lucien, and Henri-Jean Martin. *The Coming of the Book: The Impact of Printing 1450–1800*. Trans. David Gerard. London: NLB, 1976.

Ferré, Frederick. *Philosophy of Technology*. Englewood Cliffs, N. J.: Prentice Hall, 1988.

Fisher, Marvin. "The Iconology of Industrialism 1830–60." *American Quarterly*, 13 (1961): 347–64.

Florman, Samuel. *The Existential Pleasures of Engineering*. New York: St. Martin's Press, 1976.

————. *Blaming Technology: The Irrational Search for Scapegoats*. New York: St. Martin's Press, 1981.

————. *The Civilized Engineer*. New York: St. Martin's Press, 1987.

Forsyth, R. A. "The Myth of Nature and the Victorian Compromise of the Imagination." *ELH*, 31 (1964): 213–40.

————. "The Victorian Self-Image and the Emergent City Sensibility." *University of Toronto Quarterly*, 33 (1963–64): 61–77.

Geertz, Clifford. "Art as a Cultural System." *Modern Language Notes*, 91 (1976): 473–99.

————. *The Interpretation of Cultures*. New York: Basic Books, 1973.

Gellrich, Jesse M. *The Idea of the Book in the Middle Ages: Language Theory, Mythology, and Fiction*. Ithaca, N.Y.: Cornell University Press, 1985.

Gendolla, Peter. *Die lebenden Maschinen*. Marburg: Guttandin und Hoppe, 1980.

Giedion, Sigfried. *Mechanization Takes Command*. New York: Oxford University Press, 1948.

————. *Space, Time and Architecture*. Cambridge: Harvard University Press, 1949.

Gille, Bertrand. *The Renaissance Engineers*. London: Lund Humphries, 1966.

Ginestier, Paul. *The Poet and the Machine*. Trans. Martin B. Friedman. Chapel Hill: University of North Carolina Press, 1961.

Goldman, Steven Louis. "Present Strains in the Relation between Science, Technology and Society." *Science, Technology, and Human Values*, 4.27 (1978–1979): 44–51.

Goldstein, Laurence. *The Flying Machine and Modern Literature*. Bloomington: Indiana University Press, 1986.

Greenberg, Mark L. "Eighteenth-Century Poetry Represents Moments of Scientific Discovery: Appropriation and Generic Transformation." Pp. 115–38 in Peterfreund, ed. *Literature and Science*.

Hardison, O. B., Jr. *Disappearing Through the Skylight: Culture and Technology in the Twentieth Century*. New York: Viking, 1990.

Hayles, N. Katherine. "Information or Noise? Economy of Explanation in Barthes's *S/Z* and Shannon's Information Theory." Pp. 119–42 in George Levine, ed. *One Culture: Essays in Science and Literature*. Madison: University of Wisconsin Press, 1987.

————. "Self-Reflexive Metaphors in Maxwell's Demon and Shannon's Choice: Finding the Passages." Pp. 209–37 in Peterfreund, ed. *Literature and Science*.

Hebel, Franz, ed. "Technik in Sprach und Literatur," a special issue of *Der Deutsch Unterricht* 41 (1989); contains essays by Rudolf Drux, Harro Segeberg, Michael Müller, Hebel, Joachim Metzner, Hans-R. Fluck, Eberhard W. Meyer, and Hebel and Karl-Heinz Jahn.

Heckmann, Herbert. *Die andere Schöpfung*. Frankfurt: Umschau, 1982.

Heggen, Alfred. "Die 'ars volandi' in der Literatur des 17. und 18. Jahrhunderts." *Technikgeschichte,* 42 (1975): 327–37.

Heidegger, Martin. *The Question Concerning Technology and Other Essays*. Trans. William Lovitt. New York: Harper and Row, 1977.

Hunt, John Dixon. *Garden and Grove: The Italian Renaissance Garden in the English Imagination 1600–1750*. Princeton, N.J.: Princeton University Press, 1986.

Ingold, Felix Philipp. *Literatur und Aviatik*. Frankfurt: Suhrkamp, 1980.

Ivasheva, Valentina V. *On the Threshold of the Twenty-First Century: The Technological Revolution and Literature*. Trans. Doris Bradbury and Natalie Ward. Moscow: Progress, 1978.

Jennings, Humphrey. *Pandæmonium: The Coming of the Machine as Seen by Contemporary Observers 1660–1886*. Ed. Mary-Lou Jennings and Charles Madge. New York: Free Press, 1985.

Kahn, Arthur D. "Every Art Possessed by Man Comes from Prometheus: The Greek Tragedians and Science and Technology." *Technology and Culture,* 11 (1970): 133–62.

Kasson, John F. *Civilizing the Machine: Technology and Re-*

publican Values in America 1776–1900. New York: Penguin, 1977.

Keller, A. G. *A Theatre of Machines.* New York: Macmillan, 1964.

Kenner, Hugh. *The Counterfeiters.* New York: Doubleday/Anchor, 1973.

———. *The Mechanic Muse.* New York: Oxford University Press, 1987.

Kernan, Alvin. *Printing Technology, Letters, and Samuel Johnson.* Princeton, N.J.: Princeton University Press, 1987.

———. *The Imaginary Library: An Essay on Literature and Society.* Princeton, N.J.: Princeton University Press, 1982.

Knapp, Bettina. *Machine, Metaphor, and the Writer: A Jungian View.* University Park: The Pennsylvania State University Press, 1989.

Kristeller, Paul Oskar. "The Modern System of the Arts." Pp. 163–227 of his *Renaissance Thought II: Papers on Humanism and the Arts.* New York: Harper Torchbooks, 1965.

Lafitte, Jacques. *Refléxions sur la science des machines.* Paris: J. Vrin, 1972.

Layton, Edwin T. "Technology as Knowledge." *Technology and Culture,* 15 (1974): 31–41.

Lee, Judith Yaross, and Joseph W. Slade, eds. *Beyond the Two Cultures: Essays on Science, Technology, and Literature.* Ames: Iowa State University Press, 1989.

Lewis, Arthur, ed. *Of Man and Machines.* New York: Dutton, 1963.

Malraux, André. *The Voices of Silence* (1953). Trans. Stuart Gilbert. Princeton, N.J.: Princeton University Press, 1978.

———. "Two Kingdoms of Force." *Massachusetts Review,* 1 (1959): 72–95.

Marx, Leo. *The Machine in the Garden: Technology and the Pastoral Ideal in America.* New York: Oxford University Press, 1964.

Marx, Leo, ed. *The Pilot and the Passenger: Essays on Literature, Technology, and Culture in the United States.* New York: Oxford University Press, 1988.

McKay, Donald. *Information, Mechanism and Meaning.* Cambridge: MIT Press, 1969.

McLuhan, Marshall. *The Gutenberg Galaxy: The Making of Typographical Man.* Toronto: University of Toronto Press, 1962.

————. *Understanding Media: The Extensions of Man.* New York: McGraw-Hill, 1964.

Mitcham, Carl, and Robert Mackey, eds. *Philosophy and Technology: Readings in the Philosophical Problems of Technology.* New York: Free Press, 1972; paperback ed., 1983.

————. *Bibliography of the Philosophy of Technology.* Chicago: University of Chicago Press, 1973.

Moles, Abraham. *Information Theory and Esthetic Perception.* Trans. Joel E. Cohen. Urbana: University of Illinois Press, 1968.

Muller, Herbert J. *The Children of Frankenstein: A Primer on Modern Technology and Human Values.* Bloomington: Indiana University Press, 1970.

Mumby, F. A., and Ian Norrie. *Publishing and Bookselling,* 5th ed. London: Jonathan Cape, 1974.

Mumford, Lewis. *Technics and Civilization.* New York: Harcourt, Brace, and World, 1934.

————. *Art and Technics.* New York: Columbia University Press, 1952.

————. "Technics and the Future of Western Civilization," in his *In the Name of Sanity.* New York: Harcourt, Brace, 1954.

————. *The Myth of the Machine.* Vol. 1: *Technics and Human Development.* New York: Harcourt, Brace, Jovanovich, 1967; Vol. 2: *The Pentagon of Power.* New York: Harcourt, Brace, Jovanovich, 1970.

Nef, John U. *Cultural Foundations of Industrial Civilization.* Cambridge: Cambridge University Press, 1958.

Nettersheim, Josefine. *Poeta doctus oder die Poetisierung der Wissenschaft von Musäus bis Benn.* Berlin: Durcker, 1975.

Nicolson, Marjorie Hope. *Newton Demands the Muse: Newton's Opticks and the Eighteenth Century Poets.* Princeton, N.J.: Princeton University Press, 1946.

Ong, Walter J., S.J. *The Presence of the Word.* New Haven: Yale University Press, 1967.

————. *Rhetoric, Romance, and Technology.* Ithaca, N.Y.: Cornell University Press, 1971.

————. "Reading, Technology, and the Nature of Man: An Interpretation." *Yearbook of English Studies,* 10 (1980): 132–49.

————. *Orality and Literacy, The Technologizing of the Word.* London: Methuen, 1982.

Ortega y Gasset, José. "Meditación de la técnica," in his *En-*

simismamiento y alteración (1939); in *Obras completas,* vol. V. Madrid: Revista de Occidente, 1947.

Pacey, Arnold. *The Maze of Ingenuity.* Cambridge: MIT Press, 1966.

Parrinder, Patrick. *Authors and Authority: A Study of English Literary Criticism and Its Relation to Culture 1750–1900.* London: Routledge and Kegan Paul, 1977.

Peterfreund, Stuart, ed. *Literature and Science: Theory and Practice.* Boston: Northeastern University Press, 1990.

Plant, Marjorie. *The English Book Trade, An Economic History of the Making and Sale of Books.* 3d ed. London: George Allen and Unwin, 1974.

Porush, David. "Technology and Postmodernism: Cybernetic Fiction." *Sub-Stance,* 27 (1980): 92–100.

———. *The Soft Machine: Cybernetic Fiction.* London: Methuen, 1985.

Rapp, Friedrich. *Analytical Philosophy of Technology.* Trans. Stanley R. Carpenter and Theodor Langenbruch. Boston: D. Reidel, 1981.

Read, Herbert. *Art and Industry.* Bloomington: Indiana University Press, 1961.

Rivers, Isabel, ed. *Books and Their Readers in Eighteenth-Century England.* Leicester and New York: Leicester University Press and St. Martin's Press, 1982.

Sanzo, Eileen. "William Blake and the Technological Age." *Thought,* 46 (1971): 577–91.

Schatzberg, Walter, Ronald A. Waite, and Jonathan K. Johnson, eds. *The Relations of Literature and Science: An Annotated Bibliography of Scholarship 1880–1980.* New York, Modern Language Association of America, 1987.

Schivelbusch, Wolfgang. *The Railway Journey: The Industrialization of Time and Space in the Nineteenth Century.* Berkeley: University of California Press, 1977; 1986.

Schneider, Peter Paul. *Literatur im Industriezeitalter,* Bd. 1 und 2. Marbach am Neckar: Deutsche Schillergesellschaft, 1987.

Segal, Howard. *Technological Utopianism in American Culture.* Chicago: University of Chicago Press, 1985.

Segeberg, Harro. *Technic in der Literatur.* Frankfurt: Suhrkamp, 1987.

Shapin, Steven, and Simon Schaffer. *Leviathan and the Air Pump:*

Hobbes, Boyle and the Experimental Life. Princeton, N.J.: Princeton University Press, 1985.

Singer, C., E. J. Holmyard, and A. R. Hall, eds. *A History of Technology*. 5 vols. Oxford: Oxford University Press, 1954–1958.

Steinberg, S. H. *Five Hundred Years of Printing*. 3d ed. New York and London: Penguin Books, 1974.

Strong, Roy. *The Renaissance Garden in England*. London: Thames and Hudson, 1979.

Sussman, Herbert L. *Victorians and the Machine: The Literary Response to Technology*. Cambridge: Harvard University Press, 1968.

Sypher, Wylie. *Literature and Technology: The Alien Vision*. New York: Random House, 1968.

Tafuri, Manfredo. *Humanism, Technical Knowledge and Rhetoric: The Debate in Renaissance Venice*. The Walter Gropius Lecture. Cambridge: Harvard University Graduate School of Design, 1986.

Teich, Albert H., ed. *Technology and Man's Future,* 3d ed. New York: St. Martin's Press, 1981.

Tichi, Cecelia. *Shifting Gears: Technology, Literature, Culture in Modernist America*. Chapel Hill: University of North Carolina Press, 1987.

Warburg, Jeremy. "Poetry and Industrialism." *Modern Language Review,* 53 (1958): 161–70.

———. *The Industrial Muse*. London: Macmillan, 1958.

Weiss, Burghard. *Literatur und Geschichte der Naturwissenschaften und Technic*. Berlin: Berlin Verlag, 1985.

Wiener, Norbert. *Cybernetics: Or Control and Communication in the Animal and the Machine*. Cambridge: MIT Press, 1948.

Williams, Raymond. *Culture and Society 1780–1950*. New York: Columbia University Press, 1958.

———. *Keywords: A Vocabulary of Culture and Society*. New York: Oxford University Press, 1976.

Williams, Rosalind. *Notes on the Underground: An Essay on Technology, Society, and the Imagination*. Cambridge: MIT Press, 1989.

Winner, Langdon. *Autonomous Technology: Technics Out-of-Control as a Theme in Political Thought*. Cambridge: MIT Press, 1977.

Index

318